Practice Exercises for Advanced Microeconomic Theory

Practice Exercises for Advanced Microeconomic Theory

Felix Muñoz-Garcia

The MIT Press

Cambridge, Massachusetts

London, England

This book was set in CMR10 by diacriTech, Chennai.

ISBN: 978-0-262-53314-0

Contents

Preface

This textbook presents 107 exercises on microeconomic theory, with detailed answers and explanations, that can help students enrolled in Masters and PhD programs in economics and finance (as well as undergraduate seniors) practice their theoretical foundations. These exercises essentially cover the material often discussed during the first semester of the advanced microeconomics courses (and some of the second semester), such as preference relations, demand theory and applications, producer theory, partial and general equilibrium, choice under uncertainty, monopoly, oligopoly models, externalities and public goods, and contract theory.

While standard textbooks often used in microeconomics courses (e.g., Mas-Colell et al. 1995; Jehle and Reny 2011) rigorously cover the theoretical foundations, they rarely provide detailed worked-out examples. Graduate students, as a consequence, lack textbooks offering practice exercises with which to test their understanding. This textbook seeks to fill this gap by presenting several exercises with detailed step-by-step explanations. Importantly, it emphasizes the economic intuition behind the main results and avoids unnecessary notation when possible, thus allowing students to use the text as a complement of the textbook adopted in their class, *regardless* of the particular microeconomics textbook selected by the instructor.

Organization of the book The first two chapters are dedicated to consumer theory, with exercises on preference relations (testing whether different properties hold), choice rules (the weak axiom of revealed preference), and demand theory. Chapter 3 takes a more applied perspective by using the tools learned in the previous two chapters to evaluate the welfare change that results from a price change, the introduction of different types of taxes, and so on. Chapters 4 and 5 study topics on production theory and choice under uncertainty, respectively, and Chapter 6 analyzes partial and general equilibrium. The last four chapters examine equilibrium behavior under market imperfections, namely monopoly (chapter 7), imperfect competition (chapter 8), externalities and public goods (chapter 9), and contract theory (chapter 10); together they elucidate how regulation can induce private agents to voluntarily produce socially optimal outcomes. For further guidance, every chapter begins with a paragraph describing the main exercises in that chapter, their connections with one another, and their extensions.

How to use this textbook The organization of the text allows for flexible uses by instructors. Some instructors may choose to use parts of the manuscript in class, in order to clarify applications and parametric examples that are only theoretically covered in standard textbooks. Alternatively, other instructors may choose to assign certain exercises as a required reading, since these exercises can closely complement the material covered in class. This strategy could be particularly effective in preparing students for future homework assignments on similar topics, allowing instructors to dedicate more time covering the theoretical foundations in class.

Acknowledgements I would first like to thank several colleagues who encouraged me in the preparation of this book: Ron Mittlehammer, Ana Espinola-Arredondo, and Alan Love. I am, of course, especially grateful to my teachers and advisors at the University of Pittsburgh, who taught me microeconomic theory, industrial organization, and public economics, instilling a passion for applied theory that the reader will hopefully notice in the following pages. I am also thankful to the "team" of teaching and research assistants at Washington State University, who helped me with this project over several years: Eric Dunaway, Xin Zhao, Sherzod Akhundjanov, Tongzhe Li, Brett Devine, Max St. Brown, Arzu Aysin Teikindor, Matthew Campbell, Shuo Li, Xiaonan Liu, along with the review of several exercises by Modhurima Amin, Pak Sing Choi, Syed Badruddoza, Zhuang Hao, Youngran Choi, Boris Houenou, Kiana Yektansani, and Xinlong Tan. I am also grateful to the publishing team at MIT Press, especially John Conwell, Emily Taber, and Dana Andrus, who supported this project and provided motivation from the beginning. Last, but not least, I would like to thank my wife, Ana Espinola-Arredondo, for encouraging me during the preparation of the manuscript. She always believed in the potential of the following exercises as a guide for generations of students. Thanks so much for everything.

Felix Muñoz-Garcia, PhD
Associate Professor
School of Economic Sciences
Washington State University

Chapter 1 — Preferences and Utility

Summary In this chapter we first study how to test different properties of preference relations, such as completeness, transitivity, convexity, monotonicity, and local non-satiation. We examine these properties accompanying our discussion with multiple figures, which help illustrate the economic intuition behind each preference relation. In subsequent exercises we explore some of these properties, such as monotonicity and transitivity, in more detail. We then focus on the lexicographic preference relation which, despite not admitting a graphical representation through indifference curves, still allows for several economic results. Specifically, we first test whether this preference relation satisfies completeness and transitivity, and afterward show that, if we restrict our attention to finite consumption sets, we can find a utility function that represents this preference relation. We then dedicate some exercises to test the weak axiom of revealed preference (WARP) on several contexts: first on different choice rules, and then on the lexicographic preference relation. Finally, the last exercises check whether the Cobb–Douglas utility function satisfies different properties, such as as homogeneity, homotheticity, local non-satiation, and quasi-concavity.

Exercise #1 — Checking properties of preference relations—I

1. For each of the following preference relations in the consumption of two goods (1 and 2): describe the upper contour set, the lower contour set, the indifference set of bundle (2,1), and interpret them. Then check whether these preference relations are rational (by separately examining whether they are complete and transitive), monotone, and convex.

    (a) Bundle (x_1, x_2) is weakly preferred to (y_1, y_2), i.e., $(x_1, x_2) \succsim (y_1, y_2)$ if and only if $x_1 \geqslant y_1 - 1$.

      - Let us first build some intuition on this preference relation. First, note that an individual prefers a bundle x to another bundle y if and only if the first component of bundle x, x_1, contains at least one unit less than the first component of bundle y, i.e., $x_1 \geqslant y_1 - 1$. For instance, $(2, 1)$ is preferred to $(2, 6)$ since $x_1 = 2$ and $y_1 = 2$, thus implying $2 \geqslant 2 - 1 = 1$. Importantly, the individual ignores the content of the second component when comparing two bundles. Let us next describe the upper contour, lower contour, and indifference set of a given bundle, such as $(2, 1)$. You can take any other bundle of course! The upper contour set of this bundle is given by

$$UCS(2, 1) = \{(x_1, x_2) \succsim (2, 1) \Longleftrightarrow x_1 \geq 2 - 1\} = \{(x_1, x_2) : x_1 \geq 1\}$$

      while the lower contour set is defined as

$$LCS(2, 1) = \{(2, 1) \succsim (x_1, x_2) \Longleftrightarrow 2 \geq x_1 - 1\} = \{(x_1, x_2) : x_1 \leq 3\}.$$

      Finally, the consumer is indifferent between bundle (2,1) and the set of bundles where

$$IND(2, 1) = \{(x_1, x_2) \sim (2, 1) \Longleftrightarrow 1 \leq x_1 \leq 3\}.$$

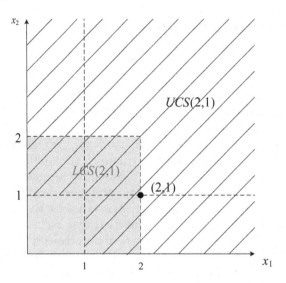

Figure 1.1 UCS, LCS, and IND of bundle (2,1).

Figure 1.1 depicts:

1. All bundles in $\mathbb{R}^2_+$ such that $x_1 \geq 1$, and thus belong to the $UCS(2,1)$, i.e., the set of bundles that are weakly preferred to (2,1);

2. All bundles such that $x_1 \leq 3$ and are therefore in the $LCS(2,1)$, i.e., the set of bundles weakly preferred by (2,1); and

3. Those bundles in between, $1 \leq x_1 \leq 3$, in the $IND(2,1)$ are indifferent between them and bundle (2,1). [Figure 1.1 represents the UCS, LCS, and IND sets, where all cutoffs we found were on the x_1 axis, since this individual ignores the amount of x_2.]

As a remark, this preference relation satisfies *continuity*. In particular, continuity requires that both the upper and the lower contour sets are closed, which is satisfied given that they both contain their boundary points.

- *Completeness.* For this property to hold, we need that, for any pair of bundles (x_1, x_2) and (y_1, y_2), either $(x_1, x_2) \succsim (y_1, y_2)$ or $(y_1, y_2) \succsim (x_1, x_2)$, or both (i.e., $(x_1, x_2) \sim (y_1, y_2)$). Since this preference relation only depends on the first component of every bundle, we have that, for every pair of bundles (x_1, x_2) and (y_1, y_2), either:

  1. $x_1 \geq y_1 - 1$, which implies that $(x_1, x_2) \succsim (y_1, y_2)$; or
  2. $x_1 < y_1 - 1$, which implies

  $$y_1 > x_1 + 1 > x_1 - 1,$$

  and hence $y_1 > x_1 - 1$, thus ultimately yielding $(y_1, y_2) \succsim (x_1, x_2)$. Hence, this preference relation is complete.

Additionally, note that this preference relation satisfies reflexivity, since completeness implies reflexivity, i.e., every bundle (x_1, x_2) is weakly preferred to itself.

- *Transitivity.* We need to show that, for any three bundles (x_1, x_2), (y_1, y_2), and (z_1, z_2) such that

$$(x_1, x_2) \succsim (y_1, y_2) \text{ and } (y_1, y_2) \succsim (z_1, z_2), \text{ then } (x_1, x_2) \succsim (z_1, z_2).$$

This property does not hold for this preference relation. In order to show this result, notice that a bundle (x_1, x_2) is preferred to another bundle (y_1, y_2) if its first component, x_1, is larger than that of the other bundle, y_1, by less than one unit, i.e., condition $x_1 \geq y_1 - 1$ is equivalent to $1 \geq y_1 - x_1$. This condition about the distance between x_1 and y_1 is depicted in the bottom left-hand side of figure 1.2. A similar argument can be extended to the comparison between two bundles (y_1, y_2) and (z_1, z_2), where the former is preferred to the latter if and only if the distance between their first components is smaller than one, i.e., $1 \geq z_1 - y_1$; also depicted at the bottom of figure 1.2, but on the right-hand side. Hence, for bundle (x_1, x_2) to be preferred to (z_1, z_2), i.e., $(x_1, x_2) \succsim (z_1, z_2)$, we need the distance between their first components to be smaller than one, i.e., $1 \geq z_1 - x_1$; as we next show with a counterexample. Consider the following three bundles (notice that the second component of every bundle is inconsequential, since the preference ordering only relies on a comparison of the first component of every vector):

$$(x_1, x_2) = (5, 4),$$
$$(y_1, y_2) = (6, 1),$$
$$(z_1, z_2) = (7, 2).$$

First, note that $(x_1, x_2) \succsim (y_1, y_2)$ since the difference in their first component is smaller (or equal) to one unit, $x_1 \geq y_1 - 1$ (i.e., $5 \geq 6 - 1$). Additionally, $(y_1, y_2) \succsim$

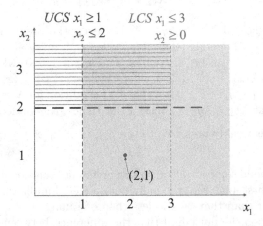

Figure 1.2 UCS, LCS, and IND of bundle (2,1).

(z_1, z_2) is also satisfied since $y_1 \geq z_1 - 1$ (i.e., $6 \geq 7 - 1$). However, $(x_1, x_2) \not\succsim (z_1, z_2)$ since the difference between z_1 and x_1 is larger than one unit, $x_1 \not\geq z_1 - 1$ (i.e., $5 \not\geq 7 - 1$). Hence, this preference relation does not satisfy transitivity.

- *Monotonicity.* This property is satisfied for this preference relation. In particular, increasing the amount of good 1 yields a new bundle $(x_1 + \varepsilon, x_2)$ that is weakly preferred to the original bundle (x_1, x_2), i.e., the comparison of their first component yields $x_1 + \varepsilon \geq x_1 - 1$, or $\varepsilon \geq -1$, which holds since $\varepsilon > 0$ by assumption. Similarly, increasing the amount of the second component produces a new bundle $(x_1, x_2 + \varepsilon)$ which is weakly preferred to the original bundle (x_1, x_2). Recall that this individual compares bundles by evaluating the first component alone. Since in this case the amount of the first component is unaffected, then he is indifferent between bundle (x_1, x_2) and $(x_1, x_2 + \varepsilon)$; an indifference that is allowed by the definition of monotonicity. Hence, the preference relation satisfies monotonicity. As a curiosity, note that, while the preference relation satisfies monotonicity, it does not satisfy strong monotonicity. Indeed, for this property to hold, we need that an increase in the amount of *any* of the goods yields a new bundle that is strictly preferred to the original bundle (x_1, x_2). While this is true if we increase the amount of good 1, it is not if we only increase the amount of good 2, thus not satisfying strict monotonicity.

- *Convexity.* This property implies that the upper contour set must be convex, that is, if bundle (x_1, x_2) is weakly preferred to (y_1, y_2), $(x_1, x_2) \succsim (y_1, y_2)$, then the convex combination of these two bundles is also weakly preferred to (y_1, y_2),

$$\lambda(x_1, x_2) + (1 - \lambda)(y_1, y_2) \succsim (y_1, y_2) \text{ for any } \lambda \in [0, 1].$$

In this case, $(x_1, x_2) \succsim (y_1, y_2)$ implies that $x_1 \geq y_1 - 1$; whereas $\lambda(x_1, x_2) + (1 - \lambda)(y_1, y_2) \succsim (y_1, y_2)$ implies

$$\lambda x_1 + (1 - \lambda)y_1 \geq y_1 - 1,$$

which simplifies to $\lambda x_1 \geq \lambda y_1 - 1$. However, the premise from $(x_1, x_2) \succsim (y_1, y_2)$, i.e., $x_1 \geq y_1 - 1$, entails that $\lambda x_1 \geq \lambda y_1 - 1$ must also hold. (To see that, note that $x_1 \geq y_1 - 1$ can be written as $(x_1 - y_1) + 1 \geq 0$, while $\lambda x_1 \geq \lambda y_1 - 1$ can be expressed as $\lambda(x_1 - y_1) + 1 \geq 0$, where $\lambda(x_1 - y_1) + 1 \leq (x_1 - y_1) + 1$ since $\lambda \in [0, 1]$.) Therefore, $(x_1 - y_1) + 1 \geq 0$ is a sufficient condition for $\lambda(x_1 - y_1) + 1 \geq 0$, ultimately implying that $\lambda x_1 \geq \lambda y_1 - 1$ must hold. Hence, this preference relation is convex.

(b) Bundle (x_1, x_2) is weakly preferred to (y_1, y_2), i.e., $(x_1, x_2) \succsim (y_1, y_2)$, if $x_1 \geq y_1 - 1$ and $x_2 \leq y_2 + 1$.

- Let us first build some intuition on this preference relation. Similarly as the preference relation we first analyzed, the individual prefers bundle x to y if the first component of x is larger than that of y in less than one unit, i.e., $x_1 \geq y_1 + 1$ or $1 \geq y_1 - x_1$; but in addition, he must find that the difference between their second components is larger than one unit, i.e., $x_2 \leq y_2 + 1$ or $1 \leq y_2 - x_2$.

- Let us next find the upper contour, lower contour, and indifference set of a given bundle, such as (2, 1). The upper contour set of this bundle is given by

$$UCS(2,1) = \{(x_1, x_2) \succsim (2,1) \Longleftrightarrow x_1 \geq 2 - 1 \text{ and } x_2 \leq 1 + 1\}$$
$$= \{(x_1, x_2) : x_1 \geq 1 \text{ and } x_2 \leq 2\},$$

  which is graphically represented in figure 1.2 by all those bundles in the lower right-hand corner (below $x_2 = 2$ and to the right of $x_1 = 1$). On the other hand, the lower contour set is defined as

$$LCS(2,1) = \{(2,1) \succsim (x_1, x_2) \Longleftrightarrow 2 \geq x_1 - 1 \text{ and } 1 \leq x_2 + 1\}$$
$$= \{(x_1, x_2) : x_1 \leq 3 \text{ and } x_2 \geq 0\},$$

  which is depicted in figure 1.2 by all those bundles in the left half of the positive quadrant (above $x_2 = 0$ and to the left of $x_1 = 3$). Finally, the consumer is indifferent between bundle (2,1) and the set of bundles where

$$IND(2,1) = \{(x_1, x_2) \sim (2,1) \Longleftrightarrow 1 \leq x_1 \leq 3 \text{ and } 0 \leq x_2 \leq 2\}$$

  graphically, represented by the rectangle in the bottom center of the figure, for all $x_2 \leq 2$ and $1 \leq x_1 \leq 3$.

- *Completeness.* From the above analysis it is easy to note that completeness is *not* satisfied, since there are bundles in the area $x_1 > 3$ and $x_2 > 2$ where our preference relation does not specify if they belong to the upper contour set, the lower contour set, or the indifference set of bundle (2, 1). Hence, any bundle in the unshaded region where $x_1 > 3$ and $x_2 > 2$ (in the top right-hand corner of figure 1.2) would be incomparable with (2, 1). Another way to prove that completeness does not hold is by finding a counterexample. In particular, we must find an example of two bundles such that neither $(x_1, x_2) \succsim (y_1, y_2)$ nor $(y_1, y_2) \succsim (x_1, x_2)$. Let us take, for instance, two bundles,

$$(x_1, x_2) = (1, 2) \text{ and } (y_1, y_2) = (4, 6).$$

We have that:

1. $(x_1, x_2) \not\succsim (y_1, y_2)$ since $1 \not\geq 4 - 1$ for the first component of the bundle (and we need $x_1 \geq y_n - 1$ for $(x_1, x_2) \succsim (y_1, y_2)$ to hold), and

2. $(y_1, y_2) \not\succsim (x_1, x_2)$ since $6 \not\leq 2 + 1$ for the second component of the bundle. Hence, for these are two bundles neither $(x_1, x_2) \succsim (y_1, y_2)$ nor $(y_1, y_2) \succsim (x_1, x_2)$, which implies that this preference relation is not complete.

- *Transitivity.* We need to show that, for any three bundles (x_1, x_2), (y_1, y_2) and (z_1, z_2) such that

$$(x_1, x_2) \succsim (y_1, y_2) \text{ and } (y_1, y_2) \succsim (z_1, z_2), \text{ then } (x_1, x_2) \succsim (z_1, z_2).$$

This property does not hold for this preference relation. In order to show that, let us consider the following three bundles (that is, we are finding a counterexample to show that transitivity does not hold):

$$(x_1, x_2) = (2, 1),$$
$$(y_1, y_2) = (3, 4),$$
$$(z_1, z_2) = (4, 6).$$

First, note that $(x_1, x_2) \succsim (y_1, y_2)$ since the distance between their first components is not larger than one unit $x_1 \geq y_1 - 1$ (i.e., $2 \geq 3 - 1$), and the distance between the second components is larger than one unit $x_2 \leq y_2 + 1$ (i.e., $1 \leq 4 + 1$). Additionally, $(y_1, y_2) \succsim (z_1, z_2)$ is also satisfied since $y_1 \geq z_1 - 1$ for the first component (i.e., $3 \geq 4 - 1$), and $y_2 \leq z_2 + 1$ for the second component (i.e., $3 \leq 4 + 1$). However, $(x_1, x_2) \not\succsim (z_1, z_2)$ since the difference of the first components is strictly larger than one unit $x_1 \not\geq z_1 - 1$ (i.e., $2 \not\geq 4 - 1$). Hence, this preference relation does not satisfy transitivity.

- *Monotonicity*. For this property to hold, we need that an increase in the amounts of one good yields a new bundle that is weakly preferred to the original bundle. Indeed, if we increase the amount of good 1 by $\varepsilon > 0$ to create bundle $(x_1 + \varepsilon, x_2)$, we have that the first component satisfies $x_1 + \varepsilon \geqslant x_1 - 1$, i.e., $\varepsilon \geqslant -1$, and the second component satisfies $x_2 \leqslant x_2 + 1$, i.e., $0 \leqslant 1$. If we only increase the amounts of good 2, a similar argument applies. Finally, if we increase the amounts of both goods 1 and 2 simultaneously, according to the definition of monotonicity we need that the newly created bundle is strictly preferred to the initial bundle, i.e., $(x_1 + \varepsilon, x_2 + \delta) \succ (x_1, x_2)$ where constants $\varepsilon, \delta > 0$ are allowed to differ for each good. For this relationship to hold, note that we need that: (1) the first components satisfy $x_1 + \varepsilon \geq x_1 - 1$, or $\varepsilon \geq -1$ (which holds by definition); and (2) the second components satisfy $x_2 + \delta \leq x_2 + 1$, which implies $\delta \leq 1$ (which does not necessarily hold by assumption). Therefore, for this preference relation to be monotonic, we need that $\delta \leq 1$. In other words, if good 2 is increased by more than one unit, the preference relation is not monotonic. For instance, if the amount of both goods is increased by two units, i.e., $\varepsilon = \delta = 2$, the new bundle $(x_1 + 2, x_2 + 2)$ is not necessarily preferred to the original bundle (x_1, x_2) since the condition on the first component, $x_1 + 2 \geq x_1 - 1$, holds but that on the second component, $x_2 + 2 \leq x_2 + 1$, does not.

- *Convexity*. This property implies that the upper contour set must be convex. That is, if bundle (x_1, x_2) is weakly preferred to (y_1, y_2), $(x_1, x_2) \succsim (y_1, y_2)$, then the convex combination of these two bundles is also weakly preferred to (y_1, y_2),

$$\lambda(x_1, x_2) + (1 - \lambda)(y_1, y_2) \succsim (y_1, y_2) \quad \text{for any } \lambda \in [0, 1].$$

In this case, $(x_1, x_2) \succsim (y_1, y_2)$ implies that $x_1 \geq y_1 - 1$ and $x_2 \leq y_2 + 1$; whereas $\lambda(x_1, x_2) + (1 - \lambda)(y_1, y_2) \succsim (y_1, y_2)$ implies

$$\lambda x_1 + (1 - \lambda) y_1 \geq y_1 - 1 \text{ for the first component, and}$$
$$\lambda x_2 + (1 - \lambda) y_2 \leq y_2 + 1 \text{ for the second component,}$$

which respectively can be rewritten as

$$\lambda\,(x_1 - y_1) \geq -1, \text{ and}$$
$$\lambda\,(x_2 - y_2) \leq 1.$$

In addition, the condition on the first component $x_1 - y_1 \geq -1$ (or alternatively, $x_1 \geq y_1 - 1$) holds by assumption since $(x_1, x_2) \succsim (y_1, y_2)$. Similarly, the condition on the second component $x_2 - y_2 \leq 1$ (or alternatively, $x_2 \leq y_2 + 1$) is also satisfied by $(x_1, x_2) \succsim (y_1, y_2)$. Hence, the preference relation satisfies convexity.

(c) Bundle (x_1, x_2) is weakly preferred to (y_1, y_2), i.e., $(x_1, x_2) \succsim (y_1, y_2)$, if and only if $\max\{x_1, x_2\} \geq \max\{y_1, y_2\}$.

- Intuitively, this relation states that a bundle (x_1, x_2) is preferred to an alternative bundle (y_1, y_2) if and only if the most abundant component of the first bundle exceeds the most abundant component of the second bundle. In this preference relation, for a given bundle $(2, 1)$, the upper contour set is defined as all those bundles that contain more than two units in its most abundant component, i.e. (x_1, x_2) where $x_i \geq 2$ for at least one good i. Figure 1.3 depicts this UCS, which contains all the bundles to the right-hand side of $x_1 = 2$ (since they all have more than two units in the first component), but also those points that, despite being to the left of $x_1 = 2$, contain more than two units of good 2, i.e., all bundles (x_1, x_2) for which $x_2 \geq 2$ in the left-hand corner of the figure. In contrast, the LCS embodies all bundles for which its most abundant component is weakly lower than 2, i.e., (x_1, x_2) where $x_i \leq 2$ for every good i, and are graphically depicted by the points below $x_2 = 2$ and to the left of $x_1 = 2$ on figure 1.3.

  As a consequence, the IND set of bundle $(2, 1)$ contains all those bundles for which its most abundant component has exactly two units, i.e., $(2, x_2)$ and $(x_1, 2)$ for all

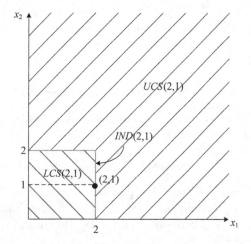

Figure 1.3 UCS, LCS, and IND of bundle (2,1).

$x_1 \in [0, 2]$ and $x_2 \in [0, 2]$, as depicted in the square area of figure 1.3, thus including the origin $(0, 0)$ as part of the IND set of bundle $(2, 1)$.

- *Completeness.* For completeness to hold, we need to show that, for any two bundles (x_1, x_2), $(y_1, y_2) \in \mathbb{R}^2$, either $\max\{x_1, x_2\} \geq \max\{y_1, y_2\}$, or $\max\{y_1, y_2\} \geq \max\{x_1, x_2\}$, or both, i.e., $\max\{x_1, x_2\} = \max\{y_1, y_2\}$.[1] Let $\max\{x_1, x_2\} = a$, and $\max\{y_1, y_2\} = b$. Since $a, b \in \mathbb{R}$, and real numbers are totally ordered, then either $a \geq b$, or $b \geq a$, or both $(a = b)$. It then follows that either $(x_1, x_2) \succsim (y_1, y_2)$, or $(y_1, y_2) \succsim (x_1, x_2)$, or both, i.e., $(x_1, x_2) \sim (y_1, y_2)$. Hence, this preference relation is complete.

  Note that this property could be anticipated by our description of the UCS, LCS, and IND sets in figure 1.3 whereby, for a given bundle $(2, 1)$, we can rank any other bundle in the positive quadrant (x_1, x_2) as being preferable to $(2, 1)$, i.e., $(x_1, x_2) \succsim (2, 1)$, or $(2, 1)$ being preferred to this bundle, i.e., $(2, 1) \succsim (x_1, x_2)$, or both, i.e. $(x_1, x_2) \sim (2, 1)$.

- *Transitivity.* Take three bundles (x_1, x_2), (y_1, y_2) and $(z_1, z_2) \in \mathbb{R}^2$ satisfying $(x_1, x_2) \succsim (y_1, y_2)$ and $(y_1, y_2) \succsim (z_1, z_2)$. Then, they must satisfy that, on one hand, $\max\{x_1, x_2\} \geq \max\{y_1, y_2\}$ and, on the other hand, $\max\{y_1, y_2\} \geq \max\{z_1, z_2\}$. Therefore, by transitivity of the "greater than or equal" relation $(\geq)$, $\max\{x_1, x_2\} \geq \max\{z_1, z_2\}$, which implies $(x_1, x_2) \succsim (z_1, z_2)$. Hence, the preference relation is transitive. Since it is also complete as shown above, this preference relation is rational.

- *Monotonicity.* Recall that, in order to check if a preference relation is monotonic, we need to show that if we increase all components of a given bundle (x_1, x_2), the newly created bundle is *strictly* preferred to (x_1, x_2). Take a bundle (y_1, y_2) such that $y_1 > x_1$ and $y_2 > x_2$, e.g., $y_1 = x_1 + \varepsilon$ and $y_2 = x_2 + \delta$ where $\varepsilon, \delta > 0$. Then, $\max\{y_1, y_2\} > \max\{x_1, x_2\}$ with strict inequality, and it follows that $(y_1, y_2) \succ (x_1, x_2)$. Hence, the preference relation satisfies monotonicity, i.e., if $y_i > x_i$ for all components $i = \{1, 2\}$, then $y \succ x$.

- *Convexity.* Recall that for a preference relation to satisfy convexity, we need that, for any three bundles (x_1, x_2), (y_1, y_2), and (z_1, z_2), where the last two bundles are weakly preferred to (x_1, x_2), that is,

$$(y_1, y_2) \succsim (x_1, x_2) \text{ and } (z_1, z_2) \succsim (x_1, x_2),$$

  it must hold that the convex combination of bundles (y_1, y_2) and (z_1, z_2) is also weakly preferred to (x_1, x_2),

$$\lambda(x_1, x_2) + (1 - \lambda)(y_1, y_2) \succsim (x_1, x_2).$$

  In order to check whether this preference relation satisfies convexity, take three bundles (x_1, x_2), (y_1, y_2) and $(z_1, z_2) \in \mathbb{R}^2$ such that $(y_1, y_2) \succsim (x_1, x_2)$ and $(z_1, z_2) \succsim (x_1, x_2)$. Therefore, it must be that $\max\{y_1, y_2\} \geq \max\{x_1, x_2\}$, and

---

[1] Intuitively, the last case occurs when the amount of the most abundant item in bundle x coincides with the amount of the most abundant item in bundle y.

similarly that $\max\{z_1, z_2\} \geqslant \max\{x_1, x_2\}$. The convex combination of (y_1, y_2) and (z_1, z_2) yields a first component of $\lambda y_1 + (1 - \lambda)z_1$ and a second component of $\lambda y_2 + (1 - \lambda)z_2$. However, the largest of these two components,

$$\max\{\lambda y_1 + (1 - \lambda)z_1, \lambda y_2 + (1 - \lambda)z_2\},$$

is not necessarily higher than $\max\{x_1, x_2\}$. In order to see that, consider an example in which the two premises of convexity hold, that is,

$$\max\{y_1, y_2\} \geqslant \max\{x_1, x_2\} \quad \text{and} \quad \max\{z_1, z_2\} \geqslant \max\{x_1, x_2\},$$

such as $(y_1, y_2) = (0, 4)$ and $(x_1, x_2) = (3, 3)$ and $(z_1, z_2) = (4, 0)$. Indeed, note that $\max\{y_1, y_2\} = 4$, $\max\{x_1, x_2\} = 3$ and $\max\{z_1, z_2\} = 4$, implying that $\max\{y_1, y_2\} = 4 \geqslant 3 = \max\{x_1, x_2\}$ and $\max\{z_1, z_2\} = 4 \geqslant 3 = \max\{x_1, x_2\}$. Now, note that the convex combination of (y_1, y_2) and (z_1, z_2) with λ, will give us values between 0 and 4. For intermediate values of λ (such as $\lambda = \frac{1}{2}$) the convex combination of bundles y and x yields

$$\max\left\{\frac{1}{2}0 + \frac{1}{2}4, \frac{1}{2}4 + \frac{1}{2}0\right\} = \max\{2, 2\} = 2,$$

which is lower than $\max\{x_1, x_2\} = 3$. Hence, the preference relation is *not* convex.

- *Alternative proof of nonconvex preferences without using a counterexample.* We could anticipate the nonconvexity of preferences, since figure 1.3 depicted a nonconvex upper contour set (which implies nonconvex preferences). As we see in figure 1.4, we can find bundles, like x, for which its upper contour set is not convex. That is,

$$y \succsim x \quad \text{but} \quad \alpha x + (1 - \alpha)y \not\succsim x \text{ for all } \alpha \in [0, 1].$$

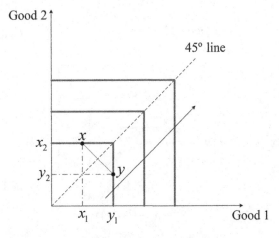

Figure 1.4 Nonconvex upper contour sets.

- In order to formally demonstrate that the upper contour set is not convex, we need to show that, for a convex combination of two bundles, i.e., $\alpha x + (1 - \alpha)y$, we have that

$$\max\{\alpha x_1 + (1 - \alpha)y_1, \alpha x_2 + (1 - \alpha)y_2\} < \max\{x_1, x_2\} = x_2, \tag{1}$$

which would imply that the upper contour set is nonconvex and, therefore, preferences are not convex. In order to prove that, we focus on the case in which $y \sim x$, i.e., bundles x and y lie on the same indifference curve, which means that $x_1 = y_2$ and that $x_2 = y_1$ (as depicted in figure 1.5).

To show that inequality (1) is indeed satisfied, we will first focus in the case in which the convex combination of bundles x and y lies below the 45°-line (i.e., low values of α), and then on the case in which this convex combination lies above the 45°-line (i.e., high values of α):

Case 1: The convex combination lies below the 45°-line, as depicted in figure 1.5. In particular, since the convex combination lies below the 45°-line, we have that

$$\alpha x_1 + (1 - \alpha)y_1 \geq \alpha x_2 + (1 - \alpha)y_2,$$

which implies that

$$\max\{\alpha x_1 + (1 - \alpha)y_1, \alpha x_2 + (1 - \alpha)y_2\} = \alpha x_1 + (1 - \alpha)y_1.$$

In addition, we have that

$$\alpha x_1 + (1 - \alpha)y_1 \leq \alpha x_2 + (1 - \alpha)y_1,$$

since $x_1 < x_2$, given that bundle x lies above 45°-line. In addition,

$$\alpha x_2 + (1 - \alpha)y_1 = x_2,$$

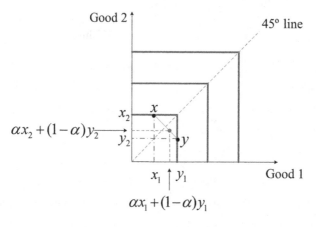

Figure 1.5 The linear combination lies below the 45°-line.

since $x_2 = y_1$ given that both bundles lie on the same indifference curve (see figure 1.5). Therefore,

$$\max\{\alpha x_1 + (1 - \alpha)y_1, \alpha x_2 + (1 - \alpha)y_2\} < \max\{x_1, x_2\},$$

implying that the consumer's utility from the convex combination of bundles x and y is strictly lower than from consuming bundle x alone, i.e., a violation of convexity in preferences.

Case 2: The convex combination now lies above the 45°-line, as depicted in figure 1.6.

In particular, since the convex combination lies above the 45°-line, we have that

$$\alpha x_1 + (1 - \alpha)y_1 \le \alpha x_2 + (1 - \alpha)y_2,$$

which implies that

$$\max\{\alpha x_1 + (1 - \alpha)y_1, \alpha x_2 + (1 - \alpha)y_2\} = \alpha x_2 + (1 - \alpha)y_2.$$

We furthermore have that

$$\alpha x_2 + (1 - \alpha)y_2 \le \alpha x_2 + (1 - \alpha)y_1,$$

since $y_1 > y_2$, given that bundle y lies below the 45°-line. Finally,

$$\alpha x_2 + (1 - \alpha)y_1 = x_2,$$

since bundles x and y lie on the same indifference curve, thus entailing that $x_2 = y_1$. As a consequence,

$$\max\{\alpha x_1 + (1 - \alpha)y_1, \alpha x_2 + (1 - \alpha)y_2\} < \max\{x_1, x_2\},$$

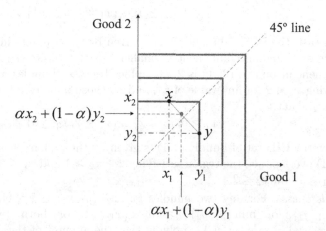

Figure 1.6 The linear combination lies above the 45°-line.

which also suggests that the consumer's utility from the convex combination of bundles x and y is strictly lower than from consuming bundle x alone, which constitutes a violation of convexity in preferences for Case 2 as well. Therefore, preferences are not convex.

- *Remark:* Note that this preference relation satisfies local nonsatiation. In order to show this property, take any bundle $(x_1, x_2) \in \mathbb{R}^2$ and $\varepsilon > 0$. Let us now generate a new bundle (y_1, y_2) in which both components of (x_1, x_2) have been increased by $\frac{\varepsilon}{2}$, i.e., $(y_1, y_2) \equiv (x_1 + \frac{\varepsilon}{2}, x_2 + \frac{\varepsilon}{2})$. Hence, $\max\{y_1, y_2\} > \max\{x_1, x_2\}$. By the preference relation in this example, it follows that $y \succsim x$, but not $x \succsim y$, so that $y \succ x$. We just need to confirm that bundles x and y are ε−close, by finding their Cartesian distance

$$\|x - y\| = \sqrt{\left[x_1 - \left(x_1 + \frac{\varepsilon}{2}\right)\right]^2 + \left[x_2 - \left(x_2 + \frac{\varepsilon}{2}\right)\right]^2} = \frac{\varepsilon}{\sqrt{2}},$$

which is smaller than ε, implying that the preference relation satisfies local nonsatiation.

(d) Bundle (x_1, x_2) is weakly preferred to (y_1, y_2), i.e., $(x_1, x_2) \succsim (y_1, y_2)$, if and only if $\max\{x_1, x_2\} \geqslant \min\{y_1, y_2\}$.

- Intuitively, this relation states that a bundle (x_1, x_2) is preferred to an alternative bundle (y_1, y_2) if and only if the most abundant component of the first bundle exceeds the least abundant component of the second bundle. For a given bundle like $(2, 1)$, its UCS comprises all those bundles whose most abundant component is larger than one unit (i.e., the least abundant component in bundle $(2, 1)$ is 1), depicted by the points in figure 1.7 for which $x_1 \geq 1$ regardless of their content of good 2, and all those bundles for which $x_2 \geq 1$ regardless of their content of good 1. That is,

$$\{x_1 \geq 1, x_2 \geq 0\} \cup \{x_1 \geq 0, x_2 \geq 1\}.$$

In contrast, the LCS of bundle $(2, 1)$ is given by those points in figure 1.7 for which their least abundant component is smaller than two units (i.e., the most abundant component in bundle $(2, 1)$ is 2). Graphically, these bundles are depicted as those satisfying $x_2 < 2$ for any value of x_1, and all those bundles for which $x_1 < 2$ for any value x_2. That is,

$$\{x_1 \geq 0, x_2 \leq 2\} \cup \{x_1 \leq 2, x_2 \geq 0\}.$$

Finally, the IND set of bundle $(2, 1)$ is given by the region where the UCS and LCS of $(2, 1)$ overlap, i.e., the region satisfying $2 \geq x_2 \geq 1$ and $x_1 \leq 2$, and that satisfying $2 \geq x_1 \geq 1$ and $x_2 \leq 2$.

- *Completeness.* For any two bundles $(x_1, x_2),(y_1, y_2) \in \mathbb{R}^2$, either $\max\{x_1, x_2\} \geq \min\{y_1, y_2\}$, or $\min\{y_1, y_2\} \geq \max\{x_1, x_2\}$, or both (which occurs when $\max\{x_1, x_2\} = \min\{y_1, y_2\}$, implying that the amount of the most abundant component of bundle x coincides with the amount in the least abundant component in

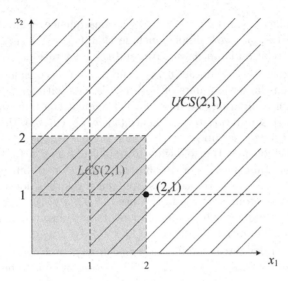

Figure 1.7 UCS and LCS of bundle $(2, 1)$.

bundle y). In the first case, we clearly have $(x_1, x_2) \succsim (y_1, y_2)$. In the second, note that $\min\{y_1, y_2\} \geq \max\{x_1, x_2\}$ implies

$$\max\{y_1, y_2\} \geqslant \min\{y_1, y_2\} \geq \max\{x_1, x_2\} \geqslant \min\{x_1, x_2\},$$

and hence, $\max\{y_1, y_2\} \geq \min\{x_1, x_2\}$, which yields $(y_1, y_2) \succsim (x_1, x_2)$. Finally, in the third case, $(x_1, x_2) \sim (y_1, y_2)$. Hence, this preference relation is complete.

- *Transitivity.* Take three bundles (x_1, x_2), (y_1, y_2) and $(z_1, z_2) \in \mathbb{R}^2$ satisfying

$$(x_1, x_2) \succsim (y_1, y_2) \quad \text{and} \quad (y_1, y_2) \succsim (z_1, z_2).$$

Then, they must satisfy that, on one hand, $\max\{x_1, x_2\} \geqslant \min\{y_1, y_2\}$, and on the other hand, $\max\{y_1, y_2\} \geqslant \min\{z_1, z_2\}$. However, it can be that $\max\{x_1, x_2\} \geqslant \min\{z_1, z_2\}$ is not satisfied, a condition we need for $(x_1, x_2) \succsim (z_1, z_2)$ and thus for transitivity to hold. For instance, consider bundle $(x_1, x_2) = (1, 0)$ and $(y_1, y_2) = (3, 0)$, which satisfy

$$\max\{x_1, x_2\} = 1 \geq 3 = \min\{y_1, y_2\};$$

and $(z_1, z_2) = (2, 2)$, which satisfies

$$\max\{y_1, y_2\} = 3 \geqslant 2 = \min\{z_1, z_2\}.$$

However, note that

$$\max\{x_1, x_2\} = 1 < 2 = \min\{z_1, z_2\},$$

which implies $(x_1, x_2) \precsim (z_1, z_2)$. As a consequence, while $(x_1, x_2) \succsim (y_1, y_2)$ and $(y_1, y_2) \succsim (z_1, z_2)$, we cannot conclude that $(x_1, x_2) \succsim (z_1, z_2)$, entailing that the preference relation is *not* transitive, and thus not rational either.

- *Monotonicity.* Take a bundle (y_1, y_2), and now let us consider another bundle (x_1, x_2) that contains larger amounts of both goods, i.e., with $x_1 > y_1$ and $x_2 > y_2$. At this point, when comparing the max $\{x_1, x_2\}$ against the min $\{y_1, y_2\}$, we can find that max $\{x_1, x_2\} \geqslant$ min $\{y_1, y_2\}$ and hence $(x_1, x_2) \succsim (y_1, y_2)$. However, we can also have that max $\{y_1, y_2\} \geqslant$ min $\{x_1, x_2\}$, which implies $(y_1, y_2) \succsim (x_1, x_2)$. In order to see that, let us consider the following example: $(x_1, x_2) = (3, 1)$ and $(y_1, y_2) = (2, 0)$. Indeed, note that max $\{x_1, x_2\} = 3 \geqslant$ min $\{y_1, y_2\} = 0$, but also that max $\{y_1, y_2\} = 2 \geqslant$ min $\{x_1, x_2\} = 1$. Hence, this preference relation doesn't satisfy monotonicity. Since, for monotonicity to hold, we need $(x_1, x_2) \succsim (y_1, y_2)$ but $(y_1, y_2) \nsucceq (x_1, x_2)$, so that the bundle in which all components have been increased, (x_1, x_2), is *strictly* preferred to the initial bundle, i.e., $(x_1, x_2) \succ (y_1, y_2)$.

- *Convexity.* Take three bundles $(x_1, x_2), (y_1, y_2)$, and $(z_1, z_2) \in \mathbb{R}^2$ with $(y_1, y_2) \succsim (x_1, x_2)$ and $(z_1, z_2) \succsim (x_1, x_2)$. Therefore, it must be that max $\{y_1, y_2\} \geqslant$ min $\{x_1, x_2\}$, and similarly that max $\{z_1, z_2\} \geqslant$ min $\{x_1, x_2\}$. However, the convex combination of (y_1, y_2) and (z_1, z_2) yields $(\lambda y_1 + (1 - \lambda)z_1, \lambda y_2 + (1 - \lambda)z_2)$ whose largest component,

$$\max\{\lambda y_1 + (1 - \lambda)z_1, \lambda y_2 + (1 - \lambda)z_2\},$$

is not necessarily higher than min $\{x_1, x_2\}$. In order to see that, consider an example in which max $\{y_1, y_2\} \geqslant$ min $\{x_1, x_2\}$, and max $\{z_1, z_2\} \geqslant$ min $\{x_1, x_2\}$, such as $(y_1, y_2) = (0, 4)$, $(x_1, x_2) = (3, 3)$ and $(z_1, z_2) = (4, 0)$. Indeed,

$$\max\{y_1, y_2\} = 4 \geqslant \min\{x_1, x_2\} = 3 \quad \text{and}$$
$$\max\{z_1, z_2\} = 4 \geq 3 = \min\{x_1, x_2\}.$$

Now, note that the convex combination of $(y_1, y_2) = (0, 4)$ and $(z_1, z_2) = (4, 0)$ with λ, will give us values between 0 and 4. Graphically, since we examine commodity bundles in $\mathbb{R}^2$, $(0, 4)$ lies on the vertical axis while $(4, 0)$ lies on the horizontal axis; thus implying that their convex combination is a downward diagonal line connecting these two points, as depicted in figure 1.8.

For instance, for intermediate values of λ (such as $\lambda = \frac{1}{2}$) we have that

$$\max\left\{\frac{1}{2}0 + \frac{1}{2}4, \frac{1}{2}4 + \frac{1}{2}0\right\} = \max\{2, 2\} = 2,$$

which does not exceed min $\{x_1, x_2\} = \min\{3, 3\} = 3$. Hence, the preference relation is *not* convex.

- *Remark:* This preference relation does not satisfy local nonsatiation (LNS). In particular, consider bundle $(x_1, x_2) = (1, 0)$. To establish LNS we must find a pair $(y_1, y_2) \in \mathbb{R}^2$ such that (y_1, y_2) is arbitrarily close to (x_1, x_2), and $(y_1, y_2) \succ (x_1, x_2)$

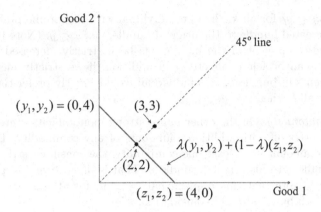

Figure 1.8 Checking for convexity.

strictly. In order to obtain $(y_1, y_2) \succ (x_1, x_2)$ we need that $(y_1, y_2) \succsim (x_1, x_2)$ and $(x_1, x_2) \not\succsim (y_1, y_2)$. By the preference relation in this example, the first condition implies

$$\max\{y_1, y_2\} \geqslant \min\{x_1, x_2\},$$

whereas the second condition requires

$$\max\{x_1, x_2\} < \min\{y_1, y_2\}.$$

However, $\min\{x_1, x_2\} = 0$ and $\max\{x_1, x_2\} = 1$. This implies that the above two conditions can be rewritten as

$$\max\{y_1, y_2\} \geqslant 0 \quad \text{and} \quad 1 < \min\{y_1, y_2\},$$

or, more compactly, as $\max\{y_1, y_2\} \geqslant \min\{y_1, y_2\} > 1$. As a consequence, *both* coordinates in bundle (y_1, y_2) must exceed 1 for this condition to be fulfilled, and points to the northeast of $(1, 1)$ cannot be found to be arbitrarily close to $(x_1, x_2) = (1, 0)$, i.e., for any $\varepsilon > 0$. Hence, this preference relation does *not* satisfy LNS.

Exercise #3 — Monotonicity and strong monotonicity

3. Explain monotonicity and strong monotonicity in preference relations, and compare them. Provide an example where a bundle x is (strictly) preferred to bundle y when preferences satisfy strong monotonicity, but x is not necessarily preferred to y under monotonicity.

- *Monotonicity* states that increasing the amount of some commodities cannot hurt, and increasing the amount of all commodities is strictly preferred. Formally, if we take bundle $y \in \mathbb{R}^L$ and weakly increase all k components, so that we generate a new bundle $x \in \mathbb{R}^L$

satisfying $x_k \geq y_k$ for all k, then an individual with monotonic preferences would prefer the newly created bundle to the original bundle, i.e., $x \succsim y$. (Note that this implies that at least one component of the bundle has been strictly increased while the remaining components can be left unaffected.) In addition, if we strictly increase the amount of all components in bundle y, this individual would strictly prefer the new bundle, i.e., if $x_k > y_k$ for all k, then $x \succ y$.

- *Strong monotonicity.* On the other hand, strong monotonicity states that the consumer is strictly better off with additional amounts of any commodity. That is, if we strictly increase the amount of at least one commodity, the consumer strictly prefers the newly created bundle x to his original bundle y. That is, if $x_k \geq y_k$ for all good k and $x \neq y$, then $x \succ y$. (Note that this implies that $x_j > y_j$ for at least one commodity j, since otherwise both bundles would coincide.)

- *Comparison.* Then, a consumer's preference relation can satisfy monotonicity (if additional amounts of one of his commodity do not harm his utility), but does not need to satisfy strong monotonicity (since for that to occur, he would need to become strictly better off as a consequence of the additional amounts in one of his commodities). However, if a consumer's preferences satisfy strong monotonicity, they must also satisfy monotonicity. That is why strong monotonicity is a more restrictive ("stronger") assumption on preferences than monotonicity.

- *Example*: Consider bundles $x = (1, 2)$ and $y = (1, 1)$. If preferences satisfy strong monotonicity, $x \succ y$ since the second component in bundle x is higher than the corresponding component in y, i.e., $x_j \geq y_j$ for some good j. However, if preferences only satisfy monotonicity, we cannot state that $x \succ y$ (strictly), since $x_k > y_k$ does not hold for all k commodities.

Exercise #5 — Convex preferences

5. Consider a concave utility function $u(x)$, where $x \in \mathbb{R}_+^N$ denotes consumption bundles with N components. In addition, consider the transformation $v(x) = f(u(x))$, where function $f(\cdot)$ is strictly increasing and concave. Show that the preferences represented by $v(x)$ must be convex, i.e., indifference curves are bowed-in towards the origin.

- *What we need to show?* In order to show convexity in preferences, we need that, for any three bundles x_1, x_2 and y satisfying $x_1 \succsim y$ and $x_2 \succsim y$, their linear combination $\overline{x} \equiv \alpha x_1 + (1 - \alpha) x_2$ also satisfies $\overline{x} \succsim y$. In terms of the utility function $u(x)$ representing the preference relation $\succsim$, this property implies that if the utility from bundles x_1 and x_2 satisfies $u(x_1) \geq u(y)$ and $u(x_2) \geq u(y)$, then the utility of their linear combination $\overline{x}$ also yields a utility level weakly higher than that of bundle y, i.e., $u(\overline{x}) \geq u(y)$.

- *Proof.* Since the transformation $v(x) = f(u(x))$ is concave, it satisfies

$$v(\overline{x}) \geq \alpha v(x_1) + (1 - \alpha) v(x_2).$$

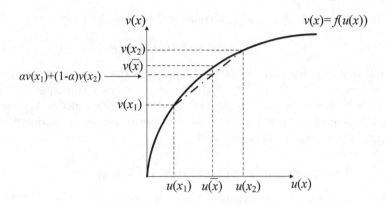

Figure 1.9 Concave utility function.

In words, the linear combination of the utility from bundles x_1 and x_2, $\alpha v(x_1) + (1 - \alpha)v(x_2)$, is lower than the utility from the linear combination of bundles x_1 and x_2, $v(\overline{x})$, as depicted in figure 1.9.

Using the definition of transformation $v(x) = f(u(x))$, we can rewrite the above inequality in terms of the $f(\cdot)$ function (rather than in terms of $v(\cdot)$), as follows:

$$f\left(u(\overline{x})\right) \geq \alpha f\left(u(x_1)\right) + (1 - \alpha)f\left(u(x_2)\right).$$

In addition, since transformation $f(u(x))$ is strictly increasing, $f\left(u(x_1)\right) \geq f\left(u(y)\right)$ since $u(x_1) \geq u(y)$, and similarly $f\left(u(x_2)\right) \geq f\left(u(y)\right)$ since $u(x_2) \geq u(y)$. Hence, we can expand the above inequality as follows:

$$f\left(u(\overline{x})\right) \geq \alpha \underbrace{f\left(u(x_1)\right)}_{\geq f(u(y))} + (1 - \alpha)\underbrace{f\left(u(x_1)\right)}_{\geq f(u(y))}$$

$$\geq \alpha f\left(u(y)\right) + (1 - \alpha)f\left(u(y)\right) = f\left(u(y)\right),$$

which simplifies to $f\left(u(\overline{x})\right) \geq f\left(u(y)\right)$. Finally, using again the property that transformation $f(u(x))$ is strictly increasing, $f\left(u(\overline{x})\right) \geq f\left(u(y)\right)$ implies $u(\overline{x}) \geq u(y)$ as we sought to show.

Exercise #7 — Monotonic transformations—I

7. Consider a utility function $u : \mathbb{R}_+^L \to \mathbb{R}$ representing a rational preference relation $\succsim$ over bundles $x \in \mathbb{R}_+^L$. Show that if $f : \mathbb{R} \to \mathbb{R}$ is a strictly increasing function, the function $v : X \to \mathbb{R}$ defined by $v(x) = f(u(x))$ is also a utility function that represents the same rational preference relation $\succsim$ as utility function $u(x)$.

- To show that $v(x) = f\left(u\left(x\right)\right)$ is also a utility function representing the same rational preference relation $\succsim$, we need to show that $v(x) \geqslant v(y)$ is equivalent to $x \succsim y$. That is,

$$f\left(u\left(x\right)\right) \geqslant f\left(u\left(y\right)\right) \Longleftrightarrow x \succsim y.$$

Since $f : \mathbb{R} \to \mathbb{R}$ is a strictly increasing function, then

$$f\left(u\left(x\right)\right) \geqslant f\left(u\left(y\right)\right) \Longleftrightarrow u\left(x\right) \geqslant u\left(y\right),$$

and since the utility function $u(\cdot)$ represents the rational preference relation $\succsim$, we can conclude that $u\left(x\right) \geqslant u\left(y\right) \Longleftrightarrow x \succsim y$. As a consequence, any function $v : X \to \mathbb{R}$ defined by $v(x) = f\left(u(x)\right)$ is also a utility function representing the same rational preference relation $\succsim$. As possible examples, consider $v(x) = [u(x)]^2$, or $v(x) = \alpha + \beta u(x)$, where $\alpha, \beta > 0$.

Exercise #9 — Lexicographic preference relation

9. Let us define a lexicographic preference relation in a consumption set $X \times Y$, as follows:

$$(x_1, x_2) \succsim (y_1, y_2) \text{ if and only if } \begin{cases} x_1 > y_1, \text{ or if} \\ x_1 = y_1 \text{ and } x_2 \geqslant y_2. \end{cases} \qquad (1)$$

Intuitively, the consumer prefers bundle x to y if the former contains more units of the first good than the latter, i.e., $x_1 > y_1$. However, if both bundles contain the same amounts of good 1, $x_1 = y_1$, the consumer ranks bundle x above y if the former has more units of good 2 than the latter, i.e., $x_2 \geq y_2$. For simplicity, assume that both components have been normalized to $X = [0, 1]$ and $Y = [0, 1]$.

(a) Show that the lexicographic preference relation satisfies rationality (i.e., it is complete and transitive).

1. *Completeness.* By definition, $\succsim$ is a complete preference relation if for all bundles $(x_1, x_2), (y_1, y_2) \in \mathbb{R}^2$, either $(x_1, x_2) \succsim (y_1, y_2)$, or $(y_1, y_2) \succsim (x_1, x_2)$, or both. Hence, we need to show that

$$(x_1, x_2) \nsucceq (y_1, y_2) \implies (y_1, y_2) \succsim (x_1, x_2).$$

Indeed, note that $(x_1, x_2) \nsucceq (y_1, y_2)$ can be expressed as

$$(x_1, x_2) \nsucceq (y_1, y_2) \text{ if } \begin{cases} y_1 \geq x_1, \text{ and if} \\ y_1 \neq x_1 \text{ or } y_2 > x_2 \end{cases}. \qquad (2)$$

Expression (2) describes that bundle (y_1, y_2) contains weakly more units of good 1 than (x_1, x_2) does, thus implying that a consumer with a lexicographic preference relation weakly prefers (y_1, y_2) to (x_1, x_2), i.e., $(y_1, y_2) \succsim (x_1, x_2)$. Therefore, we have shown that $(x_1, x_2) \nsucceq (y_1, y_2)$ implies $(y_1, y_2) \succsim (x_1, x_2)$. Hence, the preference relation is complete.

2. *Transitivity.* Let us take three bundles $(x_1, x_2), (y_1, y_2)$ and $(z_1, z_2) \in \mathbb{R}^2$ with $(x_1, x_2) \succsim (y_1, y_2)$:

$$(x_1, x_2) \succsim (y_1, y_2) \text{ if and only if } \begin{cases} x_1 > y_1, \text{ or if} \\ x_1 = y_1 \text{ and } x_2 \geqslant y_2, \end{cases}$$

and $(y_1, y_2) \succsim (z_1, z_2)$, that is,

$$(y_1, y_2) \succsim (z_1, z_2) \text{ if and only if } \begin{cases} y_1 > z_1, \text{ or if} \\ y_1 = z_1 \text{ and } y_2 \geqslant z_2. \end{cases}$$

Hence, we need to check for transitivity in the four possible cases in which $(x_1, x_2) \succsim (y_1, y_2)$ and $(y_1, y_2) \succsim (z_1, z_2)$.

(a) If $x_1 > y_1$, and $y_1 > z_1$, then by the transitivity of the "greater than or equal" operator ($\geq$), we obtain $x_1 > z_1$. As we know that $x_1 > z_1$ implies $(x_1, x_2) \succsim (z_1, z_2)$, then transitivity holds in this case.

(b) If ($x_1 = y_1$ and $x_2 \geqslant y_2$) and ($y_1 = z_1$ and $y_2 \geqslant z_2$), then ($x_1 = z_1$ and $x_2 \geqslant z_2$). In addition, we know that ($x_1 = z_1$ and $x_2 \geqslant z_2$) implies $(x_1, x_2) \succsim (z_1, z_2)$, which validates transitivity.

(c) If $x_1 > y_1$, and ($y_1 = z_1$ and $y_2 \geqslant z_2$), then $x_1 > z_1$. As we know that $x_1 > z_1$ implies $(x_1, x_2) \succsim (z_1, z_2)$, transitivity holds in this case as well.

(d) If $y_1 > z_1$ and ($x_1 = y_1$ and $x_2 \geqslant y_2$), then $x_1 > z_1$, and we know that $x_1 > z_1$ implies $(x_1, x_2) \succsim (z_1, z_2)$, entailing that transitivity holds in this case as well. We have then checked all four cases under which $(x_1, x_2) \succsim (y_1, y_2)$ and $(y_1, y_2) \succsim (z_1, z_2)$ may arise, and in all of them we obtained $(x_1, x_2) \succsim (z_1, z_2)$, confirming that this preference relation is transitive. Therefore, since the preference relation is complete and transitive, we can conclude that it is rational.

(b) Show that the lexicographic preference relation $\succsim$ *cannot* be represented by a utility function $u : X \times Y \to \mathbb{R}$.

- Let us work by contradiction. So, let us suppose that there is a utility function $u(\cdot)$ representing this lexicographic preference relation $\succsim$. Then, for any $x_1 \in X$, the pair $(x_1, 1)$ is strictly preferred to the pair $(x_1, 0)$, i.e., $(x_1, 1) \succ (x_1, 0)$. If there is a utility function $u(\cdot)$ representing this preference relation, then we must have that

$$(x_1, 1) \succ (x_1, 0) \iff u(x_1, 1) > u(x_1, 0).$$

On the other hand, from the Archimedean property, we know that we can pick a rational number $r(x_1)$ such that it lies in between $u(x_1, 1)$ and $u(x_1, 0)$.

$$u(x_1, 1) > r(x_1) > u(x_1, 0).$$

Let us take any $x_1, x_2 \in X$, and let us suppose without loss of generality that $x_1 > x_2$. Similarly to our above result, we then have that

$$u(x_2, 1) > r(x_2) > u(x_2, 0).$$

And since $x_1 > x_2$, we have that

$$u(x_1, 1) > r(x_1) > u(x_1, 0) > u(x_2, 1) > r(x_2) > u(x_2, 0),$$

which implies

$$r(x_1) > r(x_2).$$

Then, $r(\cdot)$ provides a one-to-one function from the set of real numbers, $\mathbb{R}$ (which is uncountable) to the set of rational numbers, $\mathbb{Q}$, which is countable. But this is a mathematical impossibility.[2] Thus, we conclude that there can be no utility function representing the lexicographic preferences when they are defined over a continuous set $X \times Y$, where $X = [0, 1]$ and $Y = [0, 1]$.

(c) Assume now that this preference relation is defined on a *finite* consumption set $X = X_1 \times X_2$, where $X_1 = \{x_{11}, x_{12}, ..., x_{1n}\}$ and $X_2 = \{x_{21}, x_{22}, ..., x_{2m}\}$. [*Hint:* You can define a function $N_i(x_{ij})$ as the number of elements in sequence X_i prior to element x_{ij}; that is,

$$N_i(x_{ij}) = \#\{y \in X_i | y < x_{ij}\}.$$

Then define a utility function

$$u(y_1, y_2) = mN_1(y_1) + N_2(y_2), \quad \text{where} \quad m > 0,$$

and for any pair $(y_1, y_2) \in X_1 \times X_2$.]

1. Let us first define a function $N_i(x_{ij})$ as the number of elements in sequence X_i prior to element x_{ij}:

$$N_i(x_i) = \#\{y \in X_i | y < x_{ij}\}, \text{ where } X_i = \{x_{i1}, x_{i2}, ..., x_{in}\}.$$

Then, we define a utility function $u(y_1, y_2) = mN_1(y_1) + N_2(y_2)$ for any pair $(y_1, y_2) \in X_1 \times X_2$. In order to show that this utility function indeed represents the lexicographic preference relation (when consumption sets are finite), we need to show the usual two lines of implication:

$$(y_1, y_2) \succsim (z_1, z_2) \implies u(y_1, y_2) \geq u(z_1, z_2), \text{ and}$$

$$(y_1, y_2) \succsim (z_1, z_2) \impliedby u(y_1, y_2) \geq u(z_1, z_2).$$

2. Let us first show that $(y_1, y_2) \succsim (z_1, z_2) \implies u(y_1, y_2) \geq u(z_1, z_2)$. In order to show this result, we need that

$$\begin{cases} y_1 > z_1, \text{ or} \\ y_1 = z_1 \text{ and } y_2 \geqslant z_2 \end{cases} \text{ implies } mN_1(y_1) + N_2(y_2) \geq mN_1(z_1) + N_2(z_2).$$

Hence, we first need to check if this inequality is satisfied when $y_1 > z_1$, and when $(y_1 = z_1 \text{ and } y_2 \geqslant z_2)$.

---

[2]For a review of real and rational numbers, see, for instance, Simon and Blume's *Mathematics for Economists*, pp. 848–849.

(a) Let us first check if $y_1 > z_1$ implies $mN_1(y_1) + N_2(y_2) \geq mN_1(z_1) + N_2(z_2)$. Alternatively, we can rewrite this inequality as

$$m\underbrace{[N_1(y_1) - N_1(z_1)]}_{a} + \underbrace{[N_2(y_2) - N_2(z_2)]}_{b} \geq 0. \tag{1}$$

Let us analyze if this expression can ever be negative (we will examine the infimum values) by separately evaluating the infimum of terms (a) and (b). Regarding term (a), we know that, if $y_1 > z_1$,

$$\inf\left[N_1(y_1) - N_1(z_1)\right] = k - (k-1) = 1,$$

since $N_1(y_1) > N_1(z_1)$ given that $y_1 > z_1$,

and hence, $\inf\left[m\left[N_1(y_1) - N_1(z_1)\right]\right] = m$. Thus, $m\left[N_1(y_1) - N_1(z_1)\right] \geq m$, and term (a) in expression (1) is always weakly above m. Let us now focus on term (b) of expression (1):[3]

$$\inf\left[N_2(y_2) - N_2(z_2)\right] = \inf N_2(y_2) - \sup N_2(z_2) = 0 - (m-1) = 1 - m.$$

Intuitively, the result $\inf N_2(y_2) = 0$ implies that there are no elements prior to y_2 (that is, y_2 is the first term of the sequence); in contrast, $\sup N_2(z_2) = m - 1$ means that z_2 is the last element in the sequence of length m, and hence all other $m-1$ elements in the sequence were located prior to z_2. Hence, $N_1(y_1) - N_1(z_1) \geq 1 - m$, and thus term (b) in expression (1) always lies above $1 - m$. Combining the results of the first and second term of the infimum of expression (1), we can conclude that

$$m\left[N_1(y_1) - N_1(z_1)\right] + \left[N_2(y_2) - N_2(z_2)\right] \geq m - (1-m) = 1,$$

which is clearly above 0. Recall that we needed to show that

$$m\left[N_1(y_1) - N_1(z_1)\right] + \left[N_2(y_2) - N_2(z_2)\right] \geq 0.$$

Therefore, $y_1 > z_1$ indeed implies $u(y_1, y_2) \geq u(z_1, z_2)$.

(b) Let us now check that $(y_1 = z_1$ and $y_2 \geqslant z_2)$ also implies $mN_1(y_1) + N_2(y_2) \geq mN_1(z_1) + N_2(z_2)$. Alternatively, we can rewrite this inequality as

$$m\left[N_1(y_1) - N_1(z_1)\right] + \left[N_2(y_2) - N_2(z_2)\right] \geq 0.$$

First, note that $y_1 = z_1$ implies that $N_1(y_1) = N_1(z_1)$. Second, note that $y_2 \geqslant z_2$ implies that $N_2(y_2) \geq N_2(z_2)$. Therefore, the above inequality becomes

$$0 + \underbrace{\left[N_2(y_2) - N_2(z_2)\right]}_{\geq 0} \geq 0,$$

which confirms what we needed to show. Hence, $(y_1 = z_1$ and $y_2 \geqslant z_2)$ indeed implies $u(y_1, y_2) \geq u(z_1, z_2)$.

---

[3] Note that we are not imposing any conditions on y_2 and z_2, since we only assumed that $y_1 > z_1$.

3. Let us now show the opposite direction of implication, i.e., $(y_1, y_2) \succsim (z_1, z_2) \impliedby$ $u(y_1, y_2) \geq u(z_1, z_2)$. First, note that if $u(y_1, y_2) \geq u(z_1, z_2)$, then it must be that $mN_1(y_1) + N_2(y_2) \geq mN_1(z_1) + N_2(z_2)$. Rearranging, we obtain

$$m\left[N_1(y_1) - N_1(z_1)\right] + \left[N_2(y_2) - N_2(z_2)\right] \geq 0.$$

Then, note that this inequality can be positive for two different reasons: (1) because $N_1(y_1) > N_1(z_1)$, which implies $y_1 > z_1$; or because (2) $N_1(y_1) = N_1(z_1)$ and $N_2(y_2) \geq N_2(z_2)$, which implies $y_1 = z_1$ and $y_2 \geqslant z_2$. And we know that, by definition, these two cases describe the lexicographic preference relation

$$(y_1, y_2) \succsim (z_1, z_2) \text{ if and only if } \begin{cases} y_1 > z_1, \text{ or if} \\ y_1 = z_1 \text{ and } y_2 \geqslant z_2. \end{cases}$$

Hence, $(y_1, y_2) \succsim (z_1, z_2) \impliedby u(y_1, y_2) \geq u(z_1, z_2)$. Since we have shown this implication in both directions, then we have confirmed that this utility function indeed represents the lexicographic preference relation

$$(y_1, y_2) \succsim (z_1, z_2) \iff u(y_1, y_2) \geq u(z_1, z_2).$$

Exercise #11 — WARP and rationality

11. Consider a choice rule $C(\cdot)$ defined over a budget set $\mathcal{B}$, and assume it satisfies the weak axiom of revealed preference (WARP). Does this choice structure guarantee a rational preference relation? [*Hint*: It is sufficient to find an example of a choice rule that, despite satisfying WARP, does not satisfy transitivity (one of the conditions for rationality).]

- Let us prove it using an example of a choice rule satisfying WARP, which does not satisfy transitivity. Consider a consumption set $X = \{x, y, z\}$, and the following budget sets

$$\mathcal{B} = \{\{x, y\}, \{y, z\}, \{x, z\}\}.$$

Now, let us next consider the following simple choice rule that selects a single element every time the decision maker is confronted with a pair of available bundles

$$C(\{x, y\}) = \{x\},$$

$$C(\{y, z\}) = \{y\},$$

$$C(\{x, z\}) = \{z\}.$$

Note that this choice rule satisfies WARP. However, note that such a choice rule implies

$$C(\{x, y\}) = \{x\}, \text{ which entails } x \succ y, \text{ and}$$
$$C(\{y, z\}) = \{y\}, \text{ which implies } y \succ z.$$

But, if the preference relation were rational (satisfying transitivity as a consequence), then we would have that

$$\text{if } x \succ y \text{ and } y \succ z, \text{ then } x \succ z.$$

But $x \succ z$ contradicts the choice rule $C(\{x, z\}) = \{z\}$, whereby the decision maker only selects bundle z when both x and z were available to him. Therefore, this choice rule entails $z \succ x$, alternatively implying that a choice rule, despite satisfying WARP, does *not* guarantee a rational preference relation.

Exercise #13 — Lexicographic preference and WARP

13. Does the lexicographic preference relation induce a choice structure that satisfies the weak axiom of revealed preference (WARP)? [*Hint*: Prove it in two steps. First, show whether the lexicographic preference relation is a *rational* preference relation, and then show that every rational preference relation implies a choice structure which satisfies WARP].

- We want to prove this statement in two steps:

    (1) Every lexicographic preference relation is rational, and

    (2) Every rational preference relation satisfies WARP.

- The first step was already shown in exercise 9 of this chapter.

- Let us prove here the second step (that every rational preference relation satisfies WARP).

    Let us first recall the definition of a choice rule satisfying WARP:

    if for some $B \in \mathcal{B}$ with $x, y \in B$, we have $x \in C(B)$,
    then for any $B' \in \mathcal{B}$ with $x, y \in B'$, and where $y \in C(B')$, we must have $x \in C(B')$.

    First, take some budget set $B \in \mathcal{B}$. Let us assume that $x, y \in B$, and that bundle x is revealed preferred to all other bundles in B, i.e., $x \in C^*(B, \succsim)$. Hence, $x \succsim y$.

    To check whether WARP is satisfied, suppose that for other budget set $B' \in \mathcal{B}$ that also contains bundles x and y, i.e., $x, y \in B'$, we have that bundle y is revealed preferred, i.e., $y \in C^*(B', \succsim)$. This implies that $y \succsim z$ for any $z \in B'$.

    Since we also had that $x \succsim y$. Hence, by transitivity (note that here we can use transitivity because the preference relation is rational), we obtain

    $$x \succsim y \text{ and } y \succsim z, \text{ then } x \succsim z,$$

    and $x \succsim z$ for all $z \in B'$ implies that $x \in C^*(B', \succsim)$. Therefore, WARP is satisfied.

Exercise #15 — Homogeneity and addition

15. Consider utility functions $u(x_1, x_2)$ and $v(x_1, x_2)$. Prove that if $u(x_1, x_2)$ and $v(x_1, x_2)$ are both homogeneous of degree r, then their simple sum

$$s(x_1, x_2) \equiv u(x_1, x_2) + v(x_1, x_2)$$

is also homogeneous of degree r.

- Whenever it holds that utility function $u(x_1, x_2)$ is homogeneous of degree r,

$$t^r u(x_1, x_2) = u(tx_1, tx_2),$$

and that utility function $v(x_1, x_2)$ is homogeneous of the same degree r,

$$t^r v(x_1, x_2) = v(tx_1, tx_2),$$

thus it must also be true that, if we construct the sum $s(x_1, x_2) = u(x_1, x_2) + v(s_1, s_2)$, and we increase the arguments (x_1, x_2) by a common factor t, the sum function $s(x_1, x_2)$ still exhibits homogeneity of degree r, that is,

$$s(tx_1, tx_2) = u(tx_1, tx_2) + v(tx_1, tx_2) = t^r u(x_1, x_2) + t^r v(x_1, x_2)$$
$$= t^r [u(x_1, tx_2) + v(x_1, x_2)] = t^r s(x_1, x_2),$$

or, more compactly, $s(tx_1, tx_2) = t^r s(tx_1, tx_2)$. Hence, simple addition preserves the homogeneity of the function we are adding up.

Exercise #17 — Quasi-hyperbolic discounting

17. Consider a consumer with utility function $u(x_t) = \ln x_t$ for the income x_t he enjoys in period t. Assume that he receives no income in the first two periods, but receives an income $w > 0$ in the third period. In addition, this consumer discounts his income stream (x_0, x_1, x_2) according to

$$u(x_0, x_1, x_2) = \ln x_0 + \beta\delta \ln x_1 + \beta\delta^2 \ln x_2,$$

where $\delta \in (0, 1)$ denotes his discount factor, and $\beta \leq 1$. Let us next show that this type of utility function (commonly known as the (β, δ)−model) exhibits present bias when $\beta \neq 1$. Assume that, once the individual makes plans in period 0, he does not revise these plans in the future.

(a) Assume that he borrows during periods 0 and 1, and in period 2 he uses w to pay his debt. For simplicity, assume that he pays no interest r for consumption he undertakes in periods 0 and 1, but he pays $(1 + r)(x_0 + x_1)$. Find his optimal consumption plan for (x_0, x_1, x_2).

- Since the individual's budget constraint in period 2 is $w - x_2 = (1+r)(x_0 + x_1)$, its utility maximization problem is

$$\max_{x_0, x_1, x_2} \ln(x_0) + \beta\delta \ln(x_1) + \beta\delta^2 \ln(x_2)$$

$$\text{subject to } x_2 = w - (1+r)(x_0 + x_1),$$

which can be reduced to an unconstrained maximization problem with only two choice variables:

$$\max_{x_0, x_1} \ln(x_0) + \beta\delta \ln(x_1) + \beta\delta^2 \ln\left[w - (1+r)(x_0 + x_1)\right].$$

Taking FOCs with respect to x_0 yields

$$\frac{1}{x_0} + \beta\delta^2 \frac{1}{w - (1+r)(x_0 + x_1)}(-(1+r)) = 0,$$

and rearranging,

$$w - (1+r)(x_0 + x_1) = x_0 \beta\delta^2(1+r).$$

Then solving for x_0 yields

$$x_0 = \frac{w - (1+r)x_1}{(1+r)(\beta\delta^2 + 1)}.$$

Likewise, taking FOCs with respect to x_1 yields

$$\beta\delta\frac{1}{x_1} + \beta\delta^2 \frac{1}{w - (1+r)(x_0 + x_1)}(-(1+r)) = 0,$$

and rearranging,

$$w - (1+r)(x_0 + x_1) = x_1 \delta(1+r).$$

Then solving for x_1 yields

$$x_1 = \frac{w - (1+r)x_0}{(1+r)(\delta + 1)}.$$

Simultaneously solving for x_0 and x_1, we find the optimal consumption levels

$$x_0^* = \frac{w}{(1+r)(1 + \beta\delta + \beta\delta^2)} \quad \text{and} \quad x_1^* = \frac{\beta\delta w}{(1+r)(1 + \beta\delta^2 + \beta\delta^2)}.$$

Plugging their values into the budget constraint, we obtain the optimal consumption in period 2,

$$x_2^* = \frac{\beta\delta^2 w}{1 + \beta\delta + \beta\delta^2}.$$

(b) Compare the total debt that at period 0 a present-biased individual (with $\beta \neq 1$) and an individual without present bias ($\beta = 1$) plan to have at period 2.

- The total debt of this individual is $x_0^* + x_1^*$, that is,

$$x_0^* + x_1^* = \frac{w + \beta\delta w}{(1+r)(1+\beta\delta+\beta\delta^2)} \equiv TD(\beta).$$

Therefore, in the case that he is not present biased, $\beta = 1$, the above equation becomes

$$TD(1) = \frac{w + \delta w}{(1+r)(1+\delta+\delta^2)},$$

where $TD(\beta) > TD(1)$ for all $\beta < 1$.

(c) While part (b) of the exercise focused on the debts that both types of individuals plan to have at period 2, the present-biased individual still has an opportunity to further increase his debt during period 1 given his time-inconsistent preferences. Find his optimal consumption plan (x_1, x_2) at period 1.

- The present-biased individual will reevaluate his consumption in periods 1 and 2 once he reaches period 1. In particular, he solves the utility maximization problem

$$\max_{x_1, x_2} \quad \ln(x_1) + \beta\delta \ln(x_2)$$
$$\text{subject to} \quad x_2 = w - (1+r)(x_0 + x_1).$$

This reduces to the unconstrained problem

$$\max_{x_1} \quad \ln(x_1) + \beta\delta \ln(w - (1+r)(x_0 + x_1)).$$

Taking FOCs with respect to x_1 yields

$$\frac{1}{x_1} + \beta\delta \frac{1}{w - (1+r)(x_0 + x_1)}(-(1+r)) = 0,$$

and rearranging,

$$w - (1+r)(x_0 + x_1) = x_1 \beta\delta(1+r).$$

Solving for x_1 yields the optimal consumption in period 1,

$$x_1^* = \frac{w - (1+r)x_0}{(1+r)(1+\beta\delta)},$$

whereas the optimal consumption in period 2 can be found from the budget constraint

$$x_2^* = w - (1+r)(x_0 + x_1^*) = \frac{\beta\delta[w - (1+r)x_0]}{1+\beta\delta}.$$

(d) Evaluate again the total debt of the present-biased individual against that of the decision maker who does not exhibit present bias.

- Total debt, $x_0^* + x_1^*$, for the present-biased individual is

$$\frac{w}{(1+r)(1+\beta\delta+\beta\delta^2)} + \frac{w-(1+r)x_0}{(1+r)(1+\beta\delta)}.$$

Whereas for the non-present-biased individual total debt still is the expression we found in part (b) of the exercise,

$$\frac{w+\delta w}{(1+r)(1+\delta+\delta^2)}.$$

Hence, the total debt of the present-biased individual is actually larger after he reevaluates his consumption plans at period 1 (larger than what we found for him in part (b)). In other words, his planned debt in period zero is further increased once he re-optimized at period 1.

(e) Evaluate the expression we found in part (d) for parameter values $w = 100$, $x_0 = 10$, $\delta = 0.9$, and $r = 0.3$.

- Substituting these values, the total debt for the present-biased individual is

$$\frac{100}{1.3+2.23\beta} + \frac{87}{1.3+1.17\beta}.$$

Figure 1.10 plots the total debt as a function of β.

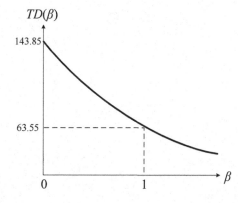

Figure 1.10 Total debt as a function of present bias.

Chapter 2 — Demand Theory

Summary This chapter analyzes Walrasian demand, its properties, and its comparative statics with respect to prices and wealth. In particular, we start analyzing a set of introductory exercises in which we study how to find the Walrasian demand on different utility functions, such as the Cobb–Douglas, CES, etc., where we also examine under which conditions they satisfy Walras' law. In exercises 5–7 we test whether different demand functions satisfy WARP. We then analyze income and substitution effects under different contexts, such as when consumer preferences are quasi-linear, when goods are inferior and Giffen, etc. Afterward, we investigate the relationship between the WARP and the so-called compensated and uncompensated law of demand, and the connection of these laws with the Slutsky matrix. We then examine the constant elasticity of substitution (CES) utility function and under which conditions it embodies standard utility functions, such as the Cobb–Douglas, and those representing preferences for perfect complements or substitutes. The chapter also studies the duality between the utility maximization problem (UMP) and the expenditure minimization problem (EMP). We next examine under which conditions the utility maximization problem of a separable utility function can be partitioned into pieces. The chapter finally explores utility functions representing a minimum amount of goods that the individual needs to consume, i.e., the Stone–Geary utility functions, finding the Walrasian demand and its properties.

Exercise #1 — Finding Walrasian demands—I

1. Determine the Walrasian demand $x(p, w) = (x_1(p, w), x_2(p, w))$ and the indirect utility function $v(p, w)$ for each of the following utility functions in $\mathbb{R}_+^2$. Briefly describe the indifference curves of each utility function and find the marginal rate of substitution, $MRS_{1,2}(x)$. Consider the following two points in your analysis:

   - *Existence.* First, in all three cases the budget set is compact (it is closed, since the bundles in the frontier are available for the consumer, and bounded). Additionally, all utility functions are continuous. Therefore, we can apply Weierstrass theorem to conclude that each of the utility maximization problems (UMPs) we consider has at least one solution.

   - *Binding constraints.* We know that if preferences are locally nonsatiated, then the budget constraint will be binding, i.e., the consumer will be exhausting all his wealth. We can easily check that these utility functions are increasing in both x_1 and x_2, which implies monotonicity and, in turn, entails local nonsatiation. Hence, we can assume thereafter that the budget constraint is binding.

   (a) Cobb–Douglas utility function, $u(x) = x_1^3 x_2^4$.

      1. This utility function is a Cobb–Douglas utility function, with smooth indifference curves that are bowed-in towards the origin. Regarding the marginal rate of

substitution between goods x_1 and x_2, MRS_{x_1,x_2}, we have

$$MRS_{x_1,x_2} = \frac{\frac{\partial u(x)}{\partial x_1}}{\frac{\partial u(x)}{\partial x_2}} = \frac{3x_1^2 x_2^4}{4x_1^3 x_2^3} = \frac{3x_2}{4x_1}.$$

2. The UMP is given by

$$\max_{x_1,x_2} u(x) = x_1^3 x_2^4$$

subject to

$$p_1 x_1 + p_2 x_2 \leq w,$$

$$x_1, x_2 \geq 0.$$

As mentioned above, the budget constraint will be binding. Furthermore, since the utility from consuming zero amounts of either of the goods is zero, i.e., $u(0, \cdot) = u(\cdot, 0) = 0$, and the consumer's wealth is strictly positive, $w > 0$, then it can never be optimal to consume zero amounts of either of the goods. Therefore, we do not need to worry about the nonnegativity constraints $x_1, x_2 \geq 0$, i.e., there are no corner solutions. The Lagrangian of this UMP is then

$$\mathcal{L}(x_1, x_2; \lambda) = x_1^3 x_2^4 - \lambda [p_1 x_1 + p_2 x_2 - w].$$

The first-order conditions are

$$\frac{\partial \mathcal{L}}{\partial x_1} = 3x_1^2 x_2^4 - \lambda p_1 = 0,$$

$$\frac{\partial \mathcal{L}}{\partial x_2} = 4x_1^3 x_2^3 - \lambda p_2 = 0,$$

Solving for λ on both first-order conditions, we obtain

$$\frac{3x_1^2 x_2^4}{p_1} = \frac{4x_1^3 x_2^3}{p_2} \Longleftrightarrow \frac{3x_2}{p_1} = \frac{4x_1}{p_2}.$$

This is the well-known "equal bang for the buck" condition across goods at utility maximizing bundles. (Intuitively, the consumer adjusts his consumption of goods 1 and 2 until the point in which the marginal utility per dollar on good 1 coincides with that of good 2.) Using now the budget constraint (which is binding), we have

$$p_1 x_1 + p_2 x_2 = w \Longleftrightarrow x_1 = \frac{w}{p_1} - \frac{p_2 x_2}{p_1},$$

and substituting this expression of x_1 into the above equality, yields the Walrasian demand for good 2

$$\frac{3x_2}{p_1} = \frac{4}{p_2} \left(\frac{w}{p_1} - \frac{p_2 x_2}{p_1} \right) \Longleftrightarrow x_2 = \frac{4}{7} \frac{w}{p_2}.$$

Then, similarly solving for x_1, we obtain the Walrasian demand for good 1,

$$\frac{3}{p_1}\left(\frac{w}{p_2} - \frac{p_1 x_1}{p_2}\right) = \frac{4x_1}{p_2} \iff x_1 = \frac{3}{7}\frac{w}{p_1}.$$

Hence, the Walrasian demand function is

$$x(p, w) = \left(\frac{3}{7}\frac{w}{p_1}, \frac{4}{7}\frac{w}{p_2}\right).$$

And the indirect utility function $v(p, w)$ is given by plugging the Walrasian demand of each good into the consumer's utility function, which provides us with his utility level in equilibrium, as follows:

$$v(p, w) = \left(\frac{3}{7}\frac{w}{p_1}\right)^3 \left(\frac{4}{7}\frac{w}{p_2}\right)^4 = \frac{3^3 \times 4^4}{7^7}\frac{w^7}{p_1^3 p_2^4}.$$

(b) Preferences for substitutes (linear utility function), $u(x) = 3x_1 + 4x_2$.

- In order to draw indifference curves for this utility function, just consider some fixed utility level, e.g., $\bar{u} = 10$, and then solve for x_2, obtaining $x_2 = \frac{\bar{u}}{4} - \frac{3}{4}x_1$. Note that the resulting expressions are functions of x_1 only, and importantly, they are *linear* in x_1, as depicted in figure 2.1. Intuitively, this indicates that both goods can be substituted at the same rate, regardless of the amount the consumer owns of every good (goods are perfect substitutes). The MRS_{x_1, x_2} confirms this intuition, since it is constant for any amount of x_1 and x_2,

$$MRS_{x_1, x_2} = \frac{\frac{\partial u(x)}{\partial x_1}}{\frac{\partial u(x)}{\partial x_2}} = \frac{3}{4}.$$

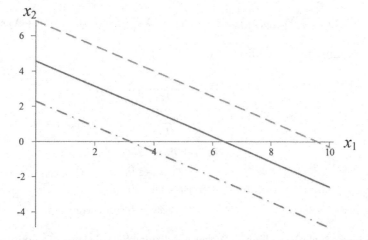

Figure 2.1 Indifference curves of $u(x) = 3x_1 + 4x_2$

The $MRS_{x_1,x_2} = \frac{p_1}{p_2}$ condition in this case entails $\frac{3}{4} = \frac{p_1}{p_2}$, or $\frac{3}{p_1} = \frac{4}{p_2}$, which represents in the left (right) the marginal utility per dollar spent on good 1 (good 2, respectively), i.e., the "bang for the buck" on each good. When $\frac{3}{p_1} > \frac{4}{p_2}$, the consumer seeks to purchase good 1 alone, giving rise to a corner solution with $x_1(p,w) = \frac{w}{p_1}$ and $x_2(p,w) = 0$ as Walrasian demands. Similarly, when $\frac{3}{p_1} < \frac{4}{p_2}$ a corner solution emerges with only good 2 being consumed, i.e., $x_1(p,w) = 0$ and $x_2(p,w) = \frac{w}{p_2}$. Finally, when $\frac{3}{p_1} = \frac{4}{p_2}$, a continuum of equilibria arise as the consumer is indifferent between dedicating more money to good 1 or good 2; that is, all (x_1, x_2)-pairs on the budget line $p_1 x_1 + p_2 x_2 = w$ are utility-maximizing bundles.

- For completeness, we next show that we can obtain the same solutions if we were to set up the consumer's UMP, his associated Lagrangian, and take Kuhn–Tucker conditions. The UMP in this case is

$$\max_{x_1, x_2} u(x) = 3x_1 + 4x_2$$

subject to

$$p_1 x_1 + p_2 x_2 \leq w,$$

$$x_1, x_2 \geq 0.$$

As mentioned above, the budget constraint will be binding. The nonnegativity constraints, however, will not necessarily be binding, implying that in certain cases the consumer might choose to select zero amounts of some good. Therefore, we face a maximization problem with inequality constraints, $x_1, x_2 \geqslant 0$, and hence must use Kuhn–Tucker conditions. First, we set up the Kuhn–Tucker style Lagrangian of this UMP

$$\mathcal{L}(x_1, x_2; \lambda_1, \lambda_2, \lambda_3) = 3x_1 + 4x_2 - \lambda_1 [p_1 x_1 + p_2 x_2 - w] + \lambda_2 x_1 + \lambda_3 x_2.$$

The Kuhn–Tucker conditions are

$$\frac{\partial \mathcal{L}}{\partial x_1} = 3 - \lambda_1 p_1 + \lambda_2 = 0,$$

$$\frac{\partial \mathcal{L}}{\partial x_2} = 4 - \lambda_1 p_2 + \lambda_3 = 0,$$

$$p_1 x_1 + p_2 x_2 \leq w,$$

$$x_1, x_2 \geq 0,$$

$$\lambda_1 [p_1 x_1 + p_2 x_2 - w] = 0,$$

$$\lambda_2 x_1 = 0, \text{ and } \lambda_1 x_2 = 0.$$

While we include all Kuhn–Tucker conditions for this type of maximization problems, some of them can be eliminated, since we know that the budget constraint is binding, i.e., $p_1 x_1 + p_2 x_2 = w$. Additionally, solving for λ_1 in the first two expressions, we obtain

$$\frac{3 + \lambda_2}{p_1} = \frac{4 + \lambda_3}{p_2}. \tag{1}$$

Now we are ready to consider the solutions that can arise in the four possible cases in which the nonnegativity constraints can be met. These cases are

1. $\lambda_2 = 0$ and $\lambda_3 = 0$ i.e., $x_1 > 0$ and $x_2 > 0$.
2. $\lambda_2 = 0$ and $\lambda_3 \neq 0$ i.e., $x_1 > 0$ and $x_2 = 0$.
3. $\lambda_2 \neq 0$ and $\lambda_3 = 0$ i.e., $x_1 = 0$ and $x_2 > 0$.
4. $\lambda_2 \neq 0$ and $\lambda_3 \neq 0$ i.e., $x_1 = 0$ and $x_2 = 0$.

- *CASE 1*: Interior solution, $x_1 > 0$ and $x_2 > 0$, i.e., $\lambda_2 = 0$ and $\lambda_3 = 0$. This implies that equation (1) becomes

$$\frac{3}{p_1} = \frac{4}{p_2} \iff \frac{p_1}{p_2} = \frac{3}{4}.$$

Hence, we can only have an interior solution when the price ratio is exactly $\frac{3}{4}$. In such a case, the budget line totally overlaps a indifference curve with the same slope, $\frac{3}{4}$ (as depicted in figure 2.2), and the consumer can choose any consumption bundle on the budget line. In particular, any bundle (x_1, x_2) satisfying $p_1 x_1 + p_2 x_2 = w$ is optimal as long as the price ratio is exactly $\frac{p_1}{p_2} = \frac{3}{4}$.

- *CASE 2*: Lower corner solution, $x_1 > 0$ and $x_2 = 0$, i.e., $\lambda_2 = 0$ and $\lambda_3 > 0$. Since wealth is fully spent on good 1, we have that $x_1 = \frac{w}{p_1}$. In order to determine when this solution is optimal, we can use expression (1), and the fact that $\lambda_2 = 0$, to obtain

$$\frac{3}{p_1} = \frac{4 + \lambda_3}{p_2} \iff \lambda_3 = 3\frac{p_2}{p_1} - 4,$$

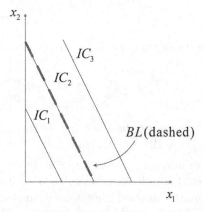

Figure 2.2 Case 1: Interior solutions

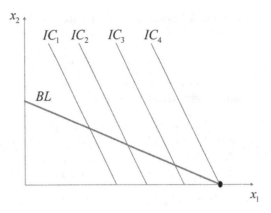

Figure 2.3 Case 2: Corner solution—I

and since $\lambda_3 > 0$ we find that this solution is optimal when

$$\lambda_3 = 3\frac{p_2}{p_1} - 4 > 0 \Longleftrightarrow \frac{p_1}{p_2} < \frac{3}{4}.$$

Graphically, this happens when the linear indifference curves are steeper than the budget line, i.e., $MRS > \frac{p_1}{p_2}$, as depicted in figure 2.3.

- *CASE 3*: Upper corner solution, $x_1 = 0$ and $x_2 > 0$, i.e., $\lambda_2 > 0$ and $\lambda_3 = 0$. Since wealth is fully spent on good 2, we have that $x_2 = \frac{w}{p_2}$. In order to determine when this solution is optimal, we can use expression (1), and the fact that $\lambda_3 = 0$, which yields

$$\frac{3 + \lambda_2}{p_1} = \frac{4}{p_2} \Longleftrightarrow \lambda_2 = 4\frac{p_1}{p_2} - 3,$$

and since $\lambda_2 > 0$ we find that this solution becomes optimal when

$$\lambda_2 = 4\frac{p_1}{p_2} - 3 > 0 \Longleftrightarrow \frac{p_1}{p_2} > \frac{3}{4}.$$

Graphically, this occurs when the linear indifference curves are flatter than the budget line, i.e., $MRS < \frac{p_1}{p_2}$, as illustrated figure 2.4.

- *CASE 4*: Corner solution, $x_1 = 0$ and $x_2 = 0$, i.e., $\lambda_2 > 0$ and $\lambda_3 > 0$. This solution would not exhaust this individual's wealth, i.e., it would imply $p_1 x_1 + p_2 x_2 < w$. Indeed, since the utility function is monotone, the budget constraint should be binding (the consumer should spend his entire wealth). Hence, case 4 cannot arise under any positive price-wealth pairs (p, w).

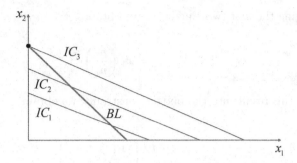

Figure 2.4 Case 3: Corner solution—II

- *SUMMARY*: We can now summarize the Walrasian demand correspondence

$$x(p,w) = \begin{cases} \left(0, \frac{w}{p_2}\right) \text{ if } \frac{p_1}{p_2} > \frac{3}{4}, \\ \text{any } (x_1, x_2) \in \mathbb{R}_+^2 \text{ s.t. } p_1 x_1 + p_2 x_2 = w \text{ if } \frac{p_1}{p_2} = \frac{3}{4}, \\ \left(\frac{w}{p_1}, 0\right) \text{ if } \frac{p_1}{p_2} < \frac{3}{4}. \end{cases}$$

- Plugging this Walrasian demand into the utility function yields the indirect utility function

$$v(p,w) = \begin{cases} 4\frac{w}{p_2} \text{ if } \frac{p_1}{p_2} \geq \frac{3}{4}, \\ 3\frac{w}{p_1} \text{ if } \frac{p_1}{p_2} < \frac{3}{4}. \end{cases}$$

Exercise #3 — Finding Walrasian demand for the CES utility function

3. Consider a consumer with CES utility function

$$u(x_1, x_2) = [x_1^\rho + x_2^\rho]^{\frac{1}{\rho}},$$

where coefficient ρ satisfies $\rho \neq 0$ and $\rho \leq 1$.

(a) Find the Walrasian demands of this consumer, $x_1(p,w)$ and $x_2(p,w)$.

- The Lagragian in this individual's UMP is

$$\mathcal{L}(x_1, x_2; \lambda) = [x_1^\rho + x_2^\rho]^{\frac{1}{\rho}} + \lambda [w - p_1 x_1 - p_2 x_2].$$

Taking first-order conditions yields

$$\frac{\partial \mathcal{L}}{\partial x_1} = [x_1^\rho + x_2^\rho]^{\frac{1-\rho}{\rho}} x_1^{\rho-1} - \lambda p_1 = 0,$$

$$\frac{\partial \mathcal{L}}{\partial x_2} = [x_1^\rho + x_2^\rho]^{\frac{1-\rho}{\rho}} x_2^{\rho-1} - \lambda p_2 = 0,$$

$$\frac{\partial \mathcal{L}}{\partial \lambda} = w - p_1 x_1 - p_2 x_2 = 0.$$

Rearranging the first two equalities, we obtain

$$x_2 = x_1 \left(\frac{p_2}{p_1} \right)^{\frac{1}{\rho - 1}}.$$

Plugging this result into the budget constraint, we obtain

$$p_1 x_1 - p_2 \left[x_1 \left(\frac{p_2}{p_1} \right)^{\frac{1}{\rho - 1}} \right] = w,$$

and solving for x_1, we find the Walrasian demand for good 1,

$$x_1(p, w) = \frac{w \cdot p_1^{\frac{1}{\rho - 1}}}{p_1^{\frac{\rho}{\rho - 1}} + p_2^{\frac{\rho}{\rho - 1}}}.$$

For compactness, this demand can be expressed as $x_1(p, w) = \frac{w \cdot p_1^{r-1}}{p_1^r + p_2^r}$ where $r \equiv \frac{\rho}{\rho - 1}$. We can finally plug $x_1(p, w)$ into $x_2 = x_1 \left(\frac{p_2}{p_1} \right)^r$ in order to find the Walrasian demand of good 2,

$$x_2(p, w) = \frac{w \cdot p_2^{r-1}}{p_1^r + p_2^r},$$

(b) What is the Walrasian demand of any good $i = \{1, 2\}$ when parameter $\rho \to 0$?

- When $\rho \to 0$ (the consumer's preferences can be represeneted with a Cobb–Douglas utility function) parameter r also approaches zero. In this setting, his Walrasian demand for good i, $x_i(p, w) = \frac{w \cdot p_i^{r-1}}{p_i^r + p_j^r}$, becomes

$$\lim_{\rho \to 0} x_i(p, w) = \frac{w \cdot p_i^{-1}}{1 + 1} = \frac{w}{2p_i}$$

which exactly coincides with the Walrasian demand of a consumer with Cobb–Douglas utility function $u(x_1, x_2) = x_1^\alpha x_2^\alpha$ for any $\alpha > 0$.

Exercise #5 — Checking WARP

5. Check whether the following demand functions satisfy the weak axiom of revealed preference (WARP).

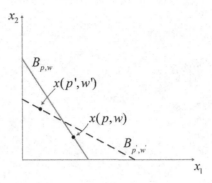

Figure 2.5 Random demand

(a) "Random demand": For any pair of prices p_1 and p_2 and wealth w, the consumer randomizes uniformly over all points in the budget frontier.[1]

- Let us prove that this demand function does not necessarily satisfy WARP by using an example, as depicted in figure 2.5. WARP states that

$$\text{if } p \cdot x\left(p', w'\right) \leq w \text{ and } x\left(p', w'\right) \neq x\left(p, w\right) \text{ then } p' \cdot x\left(p, w\right) > w'.$$

That is, if the new consumption bundle (chosen under the new prices and wealth) is affordable under the old prices and wealth, then it must be the case that the old consumption bundle is not affordable under the new prices and wealth. In the case of the random demand depicted in figure 2.4, however, we find that

$$p \cdot x\left(p', w'\right) \leq w \text{ and } x\left(p', w'\right) \neq x\left(p, w\right) \textbf{ but } p' \cdot x\left(p, w\right) < w'.$$

That is, the old consumption bundle is *still* affordable under the new prices and wealth, i.e., graphically, bundle $x(p, w)$ lies below budget line $B_{p', w'}$ (dashed line in the figure). Since there exists a positive probability that random demand assigns bundles as the ones illustrated in figure 2.4, we can conclude that random demand does not satisfy WARP.

(b) "Average demand": The expected "random demand" given p_1, p_2, and w.[2]

---

[1]For instance, this demand can arise when the consumer regards two goods as perfect substitutes and their price ratio $\frac{p_1}{p_2}$ coincides with the ratio of marginal utilities. In this case, a continuum of Walrasian demands emerges, i.e., one for each point of the consumer's budget line. Since the consumer is indifferent among all these points, he can randomly choose one of these optimal bundles.

[2]If the "random demand" could arise in the presence of perfect substitutes, the "average demand" can then emerge as the average bundle that this consumer selects after randomly choosing a bundle from his budget line (as predicted by random demand) a sufficient number of times.

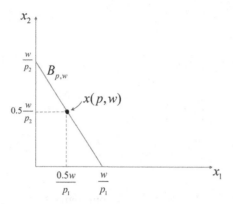

Figure 2.6 Average demand—I.

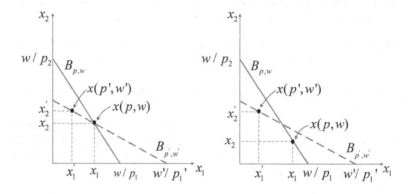

Figure 2.7 Average demand—II.

- First, note that if the consumer randomizes uniformly over all points in her budget line (as described by the random demand), then the expected random demand is allocated at the midpoint of the budget line, as depicted in figure 2.6 for budget line $B_{p,w}$.

  Let us now prove that WARP is satisfied for average demand. Let us work by contradiction, by assuming that average demand violates WARP. There are two possibilities in which this violation might take place, as the two panels in figure 2.6 illustrate. In particular, in both figures bundle $x(p',w')$ is affordable under old prices and wealth, i.e., it lies on or below budget line $B_{p,w}$, but bundle $x(p,w)$ is also affordable under the new prices and wealth, i.e., it lies on or below $B_{p',w'}$, which constitute a violation of WARP.

- Let us first determine the location of points x_1 and x_1' according to the average demand. Recall that these points must to be located at the midpoint of the budget line. Hence,

$$x_1 = \frac{1}{2}\frac{w}{p_1} \quad \text{and} \quad x_1' = \frac{1}{2}\frac{w'}{p_1'},$$

therefore $2x_1 = \frac{w}{p_1}$ and $2x_1' = \frac{w'}{p_1'}$. Moreover, we can see in both figures that $x_1' < x_1$. Therefore, $2x_1' < 2x_1$, which implies

$$\frac{w'}{p_1'} < \frac{w}{p_1}.$$

But in both figures we actually see the opposite, i.e., $\frac{w'}{p_1'} > \frac{w}{p_1}$. Hence, we have reached a contradiction, and average demand cannot violate WARP.

(c) "Conspicuous demand": The individual spends all his wealth on the most expensive good. This is often referred to as "conspicuous consumption" and includes items such as luxury cars, yachts, and private islands! For instance, if good 1 is the most expensive, $p_1 > p_2$, then the consumer spends all his wealth on good 1, $x_1(p_1, p_2, w) = \frac{w}{p_1}$, but nothing on good 2, $x_2(p_1, p_2, w) = 0$. More generally, for any p_1, p_2, and w, the demand for good $i = \{1, 2\}$ is

$$x_i(p_1, p_2, w) = \begin{cases} \frac{w}{p_i} & \text{if } p_i > p_j \text{ where } j \neq i, \text{ and} \\ 0 & \text{otherwise.} \end{cases}$$

- Let us divide it into two cases: Case 1, in which $p_1 \geq p_2$ (good 1 is the most expensive), and Case 2, in which $p_1 < p_2$ (good 2 is the most expensive). Once we represent the conspicuous demand for all price vectors, we will check if it satisfies WARP.

  – *Case 1* $(p_1 \geq p_2)$: The demand function of good 1 is $x_1(p_1, p_2, w) = \frac{w}{p_1}$, while the demand of good 2 is zero, $x_2(p_1, p_2, w) = 0$, as depicted in figure 2.8.

  – *Case 2* $(p_1 < p_2)$: In this case, the demand function of good 2 reduces to $x_2(p_1, p_2, w) = \frac{w}{p_2}$, while that of good 1 is zero, as illustrated in figure 2.9.

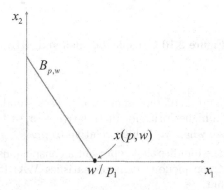

Figure 2.8 Conspicuous demand—I.

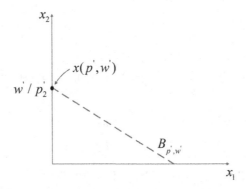

Figure 2.9 Conspicuous demand—II.

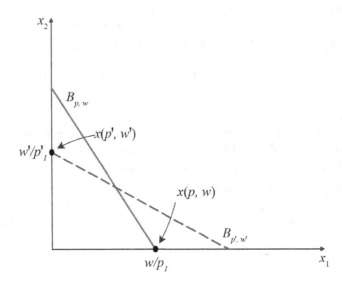

Figure 2.10 Conspicuous demand—III.

- Summarizing, figure 2.10 represents both cases simultaneously, where budget line $B_{p,w}$ represents a higher price for p_1 (relative to p_2) while budget line $B_{p',w'}$ depicts the opposite case, where p_2 is high relative to p_1.

- After depicting the bundles that represent a conspicuous demand for all price vectors, we can check if conspicuous demand satisfies WARP. As mentioned in part (a), WARP states that

$$\text{if } p \cdot x\,(p',w') \leq w \text{ and } x\,(p',w') \neq x\,(p,w)\,, \text{ then } p' \cdot x\,(p,w) > w'.$$

Figure 2.10 summarizes both cases. While bundle $x(p', w')$ is affordable under old prices and wealth, i.e., $p \cdot x(p', w') \leq w$ since it lies below the solid budget line $B_{p,w}$ in figure 2.10, bundle $x(p, w)$ is still affordable under new prices and wealth, i.e., $p' \cdot x(p, w) < w'$, since it lies below the dashed budget line $B_{p',w'}$. Intuitively, both bundles $x(p, w)$ and $x(p', w')$ are available at (p, w) and at (p', w'), but the consumer does not choose the same bundle under (p, w) as under (p', w'). Hence, conspicuous demand violates WARP.

Exercise #7 — WARP for undergrads—II

7. Jeremy has a monthly income of $60. He spends his money making telephone calls (measured in minutes) at a price p_x and on other composite good y, whose price has been normalized to one, i.e., $p_y = \$1$. His mobile phone company offers him two plans: Plan A, in which he pays no monthly fee and makes calls for $0.50 per minute; or Plan B, in which he pays a $20 monthly fee and benefits from cheaper phone calls at $0.20 per minute.

(a) Depict Jeremy's budget constraint under each of the two plans, with the number of phone calls (good x) in the horizontal axis and the composite good (good y) in the vertical axis.

- Let x denote the number of phone calls, and y denote spending on other goods. The expression of the budget line under Plan A, BL_A is $0.5x + y = 60$, or $y = 60 - 0.5x$, as depicted in the solid line of figure 2.11 that originates at $y = 60$ and which crosses the horizontal axis at $x = 120$. Under Plan B, Jeremy's budget line, BL_B, is $0.2x + y = 40$, or $y = 40 - 0.2x$, as illustrated in figure 2.11 by the dashed line that originates at $y = 40$ and crosses the horizontal axis at $x = 200$. These two budget lines intersect each other at $0.5x + (40 - 0.2x) = 60$, i.e., $x = 66.67$. Hence,

$$y = 40 - 0.2x = 40 - (0.2 \times 66.67) = 26.67.$$

Therefore, BL_A and BL_B intersect at bundle $(66.67, 26.67)$.

(b) If Jeremy mentions that Plan A is better for him, what is the set of baskets he may purchase if his behavior is consistent with the WARP?

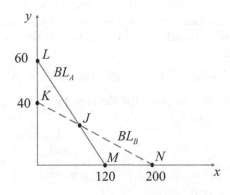

Figure 2.11 Checking WARP

- According to WARP, if the consumption bundle under new prices and wealth was affordable under the original prices and wealth, $p \cdot x(p', w') \leq w$, then the bundle selected under the old prices and wealth cannot be affordable under the new prices and wealth, i.e., $p' \cdot x(p, w) \leq w'$.

- In this context, where the consumer moves from facing budget line BL_B to BL_A, WARP states that, if the consumption bundle under BL_B, $x(p', w')$, is affordable under BL_A, it must lie on segment KJ in figure 2.11, i.e., this is equivalent to the premise of WARP, $p \cdot x(p', w') \leq w$. Hence, the bundle selected when facing budget line BL_A, $x(p, w)$, must be unaffordable under BL_B; that is, $x(p, w)$ must lie on segment LJ of budget line BL_A. Notice that bundles in segment JM are instead affordable under BL_B, thus violating WARP.

Exercise #9 — An introduction to income and substitution effect with a quasi-linear utility function

9. Michael's preferences over soda (good x) and other goods (composite good, y) are given by the quasi-linear utility function $U(x, y) = 2\sqrt{x} + y$. His income is $10. Assume that the price of the composite good is normalized to 1, i.e., $p_y = \$1$.

(a) What is Michael's optimal basket when the price of sodas is $p_x = \$0.5$? Label it basket A.

- At an interior optimum, we can use the shortcut $MRS_{x,y} = \frac{p_x}{p_y}$ to obtain the Walrasian demand for soda (good x),

$$\frac{MU_x}{MU_y} = \frac{p_x}{p_y} \Longleftrightarrow \frac{\frac{1}{\sqrt{x}}}{1} = p_x \Longleftrightarrow x = \frac{1}{(p_x)^2}.$$

Hence, when the price of soda is $p_x = 0.5$ Michael buys $x = \frac{1}{(0.5)^2} = 4$ sodas. We can find the number of units of good y (the composite good) by using the budget line $p_x x + p_y y = I$. That is, $0.5 \cdot 4 + y = 10$, which implies that Michael demands $y = 8$ units of the composite good, as depicted in the figure 2.12. Notice that the tangency point between the consumer's budget line and the indifference curve furthest from the origin occurs at bundle $A = (4, 8)$, whereby the consumer attains a utility level of $2\sqrt{4} + 8 = 12$.

(b) What is his optimal basket when the price of sodas drops to $p_x = \$0.2$? Label it basket C.

- Similarly to the previous part, the demand for sodas (good x) is

$$x = \frac{1}{(p_x)^2} = \frac{1}{(0.2)^2} = 25,$$

and for the case of the composite good, $0.2 \cdot 25 + y = 10$, which implies $y = 5$ units of the composite good.

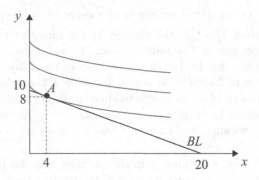

Figure 2.12 Walrasian demand when $p_x = \$0.5$

- Comparing the initial consumption bundle $A = (4, 8)$ with that arising when the price of good x changes to $p_x = \$0.2$, i.e., $C = (25, 5)$, we can see that the individual now consumes more of good x (which became cheaper) but less of good y (which became more expensive in relative terms).

- The increase in the consumption of x due to price reduction, i.e., $25 - 4 = 21$, is the total effect due to the price decrease (in the subsequent parts of this exercise, we disentangle the total effect into the substitution and income effects). Finally, note that at bundle C, the consumer attains a utility level of $2\sqrt{25} + 5 = 15$.

(c) The "decomposition" budget line, BL_d, is tangent to the initial utility level. Label this tangency point "basket B" and find the amount of goods x and y that this consumer will choose at basket B.

- The decomposition budget line BL_d can be understood as the budget line resulting after applying a Hicksian wealth compensation after the price of good x drops to $p_x = \$0.2$ (i.e., a wealth reduction that maintains the individual's initial utility level unaffected but that reflects the new price ratio).

- Hence, we know that all points in the "decomposition" budget line, BL_d, must yield the same utility level as basket A. At basket A, $x = 4$ and $y = 8$ which implies a utility level of $U_1 = 2\sqrt{4} + 8 = 12$. Therefore, basket B must satisfy that $2\sqrt{x} + y = 12$. Secondly, we know that the slope of the decomposition budget line at B must be the same as the slope of the final budget line at C. That is,

$$\frac{MU_x}{MU_y} = \frac{p_x}{p_y} \iff \frac{\frac{1}{\sqrt{x}}}{1} = \frac{0.2}{1},$$

which implies that $x = 25$ and $2\sqrt{25} + y = 12$, i.e., $y = 2$. Basket B is thus $(x, y) = (25, 2)$.

(d) Find the income and substitution effects of a decrease in the price of sodas.

- The *substitution effect* is the change in the quantity of sodas purchased as the consumer moves from the initial basket A (where he consumes 4 cans of sodas) to the decomposition basket B (where he consumes 25). The substitution effect on sodas is therefore $25 - 4 = 21$ sodas. Intuitively, the substitution effect reflects the additional amount of sodas this individual consumes which only captures the change in relative prices. In particular, keeping his purchasing power unaffected sodas become relative cheaper, and thus he wants to adjust his consumption pattern to buy more units of this good.

- The *income effect* is the change in the quantity of sodas purchased as the consumer moves from the decomposition basket B to the final basket C. Because he consumes the same number of sodas at B and C, the income effect is zero. Intuitively, the income effect captures the additional consumption that this individual experiences, not from the change in relative prices, but from the additional purchasing power that cheaper sodas provide him.

(e) Calculate the compensating variation of this price decrease.

- The compensating variation measures how much income an individual is willing to give up *before* the price change in order to be as well off as *after* the price decrease. Hence, the compensating variation is the difference between the consumer's income ($10) and the income he would need to reach the same utility level at the new price ($0.20), i.e., to purchase the decomposition basket B. Since at basket B he buys 25 cans of sodas and 2 units of the composite good, he would need an income of

$$\$0.2 \cdot 25 + \$1 \cdot 2 = \$7.$$

That is, the consumer would be willing to have his income reduced from $10 to $7 if the price of sodas falls from $0.50 to $0.20, and still keep his utility unaffected. Thus, the compensating variation is $3. This is also the so-called "Hicksian wealth compensation" necessary to keep the consumer's utility level unaffected after the price of soda decreases to $p_x = \$0.2$.

(f) Calculate the equivalent variation of the price decrease.

- The equivalent variation is the measure of how much additional income a consumer would need *before* a price reduction to be as well off as *after* the price decrease. Hence, we first need to determine the location of basket E (a basket in which the consumer faces a budget line parallel to his initial budget line, thus reflecting the initial price ratio, but tangent to the indifference curve that the consumer can reach after the price reduction). First, we know that basket E lies on the final indifference curve U_2, which reaches a utility level of 15 (see part b of the exercise). Therefore, at basket E, $2\sqrt{x} + y = 15$. Second, we know that at basket E, the final indifference curve must be tangent to the initial budget line,

$$\frac{MU_x}{MU_y} = \frac{p_x}{p_y} \Longleftrightarrow \frac{\frac{1}{\sqrt{x}}}{1} = \frac{0.5}{1},$$

which, solving for x, yields $x = 4$ units. When we substitute this value of x into the equation $2\sqrt{x} + y = 15$ we find that $y = 11$. Then, at basket E the consumer purchases 4 cans of soda and 11 units of the composite good.

- To purchase basket E at the *initial* price of $0.50, the consumer would need an income of

$$\$0.5 \cdot 4 + \$1 \cdot 11 = \$13.$$

Hence, the equivalent variation is the difference between this income level ($13) and his initial income ($10), or $3. Thus, the compensating variation and the equivalent variation coincide.

- *Remark:* If income effects are absent, the compensating variation and the equivalent variation of a price change will be *equal* to each other, and also equal to the change in the consumer surplus. In particular, change in consumer surplus is the area below the Walrasian demand curve $x = \frac{1}{(p_x)^2}$ between prices $p_x = \$0.5$ and $p_x = \$0.2$, that is,

$$\triangle CS = \int_{0.2}^{0.5} \frac{1}{(p_x)^2} = \left[-\frac{1}{p_x} \right]_{0.2}^{0.5} = 3.$$

However, if income effects are present, the compensating and the equivalent variation will give us *different* measures of the welfare change that the consumer experiences as a result of the price change. Moreover, these measures will not generally coincide with the change in consumer surplus.

Exercise #11 — Relationship between WARP and CLD

11. Figure 2.13 illustrates the change in a decrease in the price of good 1, thus producing an outward pivoting effect on the consumer's budget line, from $B_{p,w}$ to $B_{p',w}$, where the price of good 2 and wealth remain constant. This corresponds to the case where the consumer receives a wealth compensation (changing his wealth level from w to w') that guarantees he can still afford his initial consumption bundle, $x(p, w)$. (This type of wealth compensation is often referred to as the "Slutsky wealth compensation.") Assuming that the Walrasian demand satisfies the weak axiom of revealed preference (WARP), answer the following questions.

   (a) Bundle $x(p', w')$ cannot lie on segment A, which is to the left-hand side of bundle $x(p, w)$, but it must lie on segment B, which is to the right-hand side of bundle $x(p, w)$.

      - In order to check whether bundle $x(p', w')$ being in segment A or B is compatible with WARP, let us separately assume that it lies in each segment:
      - *Segment A.* Let us start checking that $x(p', w')$ cannot lie on segment A. Applying WARP, first note that both bundles $x(p, w)$ and $x(p', w')$ are affordable under initial prices and wealth, $B_{p,w}$, i.e., graphically they both lie on or below budget line $B_{p,w}$

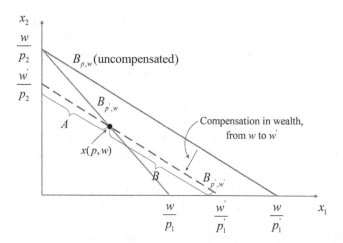

Figure 2.13 WARP and the compensated law of demand

in figure 2.13. However, in the second step of WARP, we see that $x(p,w)$ is affordable under $B_{p',w'}$, i.e., it lies on the dashed budget line $B_{p',w'}$, which constitutes a violation of WARP. Hence, $x(p',w')$ cannot lie on segment A.

- *Segment B.* Let us now check if $x(p',w')$ can lie on segment B. In the first step of WARP, we see that $x(p,w)$ is affordable under initial prices and wealth, $B_{p,w}$, but $x(p',w')$ is not, i.e., bundle $x(p',w')$ lies strictly above budget line $B_{p,w}$ in figure 2.8. Hence, the premise of WARP does not hold, and as a consequence WARP is not violated if $x(p',w')$ lies on segment B.

(b) What conclusions can you infer from your results in part (a) about the slope of the Walrasian demand function? And the slope of the Hicksian demand function?

- *Hicksian demand.* From the previous result, we can conclude that $x(p',w')$ must contain more of good 1 (note that graphically, bundle $x(p',w')$ lies in segment B, which is to the right-hand side of bundle $x(p,w)$). Then, a decrease in the price of good 1 (when we appropriately compensate for wealth effects) leads to an increase in the quantity demanded. This is the Compensated Law of Demand (CLD), and it implies that the Hicksian (compensated) demand curve must be negatively sloped (a decrease in prices leads to an increase in the consumption of that good).

- *Walrasian demand.* From this result, however, we cannot guarantee that the uncompensated law of demand (ULD) is satisfied. Therefore, we cannot conclude that the Walrasian demand curve (in which wealth effects are left uncompensated) is also negatively sloped. It can be positively or negative sloped, depending on whether the good is Giffen or not, respectively.

Exercise #13 — Quasi-linear preferences

13. Consider a consumer with a quasi-linear preference relation over two goods, x_1 and x_2, and assume that it is quasilinear with respect to good 1. Show that the wealth effects for good 2 are eliminated, i.e., all additional income is spent in good 1 alone.

   - Let us first recall some properties of quasi-linear preferences. Figure 2.14 depicts indifference curves of a quasi-linear preference relation, assuming that good 1 is desirable.

   - Good 1 is desirable: For any bundle $x \in (-\infty, +\infty) \times \mathbb{R}_+^{L-1}$, we have that adding extra units of good 1 yields a more desirable bundle. That is, for a vector $e_1 = (1, 0, ..., 0)$ and $\alpha > 0$,

$$x + \alpha e_1 \succ x,$$

   as depicted in figure 2.16. Note that bundle $x + \alpha e_1$ contains only α more units of good 1 than bundle x, while it has the same units of all other goods. In addition, bundle $x + \alpha e_1$ lies on an indifference curve, IC_2, associated to a higher utility than that in which the original bundle x lies, IC_1.

   - All indifference curves are parallel displacements to each other along good 1 axis. That is, for all bundles $x, y \in (-\infty, +\infty) \times \mathbb{R}_+^{L-1}$, we have that if the consumer is indifferent between bundles x and y, $x \sim y$, then he is also indifferent between bundles $x + \alpha e_1$ and $y + \alpha e_1$, whereby only the amount of good 1 has been increased by the same factor $\alpha > 0$ on both bundles. That is,

$$x + \alpha e_1 \sim y + \alpha e_1 \quad \text{for } \alpha > 0 \text{ and } e_1 = (1, 0, ..., 0).$$

   - We need to show that the wealth effects for all the remaining goods (other than good 1) are eliminated. That is, all additional wealth is spent on good 1. More formally, for every

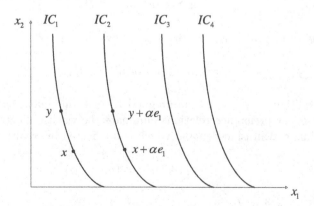

Figure 2.14 Quasi-linear preferences

price vector $p \in \mathbb{R}^{L}_{++}$, for wealth $w \geq 0$, for every consumption bundle $x \in (-\infty, +\infty) \times \mathbb{R}^{L-1}_{+}$, for all $\alpha > 0$ and $e_1 = (1, 0, ..., 0)$, we need to show that, if $x = x(p, w)$ is the consumer's demand vector at prices p and wealth w, then his demand vector when prices are unchanged but his wealth increases in α, $x(p, w + \alpha)$, is given by $x + \alpha e_1$. That is,

$$x + \alpha e_1 = x(p, w + \alpha).$$

The left-hand side of the equality illustrates that, relative to his initial Walrasian demand under wealth level w, x, when the consumer's wealth increases to $w + \alpha$ he only increases his consumption of good 1 in αe_1 units.

Proof. For any given price vector $p \in \mathbb{R}^{L}_{++}$ and wealth level $w \geq 0$, the consumer demands a consumption bundle $x \in (-\infty, +\infty) \times \mathbb{R}^{L-1}_{+}$. When the consumer's income increases to $w + \alpha$ (and prices are unaffected), his optimal consumption bundle becomes $x + \alpha e_1$, which is affordable at $(p, w + \alpha)$, that is,

$$p \cdot (x + \alpha e_1) \leq w + \alpha.$$

Let us now take a new consumption bundle $y \in (-\infty, +\infty) \times \mathbb{R}^{L-1}_{+}$, such that it is also affordable at $(p, w + \alpha)$,

$$p \cdot y \leq w + \alpha.$$

Hence, consumption bundle $y - \alpha e_1$ is affordable at (p, w),

$$p \cdot (y - \alpha e_1) \leq w.$$

But we previously stated that bundle x was also affordable at (p, w). Therefore,

$$x \succsim z \quad \text{for all } z \in B_{p,w}.$$

Then, $x \succsim y - \alpha e_1$ given that $y - \alpha e_1 \in B_{p,w}$, which implies

$$x + \alpha e_1 \succsim y \quad \text{for all } y \in B_{p,w+\alpha}.$$

Hence, all additional wealth is spent on good 1. As a consequence, $x + \alpha e_1 = x(p, w + \alpha)$. Thus, quasi-linear preference relations eliminate the wealth effects in all the remaining goods, yielding a Walrasian demand which is unaffected by wealth effects

$$x_l(p, w) = x_l(p, w + \alpha)$$

for all goods $l = 2, 3, ..., L$.

Exercise #15 — CES utility function

15. Consider the following utility function with constant elasticity of substitution (CES): $u(x_1, x_2) = [\alpha_1 x_1^\rho + \alpha_2 x_2^\rho]^{\frac{1}{\rho}}$ where $\rho \neq 0$ and $\rho \leq 1$. Show that:

(a) When $\rho = 1$, indifference curves are linear (goods 1 and 2 are perfect substitutes).

- If $\rho = 1$, then $u(x_1, x_2) = \alpha_1 x_1 + \alpha_2 x_2$. Then, the utility function becomes linear (goods are perfect substitutes). The equation of an indifference curve can be obtained solving for x_2,

$$x_2 = \frac{U}{\alpha_2} - \frac{\alpha_1}{\alpha_2} x_1.$$

For instance, for $U = 10$, the linear indifference curve originates at $\frac{10}{\alpha_2}$ and crosses the x_1−axis at $0 = \frac{10}{\alpha_2} - \frac{\alpha_1}{\alpha_2} x_1$, i.e., at $x_1 = \frac{10}{\alpha_1}$.

(b) When $\rho \to 0$, the utility function represents a Cobb–Douglas utility function, $u(x_1, x_2) = x_1^{\alpha_1} x_2^{\alpha_2}$, where the exponents satisfy $\alpha_1 + \alpha_2 = 1$.

- Let us define $\widetilde{u}(x) \equiv \ln u(x)$, where

$$\ln u(x) = \frac{1}{\rho} \ln \left[\alpha_1 x_1^\rho + \alpha_2 x_2^\rho \right].$$

Then, the limit of this utility function when $\rho \to 0$ is

$$\lim_{\rho \to 0} \widetilde{u}(x) = \lim_{\rho \to 0} \frac{\ln \left[\alpha_1 x_1^\rho + \alpha_2 x_2^\rho \right]}{\rho} = \frac{0}{0}.$$

Hence, we need to use l'Hopital's rule, as follows,

$$\lim_{\rho \to 0} \frac{\frac{\partial \ln\left[\alpha_1 x_1^\rho + \alpha_2 x_2^\rho\right]}{\partial \rho}}{\frac{\partial \rho}{\partial \rho}} = \lim_{\rho \to 0} \frac{\partial \ln \left[\alpha_1 x_1^\rho + \alpha_2 x_2^\rho \right]}{\partial \rho}$$

$$= \lim_{\rho \to 0} \frac{1}{\alpha_1 x_1^\rho + \alpha_2 x_2^\rho} \left[\alpha_1 \ln(x_1) x_1^\rho + \alpha_2 \ln(x_2) x_2^\rho \right]$$

$$= \frac{\alpha_1 \ln(x_1) + \alpha_2 \ln(x_2)}{\alpha_1 + \alpha_2} = \frac{[x_1^{\alpha_1} x_2^{\alpha_2}]}{\alpha_1 + \alpha_2}.$$

Recall that so far we have been dealing with the limit $\lim_{\rho \to 0} \widetilde{u}(x)$, while in fact we are interested in $\lim_{\rho \to 0} u(x)$. So, given that $\widetilde{u}(x) \equiv \ln u(x)$, we have that $\lim_{\rho \to 0} \widetilde{u}(x) = x_1^{\alpha_1} x_2^{\alpha_2}$.

Solving for x_2 yields the equation of an indifference curve $x_2 = \left(\frac{\widetilde{u}}{x_1^{\alpha_1}} \right)^{\frac{1}{\alpha_2}}$, e.g., if $\alpha_1 = \alpha_2 = 0.5$, the indifference curve becomes $x_2 = \frac{\widetilde{u}}{x_1}$. Hence, indifference curves are decreasing in x_1, but at a decreasing rate (i.e., indifference curves are bowed-in towards the origin).

(c) When $\rho \to -\infty$, the utility function becomes a Leontief utility function given by $u(x_1, x_2) = \min\{x_1, x_2\}$, and thus represents two goods that are perfect complements. [*Hint:* Since in this case $\rho \to -\infty$, you can consider that ρ is a negative number.]

- We need to show that if $x_2 \geq x_1$, then

$$\lim_{\rho \to -\infty} [\alpha_1 x_1^\rho + \alpha_2 x_2^\rho]^{\frac{1}{\rho}} = \min\{x_1, x_2\} = x_1.$$

- Suppose, without loss of generality, that $x_2 \geq x_1$. Then $x_2^\rho \leq x_1^\rho$ since parameter ρ satisfies $0 \neq \rho \leq 1$ and approaches $-\infty$ (i.e., it is a negative number). Hence, multiplying both sides of the inequality by $\alpha_2 \geq 0$ yields $\alpha_2 x_2^\rho \leq \alpha_2 x_1^\rho$. Adding $\alpha_1 x_1^\rho$ on both sides of the inequality,

$$\alpha_1 x_1^\rho + \alpha_2 x_2^\rho \leq \alpha_1 x_1^\rho + \alpha_2 x_1^\rho,$$

and rearranging,

$$\alpha_1 x_1^\rho + \alpha_2 x_2^\rho \leq (\alpha_1 + \alpha_2) x_1^\rho,$$

and since ρ is a negative number,

$$\underbrace{[\alpha_1 x_1^\rho + \alpha_2 x_2^\rho]^{\frac{1}{\rho}}}_{B} \geq \underbrace{[(\alpha_1 + \alpha_2) x_1^\rho]^{\frac{1}{\rho}}}_{C}. \tag{2}$$

- In addition, if $x_1 \geq 0$ and $x_2 \geq 0$, then $0 \leq \alpha_2 x_2^\rho$. If we add $\alpha_1 x_1^\rho$ on both sides of the inequality, we obtain

$$\alpha_1 x_1^\rho \leq \alpha_1 x_1^\rho + \alpha_2 x_2^\rho$$

and since ρ is a negative number,

$$\underbrace{[\alpha_1 x_1^\rho]^{\frac{1}{\rho}}}_{A} \geq \underbrace{[\alpha_1 x_1^\rho + \alpha_2 x_2^\rho]^{\frac{1}{\rho}}}_{B}.$$

Combining this result with that of expression (2), yields

$$\underbrace{[\alpha_1 x_1^\rho]^{\frac{1}{\rho}}}_{A} \geq \underbrace{[\alpha_1 x_1^\rho + \alpha_2 x_2^\rho]^{\frac{1}{\rho}}}_{B} \geq \underbrace{[(\alpha_1 + \alpha_2) x_1^\rho]^{\frac{1}{\rho}}}_{C} \tag{3}$$

We can use the "Squeezing Theorem" to obtain the limits of terms A and C, where $\rho \to -\infty$, in order to obtain the limit of term B, which must be between A and C. Let us first find the limit of term A,

$$\lim_{\rho \to -\infty} [\alpha_1 x_1^\rho]^{\frac{1}{\rho}} = x_1$$

Let us now find the limit of term C,

$$\lim_{\rho \to -\infty} [(\alpha_1 + \alpha_2)\, x_1^{\rho}]^{\frac{1}{\rho}} = x_1.$$

Hence, since the limits of both terms A and C coincide (both of them are x_1), the limit of term B must also be x_1. That is,

$$\lim_{\rho \to -\infty} [\alpha_1 x_1^{\rho} + \alpha_2 x_2^{\rho}]^{\frac{1}{\rho}} = x_1,$$

which is exactly what we needed to show: if $x_2 \geq x_1$, then

$$\lim_{\rho \to -\infty} [\alpha_1 x_1^{\rho} + \alpha_2 x_2^{\rho}]^{\frac{1}{\rho}} = \min\{x_1, x_2\} = x_1.$$

A similar argument applies to the case in which $x_2 < x_1$, whereby

$$\lim_{\rho \to -\infty} [\alpha_1 x_1^{\rho} + \alpha_2 x_2]^{\frac{1}{\rho}} = \min\{x_1, x_2\} = x_2.$$

Exercise #17 — Concavity of the support function

17. Prove the concavity of the support function $\mu_K(p)$. That is, show that

$$\mu_K\left(\alpha p + (1 - \alpha)\, p'\right) \geqslant \alpha \mu_K(p) + (1 - \alpha)\, \mu_K(p')$$

for every two price vectors $p, p' \in \mathbb{R}^L$ and for any $\alpha \in [0, 1]$.

- First, from the definition of the support function $\mu_K(p)$ we know that, for a given price vector p, $\mu_K(p)$ identifies the bundle x^* that minimizes $p \cdot x$ (i.e., it minimizes the cost of buying bundle x) subject to reaching a utility level u, i.e., $u(x) \geq u$. Hence, $p \cdot x^* \leq p \cdot x$ holds for all bundles x in set K, or

$$\mu_K(p) \equiv p \cdot x^* \leq p \cdot x.$$

Thus, multiplying by $\alpha \in [0, 1]$ on both sides of inequality $\mu_K(p) \leq p \cdot x$,

$$\alpha \mu_K(p) \leq \alpha p \cdot x. \tag{4}$$

And similarly for any other price vector p', where $\mu_K(p') \leq p' \cdot x$, thus implying that, if we multiply both sides of the inequality by $(1 - \alpha)$, we obtain

$$(1 - \alpha)\, \mu_K(p') \leq (1 - \alpha)\, p' \cdot x. \tag{5}$$

Summing up expressions (4) and (5) yields

$$\alpha \mu_K(p) + (1 - \alpha)\, \mu_K(p') \leq \alpha p \cdot x + (1 - \alpha)\, p' \cdot x,$$

which can be simplified to

$$\alpha \mu_K(p) + (1 - \alpha) \mu_K(p') \le [\alpha p + (1 - \alpha) p'] \cdot x, \tag{6}$$

and by the definition of the support function, we know that $\mu_K(\alpha p + (1 - \alpha) p') = [\alpha p + (1 - \alpha) p'] \cdot x$. Therefore, expression (6) can be rewritten as

$$\alpha \mu_K(p) + (1 - \alpha) \mu_K(p') \le \mu_K(\alpha p + (1 - \alpha) p'),$$

and hence the support function, $\mu_K(p)$, is concave.

Exercise #19 — Separable utility function

19. Consider an individual with a separable utility function over L goods

$$u(x) = \sum_{i=1}^{L} \alpha_i \ln x_i,$$

where $\sum_{i=1}^{L} \alpha_i = 1$ and $\alpha_i > 0$ for every good i. Assume that the consumer faces a strictly positive price vector $p \gg 0$ and his wealth is given by $w > 0$.

(a) Find the Walrasian demands, and the shadow price of wealth.

- The consumer solves a UMP given by

$$\max_{x \ge 0} \quad u(x)$$

subject to $p \cdot x \le w$.

Using the shortcut $MRS_{i,j} = \frac{p_i}{p_j}$, we obtain interior solutions $\frac{\alpha_i}{x_i} = \frac{p_i}{p_j}$, or $\frac{\alpha_i}{p_i} \cdot p_j = x_i$, which together with the budget constraint yields a Walrasian demand of

$$x_i(p, w) = \frac{\alpha_i w}{p_i} \quad \text{for every good } i \tag{7}$$

In addition, we can obtain the Lagrange multiplier, λ, from the first-order condition

$$\frac{\partial u}{\partial x_i} = \lambda p_i, \text{ or } \frac{\alpha_i}{x_i} = \lambda p_i$$

which, combined with (7) yields

$$\frac{\alpha_i}{\frac{\alpha_i x}{p_i}} = \lambda p_i,$$

and solving for λ, we obtain

$$\lambda(p, w) = \frac{1}{w}.$$

Hence, the marginal value of relaxing the constraint (i.e., the shadow price of wealth) is $\frac{1}{w}$.

(b) Let us next find the shadow price of wealth using an alternative approach. First, find the indirect utility function, $v(p, w)$, resulting from the previous UMP. Then, measure how it is affected by a marginal increase in wealth, i.e., find the derivative $\frac{\partial v(p,w)}{\partial w}$. Does your result coincide with what you found in part (a)?

- The indirect utility function is

$$v(p, w) = \sum_{i=1}^{L} \alpha_i \cdot \ln\left(\frac{\alpha_i w}{p_i}\right).$$

  Hence, the marginal utility of wealth is

$$\frac{\partial v(p, w)}{\partial w} = \sum_{i=1}^{L} \alpha_i \cdot \frac{1}{\frac{\alpha_i w}{p_i}} \cdot \frac{\alpha_i}{p_i} = \frac{1}{w} \sum_{i=1}^{L} \alpha_j = \frac{1}{w},$$

  which coincides with the Lagrange multiplier $\lambda(p, w)$ we found in part (a).

- Interestingly, this result is generalizable to settings in which, given the separable nature of the utility function, the consumer focuses on a subset of goods $\{1, 2, ..., L_1\}$ where $L_1 < L$, $\{L_1 + 1, ..., L_2\}$, etc. and solves a separated UMP for each of these subsets of goods, i.e., one UMP for goods $\{1, 2, ..., L_1\}$, another UMP for goods $\{L_1+1, ..., L_2\}$, etc.. The consumer's solution to these separated UMPs must coincide with that in part (a), where the consumer simultaneously considers all L goods.

Exercise #21 — Stone–Geary utility function with three goods

21. Consider a three-good setting in which the consumer has a Stone–Geary utility function

$$u(x) = (x_1 - b_1)^\alpha (x_2 - b_2)^\beta (x_3 - b_3)^\gamma,$$

where $b_1, b_2, b_3 > 0$ represent the minimal amounts of goods 1, 2, and 3 that this individual must consume at any given period in order to remain alive (e.g., calories, water, and shelter).

(a) Find the consumer's Walrasian demand and indirect utility function.[3]

- We can use $\widetilde{x}_i = x_i - b_i$ for every good $i = \{1, 2, 3\}$ to denote each term in parenthesis in the above utility function, which yields the following Cobb–Douglas type utility function with three goods,

$$u(\widetilde{x}) = \widetilde{x}_1^\alpha \widetilde{x}_2^\beta \widetilde{x}_3^\gamma.$$

  We can now transform the income of this individual from w to $\widetilde{w} = w - (p_1 b_1 + p_2 b_2 + p_3 b_3)$ in order to account for the money spent on the minimal amounts of goods 1,

---

[3]This system of demands is known as the "linear expenditure system" and it is due to Stone (1954).

2, and 3 that the individual needs for his survival. Then, the Walrasian demands of this Cobb–Douglas type utility function become

$$\tilde{x}_1(p, w) = \frac{\alpha}{\alpha + \beta + \gamma} \frac{\tilde{w}}{p_1}.$$

and similarly for goods 2 and 3,

$$\tilde{x}_2(p, w) = \frac{\beta}{\alpha + \beta + \gamma} \frac{\tilde{w}}{p_2} \quad \text{and} \quad \tilde{x}_3(p, w) = \frac{\gamma}{\alpha + \beta + \gamma} \frac{\tilde{w}}{p_3}.$$

(b) Verify that the Walrasian demand functions $x(p, w)$ obtained in part (a) satisfy homogeneity of degree zero in prices and Walras' law.

- *Homogeneity.* To check the homogeneity of degree zero of the Walrasian demand function, we increase all prices and wealth by a common factor λ, which yields a Walrasian demand for good 1 of

$$\tilde{x}_1(\lambda p, \lambda w) = \frac{\alpha}{\alpha + \beta + \gamma} \frac{\lambda w - \lambda pb}{\lambda p_1}$$

$$= \frac{\alpha}{\alpha + \beta + \gamma} \frac{\lambda (w - pb)}{\lambda p_1}$$

$$= \frac{\alpha}{\alpha + \beta + \gamma} \frac{w - pb}{p_1} = \tilde{x}_1(p, w),$$

thus confirming homogeneity of degree zero. (A similar argument applies to the Walrasian demand of goods 2 and 3, as they are symmetric to that of good 1.) As a remark, note that in order to test for homogeneity we did not need to use the $\alpha + \beta + \gamma = 1$ assumption. We will next use this assumption when testing for Walras' law.

- *Walras' law.* In order to check Walras' law, we evaluate the total expenditure that emerges from the Walrasian demands, to test if the consumer exhausts his wealth, as follows:

$$p \cdot \tilde{x}(p, w) = p_1 \frac{\alpha}{\alpha + \beta + \gamma} \frac{\tilde{w}}{p_1} + p_2 \frac{\beta}{\alpha + \beta + \gamma} \frac{\tilde{w}}{p_2} + p_3 \frac{\gamma}{\alpha + \beta + \gamma} \frac{\tilde{w}}{p_3}$$

$$= \frac{\alpha}{\alpha + \beta + \gamma} \tilde{w} + \frac{\beta}{\alpha + \beta + \gamma} \tilde{w} + \frac{\gamma}{\alpha + \beta + \gamma} \tilde{w}$$

$$= \frac{\tilde{w}}{\alpha + \beta + \gamma} (\alpha + \beta + \gamma) = \tilde{w},$$

and, hence, Walras' law holds. Finally, note that the demand function is unique: for a given price vector and wealth, the consumer demands a particular amount of every good.

(c) Let us now restrict our analysis to a utility function with only two goods,

$$u(x) = (x_1 - b_1)^\alpha (x_2 - b_2)^\beta,$$

where $\alpha + \beta = 1$. Are the preferences represented by this utility function homothetic?

- This preference relation is *not* homothetic. In order to see why, let us first find the marginal rate of substitution between goods 1 and 2, $MRS_{1,2}$,

$$MRS_{1,2}(x_1, x_2) = \frac{MU_1}{MU_2} = \frac{\alpha(x_1 - b_1)^{\alpha-1}(x_2 - b_2)^\beta}{\beta(x_2 - b_2)^{\beta-1}(x_1 - b_1)^\alpha} = \frac{\alpha}{\beta}\frac{x_2 - b_2}{x_1 - b_1}.$$

Scaling up all goods by a common factor t, the $MRS_{1,2}$ becomes

$$MRS_{1,2}(tx_1, tx_2) = \frac{\alpha}{\beta}\frac{tx_2 - b_2}{tx_1 - b_1},$$

which does not coincide with $MRS_{1,2}(x_1, x_2)$. Therefore, the slope of this individual's indifference curve changes as this individual's consumption of both goods increases by the same factor t, for a given proportion of goods 1 and 2 (i.e., for a given ray from the origin).

- Finally, note that if $b_1 = b_2 = 0$ (intuitively, when there is no minimal amount of goods 1 and 2 that the individual must consume in order to survive), then the above utility function becomes a Cobb–Douglas utility function, i.e., $u(x) = x_1^\alpha x_2^\beta$ and this utility function is homothetic. This is easy to check by making $b_1 = b_2 = 0$ both in $MRS_{1,2}(x_1, x_2)$ and in $MRS_{1,2}(tx_1, tx_2)$, obtaining the same ratio on both cases.

Exercise #23 — Properties of the expenditure function

23. Consider a continuous and strictly increasing utility function $u : \mathbb{R}_+^N \to \mathbb{R}$, and a vector of positive prices $p >> 0$.

(a) Show that the expenditure function $e(p, u)$ is concave in prices.

- Using a similar notation as in part (b) of exercise 22, concavity of the expenditure function can be formally expressed as

$$\alpha e(p^1, u) + (1 - \alpha)e(p^2, u) \leq e(p^\alpha, u),$$

where $p^\alpha \equiv \alpha p^1 + (1 - \alpha)p^2$ and $\alpha \in (0, 1)$. Intuitively, this property entails that the consumer's minimal expenditure is lower when facing a extreme budget set than with the average of the two. By expenditure minimization, bundle x^1 solves EMP when facing price vector p^1, i.e., $p^1 \cdot x^1 \leq p^1 \cdot x$ for all $x \in B^1$. A similar argument applies when the price vector changes to p^2, i.e, the expenditure-minimizing bundle x^2 satisfies $p^2 \cdot x^2 \leq p^2 \cdot x$ for all $x \in B^2$. Since these two inequalities hold for any feasible x, they must also hold true for a specific bundle $\overline{x}$, that is $p^1 \cdot x^1 \leq p^1 \cdot \overline{x}$

and $p^2 \cdot x^2 \leq p^2 \cdot \overline{x}$. Multiplying the first inequality by α and the second by $(1 - \alpha)$, we obtain

$$\alpha p^1 \cdot x^1 \leq \alpha p^1 \cdot \overline{x} \quad \text{and}$$
$$(1 - \alpha) p^2 \cdot x^2 \leq (1 - \alpha) p^2 \cdot \overline{x},$$

and adding them up yields

$$\alpha p^1 \cdot x^1 + (1 - \alpha) p^2 \cdot x^2 \leq \alpha p^1 \cdot \overline{x} + (1 - \alpha) p^2 \cdot \overline{x},$$

which, rearranging, and noting that $p^1 \cdot x^1 \equiv e(p^1, u)$ and $p^2 \cdot x^2 \equiv e(p^2, u)$, yields

$$\underbrace{\alpha p^1 \cdot x^1}_{e(p^1, u)} + \underbrace{(1 - \alpha) p^2 \cdot x^2}_{e(p^2, u)} \leq \underbrace{\left[\alpha p^1 + (1 - \alpha) p^2\right]}_{p^\alpha} \cdot \overline{x}.$$

That is,

$$\alpha e(p^1, u) + (1 - \alpha) e(p^2, u) \leq e(p^\alpha, u)$$

as required. Hence, the expenditure function is concave in prices. (For a graphical representation of this property, see figure 2.41 in the textbook.)

(b) Show that the expenditure function $e(p, u)$ is strictly increasing in the utility level that the consumer seeks to reach, u.

- Before presenting a formal proof, here is some intuition: When solving the EMP, the consumer chooses a bundle x satisfying the constraint $u(x) \geq u$ with equality. (Otherwise, he could choose a cheaper bundle that still satisfies $u(x) \geq u$.) If the target utility level u increases, then the consumer needs to purchase more units of at least one good, thus raising his minimal expenditure $e(p, u)$. We next present a detailed proof of this property.

- *Plan of the proof.* Let us work by contradiction, assuming that $e(p, u)$ is *not* strictly increasing in u. Hence, as a premise, consider two different utility levels $u^B > u^A$, and let x^A and x^B be the optimal consumption bundles (those solving the EMP) when the utility level that the consumer seeks to reach is u^A and u^B, respectively, that is,

$$x^A \in h(p, u^A) \quad \text{and} \quad x^B \in h(p, u^B).$$

By contradiction, let us assume that the minimal expenditure $e(p, u)$ was *not* increasing in u, thus implying that $p \cdot x^A \geq p \cdot x^B$. In words, the minimal expenditure that the consumer needs to incur when purchasing the optimal bundle that reaches the high utility level u^B is lower or equal than that when he purchases the optimal bundle that reaches the lower utility level u^A.

- *Proof.* Let us consider a "scaled-down" version of bundle x^B, where all components are reduced by a common factor λ, i.e., $\widehat{x}^B \equiv \lambda x^B$ where $\lambda \in (0,1)$. Note that such a bundle is strictly cheaper than bundle x^B, since it contains fewer units of all goods than bundle x^B, thus implying that

$$p \cdot x^A \geq p \cdot x^B > p \cdot \widehat{x}^B.$$

  Since the utility function $u(x)$ is continuous, we can find make bundle $\widehat{x}^B$ close enough to x^B (i.e., approaching λ to 1) such that its associated utility level $u(\widehat{x}^B)$ is close to that of bundle x^B, i.e., $u(\widehat{x}^B)$ is close to $u(x^B) = u^B$. In addition, since $u^B > u^A$ by assumption, then $u(\widehat{x}^B) > u^A$. However, as described above, the minimal expenditures in this context satisfies $p \cdot x^A > p \cdot \widehat{x}^B$, which contradicts that bundle x^A could solve the EMP when reaching for utility level u^A. (The consumer could have reached utility level u^A by purchasing the cheaper bundle $\widehat{x}^B$ rather than x^A.) We have thus reached a contradiction, implying that expenditure function $e(p,u)$ must be strictly increasing in u.

- Intuitively, in order to reach a higher utility level the consumer needs to purchase larger amounts of at least one of the goods, and thus his minimal expenditure raises in u. (For a graphical representation, see figure 2.40 in the textbook.)

Exercise #25 — Duality: equivalence between the UMP and EMP

25. Consider a consumer with utility function $u(x)$ satisfying continuity and local non-satiation, where $x \in \mathbb{R}_+^L$.

  (a) Show that if bundle x^* solves this consumer's UMP, then it must also solve his EMP when he seeks to reach a utility level $u = v(p,w)$.

    - Let us work by contradiction, by assuming that bundle x^* solves this consumer's UMP but does not solve his EMP. Then, there must be a cheaper bundle x' that still helps this consumer reach utility level u (or higher), that is

    $$p \cdot x' < p \cdot x^* \text{ and } u(x') \geq u$$

    But if that is the case, we can then find another bundle x'' close to x' that is feasible, i.e., $p \cdot x'' \leq p \cdot x^* \leq w$, but helps this consumer reach a higher utility level, i.e., $u(x'') \geq u(x^*) = v(p,w)$. However, that contradicts our premise, i.e., bundle x^* cannot be utility maximizing because we found a feasible bundle that reaches a higher utility level than x^* does. Then, if bundle x^* solves a consumer's UMP it must also solve his EMP.

  (b) Show the opposite result: if bundle x^* solves this consumer's EMP, then it must also solve his UMP when his wealth level is $w = e(p,u)$. [For simplicity, assume that $p \cdot x^*$ is strictly positive.]

- Since bundle x^* solves the EMP, let $p \cdot x^* \equiv e(p, u)$ denote this consumer's expenditure function. In order to show that bundle x^* solves the UMP, we seek to demonstrate that all other bundles $x \neq x^*$ in the set of feasible bundles, $p \cdot x \leq e(p, u)$, yield a lower utility level than x^* does, i.e., $u(x) \leq u(x^*)$ for all $x \neq x^*$.

- *Proof.* In order to show the above claim, consider a "scaled down" version of the feasible bundle x, i.e., $x' = \lambda x$ where $\lambda \in (0, 1)$. Since bundle x satisfies $p \cdot x \leq e(p, u)$ bundle x' must satisfy this condition strictly, i.e., $p \cdot x' < e(p, u)$. In words, bundle x' must be cheaper than x^*, implying that, if x^* minimizes this consumer's expenditure it must be that x' does not reach the required utility level u, i.e., $u(x') < u(x^*)$. Since we can approach bundle x' to x (by making $\lambda \to 1$), and since utility function is continuous, we obtain the same result for bundle x, i.e., $u(x) < u(x^*)$; as required. In summary, if bundle x^* solves a consumer's EMP, it must also be the bundle yielding the highest utility level, and thus solves his UMP.

- The results in parts (a) and (b) are often represented algebraically as follows:

$$e(p, v(p, w)) = w \quad \text{and} \quad v(p, e(p, u)) = u$$

In words, $e(p, v(p, w)) = w$ means that if we asked a consumer to solve his EMP and reach the same utility level as the utility he obtains in the UMP, $v(p, w)$, he would need to incur a minimal expenditure of $e(p, v(p, w))$, which exactly coincides with the wealth level in his UMP, w. Similarly, $v(p, e(p, u)) = u$ represents that, if we asked a consumer to solve his UMP by providing him with a wealth level exactly equal to the minimal expenditure he incurs in his EMP, $w = e(p, u)$, he would reach a utility level $v(p, e(p, u))$, which coincides with the utility he targets in his EMP, u.

Exercise #27 — Compensated (Hicksian) elasticities

27. Camo, an excellent economics student, can choose among N different goods. Using Shephard's lemma, show that for any two goods i and j, the price elasticity of Camo's Hicksian demands,

$$\varepsilon_{h_i, p_i} \equiv \frac{\partial h_i(p, u)}{\partial p_i} \frac{p_i}{h_i(p, u)}$$

(also referred to as compensated demand price elasticities) must satisfy $\varepsilon_{h_i, p_i} \varepsilon_{h_j, p_j} \geq \varepsilon_{h_i, p_j} \varepsilon_{h_j, p_i}$. [*Hint*: Recall that the expenditure function $e(p, u)$ is convex in prices.]

- From Shephard's lemma,

$$\frac{\partial e(p, u)}{\partial p_i} = h_i(p, u).$$

That is, the derivative of the expenditure function $e(p, u)$ with respect to the price of good i helps us recover the Hicksian (compensated) demand of good i, $h_i(p, u)$. Differentiating both sides of Shephard's lemma with respect to the price of good $j \neq i$, yields

$$\frac{\partial^2 e(p, u)}{\partial p_i \partial p_j} = \frac{\partial h_i(p, u)}{\partial p_j}.$$

Since the expenditure function is convex in prices, the Hessian matrix $\frac{\partial^2 e(p,u)}{\partial p_i \partial p_j}$ must be positive semi-definite. That is, its determinant is weakly positive

$$\begin{vmatrix} \frac{\partial^2 e(p,u)}{\partial p_i \partial p_i} & \frac{\partial^2 e(p,u)}{\partial p_j \partial p_i} \\ \frac{\partial^2 e(p,u)}{\partial p_i \partial p_j} & \frac{\partial^2 e(p,u)}{\partial p_j \partial p_j} \end{vmatrix} = \frac{\partial^2 e(p,u)}{\partial p_i \partial p_i} \frac{\partial^2 e(p,u)}{\partial p_j \partial p_j} - \frac{\partial^2 e(p,u)}{\partial p_i \partial p_j} \frac{\partial^2 e(p,u)}{\partial p_j \partial p_i} \geq 0.$$

- We can now use Shephard's lemma to more compactly express the above expression as

$$\frac{\partial h_i(p,u)}{\partial p_i} \frac{\partial h_j(p,u)}{\partial p_j} \geq \frac{\partial h_i(p,u)}{\partial p_j} \frac{\partial h_j(p,u)}{\partial p_i}.$$

Finally, multiplying by $\frac{p_i}{h_i(p,u)}$ and $\frac{p_j}{h_j(p,u)}$ on both sides of the inequality (thus leaving the inequality unaffected) yields

$$\underbrace{\frac{\partial h_i(p,u)}{\partial p_i} \frac{p_i}{h_i(p,u)}}_{\varepsilon_{h_i,p_i}} \underbrace{\frac{\partial h_j(p,u)}{\partial p_j} \frac{p_j}{h_j(p,u)}}_{\varepsilon_{h_j,p_j}} \geq \underbrace{\frac{\partial h_i(p,u)}{\partial p_j} \frac{p_j}{h_i(p,u)}}_{\varepsilon_{h_i,p_j}} \underbrace{\frac{\partial h_j(p,u)}{\partial p_i} \frac{p_i}{h_j(p,u)}}_{\varepsilon_{h_j,p_i}},$$

which in terms of Hicksian (compensated) elasticities entails the inequality we sought to show $\varepsilon_{h_i,p_i} \varepsilon_{h_j,p_j} \geq \varepsilon_{h_i,p_j} \varepsilon_{h_j,p_i}$.

Chapter 3 — Applications of Demand Theory

Summary This chapter makes use of the main results from previous chapters to analyze applied questions. The first exercise considers as a motivation a consumer asking for public support, and uses the indirect utility function to evaluate under which conditions this consumer prefers a sales tax reduction over a cash subsidy. Exercises 2–5 also examine the compensating and equivalent variation of different price or tax changes. Exercise 6 deals with a consumer whose preferences lead to corner solutions in his Walrasian demand and, in this setting, measures the welfare changes due to a price change (either using the compensating variation or the change in consumer surplus). This is particularly problematic since the consumer's demand may "jump" from one corner to another as a result of a sufficiently strong price variation. The following two exercises also study price changes and how the welfare of a representative consumer changes as a consequence. Exercise 7 examines the opposite argument, by considering that we are informed about the compensating variation but need to identify the extent of the price change that gave rise to such welfare change. The next exercises analyze how to find the compensating and equivalent variation: (1) under relatively little information, namely, only observing that all prices increase in the same proportion; and (2) under a setting in which a tax is introduced on spaghetti (where we also find the deadweight loss arising from the tax). Exercise 12 contemplates a scenario in which a government needs to collect large sums to implement a new health care plan, and considers increasing either income or sales taxes. In this context, we evaluate the indirect utility function emerging from the introduction of each type of tax, in order to identify which tax plan would be preferred. The remaining exercises in this chapter explore aggregation in consumer preferences, considering the effect of additively separable utility functions for each individual consumer.

Exercise #1 — Taxes versus subsidies

1. Consider a representative consumer with utility function

$$u(q_1, q_2) = \ln q_1 + q_2,$$

where q_1 denotes gallons of gas and q_2 is a numeraire representing all other goods. The price of q_2 is therefore normalized to one, $p_2 = 1$, while the price of gas is $p_1(1 + t)$, where $t \in [0, 1]$ represents a specific tax per gallon of gas. For simplicity, assume that the consumer's income is $m > 0$.

   (a) Find the Walrasian demand for q_1 and q_2, denoting them as q_1^W and q_2^W, and distinguish the case in which $m > 1$ and that when $m \leq 1$.

   - The consumer's utility maximization problem (UMP) is selecting q_1 and q_2 to solve

$$\max_{q_1, q_2} \quad u(q_1, q_2) = \ln q_1 + q_2$$

   subject to $\quad p_1(1 + t)q_1 + q_2 = m.$

Plugging the constraint into the objective function, the UMP can be simplified to a maximization problem with a single choice variable, q_1, as follows:

$$\max_{q_1} u(q_1, q_2) = \ln q_1 + [m - p_1(1+t)q_1].$$

Taking first-order conditions with respect to q_1, we obtain $\frac{1}{q_1} - p_1(1+t) = 0$. Solving for q_1 yields the Walrasian demand for good 1

$$q_1^W(\mathbf{p}, m; t) = \frac{1}{p_1(1+t)},$$

where $\mathbf{p} \equiv (p_1, p_2) \in \mathbb{R}^2_{++}$ denotes the price vector. Plugging this result into the budget constraint, we find the Walrasian demand for good 2:

$$q_2^W(\mathbf{p}, m; t) = m - p_1(1+t)\frac{1}{p_1(1+t)} = m - 1.$$

Note that there is a corner solution when $m \leq 1$ in which good 2 is not consumed. In this case, the trucker spends all his income on good 1, i.e., $p_1(1+t)q_1 + 0 = m$ which, solving for q_1, yields $q_1 = \frac{m}{p_1(1+t)}$. We can, hence, summarize the Walrasian demand correspondence as follows:

$$(q_1^W(\mathbf{p}, m; t), q_2^W(\mathbf{p}, m; t)) = \begin{cases} \left(\frac{1}{p_1(1+t)}, m - 1\right) & \text{if } m > 1, \text{ and} \\ \left(\frac{m}{p_1(1+t)}, 0\right) & \text{if } m \leq 1. \end{cases}$$

Note that in the interior solution (when $m > 1$) the demand for gas (good 1) does not depend on income m, i.e., its income effect is zero.

(b) Find the associated indirect utility function, $v\left(q_1^W, q_2^W\right)$.

- Plugging the above results into the trucker's utility function, we obtain an indirect utility function $v_1(\mathbf{p}, m; t) = \ln q_1^W + q_2^W$, that is,

$$v_1(\mathbf{p}, m; t) = \begin{cases} \ln\left(\frac{1}{p_1(1+t)}\right) + m - 1 & \text{if } m > 1, \text{ and} \\ \ln\left(\frac{m}{p_1(1+t)}\right) & \text{if } m \leq 1. \end{cases}$$

After months of lobbying from consumers' associations, the government is considering implementing either of the following policies: (1) reduce the tax on gas, from t to $t' = t - \alpha$; or (2) maintain the tax at t but give a subsidy of S dollars to the consumer equal to the tax revenue collected by the tax on gas.

(c) Let us first consider that the consumer's income satisfies $m > 1$, i.e., the consumer is relatively rich. Find the consumer's indirect utility function if the government implements the first policy, $v^I\left(q_1^W, q_2^W\right)$, and if the government implements the second policy, $v^{II}\left(q_1^W, q_2^W\right)$. Under which conditions does the consumer prefer the first policy?

- Since $m > 1$ we are at the interior solution. If the *first* policy is implemented, reducing the tax rate to $t' = t - \alpha$, the consumer's indirect utility function becomes

$$v^I\left(q_1^W, q_2^W\right) = \ln\left(\frac{1}{p_1(1+t-\alpha)}\right) + m - 1.$$

If, instead, the *second* policy is implemented, then the tax rate is unaltered, but tax revenue

$$R = tp_1 q_1^W = tp_1 \frac{1}{p_1(1+t)} = \frac{t}{1+t}$$

is given to the consumer in the form of a subsidy, yielding an indirect utility function of

$$v^{II}\left(q_1^W, q_2^W\right) = \ln\left(\frac{1}{p_1(1+t)}\right) + m - 1 + \overbrace{\frac{t}{1+t}}^{\text{subsidy}},$$

since we know that any increase in his wealth is only used to increase the amount of q_2 being consumed (the amount of good q_1 does not increase in income).

- We can now compare $v^I\left(q_1^W, q_2^W\right)$ and $v^{II}\left(q_1^W, q_2^W\right)$, obtaining that

$$v^I\left(q_1^W, q_2^W\right) > v^{II}\left(q_1^W, q_2^W\right) \iff \ln\left(\frac{1+t}{1+t-\alpha}\right) > \frac{t}{1+t},$$

which implies that if the tax reduction α is sufficiently high, the consumer prefers the first to the second policy. Indeed, solving for α, we find that $\alpha > \overline{\alpha}$, where $\overline{\alpha} \equiv (1+t)\left(1 - e^{-\frac{t}{1+t}}\right)$.

- Figure 3.1 depicts cutoff $\overline{\alpha}$, for different values of t. Hence, the region of (t, α)-pairs above cutoff $\overline{\alpha}$ describe settings in which the consumer prefers the first policy (tax reduction), while for (t, α)-pairs below cutoff $\overline{\alpha}$ the consumer prefers the second policy (subsidy).

- *Numerical example—I.* If the initial tax on gas is $t = 0.5$, then we obtain that $\ln\left(\frac{1+0.5}{1+0.5-\alpha}\right) > \frac{0.5}{1+0.5}$ holds if the tax reduction, α, satisfies $\alpha > 0.42$. If the initial tax is higher, $t = 0.8$, then we obtain that $\ln\left(\frac{1+0.8}{1+0.8-\alpha}\right) > \frac{0.8}{1+0.8}$ holds only if $\alpha > 0.64$. Intuitively, as the tax rate becomes higher, the consumer needs a larger tax reduction, α, in order to make the first policy preferable.

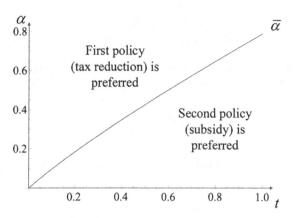

Figure 3.1 Policy comparison when $m > 1$.

(d) Let us now consider that the consumer's income satisfies $m \leq 1$, i.e., the consumer is relatively poor. Find the consumer's indirect utility function if the government implements the first policy, $v^I\left(q_1^W, q_2^W\right)$, and if the government implements the second policy, $v^{II}\left(q_1^W, q_2^W\right)$. Under which conditions does the consumer prefer the first policy?

- Since $m \leq 1$, we are at the corner solution, which is $\left(q_1^W, q_2^W\right) = \left(\frac{m}{p_1(1+t)}, 0\right)$. If the *first* policy is implemented, reducing the tax rate to $t' = t - \alpha$, the consumer's indirect utility function becomes

$$v^I\left(q_1^W, q_2^W\right) = \ln\left(\frac{m}{p_1(1 + t - \alpha)}\right).$$

If, instead, the *second* policy is implemented, then the tax rate is unaltered, but tax revenue $R = tp_1\frac{m}{p_1(1+t)} = \frac{t}{1+t}m$ is given to the consumer in the form of a subsidy, yielding a total income of $m + \frac{t}{1+t}m = \frac{1+2t}{1+t}m$. Note that $m \leq 1$ does not guarantee that $\frac{1+2t}{1+t}m \leq 1$, so with this new income, the consumer is still at a corner solution if $\frac{1+2t}{1+t}m \leq 1$, or moves to an interior solution if $\frac{1+2t}{1+t}m > 1$, i.e., where $\frac{1+2t}{1+t}m > 1 > m$. Let us analyze each case separately:

- *CASE 1:* When $\frac{1+2t}{1+t}m \leq 1$, Walrasian demands are given by

$$\left(q_1^W(\mathbf{p}, m; t), q_2^W(\mathbf{p}, m; t)\right) = \left(\frac{m(1 + 2t)}{p_1(1 + t)^2}, 0\right),$$

yielding an indirect utility function of

$$v^{II-1^{st}}\left(q_1^W, q_2^W\right) = \ln\left(\frac{m(1 + 2t)}{p_1(1 + t)^2}\right).$$

We can now compare the indirect utility function of the consumer in the first and second policy, i.e., $v^I\left(q_1^W, q_2^W\right)$ and $v^{II-1^{st}}\left(q_1^W, q_2^W\right)$, which implies that the consumer prefers the first policy if

$$\ln\left(\frac{m}{p_1(1+t-\alpha)}\right) > \ln\left(\frac{m(1+2t)}{p_1(1+t)^2}\right) \iff \ln\left(\frac{(1+t)^2}{(1+t-\alpha)(1+2t)}\right) > 0$$

Solving for α, we obtain that for $\alpha > \frac{t(1+t)}{1+2t} \equiv \widetilde{\alpha}$, a tax reduction is preferred over a subsidy.

- CASE 2: When $\frac{1+2t}{1+t}m > 1$, Walrasian demands are now both interior, and given by

$$\left(q_1^W(\mathbf{p}, m; t), q_2^W(\mathbf{p}, m; t)\right) = \left(\frac{1}{p_1(1+t)}, \frac{1+2t}{1+t}m - 1\right),$$

yielding an indirect utility function of

$$v^{II-2^{nd}}\left(q_1^W, q_2^W\right) = \ln\left(\frac{1}{p_1(1+t)}\right) + \frac{1+2t}{1+t}m - 1.$$

We can now compare the indirect utility function of the consumer in the first and second policy, i.e., $v^I\left(q_1^W, q_2^W\right)$ and $v^{II-2^{nd}}\left(q_1^W, q_2^W\right)$, which implies that the consumer prefers the first policy if

$$\ln\left(\frac{m}{p_1(1+t-\alpha)}\right) > \ln\left(\frac{1}{p_1(1+t)}\right) + \frac{1+2t}{1+t}m - 1,$$

or rearranging,

$$\ln\left(\frac{m(1+t)}{1+t-\alpha}\right) > \frac{1+2t}{1+t}m - 1.$$

Solving for α, we find that $\alpha > 1 + t - (1+t)me^{1+m\left(\frac{t}{1+t}-2\right)} \equiv \widehat{\alpha}$.

- Numerical example—II. If the initial tax rate is $t = 0.5$ and the consumer's income is $m = 0.8$, then the above condition holds as long as $\alpha > \widehat{\alpha} = 0.37$. Similarly as in part (c) of the exercise, if the tax rate is higher, $t = 0.8$, then the above condition holds as long as $\alpha > \widehat{\alpha} = 0.56$, suggesting that, as the tax rate increases the consumer only prefers the first policy if the size of the tax reduction, α, becomes sufficiently large.

- Summary. Finally, note that if the tax reduction is sufficiently larger, i.e., α exceeds all the cutoffs identified in the previous section of the exercise $\alpha > \max\{\overline{\alpha}, \widetilde{\alpha}, \widehat{\alpha}\}$, then the consumer unambiguously prefers a tax reduction than a subsidy regardless of his actual income level, m. If, instead, the tax reduction is extremely low, i.e., α falls below all cutoffs $\alpha < \min\{\overline{\alpha}, \widetilde{\alpha}, \widehat{\alpha}\}$, the consumer prefers the subsidy policy independently of his income level, m. If the tax reduction is, however, intermediate, i.e., $\min\{\overline{\alpha}, \widetilde{\alpha}, \widehat{\alpha}\} < \alpha < \max\{\overline{\alpha}, \widetilde{\alpha}, \widehat{\alpha}\}$, then the consumer's preference for one particular policy depends on his income level.

Exercise #3 — Compensating and equivalent variation

3. An individual consumes only good 1 and 2, and his preferences over these two goods can be represented by Cobb–Douglas utility function

$$u(x_1, x_2) = x_1^\alpha x_2^\beta \quad \text{where } \alpha, \beta > 0.$$

(For generality, we do not impose any assumptions on the sum of the exponents, i.e., $\alpha + \beta$ can satisfy $\alpha + \beta > 1$ or $\alpha + \beta < 1$.) This individual currently works for a firm in a city where initial prices are $p^0 = (p_1, p_2)$, and his wealth is w.

(a) Find the Walrasian demand for goods 1 and 2 of this individual, $x_1(p, w)$ and $x_2(p, w)$.

- We know that the Walrasian demand in the Cobb–Douglas case are $x_1(p, w) = \frac{\alpha}{\alpha+\beta} \frac{w}{p_1}$ and $x_2(p, w) = \frac{\beta}{\alpha+\beta} \frac{w}{p_2}$; as shown in previous chapters. As a practice we next demonstrate this result again.

- The Lagrangian of this UMP is

$$\mathcal{L}(x_1, x_2; \lambda) = x_1^\alpha x_2^\beta - \lambda \left[p_1 x_1 + p_2 x_2 - w \right].$$

The first order conditions are

$$\frac{\partial \mathcal{L}}{\partial x_1} = \alpha x_1^{\alpha-1} x_2^\beta - \lambda p_1 = 0,$$

$$\frac{\partial \mathcal{L}}{\partial x_2} = \beta x_1^\alpha x_2^{\beta-1} - \lambda p_2 = 0.$$

Solving for λ on both first-order conditions, we obtain

$$\frac{\alpha x_1^{\alpha-1} x_2^\beta}{p_1} = \frac{\beta x_1^\alpha x_2^{\beta-1}}{p_2} \iff x_2 = \frac{\beta p_1 x_1}{\alpha p_2}.$$

Using the budget constraint (which is binding), we have

$$p_1 x_1 + p_2 x_2 = w \iff x_1 = \frac{w}{p_1} - \frac{p_2 x_2}{p_1},$$

and plugging this expression of x_2 we found above, yields the Walrasian demand for good 1,

$$x_1 = \frac{w}{p_1} - \frac{p_2 \left(\frac{\beta p_1 x_1}{\alpha p_2} \right)}{p_1} \iff x_1 = \frac{\alpha w}{(\alpha + \beta) p_1},$$

and, hence, the Walrasian demand for good 2 is

$$x_2 = \frac{\beta p_1 \left(\frac{\alpha w}{(\alpha+\beta) p_1} \right)}{\alpha p_2} = \frac{\beta w}{(\alpha + \beta) p_2}.$$

Hence, the Walrasian demand function is

$$x_1(p,w) = \frac{\alpha w}{(\alpha + \beta)\, p_1} \quad \text{and} \quad x_2(p,w) = \frac{\beta w}{(\alpha + \beta)\, p_2}.$$

(b) Find his indirect utility function at price vector p, and denote it as $v(p,w)$.

- Plugging the above Walrasian demand functions in the consumer's utility function, we obtain

$$v(p,w) = \left[\frac{\alpha w}{(\alpha + \beta)\, p_1}\right]^{\alpha} \left[\frac{\beta w}{(\alpha + \beta)\, p_2}\right]^{\beta}$$

$$= \left(\frac{w}{\alpha + \beta}\right)^{\alpha + \beta} \left(\frac{\alpha}{p_1}\right)^{\alpha} \left(\frac{\beta}{p_2}\right)^{\beta}.$$

(c) The firm that this individual works for is considering moving its office to a different city, where good 1 has the same price, but good 2 (e.g., housing) is twice as expensive, i.e., the new price vector is $p' = (p_1, 2p_2)$. Find the value of the indirect utility function in the new location. Let us denote this indirect utility function $v(p',w)$.

- The indirect utility function $v(p',w)$ is

$$v(p',w) = \left(\frac{w}{\alpha + \beta}\right)^{\alpha + \beta} \left(\frac{\alpha}{p_1}\right)^{\alpha} \left(\frac{\beta}{2p_2}\right)^{\beta},$$

where, relative to $v(p,w)$, only the price of good 2 has changed (namely, it has doubled), while all other elements remain unaffected.

(d) This individual's expenditure function is[1]

$$e(p,u) = (\alpha + \beta) \left(\frac{p_1}{\alpha}\right)^{\frac{\alpha}{\alpha + \beta}} \left(\frac{p_2}{\beta}\right)^{\frac{\beta}{\alpha + \beta}} u^{\frac{1}{\alpha + \beta}}.$$

Evaluate this expenditure function in the following cases:

1. Under initial prices, p, and maximal utility level $u \equiv v(p,w)$, and denote it by $e(p,u)$.

$$e(p,u) = (\alpha + \beta) \left(\frac{p_1}{\alpha}\right)^{\frac{\alpha}{\alpha + \beta}} \left(\frac{p_2}{\beta}\right)^{\frac{\beta}{\alpha + \beta}} \underbrace{\left[\left(\frac{w}{\alpha + \beta}\right)^{\alpha + \beta} \left(\frac{\alpha}{p_1}\right)^{\alpha} \left(\frac{\beta}{p_2}\right)^{\beta}\right]^{\frac{1}{\alpha + \beta}}}_{u} = w.$$

---

[1] As a practice, you can set up the consumer's expenditure minimization problem (EMP), find the Hicksian demands that emerge from solving this EMP, $h_1(p,u)$, and $h_2(p,u)$, and afterwards plug them into $p_1 x_1 + p_2 x_2$ to obtain the expenditure function $e(p,u) \equiv p_1 h_1(p,u) + p_2 h_2(p,u)$. After some algebra, you should find an expression of $e(p,u)$ that coincides with that provided in the exercise.

2. Under initial prices, p, and maximal utility level $u' \equiv v(p', w)$, and denote it by $e(p, u')$.

$$e(p, u') = (\alpha + \beta) \left(\frac{p_1}{\alpha}\right)^{\frac{\alpha}{\alpha+\beta}} \left(\frac{p_2}{\beta}\right)^{\frac{\beta}{\alpha+\beta}} \left[\left(\frac{w}{\alpha+\beta}\right)^{\alpha+\beta} \left(\frac{\alpha}{p_1}\right)^{\alpha} \left(\frac{\beta}{2p_2}\right)^{\beta}\right]^{\frac{1}{\alpha+\beta}} = \frac{1}{2^{\frac{\beta}{\alpha+\beta}}} w.$$

3. Under new prices, p', and maximal utility level $u \equiv v(p, w)$, and denote it by $e(p', u)$.

$$e(p', u) = (\alpha + \beta) \left(\frac{p_1}{\alpha}\right)^{\frac{\alpha}{\alpha+\beta}} \left(\frac{2p_2}{\beta}\right)^{\frac{\beta}{\alpha+\beta}} \left[\left(\frac{w}{\alpha+\beta}\right)^{\alpha+\beta} \left(\frac{\alpha}{p_1}\right)^{\alpha} \left(\frac{\beta}{p_2}\right)^{\beta}\right]^{\frac{1}{\alpha+\beta}} = 2^{\frac{\beta}{\alpha+\beta}} w.$$

4. Under new prices, p', and maximal utility level $u' \equiv v(p', w)$, and denote it by $e(p', u')$.

$$e(p', u') = (\alpha + \beta) \left(\frac{p_1}{\alpha}\right)^{\frac{\alpha}{\alpha+\beta}} \left(\frac{2p_2}{\beta}\right)^{\frac{\beta}{\alpha+\beta}} \left[\left(\frac{w}{\alpha+\beta}\right)^{\alpha+\beta} \left(\frac{\alpha}{p_1}\right)^{\alpha} \left(\frac{\beta}{2p_2}\right)^{\beta}\right]^{\frac{1}{\alpha+\beta}} = w.$$

(e) Find this individual's equivalent variation due to the price change. Explain how your result can be related with this proposal of the worker to his boss: "I would really prefer to stay in this city. In fact, I would accept a salary reduction if I could keep working for the firm in this city."

- The equivalent variation of a price change is given by

$$EV = e(p', u') - e(p, u').$$

Using the results from the previous part, we have that $e(p', u') = w$, while $e(p, u') = \frac{1}{2^{\frac{\beta}{\alpha+\beta}}} w$, thus implying that the equivalent variation is

$$EV = w - \frac{1}{2^{\frac{\beta}{\alpha+\beta}}} w.$$

That is, this individual would be willing to accept a reduction in his wealth of $w - \frac{1}{2^{\frac{\beta}{\alpha+\beta}}} w$ in order to avoid moving to a different city. [Alternatively, the individual is willing to accept a reduction of $\left(1 - \frac{1}{2^{\frac{\beta}{\alpha+\beta}}}\right)$ % of his wealth.] Figure 3.2 depicts the equivalent variation for the case in which $\alpha = \beta = \frac{1}{2}$, i.e., $EV = w\left(1 - \frac{1}{\sqrt{2}}\right)$. In particular, the figure depicts the wealth level of this individual, w, in the $45°$-line; and the equivalent variation (in the shaded area). Hence, the unshaded region below the $45°$-line represents the remaining income that this individual would retain after giving up the amount found in the equivalent variation.

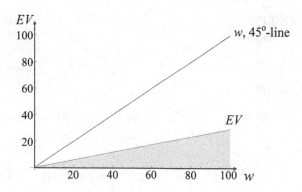

Figure 3.2 Equivalent variation (shaded area).

(f) How is this individual's consumer surplus affected by the price change? (The change in consumer surplus is often referred to as the "area variation (AV).")

- The area variation is given by the area below the Walrasian demand of good 2 (since only the price of this good changes), between the initial and final price level. That is,

$$AV = \int_{p_2}^{2p_2} x_2(p, w)dp = \int_{p_2}^{2p_2} \frac{\beta}{(\alpha + \beta)\,p}\,w\,dp$$

and rearranging

$$= \frac{\beta}{(\alpha + \beta)}\,w \int_{p_2}^{2p_2} \frac{1}{p}\,dp = \frac{\beta}{(\alpha + \beta)}\,w\ln 2.$$

Hence, moving to the new city would imply a reduction in this individual's welfare of $\frac{\beta}{(\alpha+\beta)}w\ln 2$, or $\left(\frac{\beta}{(\alpha+\beta)}\ln 2\right)\%$ of his wealth. Figure 3.3 depicts the AV for the case in which $\alpha = \beta = \frac{1}{2}$, i.e., $AV = \frac{\ln 2}{2}w$, and compares it with the EV found in part (e) of the exercise.

(g) Which of the previous welfare measures in questions (e) and (f) coincide? Which of them do *not* coincide? Explain.

- None of them coincide, since this individual's preferences produces a positive income effect.

(h) Consider how the welfare measures from questions (e) and (f) would be modified if this individual's preferences were represented, instead, by the utility function $v(x_1, x_2) = \alpha \ln x_1 + \beta \ln x_2$.

- Since we have just applied a monotonic transformation to the initial utility function, $u(x_1, x_2)$, the new utility function $v(x_1, x_2)$ represents the same preference relation as utility function $v(x_1, x_2)$. Hence, the welfare results that we would obtain from function $v(x_1, x_2)$ would be the same as those with utility function $u(x_1, x_2)$. This is, in fact, one of the advantages of using monetary measures of welfare change (such

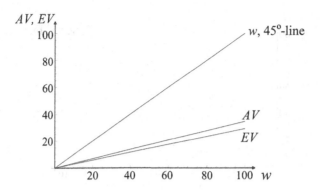

Figure 3.3 Area variation and equivalent variation.

as the equivalent, compensating, or area variation) rather than the simple difference in utility levels before and after the price change, i.e., $u' - u$. In particular, while the monetary measures are insensitive to monotonic transformations of the utility function, the utility difference when the consumer has utility function $u(x)$, i.e., $u' - u$, may differ from that when his utility experiences a monotonic transformation, $v' - v$.

Exercise #5 — Welfare measures with a quasi-linear utility

5. Consider a consumer with quasilinear utility function $u(x_1, x_2) = ax_1^\alpha + bx_2$, where $\alpha \neq 1$ and $a, b > 0$.

   (a) Find the Walrassian demand of the individual.

   - We need to solve the UMP

   $$\max_{x_1, x_2} \ u(x_1, x_2) = ax_1^\alpha + bx_2$$

   subject to $p_1 x_1 + p_2 x_2 \leq w$.

   Taking first-order conditions with respect to x_1 yields

   $$a\alpha x_1^{\alpha-1} - \lambda p_1 \leq 0,$$

   where λ denotes the Lagrange multiplier. Similarly, taking first-order conditions with respect to x_2, we find

   $$b - \lambda p_2 \leq 0.$$

   In the case of interior solutions, the above first-order conditions hold with equality. Solving for λ in both of them, we obtain

   $$\frac{a\alpha x_1^{\alpha-1}}{p_1} = \frac{b}{p_2}, \quad \text{or} \quad x_1 = \left(\frac{bp_1}{a\alpha p_2}\right)^{\frac{1}{\alpha-1}}.$$

Hence, this consumer's Walrasian demands are

$$x_1(p,w) = \left(\frac{bp_1}{a\alpha p_2}\right)^{\frac{1}{\alpha-1}} \quad \text{and} \quad x_2(p,w) = \frac{w}{p_2} - \left(\frac{bp_1^\alpha}{a\alpha p_2^\alpha}\right)^{\frac{1}{\alpha-1}},$$

and the indirect utility function becomes

$$v(p,w) = a\left[\left(\frac{bp_1}{a\alpha p_2}\right)^{\frac{1}{\alpha-1}}\right]^\alpha + b\left[\frac{w}{p_2} - \left(\frac{bp_1^\alpha}{a\alpha p_2^\alpha}\right)^{\frac{1}{\alpha-1}}\right]$$

$$= \frac{bw}{p_2} + \left(\frac{b^\alpha p_1^\alpha}{a\alpha p_2^\alpha}\right)^{\frac{1}{\alpha-1}}\left(\frac{1}{\alpha^\alpha} - 1\right).$$

- Note that $x_1(p,w) > 0$ for all admissible parameter values (i.e., $a, b, \alpha, p_1, p_2 > 0$). However, corner solutions in which $x_2(p,w) = 0$ can emerge if $\frac{w}{p_2} = \left(\frac{bp_1^\alpha}{a\alpha p_2^\alpha}\right)^{\frac{1}{\alpha-1}}$, i.e., for an income level of $w = p_2\left(\frac{bp_1^\alpha}{a\alpha p_2^\alpha}\right)^{\frac{1}{\alpha-1}}$. In such a case, the indirect utility function becomes $v(p,w) = a\left[\left(\frac{bp_1}{a\alpha p_2}\right)^{\frac{1}{\alpha-1}}\right]^\alpha$.

(b) Find the Hicksian demand for goods 1 and 2.

- Let us solve the following EMP:

$$\min_{x_1,x_2} \quad p_1x_1 + p_2x_2$$

subject to $ax_1^\alpha + bx_2 \geq u$.

Taking first-order conditions with respect to x_1 and x_2, yields

$$p_1 \geq \mu a\alpha x_1^{\alpha-1} \text{ and}$$

$$p_2 \geq \mu b,$$

where μ denotes the Lagrange multiplier of this minimization problem. In the case of interior solutions, the above first-order conditions become

$$\begin{cases} p_1 = \mu a\alpha x_1^{\alpha-1}, \\ p_2 = \mu b, \\ ax_1^\alpha + bx_2 = u. \end{cases}$$

Thus, simultaneously solving for x_1 and x_2, we find the Hicksian demands for good 1 and 2 are

$$h_1(p,u) = \left(\frac{bp_1}{a\alpha p_2}\right)^{\frac{1}{\alpha-1}}, \quad h_2(p,u) = \frac{u}{b} - \left(\frac{bp_1^\alpha}{a\alpha^\alpha p_2^\alpha}\right)^{\frac{1}{\alpha-1}},$$

and the expenditure function becomes

$$e(p, u) = p_1 \left[\left(\frac{bp_1}{a\alpha p_2} \right)^{\frac{1}{\alpha-1}} \right] + p_2 \left[\frac{u}{b} - \left(\frac{bp_1^\alpha}{a\alpha^\alpha p_2^\alpha} \right)^{\frac{1}{\alpha-1}} \right]$$

$$= \frac{p_2 u}{b} - \left(\frac{bp_1^\alpha}{a\alpha p_2} \right)^{\frac{1}{\alpha-1}} \left(\frac{1}{\alpha^\alpha} - 1 \right).$$

- Similarly as for the Walrasian demand in part (a), the Hicksian demand for good 1 is positive for all parameter values. The Hicksian demand for good 2, however, can become zero if $\frac{u}{b} = \left(\frac{bp_1^\alpha}{a\alpha^\alpha p_2^\alpha} \right)^{\frac{1}{\alpha-1}}$, i.e., for $u = b \left(\frac{bp_1^\alpha}{a\alpha^\alpha p_2^\alpha} \right)^{\frac{1}{\alpha-1}}$, thus yielding a expenditure function of $(p, u) = p_1 \left[\left(\frac{bp_1}{a\alpha p_2} \right)^{\frac{1}{\alpha-1}} \right]$.

(c) Assume that the consumer's wealth is $w = \$10$, and prices are $p_1 = p_2 = 2$. For simplicity, consider parameters $a = 2, b = 1$ and $\alpha = \frac{1}{2}$. Find the AV, CV and EV.

- For these parameters, the Walrasian demand of both goods are strictly positive (check as a practice). Hence, the indirect utility function is

$$v(p, w) = \frac{bw}{p_2} + \left(\frac{b^\alpha p_1^\alpha}{a\alpha p_2^\alpha} \right)^{\frac{1}{\alpha-1}} \left(\frac{1}{\alpha^\alpha} - 1 \right)$$

$$= \frac{1 \times 10}{2} + \left(\frac{1^{\frac{1}{2}} \times 2^{\frac{1}{2}}}{2 \times \frac{1}{2} \times 2^{\frac{1}{2}}} \right)^{\frac{1}{\frac{1}{2}-1}} \left(\frac{1}{\frac{1}{2}^{\frac{1}{2}}} - 1 \right)$$

$$= 5 + (1) \left(\sqrt{2} - 1 \right) = 4 + \sqrt{2} \approx 5.4142.$$

- *Area variation.* Hence, if the price of good 1 decreases by 50%, i.e., from $p_1 = 2$ to $p_1' = 1$, the area variation is

$$AV = \int_1^2 x_1(p, w) dp_1 = \int_1^2 \left(\frac{bp_1}{a\alpha p_2} \right)^{\frac{1}{\alpha-1}} dp_1$$

$$= \int_1^2 \left(\frac{2}{p_1} \right)^2 dp_1 = \left[-\frac{4}{p_1} \right]_1^2 = 2$$

- *Compensating variation.* Let us now examine the compensating variation associated with this price decrease. First, recall that the Hicksian demands (found in part b) are

$$h_1(p, u) = \left(\frac{bp_1}{a\alpha p_2} \right)^{\frac{1}{\alpha-1}}, \qquad h_2(p, u) = \frac{u}{b} - \left(\frac{bp_1^\alpha}{a\alpha^\alpha p_2^\alpha} \right)^{\frac{1}{\alpha-1}}.$$

Hence, the compensating variation associated to a 50% decrease in the price of good 1 is

$$CV = \int_1^2 h_1(p, u^0)dp_1 = \int_1^2 \left(\frac{bp_1}{a\alpha p_2}\right)^{\frac{1}{\alpha-1}} dp_1$$

$$= \int_1^2 \left(\frac{2}{p_1}\right)^2 dp_1 = \left[-\frac{4}{p_1}\right]_1^2 = 2.$$

- *Equivalent variation.* Let us finally identify the equivalent variation of this price change. In order to do this, we first need to evaluate the indirect utility function $v(p, w)$ at the final prices $p_1 = 1$ and $p_2 = 2$, which yields $u^1 = 3 + 2\sqrt{2} \approx 5.8284$. Plugging this utility level u^1 on the Hicksian demand for good 1 (also evaluated at final prices $p_1 = 1$ and $p_2 = 2$), we obtain

$$h_1(p, u^1) = \left(\frac{bp_1}{a\alpha p_2}\right)^{\frac{1}{\alpha-1}} = 4.$$

Hence, the equivalent variation of the price decrease is

$$EV = \int_1^2 h_1(p, u^1)dp_1 = \int_1^2 \left(\frac{bp_1}{a\alpha p_2}\right)^{\frac{1}{\alpha-1}} dp_1$$

$$= \int_1^2 \left(\frac{2}{p_1}\right)^2 dp_1 = \left[-\frac{4}{p_1}\right]_1^2 = 2.$$

Therefore, since the utility function is quasi-linear, we confirmed that all welfare measures coincide, i.e., $AV = CV = EV$.

Exercise #7 — Consumer theory and welfare

7. Consider a representative consumer in an economy with J goods, $j = 1, 2, ..., J$. Since we are mainly interested in this individual's consumption of goods 1 and 2, we group all the remaining goods $j = 3, 4, ..., J$ as good zero, q_0. The price of good zero is normalized to $p_0 = 1$ (i.e., good zero thus becomes the numeraire). The prices of goods 1 and 2 are p_1 and p_2, and income is $m > 0$. This consumer's preferences are represented by utility function

$$u(q_1, q_2, q_0) = q_1^{\frac{1}{4}} q_2^{\frac{1}{4}} + q_0.$$

(a) Find the Walrasian demands and the associated indirect utility function.

- **UMP:** In order to solve this problem, we use a standard argument for additively separate utility functions: define $e^R(\mathbf{p}, m) \equiv p_1 q_1^W + p_2 q_2^W$ to be the amount of money spent on purchasing the Walrasian demand of goods 1 and 2 alone. Then, the pair $\left(q_1^W, q_2^W\right)$ must solve the auxiliary problem

$$\max_{q_1, q_2} q_1^{\frac{1}{4}} q_2^{\frac{1}{4}} \tag{1}$$

$$\text{subject to} \quad p_1 q_1 + p_2 q_2 = e^R(\mathbf{p}, m).$$

Solving for q_2 in the constraint, $q_2 = \frac{e^R}{p_2} - \frac{p_1}{p_2}q_1$, and plugging it into the objective function, the maximization problem reduces to one with a single choice variable, q_1, as follows:

$$\max_{q_1} \; q_1^{\frac{1}{4}} \left(\frac{e^R}{p_2} - \frac{p_1}{p_2}q_1 \right)^{\frac{1}{4}}.$$

Taking first-order conditions with respect to q_1,

$$\frac{e^R - 2p_1 q_1}{4p_2 q_1^{\frac{3}{4}} \left(\frac{e^R - p_1 q_1}{p_2} \right)^{\frac{3}{4}}} = 0,$$

and solving for q_1 yields

$$q_1^W(\mathbf{p}, e^R) = \frac{e^R}{2p_1}.$$

Plugging $q_1^W(\mathbf{p}, e^R) = \frac{e^R}{2p_1}$ into the constraint, $q_2 = \frac{e^R}{p_2} - \frac{p_1}{p_2}q_1$, we obtain

$$q_2^W(\mathbf{p}, e^R) = \frac{e^R}{2p_2}.$$

In addition, note that $q_1^W(\mathbf{p}, e^R)$ and $q_2^W(\mathbf{p}, e^R)$ do not depend on the overall income of the individual, m, but on the amount of income he spends on good 1 and 2 alone, e^R. Expressions $q_1^W(\mathbf{p}, e^R)$ and $q_2^W(\mathbf{p}, e^R)$ yield an associated utility level of

$$v^R(\mathbf{p}, e^R) = \left(\frac{1}{p_1} \right)^{1/4} \left(\frac{1}{p_2} \right)^{1/4} \left(\frac{e^R}{2} \right)^{1/2},$$

which can be interpreted as the indirect utility function of the auxiliary maximization problem (1).

- Given these results for goods 1 and 2, we can analyze good 0. In particular, the Walrasian demand for good 0, q_0^W, and the amount of income spent on goods 1 and 2, $e^R(\mathbf{p}, m)$, must solve

$$\max_{q_0, e^R} \; v^R(\mathbf{p}, e^R) + q_0$$

subject to $\; e^R(\mathbf{p}, m) + q_0 = m$.

Furthermore, since $q_0 = m - e^R(\mathbf{p}, m)$, the above program can be simplified to the following maximization problem (with only one choice variable):

$$\max_{e^R} \; g(e^R, \mathbf{p}) = v^R(\mathbf{p}, e^R) + \left[m - e^R(p, m) \right].$$

Taking first-order conditions with respect to e^R, we obtain

$$\frac{\partial g(e^R, \mathbf{p})}{\partial e^R} = \frac{\left(\frac{1}{p_1}\right)^{1/4} \left(\frac{1}{p_2}\right)^{1/4}}{2\sqrt{2}\sqrt{e^R}} - 1, \tag{2}$$

and second-order conditions

$$\frac{\partial^2 g(e^R, \mathbf{p})}{\partial e^R\,^2} = -\frac{\left(\frac{1}{p_1}\right)^{1/4} \left(\frac{1}{p_2}\right)^{1/4}}{4\sqrt{2}\left(e^R\right)^{3/2}} < 0 \tag{3}$$

showing that the objective function $g(e^R, \mathbf{p})$ is strictly concave.

- Therefore, from the first order conditions in (2), the value of $e^R(\mathbf{p}, m)$ that maximizes $g(e^R, \mathbf{p})$ is $e^*(\mathbf{p}) = \frac{1}{8\sqrt{p_1 p_2}}$. This implies that:

  – When $m > \frac{1}{8\sqrt{p_1 p_2}}$, Walrasian demands are

  $$q_1^W = \frac{\frac{1}{8\sqrt{p_1 p_2}}}{2p_1} = \frac{1}{16\sqrt{p_1^3 p_2}} \quad \text{and} \quad q_2^W = \frac{\frac{1}{8\sqrt{p_1 p_2}}}{2p_2} = \frac{1}{16\sqrt{p_1 p_2^3}}$$

  for goods 1 and 2, and the rest of income, $q_0^W = m - \frac{1}{8\sqrt{p_1 p_2}}$, is spent on good 0 (Interior solutions).

  – By contrast, when $m \leq \frac{1}{8\sqrt{p_1 p_2}}$, no income is spent on good 0, $q_0^W = 0$, but only on goods 1 and 2, that is,

  $$q_1^W = \frac{m}{2p_1} \quad \text{and} \quad q_2^W = \frac{m}{2p_2}$$

  at a corner solution.

- Hence, the Walrasian demand correspondence can be summarized as

$$(q_1^W, q_2^W, q_0^W) = \begin{cases} \left(\frac{1}{16\sqrt{p_1^3 p_2}}, \frac{1}{16\sqrt{p_1 p_2^3}}, m - \frac{1}{8\sqrt{p_1 p_2}}\right) & \text{if } m > \frac{1}{8\sqrt{p_1 p_2}}, \text{ and} \\ \left(\frac{m}{2p_1}, \frac{m}{2p_2}, 0\right) & \text{if } m \leq \frac{1}{8\sqrt{p_1 p_2}}. \end{cases}$$

Note that, at the interior solution, the Walrasian demands of goods 1 and 2 do not depend on income, implying that these goods do not exhibit income effects, since all additional income effect is entirely spent on the numeraire good.

- From the above Walrasian demands, it is easy to obtain the associated indirect utility function

$$v(\mathbf{p}, m) = \begin{cases} m + \frac{1}{8\sqrt{p_1 p_2}} & \text{if } m > \frac{1}{8\sqrt{p_1 p_2}}, \text{ and} \\ \left(\frac{m^2}{4 p_1 p_2}\right)^{1/4} & \text{if } m \leq \frac{1}{8\sqrt{p_1 p_2}}. \end{cases}$$

(b) Invert the indirect utility function $v(\mathbf{p}, m)$ to obtain the expenditure function $e(\mathbf{p}, u)$.

- Note that in order to obtain the expenditure function $e(\mathbf{p}, u)$, we just need to invert the indirect utility function $v(\mathbf{p}, m)$, i.e., solving for m, which yields

$$e(\mathbf{p}, u) = \begin{cases} u - \frac{1}{8\sqrt{p_1 p_2}} & \text{if } u > \frac{1}{4\sqrt{p_1 p_2}}, \text{ and} \\ 2u^2\sqrt{p_1 p_2} & \text{if } u \le \frac{1}{4\sqrt{p_1 p_2}}. \end{cases}$$

(c) Consider that the price vector increases from $\mathbf{p}^0 = (p_1^0, p_2^0) = (1, 1)$ to $\mathbf{p}^1 = (p_1^1, p_2^1) = (2, 1)$, i.e., only the price of good 1 doubles. Let us next use the equivalent variation (EV) to evaluate the welfare loss that the consumer suffers from the increase in the price of good 1. In order to keep track of the possible corner solutions that arise at different income levels, we separately evaluate the EV at different values of m.

1. What is the EV when income satisfies $m > \frac{1}{8}$, i.e., the consumer is relatively rich?

- In this case, the consumer is at the interior solution both *before* and *after* the price change. In particular,

$$u^0 = v(\mathbf{p}^0, m) = m + \frac{1}{8} \quad \text{and} \quad u^1 = v(\mathbf{p}^1, m) = m + \frac{1}{8\sqrt{2}},$$

and the corresponding expenditure functions are

$$e(\mathbf{p}^0, u^0) = u^0 - \frac{1}{8} = m \quad \text{and} \quad e(\mathbf{p}^1, u^1) = u^1 - \frac{1}{8\sqrt{2}} = m$$

and

$$e(\mathbf{p}^0, u^1) = u^1 - \frac{1}{8} = m + \frac{1}{8\sqrt{2}} - \frac{1}{8} \quad \text{and} \quad e(\mathbf{p}^1, u^0) = u^0 - \frac{1}{8\sqrt{2}} = m + \frac{1}{8} - \frac{1}{8\sqrt{2}}.$$

- Therefore, the equivalent variation (EV) is

$$EV = e(\mathbf{p}^0, u^0) - e(\mathbf{p}^0, u^1) = m - \left(m + \frac{1}{8\sqrt{2}} - \frac{1}{8} \right) \simeq 0.036,$$

where note that we define the EV as the negative of the standard definition, since in this case we measure a loss in consumer welfare. Intuitively, the EV measures the additional income that we need to give to this consumer after the price increase, for him to maintain the same utility level he reached before the price increase.

2. What is the EV when income satisfies $\frac{1}{8} > m > \frac{1}{8\sqrt{2}}$, i.e., the consumer is moderately rich?

- *Utility levels.* In this case, the initial equilibrium *before* the price change is at a corner solution, while the equilibrium *after* the price change is interior. In particular,

$$u^0 = v(\mathbf{p}^0, m) = \left(\frac{m^2}{4} \right)^{1/4} \quad \text{and} \quad u^1 = v(\mathbf{p}^1, m) = m + \frac{1}{8\sqrt{2}}.$$

- *Expenditure function* $e(\mathbf{p}^0, u^0)$. The expenditure functions that we need to use in each case depend on whether the utility level we are using (u^0 or u^1) exceed the cutoff $\frac{1}{4\sqrt{p_1 p_2}}$, as we described in the previous part of the exercise when we found the piecewise expenditure function $e(p, u)$. In particular, for utility level $u^0 = \left(\frac{m^2}{4}\right)^{1/4}$, we have that $u^0 \leq \frac{1}{4\sqrt{p_1 p_2}}$ since $\left(\frac{m^2}{4}\right)^{1/4} < \frac{1}{4}$ holds given that $m < \frac{1}{8}$. Hence, for utility level u^0 we need to use expenditure function $2u^2 \sqrt{p_1 p_2}$, as follows

$$e(\mathbf{p}^0, u^0) = 2 \left[\left(\frac{m^2}{4}\right)^{1/4} \right]^2 = 2\sqrt{\frac{m^2}{4}} = m.$$

- *Expenditure function* $e(\mathbf{p}^1, u^1)$. For the case of utility level u^1 we have that $u^1 > \frac{1}{4\sqrt{p_1 p_2}}$ holds given that $m + \frac{1}{8\sqrt{2}} > \frac{1}{4\sqrt{2}}$ is satisfied for all $m > \frac{1}{8\sqrt{2}}$. Since this part of the exercise assumes that m satisfies $\frac{1}{8} > m > \frac{1}{8\sqrt{2}}$, we need to use $u - \frac{1}{8\sqrt{p_1 p_2}}$ as the expenditure function. In particular,

$$e(\mathbf{p}^1, u^1) = \underbrace{\left(m + \frac{1}{8\sqrt{2}}\right)}_{u^1} - \frac{1}{8\sqrt{2}} = m.$$

- *Expenditure function* $e(\mathbf{p}^0, u^1)$. Similarly, in order to find expenditure function $e(\mathbf{p}^0, u^1)$, notice that for utility level u^1 we have that $u^1 > \frac{1}{4\sqrt{p_1 p_2}}$ holds (as discussed above). Hence, we need to use $u - \frac{1}{8\sqrt{p_1 p_2}}$ as the expenditure function. Importantly, note that our testing of whether u^1 exceeds cutoff $\frac{1}{4\sqrt{p_1 p_2}}$ must always be evaluated at the prices at which u^1 is evaluated ($\mathbf{p}^1$ price vector), regardless of the prices at which we afterwards seek to evaluate the expenditure function. In particular, for expenditure function $e(\mathbf{p}^0, u^1)$, which is evaluated at the original price vector $\mathbf{p}^0$, we have

$$e(\mathbf{p}^0, u^1) = u_1 - \frac{1}{8\sqrt{1}} = \underbrace{\left(m + \frac{1}{8\sqrt{2}}\right)}_{u^1} - \frac{1}{8}.$$

- Therefore, the equivalent variation (EV) is

$$EV = e(\mathbf{p}^0, u^0) - e(\mathbf{p}^0, u^1)$$
$$= m - \left(m + \frac{1}{8\sqrt{2}} - \frac{1}{8}\right) = \frac{1}{8} - \frac{1}{8\sqrt{2}} \simeq 0.036.$$

3. What is the EV when income satisfies $\frac{1}{8\sqrt{2}} > m$, i.e., the consumer is poor?

- In this case, the equilibrium is at a corner solution, both *before* and *after* the price change. In particular,

$$u^0 = v(\mathbf{p}^0, m) = \left(\frac{m^2}{4}\right)^{1/4} \quad \text{and} \quad u^1 = v(\mathbf{p}^1, m) = \left(\frac{m^2}{8}\right)^{1/4},$$

and the corresponding expenditure functions are

$$e(\mathbf{p}^0, u^0) = 2\sqrt{\frac{m^2}{4}} = m \quad \text{and} \quad e(\mathbf{p}^1, u^1) = 2\sqrt{2\frac{m^2}{8}} = m$$

and

$$e(\mathbf{p}^0, u^1) = 2\sqrt{\frac{m^2}{8}} = \frac{m}{\sqrt{2}}.$$

- Therefore, the equivalent variation (EV) is

$$EV = e(\mathbf{p}^0, u^0) - e(\mathbf{p}^0, u^1)$$
$$= m - \frac{m}{\sqrt{2}} = \left(1 - \frac{1}{\sqrt{2}}\right) m \simeq 0.29m.$$

Exercise #9 — Using the compensating variation to identify price changes

9. The preferences of a given consumer are represented by $u(x_1, x_2) = \min\{x_1, x_2\}$. We have been informed that only the price of the good 2 has increased, from p_2^0 to p_2^1, but we cannot observe how much this price changed. We know, however, that the amount of income that has to be transferred to the consumer in order for him to recover his initial utility level is

$$\frac{p_2^0 w}{p_1^0 + p_2^0} \quad \text{dollars,}$$

where w is the initial income, and p_1^0 and p_2^0 are the initial prices of goods 1 and 2, respectively. Can you provide some information about the size of the price increase, i.e., the difference between p_2^0 and p_2^1?

- According to the information, $\frac{p_2^0 w}{p_1^0 + p_2^0}$ is the amount of income that, at the new price ratio, has to be transferred to the consumer in order to recover his initial utility level, which is the definition of the compensating variation (CV). Then,

$$CV = \frac{p_2^0 w}{p_1^0 + p_2^0}.$$

Since we can calculate the CV using the indirect utility function as

$$CV = v(\mathbf{p^1}; \mathbf{p^0}, w^0) - v(\mathbf{p^1}; \mathbf{p^1}, w^1),$$

or, using the expenditure function, as follows

$$CV = e(\mathbf{p^1}; u^0) - e(\mathbf{p^0}; u^0).$$

- In addition, you can easily find that for utility function $u(x_1, x_2) = \min\{x_1, x_2\}$, Walrasian demands are[2]

$$x_1(p, w) = x_2(p, w) = \frac{w}{p_1 + p_2}.$$

Hence, the indirect utility function is

$$v(p, w) = \min\left\{\frac{w}{p_1 + p_2}, \frac{w}{p_1 + p_2}\right\} = \frac{w}{p_1 + p_2}.$$

Using the identity $v(p, e(p, u^0)) = u^0$ into the previous indirect utility function we obtain

$$\frac{e(p, u^0)}{p_1 + p_2} = u^0,$$

and solving for $e(p, u^0)$, we find $e(p, u^0) = (p_1 + p_2)u^0$. On the other hand, we also know that

$$e(\mathbf{p}; v(\mathbf{p^0}, w)) = e(\mathbf{p}; u^0) = (p_1 + p_2)\frac{w}{p_1^0 + p_2^0}.$$

We can use this expression to calculate CV, since we know that the price of good 1 did not change, i.e., $p_1^0 = p_1^1$,

$$CV = e(\mathbf{p^1}; u^0) - e(\mathbf{p^0}; u^0) = (p_1^1 + p_2^1)\frac{w}{p_1^0 + p_2^0} - (p_1^0 + p_2^0)\frac{w}{p_1^0 + p_2^0} = \frac{(p_2^1 - p_2^0)w}{p_1^0 + p_2^0}.$$

- We can finally check that this expression coincides with $CV = \frac{p_2^0 w}{p_1^0 + p_2^0}$ given in the introduction of the exercise, if and only if

$$\frac{(p_2^1 - p_2^0)w}{p_1^0 + p_2^0} = \frac{p_2^0 w}{p_1^0 + p_2^0} \Longleftrightarrow p_2^1 - p_2^0 = p_2^0.$$

And rearranging, we obtain $p_2^1 = 2p_2^0$, implying that the price of good 2 has doubled if the consumer needs to receive a compensating variation of $CV = \frac{p_2^0 w}{p_1^0 + p_2^0}$ to keep his utility level unaffected.

---

[2]In particular, this consumer must consume the same amounts of both goods, i.e., $x_1 = x_2$, at the kink of his indifference curves. Plugging condition $x_1 = x_2$ on his budget line, we obtain $p_1 x_1 + p_2 x_1 = w$, or $(p_1 + p_2)x_1 = w$ which, solving for x_1, yields a Walrasian demand of $x_1(p, w) = \frac{w}{p_1 + p_2}$. Applying a similar argument to good 2 yields a Walrasian demand of $x_2(p, w) = \frac{w}{p_1 + p_2}$.

Exercise #11 — Finding the compensating and equivalent variation with little information

11. Consider a consumer who, facing a initial price vector $p^0 \in \mathbb{R}^n_{++}$ for n commodities, purchases a bundle $x \in \mathbb{R}^n_+$ with an income of w dollars. Assume that the price of all goods experience a common increase measured by factor $\theta > 1$.

(a) Compute the compensating variation (CV) of this price increase.

- Using the expenditure function, the CV is

$$CV = e(p^1, u^0) - e(p^0, u^0),$$

where p^1 and p^0 denote the final and initial price vector, respectively, and u^0 represents the utility level that the consumer achieves at the initial price-wealth pair (p^0, w). In this exercise, we are informed that final prices p^1 satisfy $p^1 = \theta p^0$, thus implying that the above expression for CV can be rewritten as

$$CV = e(\theta p^0, u^0) - e(p^0, u^0).$$

Recall that the expenditure function is homogeneous of degree one in prices, i.e., $e(\theta p^0, u^0) = \theta e(p^0, u^0)$. In words, increasing the prices of all goods by a common factor θ increases the consumer's minimal expenditure (the expenditure he needs to reach utility level u^0) by exactly θ. In addition, the consumer spends w dollars, i.e., $e(p^0, u^0) = w$. These properties reduce the expression of the CV to

$$CV = e(\theta p^0, u^0) - e(p^0, u^0)$$
$$= \theta \underbrace{e(p^0, u^0)}_{w} - \underbrace{e(p^0, u^0)}_{w}$$
$$= \theta w - w = w(\theta - 1).$$

For instance, increasing all prices by 50%, i.e., $\theta = 1.5$, yields a compensating variation of $CV = 0.5w$, which implies that the consumer needs to receive half of his initial wealth in order to be able to reach the same utility level as before the price change.

(b) Compute the equivalent variation (EV) of this price increase.

- Using the expenditure function, the EV is

$$EV = e(p^1, u^1) - e(p^0, u^1),$$

where u^1 represents the utility level that the consumer achieves at the final price-wealth pair (p^1, w). In this exercise, we are informed that $p^1 = \theta p^0$, or $p^0 = \frac{1}{\theta} p^1$, implying that the above expression for EV can be rewritten as

$$EV = e(p^1, u^1) - e\left(\frac{1}{\theta} p^1, u^1\right),$$

since the expenditure function is homogeneous of degree one in prices, i.e., $e\left(\frac{1}{\theta}p^1, u^1\right) = \frac{1}{\theta}e\left(p^1, u^1\right)$, and the consumer spends w dollars, $e(p^1, u^1) = w$. These properties reduce the EV to

$$EV = e(p^1, u^1) - e\left(\frac{1}{\theta}p^1, u^1\right)$$

$$= \underbrace{e(p^0, u^0)}_{w} - \frac{1}{\theta}\underbrace{e\left(p^1, u^0\right)}_{w}$$

$$= w - \frac{1}{\theta}w = w\left(1 - \frac{1}{\theta}\right).$$

Following the same numerical example as in section (a), if all prices experience a 50% increase, i.e., $\theta = 1.5$, the equivalent variation would be $EV = \frac{w}{3}$, thus suggesting that, before the price increase, the consumer would need to give up a third of his wealth in order to be as worse off as he will be after the price increase.

Exercise #13 — Consumer and producer theory within the household

13. Consider a household consisting of a husband (H) and wife (W). Each is endowed with one unit of time which has three possible uses: market production (m), home production (h), and leisure (l). Labor devoted to market production by agent $i = \{H, W\}$, L^{im}, is paid at the wage w^i per hour, where the wife receives a lower per-hour wage, $w^W < w^H$. The market price of m is normalized to 1, and we assume that all of the couple's earnings are devoted to purchasing the market good m. The household good (e.g., cook prepared at home, doing laundry, etc.) is produced according to the production technology

$$h = \sqrt{L^{Hh}} + \sqrt{L^{Wh}},$$

where L^{ih} denotes the amount of time individual i dedicates to home production. Husband and wife consume the entire amount of the market good, m, purchased by the household and the entire amount of home production, h, produced in the household. However, they consume only their own leisure time, l^i. Agent i's utility is given by

$$u^i(m, h, l^i),$$

which is increasing, strictly concave and twice continuously differentiable. Answer the following questions:

(a) Assuming the couple seeks to maximize their joint welfare, i.e., their objective function is $u^H(m, h, l^H) + u^W(m, h, l^W)$, write down the couple's constrained maximization problem. [*Hint:* You should identify eight choice variables.]

- The couple solves the following joint utility maximization problem, whereby they select: the amount of market good to purchase, m, house production to produce, h, leisure for each member in the household, l^H and l^W, labor in the market for each member, L^{Hm} and L^{Wm}, and labor in home production for each member, L^{Wm} and L^{Wm}.

$$\max_{m,h,l^H,L^{Hm},L^{Hh},l^W,L^{Wm},L^{Wh}} u^H(m,h,l^H) + u^W(m,h,l^H)$$

subject to the following four constraints: (1) the labor constraint for the husband (i.e., the amount of time he dedicates to leisure, market production and home production cannot exceed 1),

$$l^H + L^{Hm} + L^{Hh} = 1,$$

(2) the labor constraint for the wife,

$$l^W + L^{Wm} + L^{Wh} = 1,$$

(3) the amount of total purchases of the market good, m, cannot exceed the total wages received by husband and wife,

$$w^H L^{Hm} + w^W L^{Wm} = m,$$

and (4) home production behaves according to the technology described above

$$h = \sqrt{L^{Hh}} + \sqrt{L^{Wh}}.$$

(b) Using the binding constraints in the above maximization problem, simplify it in order to write down an unconstrained maximization problem (with only four choice variables, two for the husband and two for the wife). Then identify the first-order conditions that characterize an interior optimum. Interpret.

- Substituting for m, h, l^H and l^W, we obtain

$$\max_{L^{Hm},L^{Hh},L^{Wm},L^{Wh}} u^H(w^H L^{Hm} + w^W L^{Wm}, \sqrt{L^{Hh}} + \sqrt{L^{Wh}}, 1 - L^{Hm} - L^{Hh})$$
$$+ u^W(w^H L^{Hm} + w^W L^{Wm}, \sqrt{L^{Hh}} + \sqrt{L^{Wh}}, 1 - L^{Wm} - L^{Wh}),$$

which reduces our original constrained maximization problem to an unconstrained maximization problem. Taking first-order conditions with respect to the two choice variables of each agent i, L^{im} and L^{ih}, i.e., agent i's labor on market and home production, yields

$$w^i u_m^H - u_l^i + w^i u_m^W = 0, \text{ and}$$
$$\frac{u_h^H}{2\sqrt{L^{ih}}} - u_l^i + \frac{u_h^W}{2\sqrt{L^{ih}}} = 0.$$

- *First FOC:* Intuitively, the first equation reflects that an increase in, for instance, the husband's working hours in market production provides a salary, which can be used in buying market goods to the household, increasing the husband's and wife's utility (first and third component of the equation, respectively), but reduce the husband's utility since he can enjoy fewer leisure hours, as indicated in the second component, which enters negatively.

- *Second FOC:* A similar intuition applies to an additional hour of home production, which increases the amount of home goods the couple can enjoy (after the husband's extra hour is transformed through the home production technology into, for instance, a nice dinner prepared at home), as indicated in the first and third element of the second equation, but he can devote fewer hours to leisure (second component).

(c) Use the above first-order conditions to argue that, if the agents have identical preferences, i.e., their utility functions satisfy $u^H(\cdot) = u^W(\cdot)$, it is optimal for the husband to supply more market labor than the wife, and for wife to devote more time to home production than the husband.

- From the FOCs for L^{im} (first equation in the previous part of the exercise), we can rearrange the FOC of the husband to obtain $u_l^H = w^H(u_m^H + u_m^W)$. Since the husband's wage is higher, $w^H > w^W$, we then find that

$$u_l^H = w^H(u_m^H + u_m^W) > w^W(u_m^W + u_m^H) = u_l^W.$$

The marginal utilities from market labor are represented in figure 3.4. In particular, note that the marginal utility of both agents is positive but decreasing (by concavity). Hence, each additional hour of market production is more beneficial to the household if it originates from the husband than from the wife, since the utility function is concave $L^{Hm} > L^{Wm}$.

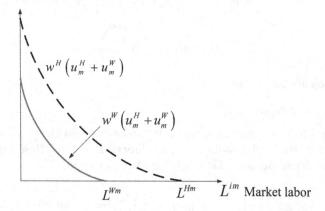

Figure 3.4 Marginal utility of market labor.

- In addition, since the utility function of both agents coincide, $u^H(\cdot) = u^W(\cdot)$, then $u_l^H > u_l^W$ can only occur because the husband enjoys less leisure than the wife (by concavity).
- Using the above results and the FOC for L^{ih} (second equation in the previous part of the exercise), we obtain

$$u_l^H = \frac{u_h^H}{2\sqrt{L^{Hh}}} + \frac{u_h^W}{2\sqrt{L^{Hh}}} > \frac{u_h^H}{2\sqrt{L^{Wh}}} + \frac{u_h^W}{2\sqrt{L^{Wh}}} = u_l^W,$$

ultimately implying that the wife dedicates more hours to house production than the husband, i.e., $L^{Wh} > L^{Hh}$.

(d) For the general case in which the agents' preferences might differ, $u^H(\cdot) \neq u^W(\cdot)$, could there be an interior optimum in which agents devote equal amounts of time to home production, $L^{Wh} = L^{Hh}$, even though $w^W < w^H$? [*Hint:* Do not overthink it.]

- No. Reversing the findings in part (c), if $L^{Wh} = L^{Hh}$, then it must be that $u_l^H = u_l^W$. From the FOCs for L^{im}, this requires that the salaries of husband and wife coincide, $w^H = w^W$.

Exercise #15 — Aggregation: properties of the social welfare function

15. Consider the following social welfare function:

$$W(u_1(x_1), u_2(x_2), ..., u_I(x_x)),$$

which is increasing in every individual's utility level, i.e., $\frac{\partial W}{\partial u_i} \geq 0$ for all $i = 1, 2, ..., I$. Verify that the social indirect utility function, $v(p, w)$, which is the optimal value of the social welfare maximization problem

$$\max_{w_1, ..., w_I} W(u_1(x_1), u_2(x_2), ..., u_I(x_I))$$

$$\text{subject to } p \cdot \left(\sum_i x_i\right) \leq w,$$

satisfies the following properties:

(a) Homogeneous of degree zero.

- We need to show that an increase in prices and wealth by a common factor λ does not affect the social indirect utility function, $v(p, w)$ that arises from the above maximization problem. That is, $v(\lambda p, \lambda w) = v(p, w)$. Hence,

$$\lambda p \left(\sum_i x_i(\lambda p, \lambda w)\right) \leq \lambda w \qquad \text{for all } \lambda > 0.$$

And since the Walrasian demand $x_i(p, w)$ is homogeneous of degree zero, we have that,

$$x_i(\lambda p, \lambda w) = x_i(p, w).$$

Using this property into the above expression,

$$\lambda p \cdot \left(\sum_i x_i(\lambda p, \lambda w) \leq \lambda w \right), \tag{1}$$

which, by homogeneity of degree zero of every individual Walrasian demand, simplifies to

$$\lambda p \cdot \left(\sum_i x_i(p, w) \right) \leq \lambda w.$$

Then dividing both sides of the inequality by λ yields

$$p \cdot \left(\sum_i x_i(p, w) \right) \leq w.$$

Therefore, the constraint in the social welfare maximization problem coincides with the constraint where both prices and wealth have increased by λ (inequality (1)). Since, in addition, the objective function is unaffected, the maximization problem leads to the same optimal value. Hence, $v(p, w) = v(\lambda p, \lambda w)$, and, as a consequence, the indirect utility function satisfies homogeneity of degree zero.

(b) Increasing in wealth, w.

- Let us take a wealth level w' such that $w' \geq w$, and denote by $(w_1, w_2, ..., w_I)$ the distribution of wealth w among the I individuals in this economy, which solves the social welfare maximization problem given the price-wealth pair (p, w).

- In addition, let $v(p, w) = W(v_1(p, w_1), v_2(p, w_2), ..., v_I(p, w_I))$ represent the social indirect utility function that arises from this welfare-maximizing distribution of wealth.[3] Furthermore, we also have that

$$\sum_i w_i \leq w \Longrightarrow \sum_i w_i \leq w'.$$

---

[3]Intuitively, note that every individual i receives a wealth w_i from the social planner, then independently solves his own utility maximization problem yielding an individual indirect utility function of $v_i(p, w)$. Finally, all these individuals' indirect utility functions are plugged into the social welfare function to evaluate the social welfare at the welfare-maximizing wealth distribution.

Hence, by the definition of $v(p, w)$ and $v(p, w')$,

$$v\left(p, w\right) = W\left(v_i\left(p, w_1\right),\; v_2\left(p, w_2\right), ..., v_I\left(p, w_I\right)\right) \leq v\left(p, w'\right).$$

Intuitively, the social planner cannot induce a lower aggregate welfare level when he distributes a total wealth $w' > w$ among all I individuals than when he only distributes a (lower) wealth level w. Even if individuals were satiated at w, they could simply choose to not spend the additional wealth they receive when w' is distributed among them.

c) Nonincreasing in prices, p.

- Let us take a price vector p' such that $p' \geq p$. Like in the previous part of the exercise, let $(v_1, v_2, ..., v_I)$ be the solution to the maximization problem given a price-wealth pair (p', w). Hence, the social indirect utility function is

$$v\left(p', w\right) = W\left(v_1\left(p'_1, w_1\right), v_2\left(p'_1, w_2\right), ..., v_I\left(p'_1, w_I\right)\right).$$

As price vector p' satisfies $p' \geq p$, we have that the individual indirect utility function of any consumer i yields a lower utility level when the prices the consumer faces are higher, p', than otherwise. That is,

$$v_i\left(p', w_i\right) \leq v_i\left(p, w_i\right) \quad \text{for all individual } i.$$

Since $W\left(\cdot\right)$ is increasing in the utility levels of every individual,

$$v_i\left(p', w_i\right) \leq v_i\left(p, w_i\right) \Longleftrightarrow W\left(v_i\left(p', w_i\right), ..., v_I\left(p', w_I\right)\right) \leq W\left(v_I\left(p, w_I\right), ..., v_I\left(p, w_I\right)\right).$$

Then, by the definition of $v\left(p, w\right)$, we obtain

$$v(p', w) \leqslant v(p, w) \text{ for all } p' > p.$$

Hence, the social indirect utility function $v(p, w)$ is nonincreasing in p.

d) Quasi-convex. [*Hint*: Use the definition of quasi-convexity for the individual's indirect utility function.]

- We know that a function is quasi-convex when its lower contour set is convex. (Alternatively, a function is quasi-convex if its upper contour set is concave.) Then we need to show that the set of price-wealth pairs

$$I = \{(p, w) : v\left(p, w\right) \leq v \; \text{ for all } v \in \mathbb{R}_+\} \quad \text{is convex.}$$

Intuitively, this is the set of price-wealth pair in which, if we allowed the social planner to solve his social welfare maximization problem by optimally distributing wealth among the I individuals, the aggregate social welfare arising from such optimal wealth distribution would be lower than a given level v. That is, this set embodies high(low) price vectors (wealth, respectively). Therefore, the convexity of this set implies that the social welfare emerging from a combination of prices and a combination of wealth levels, both of them independently yielding welfare levels below v, would also be below v. More formally, for this set to be convex we need that, for any two price-wealth pairs (p, w) and (p', w') that belong to the lower contour set, i.e., $(p, w) \in I$ and $(p', w') \in I$, their convex combination satisfies

$$\lambda \cdot v(p, w) + (1 - \lambda) \cdot v(p', w') \leq v \text{ for all } \lambda \in [0, 1], \text{ all } v \in \mathbb{R}_+$$

and for all $p \gg 0$ and $w > 0$.

- *Proof.* Using the definition of the lower contour set of $v(p, w)$, we have that

$$v(p, w) \leq v \Longleftrightarrow \lambda v(p, w) \leq \lambda v, \text{ and}$$

$$v(p', w') \leq v \Longleftrightarrow (1 - \lambda) v(p', w') \leq (1 - \lambda) v.$$

Adding up these two inequalities, we obtain

$$\lambda v(p, w) + (1 - \lambda) v(p', w') \leq \lambda v + (1 - \lambda) v,$$

which simplifies into

$$\lambda v(p, w) + (1 - \lambda) v(p', w') \leq v,$$

which implies that the lower contour set of $v(p, w)$ is convex.

Exercise #17 — Gorman form for $v_i(p, w_i)$

17. Some indirect utility functions $v_i(p, w_i)$, such as those originating from a quasi-linear preference relation, can be represented as a convex combination of individual i's wealth, w_i, as follows:

$$v_i(p, w_i) = a_i(p) + b(p)w_i,$$

which are often referred as the Gorman form indirect utility function.

(a) Show that if the indirect utility function can be expressed using the Gorman form, then all consumers exhibit parallel, straight wealth expansion paths at any price vector p. [*Hint:* Use Roy's identity.]

- To know the form of the wealth expansion paths, we need to know how the Walrasian demand $x_i(p, w)$ responds to changes in wealth levels. Since we have the consumer's indirect utility function $v_i(p, w_i)$, we can use Roy's identity in order to find his Walrasian demand $x_i(p, w)$:

$$x_i(p, w) = -\frac{\frac{\partial v_i(p, w_i)}{\partial p}}{\frac{\partial v_i(p, w_i)}{\partial w}} = -\frac{a_i'(p) + b'(p)w_i}{b(p)}.$$

We can next evaluate how the consumer's Walrasian demand $x_i(p, w)$ responds to changes in wealth, as follows:

$$\frac{\partial x_i(p, w)}{\partial w} = -\frac{b'(p)b(p) - 0}{[b(p)]^2} = -\frac{b'(p)}{b(p)}.$$

Hence, the slope of wealth expansion paths is given by $-\frac{b'(p)}{b(p)}$. In order to determine if wealth expansion paths are straight, we just have to check that their curvature does not change in w. Observing the above expression, we clearly see that wealth expansion paths have a slope which is constant in w. Additionally, note that the slope of the wealth expansion paths coincide across customers (no subscripts in the slope). Hence, the only difference in wealth expansion paths across consumers must be in the origin of this line, given by $-\frac{a_i'(p)}{b(p)}$, which varies across consumers.

(b) Show also that, if the indirect utility function can be represented using the Gorman form, $v_i(p, w_i) = a_i(p) + b(p)w_i$, with the same $b(p)$ for all individuals, then the associated expenditure function, $e_i(p, u_i)$, can be expressed as

$$e_i(p, u_i) = c(p)u_i + d_i(p).$$

- By the duality theorem, we have that the minimal expenditure needed to reach the utility level resulting from solving the UMP, $v_i(p, w_i)$, is

$$e_i\left(p, v_i(p, w_i)\right) = w_i.$$

Solving for w_i in the Gorman form indirect utility function $v_i(p, w_i) = a_i(p) + b(p)w_i$, we obtain

$$w_i = \frac{v_i(p, w_i) - a_i(p)}{b(p)}.$$

Hence,

$$e_i\left(p, v_i(p, w_i)\right) = \frac{v_i(p, w_i) - a_i(p)}{b(p)},$$

and rearranging terms,

$$e_i\left(p, v_i(p, w_i)\right) = \frac{1}{b(p)}v_i(p, w_i) - \frac{a_i(p)}{b(p)},$$

or more compactly,

$$e_i\left(p, v_i(p, w_i)\right) = c(p) \cdot v_i(p, w_i) - d_i(p),$$

where we defined $c(p) \equiv \frac{1}{b(p)}$, which is constant for all i, and $d_i(p) \equiv \frac{a_i(p)}{b(p)}$, which is type-dependent. Therefore, we obtained that, if preferences admit Gorman-form indirect utility function with the same $b(p)$ for all individuals, then preferences admit expenditure functions of the form $e_i(p, v_i(p, w_i)) = c(p) \cdot v_i(p, w_i) - d_i(p)$.

Exercise #19 — Aggregate demand

19. Consider a society where every individual i has the following (discontinuous) Walrasian demand function:

$$x_i(p) = \begin{cases} \frac{w}{4p} & \text{if } p > k, \\ \frac{w}{2p} & \text{if } p < k, \text{ and} \\ \frac{w}{4p} \text{ or } \frac{w}{2p} & \text{if } p = k, \end{cases}$$

where k is a positive constant, while $w > 0$ denotes income.

(a) Assume that there are only two individuals in this society, 1 and 2. If they both have the same income $w > 0$, find their average demand, i.e., $\frac{x_1 + x_2}{2}$. Then show that the average demand $\frac{x_1 + x_2}{2}$ takes three possible values at $p = k$.

- There are three situations we need to consider:

    1. If the demand of both consumers 1 and 2 is $x_i(p) = \frac{w}{4p}$, which can be expressed as $\frac{w}{4k}$ since $p = k$, then average demand is

    $$\frac{x_1 + x_2}{2} = \frac{\frac{w}{4k} + \frac{w}{4k}}{2} = \frac{w}{4k}.$$

    2. If both consumer 1's and 2's demand is $x_i(p) = \frac{w}{2p}$, which can be expressed as $\frac{w}{2k}$ since $p = k$, average demand becomes

    $$\frac{x_1 + x_2}{2} = \frac{\frac{w}{2k} + \frac{w}{2k}}{2} = \frac{w}{2k}.$$

    3. Finally, if one of the consumers demands $x_i(p) = \frac{w}{4p}$ while the other demands $x_j(p) = \frac{w}{2p}$ where $j \neq i$, average demand in this case is

    $$\frac{x_i + x_j}{2} = \frac{\frac{w}{4k} + \frac{w}{2k}}{2} = \frac{3w}{8k}.$$

(b) Now consider a society with an infinite number of individuals, all with the above Walrasian demand $x_i(p)$ and the same income $w > 0$. Show that now the average demand at $p = k$ now takes all the values between $\frac{w}{4p}$ and $\frac{w}{2p}$.

- If the number of individuals is now generically N, we can still reproduce the analysis in part (b) by noticing that, at $p = k$, N_1 indviduals demand $x_i(p) = \frac{w}{4p} = \frac{w}{4k}$ while the remaining N_2 individuals demand $x_i(p) = \frac{w}{2p} = \frac{w}{2k}$, where $N_1 + N_2 = N$. As a consequence, average demand becomes

$$\frac{N_1 \frac{w}{4k} + (N - N_1) \frac{w}{2k}}{N},$$

which simplifies to

$$\frac{w}{2k}\left(1 - \frac{N_1}{2N}\right).$$

Hence, average demand must belong to the set $\frac{w}{2k}\left(1 - \frac{N_1}{2N}\right)$ for all $N_1 = 1, 2, ..., N$. When $N \to \infty$, this set becomes dense in the segment $\left[\frac{w}{4k}, \frac{w}{2k}\right]$. As a consequence, aggregate demand "fills" the discontinuity segment of every individual i's Walrasian demand.

Chapter 4 — Production Theory

Summary The chapter starts with a few introductory exercises testing properties on standard production functions, such as nonincreasing returns to scale, Shephard's lemma, increasing average and marginal product, etc. Afterward, we examine the profit function that results from the firm's profit-maximization problem, testing for properties such as convexity in prices, and Hotelling's lemma, while we then study how to find the output and the cost function associated to a given profit function. We then apply the duality theorem to production theory. Finally, the chapter considers two applied exercises that make use of the properties and results learned in previous exercises: one about a firm that can use two types of technologies in its production process, and another in which N firms merge and experience an increase or decrease in their costs upon merging.

Exercise #1 — Properties of a standard production function

1. Consider a Cobb–Douglas production function $f : \mathbb{R}_+^2 \longrightarrow \mathbb{R}_+$, given by $f(z) = 2^{3/4} z_1^{1/4} z_2^{1/4}$, where $z_1 \geqslant 0$ and $z_2 \geqslant 0$ denote inputs in the production process.

   (a) Check if the production function has nonincreasing, nondecreasing, or constant returns to scale.

   - *Nonincreasing returns to scale.* If the production function satisfies nonincreasing returns to scale, for all inputs $z \in \mathbb{R}_+^2$ and for all $\alpha > 1$, we must have $\alpha f(z) \geq f(\alpha z)$. Intuitively, increasing all inputs by a common factor α, yields a less-than-proportional increase in output, $f(\alpha z)$, i.e., $\alpha f(z) \geq f(\alpha z)$. In this exercise, this condition implies

   $$\alpha \left(2^{3/4} z_1^{1/4} z_2^{1/4} \right) \geq 2^{3/4} (\alpha z_1)^{1/4} (\alpha z_2)^{1/4}.$$

   Simplifying the right-hand side, we obtain

   $$\alpha \left(2^{3/4} z_1^{1/4} z_2^{1/4} \right) \geq \alpha^{1/2} \left(2^{3/4} z_1^{1/4} z_2^{1/4} \right) \Leftrightarrow \alpha \geq \alpha^{\frac{1}{2}},$$

   which is satisfied for all $\alpha > 1$. Hence, this production function satisfies nonincreasing returns to scale.

   - *Nondecreasing returns to scale.* (Since this production function exhibits nonincreasing returns to scale, and such property holds strictly, we can actually anticipate that it will not satisfy nondecreasing returns to scale. However, and as a practice, we go over these properties nevertheless.) If the production function satisfies nondecreasing returns to scale, for all inputs $z \in \mathbb{R}_+^2$ and for all $\alpha > 1$, we must have $\alpha f(z) \leq f(\alpha z)$. In this case, a common increase in all inputs by a common factor α, yields a more-than-proportional increase in output, $f(\alpha z)$, i.e., $\alpha f(z) \leq f(\alpha z)$. In this exercise, this condition implies

   $$\alpha \left(2^{3/4} z_1^{1/4} z_2^{1/4} \right) \leq \alpha^{1/2} \left(2^{3/4} z_1^{1/4} z_2^{1/4} \right) \Leftrightarrow \alpha \leq \alpha^{\frac{1}{2}},$$

and this inequality cannot hold for any $\alpha > 1$. Then, this production function cannot exhibit nondecreasing returns to scale.

- *Constant returns to scale.* If the production function satisfies constant returns to scale, it must satisfy nonincreasing and nondecreasing returns to scale. Since this production function does not satisfy both, it cannot exhibit constant returns to scale. In particular, when a production function exhibits constant returns to scale, a common increase of all inputs by a common factor $\alpha > 1$, yields a proportional increase in output, $f(\alpha z)$, i.e., $\alpha f(z) = f(\alpha z)$.

- *Remark*: This production function is a standard Cobb–Douglas production function $f(z) = Az_1^{\alpha} z_2^{\beta}$. It is good to remember that when $\alpha + \beta \le 1$ the production function has nonincreasing returns to scale, when $\alpha + \beta \ge 1$ it has nondecreasing returns to scale, and when $\alpha + \beta = 1$ it exhibits constant returns to scale.

(b) Let $w \in \mathbb{R}^2_{++}$ denote the vector of input prices and $p > 0$ the output price. Determine for each output level $q \geqslant 0$ the cost function $c(w, q)$ and the conditional factor demand $z(w, q)$.

- We first need to find the conditional factor demand (solving the cost minimization problem, CMP, of the firm), and afterwards we can compute the firm's cost function, as the value function emerging from the CMP.

$$\text{CMP} : \min_{z \geq 0} \; w \cdot z$$

$$\text{subject to} \quad 2^{3/4} z_1^{1/4} z_2^{1/4} \geq q,$$
$$z \geq 0.$$

First, note that $z = 0$ can be ruled out. Indeed, from the production function we know that output would be zero when either of the inputs are zero, i.e., $z_1 = 0$ or $z_2 = 0$. Secondly, the production function constraint $2^{3/4} z_1^{1/4} z_2^{1/4} \geq q$ must be binding since the production function is strictly increasing in both inputs and inputs are costly (they are not free since the vector of input prices $w \in \mathbb{R}^2_{++}$ is strictly positive in all components).[1] Thus, we can solve for z_1 in this constraint, finding

$$2^{3/4} z_1^{1/4} z_2^{1/4} = q \iff z_1 = \frac{1}{8} \frac{q^4}{z_2}.$$

We can now substitute this result into the previous cost minimization problem, thus reducing the number of choice variables to only one, z_2, as follows

$$\min_{z_2} w_1 \cdot z_1 + w_2 \cdot z_2 = w_1 \cdot \left(\frac{1}{8} \frac{q^4}{z_2} \right) + w_2 \cdot z_2.$$

---

[1] Alternatively, one can set up the Lagrangian of the firm's profit maximization problem (PMP) using λ as the Lagrange multiplier of constraint $2^{3/4} z_1^{1/4} z_2^{1/4} \geq q$, then take first-order conditions with respect to inputs z_1 and z_2, and obtain that $\lambda > 0$, which implies that the above constraint holds with equality.

The first-order condition with respect to z_2 is

$$-w_1 \left(\frac{1}{8} \frac{q^4}{z_2^2} \right) + w_2 = 0,$$

and solving for z_2, yields

$$z_2 = \frac{1}{2} q^2 \sqrt{\frac{w_1}{2w_2}}.$$

Substituting z_2 into the expression for z_1 we found above, we obtain

$$z_1 = \frac{1}{8} \frac{q^4}{z_2} \implies z_1 = \frac{1}{8} \frac{q^4}{\left(\frac{1}{2} q^2 \sqrt{\frac{w_1}{2w_2}} \right)} = \frac{1}{2} q^2 \sqrt{\frac{w_2}{2w_1}}.$$

Therefore, the conditional factor demand is

$$z(w,q) = \left(\frac{1}{2} q^2 \sqrt{\frac{w_2}{2w_1}}, \frac{1}{2} q^2 \sqrt{\frac{w_1}{2w_2}} \right).$$

As a consequence, the cost function (i.e., the minimal cost that the firm must incur in order to attain output level of q) is

$$c(w,q) = w_1 \cdot z_1(w,q) + w_2 \cdot z_2(w,q)$$
$$= w_1 \frac{1}{2} q^2 \sqrt{\frac{w_2}{2w_1}} + w_2 \frac{1}{2} q^2 \sqrt{\frac{w_1}{2w_2}}$$
$$= \frac{1}{2} q^2 \sqrt{2 w_1 w_2},$$

which can be interpreted as the value function of the CMP, since we evaluated the objective function at the arguments that solved the CMP.

(c) Verify Shephard's lemma.

- Let us first recall Shephard's lemma: If the production set is *closed* and satisfies the *free-disposal* property, and the conditional factor demand $z(\overline{w}, q)$ consists of a single point $\overline{z}$, then the cost function $c(w,q)$ is differentiable with respect to w at $\overline{w}$, and this derivative is

$$\frac{\partial c(\overline{w}, q)}{\partial w_l} = \overline{z}_l.$$

Hence, in order to verify Shephard's lemma, we must first check that the production set Y is closed, and that it satisfies the free disposal property.

- *Closedness.* The production set associated with the production function is given by

$$Y = \left\{ (-z, q) \in \mathbb{R}^3 : q \le f(z) \text{ and } z \in \mathbb{R}_+^2 \right\},$$

and for convenience, we can rewrite this set as

$$Y = \left\{y \in \mathbb{R}^3 : y_1 \le 0\right\} \cap \left\{y \in \mathbb{R}^3 : y_2 \le 0\right\} \cap \left\{y \in \mathbb{R}^3 : y_3 \le f(-y_1, -y_2)\right\},$$

which is the intersection of three closed sets (the first two representing inputs, and the third representing output), and as a consequence it is closed. [Recall that the intersection of finitely many closed sets is also closed.]

- *Free-disposal.* Consider two input-output pairs that belong to production set Y, $(-z, q) \in Y$ and $(-z', q')$, where $(-z', q') \le (-z, q)$, as depicted in the figure below. This means that the second pair either uses more inputs as the first pair (producing the same output) or uses the same amount of inputs (but produces a smaller output). That is, either (1) $z_1' \ge z_1$, or $z_2' \ge z_2$, but producing the same output $q' = q$, or (2) $z_1' = z_1$ and $z_2' = z_2$, but producing less output $q' \le q$. In order to show that the free-disposal property is satisfied, we must show that $(-z', q')$ also belongs to the production set Y. Since the production function $f(\cdot)$ is weakly increasing in both inputs z_1 and z_2, we find that

$$q' \le q \le f(z) \le f(z'),$$

as illustrated in figure 4.1. That is, $(-z', q')$ also belongs to the production set Y.

- Hence, the production set Y is closed and satisfies free-disposal, implying that all conditions for Shephard's lemma hold.[2] We can thus determine the conditional factor demand function for input 1, $z_1(w, q)$, by differentiating the cost function, $c(w, q)$, with respect to the price of input 1, as follows:

$$\frac{\partial c(w, q)}{\partial w_1} = \frac{\partial \left(\frac{1}{2} q^2 \sqrt{2 w_1 w_2}\right)}{\partial w_1} = \frac{1}{2} q^2 \sqrt{\frac{w_2}{2 w_1}},$$

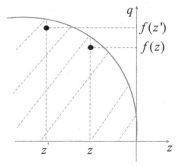

Figure 4.1 Production function $f(z)$ satisfies free disposal.

---

[2]Note that there is an additional condition, which states that conditional factor demand correspondences consist of a single point (they are functions); and this was clearly satisfied in our exercise. For a given input price vector $w = (w_1, w_2)$ and output q, the function $z(w, q)$ yields a real number for the input usage of z_1 and another for z_2.

and similarly for the conditional factor demand of input 2, $z_2(w, q)$,

$$\frac{\partial c(w, q)}{\partial w_2} = \frac{\partial \left(\frac{1}{2} q^2 \sqrt{2 w_1 w_2}\right)}{\partial w_2} = \frac{1}{2} q^2 \sqrt{\frac{w_1}{2 w_2}}.$$

(d) Determine the profit function $\pi(p, w)$.

- To determine the profit function, we can solve the profit maximization problem, using the cost function

$$\max_{q \geq 0} \; pq - \frac{1}{2} q^2 \sqrt{2 w_1 w_2}.$$

Taking first-order conditions with respect to q yields

$$p - q^* \sqrt{2 w_1 w_2} \leq 0,$$

which holds with equality in interior solutions, $q^* > 0$. In the case of interior solutions, we can solve for q^* to obtain the following profit-maximizing output:

$$q^* = \frac{p}{\sqrt{2 w_1 w_2}}.$$

And the profit arising from producing this output level is

$$\begin{aligned} \pi(p, w) &= p q^* - \frac{1}{2} (q^*)^2 \sqrt{2 w_1 w_2} \\ &= \frac{p^2}{2 \sqrt{2 w_1 w_2}}. \end{aligned}$$

Again we can see that since $p > 0$ and $w > 0$, the profit from producing q^* is positive for all parameter values. It is therefore never optimal to remain inactive, i.e., set $q^* = 0$ (which gives zero profits).

- *Sufficiency.* Let us now check second-order conditions. The above PMP is striclty concave, and thus the output level q^* that we found is profit maximizing, if the cost function is convex in q, which holds in this case since

$$\frac{\partial c(w, q)}{\partial q} = q \sqrt{2 w_1 w_2} \quad \text{and} \quad \frac{\partial^2 c(w, q)}{\partial q^2} = \sqrt{2 w_1 w_2} > 0$$

for all $w_1, w_2 > 0$.

Exercise #3 — Increasing average product

3. Show that, if a production function $f : \mathbb{R}^{L-1} \to \mathbb{R}$ satisfies increasing returns to scale, that is,

$$\text{for every } z \in \mathbb{R}^{L-1} \text{ and for every } t \geq 1, \; f(tz) \geq t \, f(z),$$

then $f(z)$ also satisfies *increasing average product* property.

- Let the common increase in all inputs, t, be $t = \frac{z'}{z}$, where $z' \geq z$. We therefore have $t \geq 1$ and, plugging $t = \frac{z'}{z}$ into the definition of increasing returns to scale, we obtain

$$f\left(\frac{z'}{z}z\right) \geq \frac{z'}{z} f(z).$$

Then multiplying both sides now by $\frac{1}{z'}$ yields

$$\frac{1}{z'}f\left(\frac{z'}{z}z\right) \geq \frac{1}{z'}\frac{z'}{z} f(z),$$

which simplifies to

$$\frac{f(z')}{z'} \geq \frac{f(z)}{z},$$

which exactly represents increasing *average* product. Hence, increasing returns to scale imply increasing average product.

Exercise #5 — Average and marginal product—II

5. Consider a firm with a production function $q = f(z_1, z_2)$ that satisfies constant returns to scale, i.e., $f(z_1, z_2) = f(\lambda z_1, \lambda z_2)$ for any $\lambda > 0$. What is the relationship between the average product of input z_1, $\frac{f(z_1, z_2)}{z_1}$, and the marginal product of the input z_2?

- First, note that constant returns to scale, i.e., $f(z_1, z_2) = f(\lambda z_1, \lambda z_2)$ entails homogeneity of degree zero. Second, recall that when applying Euler's theorem to functions that are homogeneous of degree zero, we obtain

$$f(z_1, z_2) = \frac{\partial f(z_1, z_2)}{\partial z_1} z_1 + \frac{\partial f(z_1, z_2)}{\partial z_2} z_2.$$

Dividing both sides by z_1 yields

$$\underbrace{\frac{f(z_1, z_2)}{z_1}}_{AP_1} = \underbrace{\frac{\partial f(z_1, z_2)}{\partial z_1}}_{MP_1} + \underbrace{\frac{\partial f(z_1, z_2)}{\partial z_2} \frac{z_2}{z_1}}_{MP_2},$$

that is, $AP_1 = MP_1 + MP_2\frac{z_2}{z_1}$. Solving for MP_2, we find

$$MP_2 = \frac{AP_1 - MP_1}{\frac{z_2}{z_1}}.$$

- Hence, assuming that $z_1, z_2 > 0$, if $AP_1 > MP_1$ the marginal product MP_2 is positive, but if $AP_1 < MP_1$, the marginal product MP_2 becomes negative. Since the average product of an input can be graphically interpreted as the slope of a ray connecting the output function with the origin, the first (second) case arises in production functions that are concave (convex) with respect to input 1.

Exercise #7 — Law of supply

7. Consider a firm with production set Y and a price vector $p \in \mathbb{R}^L_{++}$. Suppose the price of one commodity $l \in \{1, 2, ..., L\}$ is increased by an amount $\varepsilon > 0$. Let $y^0 \in Y$ be a profit-maximizing plan at the old prices and $y^1 \in Y$ at the new prices. (Recall that production plans, such as y^0, contain information about the inputs being used in the production process, z, as well as the output generated, q.) Prove that $y^1_l \geqslant y^0_l$, i.e., the net supply of commodity l weakly increases as its price increases.

- First note that since y^0 is profit maximizing at the old prices p^0, then it must satisfy

$$p^0 \cdot y^0 \geq p^0 \cdot y^1,$$

and since y^1 is profit maximizing at the new prices p^1, then

$$p^1 \cdot y^1 \geq p^1 \cdot y^0.$$

Adding these inequalities, we obtain

$$p^0 \cdot y^0 + p^1 \cdot y^1 \geq p^0 \cdot y^1 + p^1 \cdot y^0.$$

Rearranging yields

$$\left(p^1 - p^0\right) \cdot y^1 \geq \left(p^1 - p^0\right) \cdot y^0,$$

or

$$\left(p^1 - p^0\right) \cdot \left(y^1 - y^0\right) \geq 0,$$

which is the standard expression of the "law of supply:" firms' net supply increases as output prices increase or, alternatively, output prices and supply move in the same direction.

- Note that only the price of *one* commodity (good l) is increased $\left(p^1_l - p^0_l\right) > 0$, while the price of all other commodities remains constant, i.e. $\left(p^1_k - p^0_k\right) = 0$ for all other goods $k \neq l$. Moreover, we know that the price change for good l is $\left(p^1_l - p^0_l\right) = \varepsilon$. Then the previous expression from the law of supply can be reduced to

$$\left(p^1_l - p^0_l\right) \cdot \left(y^1_l - y^0_l\right) = \varepsilon \cdot \left(y^1_l - y^0_l\right) \geq 0,$$

and since $\varepsilon > 0$, then $y^1_l \geq y^0_l$, i.e., the net supply of commodity l weakly increases as its price increases.

Exercise #9 — Shephard's lemma

9. State and prove Shephard's lemma. [*Hint:* Use the Duality Theorem].

- *Shephard's lemma.* Let us assume that the production set Y satisfies the free-disposal property and is closed. If the conditional factor demand correspondence $z(\overline{w}, q)$ resulting from the cost minimization problem consists of a single element, then the firm's cost function $c(\overline{w}, q)$ is differentiable with respect to w evaluated at $w = \overline{w}$, and this derivative is $\nabla_w c(\overline{w}, q) = z(\overline{w}, q)$.

- *Proof.* [Here we prove it using the duality theorem, but notice that it can also be proved by using first-order conditions and by the envelope theorem.] The firm's cost function can be understood as the support function of the feasible set $F(y) \leq 0$. That is,

$$c(\overline{w}, q) = \inf \{\overline{w} \cdot z : z \in F(y)\}.$$

Hence, we can denote this expression as the support function $\mu_Y(\overline{w})$. Applying the duality theorem to this support function, we have:

- Let Y be a nonempty and closed production set Y, and let $\mu_Y(\overline{w}) = c(\overline{w}, q)$ be its support function. Then, there exists a unique conditional factor demand correspondence $z(\overline{w}, q) \in Y$ such that $c(\overline{w}, q) = \overline{w} \cdot z(\overline{w}, q)$ if and only if $c(\overline{w}, q)$ is differentiable at $\overline{w}$; moreover, this derivative is $\nabla_w c(\overline{w}, q) = z(\overline{w}, q)$. This final result is exactly what the Shephard's lemma states.

Exercise #11 — CES production function

11. Find the cost function of the following firms with different CES production functions:

(a) $f(z_1, z_2) = \sqrt{z_1} + \sqrt{z_2}$.

- Set up the firm's cost minimization problem

$$\min_{z_1, z_2} \quad p_1 z_1 + p_2 z_2$$
$$\text{subject to} \quad q \leq \sqrt{z_1} + \sqrt{z_2}.$$

Taking first-order conditions yields

$$p_1 - \frac{\lambda}{2\sqrt{z_1}} = 0 \Longleftrightarrow p_1 2\sqrt{z_1} = \lambda,$$

$$p_2 - \frac{\lambda}{2\sqrt{z_2}} = 0 \Longleftrightarrow p_2 2\sqrt{z_2} = \lambda,$$

$$\lambda \left(q - \sqrt{z_1} + \sqrt{z_2}\right) = 0,$$

where λ denotes the Lagrange multiplier of constraint $q \leq \sqrt{z_1} + \sqrt{z_2}$. Combining the first two first-order conditions gives $p_1 2\sqrt{z_1} = p_2 2\sqrt{z_2}$, or the tangency condition for cost minimization $\frac{p_1}{p_2} = \frac{\sqrt{z_2}}{\sqrt{z_1}}$. Rearranging, we obtain $\sqrt{z_2} = \frac{p_1}{p_2}\sqrt{z_1}$. Plugging this result into the third first-order condition

$$q = \sqrt{z_1} + \frac{p_1}{p_2}\sqrt{z_1}$$

and solving for z_1 yields the conditional factor demand for good 1,

$$z_1^* = \frac{p_2^2 q^2}{(p_1 + p_2)^2}.$$

- Plugging this value into our $\sqrt{z_2} = \frac{p_1}{p_2}\sqrt{z_1}$ equation above also yields the conditional factor demand for good 2,

$$z_2^* = \frac{p_1^2}{p_2^2}z_1^* = \frac{p_1^2 q^2}{(p_1 + p_2)^2}.$$

- Last, we can insert these factor demands into the objective function to derive our cost function

$$c(p_1, p_2, q) = p_1 z_1^* + p_2 z_2^* = p_1 \frac{p_2^2 q^2}{(p_1 + p_2)^2} + p_2 \frac{p_1^2 q^2}{(p_1 + p_2)^2}$$

$$= \frac{p_1 p_2 q^2}{p_1 + p_2}.$$

(b) $f(z_1, z_2) = \left(\sqrt{z_1} + \sqrt{z_2}\right)^2.$

- Setting up the firm's cost minimization problem

$$\min_{z_1, z_2} \quad p_1 z_1 + p_2 z_2$$

$$\text{subject to} \quad q = \left(\sqrt{z_1} + \sqrt{z_2}\right)^2$$

and taking first-order conditions yields

$$p_1 - \frac{\lambda(\sqrt{z_1} + \sqrt{z_2})}{\sqrt{z_1}} = 0,$$

$$p_2 - \frac{\lambda(\sqrt{z_1} + \sqrt{z_2})}{\sqrt{z_2}} = 0,$$

$$q = \left(\sqrt{z_1} + \sqrt{z_2}\right)^2.$$

Combining the first two first-order conditions gives $\frac{p_1}{p_2} = \frac{\sqrt{z_2}}{\sqrt{z_1}}$ and after rearranging, $\sqrt{z_2} = \frac{p_1}{p_2}\sqrt{z_1}$. Plugging this result into the third first-order condition,

$$q = \left(\sqrt{z_1} + \frac{p_1}{p_2}\sqrt{z_1}\right)^2,$$

and solving for z_1 yields the conditional factor demand for good 1,

$$z_1^* = \frac{p_2^2 q}{(p_1 + p_2)^2}.$$

- Plugging this value into our $\sqrt{z_2} = \frac{p_1}{p_2}\sqrt{z_1}$ equation from above also yields the conditional factor demand for good 2:

$$z_2^* = \frac{p_1^2}{p_2^2}z_1^* = \frac{p_1^2 q}{(p_1 + p_2)^2}.$$

- Finally, we can plug these factor demands into the objective function to obtain our cost function,

$$c(p_1, p_2, q) = p_1 z_1^* + p_2 z_2^* = p_1 \frac{p_2^2 q}{(p_1 + p_2)^2} + p_2 \frac{p_1^2 q}{(p_1 + p_2)^2}$$
$$= \frac{p_1 p_2 q}{p_1 + p_2}.$$

Exercise #13 — Output distribution between two plants

13. Suppose that a firm owns two plants, each producing the same good. Every plant j's average cost is given by

$$AC_j(q_j) = \alpha + \beta_j q_j \quad \text{for} \quad q_j \geq 0, \text{ where } j = \{1, 2\}.$$

Coefficient β_j may differ from plant to plant, i.e., if $\beta_1 > \beta_2$ plant 2 is more efficient than plant 1, since its average costs increase less rapidly in output. Assume that you are asked to determine the cost-minimizing distribution of aggregate output $q = q_1 + q_2$, among the two plants (i.e., for a given aggregate output q, how much q_1 to produce in plant 1 and how much q_2 to produce in plant 2). For simplicity, consider that aggregate output q satisfies $q < \frac{\alpha}{\max_j |\beta_j|}$.

(You will be using this condition in part b.)

(a) If $\beta_j > 0$ for every plant j, how should output be located among the two plants?

- The cost minimization problem in which we find the optimal combination of output q_1 and q_2 that minimizes the total cost of production across plants is

$$\min_{q_1, q_2} \ TC_1(q_1) + TC_2(q_2)$$
$$\text{subject to} \quad q_1 + q_2 = q,$$

or equivalently, the profit maximization problem in which firms choose the optimal combination of output q_1 and q_2 that maximizes the total profits across all plants is

$$\max_{q_1, q_2} \ \underbrace{pq_1 - TC_1(q_1)}_{\pi_1} + \underbrace{pq_2 - TC_2(q_2)}_{\pi_2}$$

$$\text{subject to} \quad q_1 + q_2 = q.$$

- If the average cost is $AC_j(q_j) = \alpha + \beta_j q_j$ then the total cost is $TC_j(q_j) = (\alpha + \beta_j q_j)q_j$. Thus, we can rewrite the above PMP as

$$\max_{q_1, q_2} \ pq_1 - (\alpha + \beta_1 q_1)q_1 + pq_2 - (\alpha + \beta_2 q_2)q_2$$
$$\text{subject to} \quad q_1 + q_2 = q.$$

Taking first-order conditions with respect to q_1 and q_2 yields

$$\frac{\partial (\pi_1 + \pi_2)}{\partial q_1} = p - \alpha - 2\beta_1 q_1 = \lambda,$$

$$\frac{\partial (\pi_1 + \pi_2)}{\partial q_2} = p - \alpha - 2\beta_2 q_2 = \lambda,$$

$$\frac{\partial (\pi_1 + \pi_2)}{\partial \lambda} = q_1 + q_2 = q.$$

Using the first two order conditions, we obtain

$$p - \alpha - 2\beta_1 q_1 = p - \alpha - 2\beta_2 q_2,$$

and after rearranging, $q_2 = \frac{\beta_1}{\beta_2} q_1$. Replacing this expression into the constraint $q_1 + q_2 = q$ yields

$$q_1 + \underbrace{\frac{\beta_1}{\beta_2} q_1}_{q_2} = q,$$

and solving for q_1 entails the cost-minimizing production in plant 1,

$$q_1 \left(1 + \frac{\beta_1}{\beta_2}\right) = q, \quad \text{thus} \quad q_1 = \frac{\beta_2}{\beta_1 + \beta_2} q.$$

Operating similarly for q_2, we find

$$q_2 = \frac{\beta_1}{\beta_1 + \beta_2} q.$$

- *Extension:* Note that, generally for J plants, the average cost of plant j is $AC_j(q_j) = \alpha + \beta_j q_j$, implying that the total cost must be $TC_j(q_j) = (\alpha + \beta_j q_j)q_j$. Therefore, plant j's marginal cost is $MC_j(q_j) = \alpha + 2\beta_j q_j$. Since $\beta_j > 0$ for every j, the first-order necessary and sufficient conditions for cost minimization are (1) that firms' marginal costs coincide (otherwise, we would still have incentives to distribute a larger production to those firms with the lowest marginal cost)

$$MC_j(q_j) = MC_{j'}(q_{j'}) \quad \text{for any two plants } j \text{ and } j',$$

and (2) that the aggregate output constraint holds,

$$q_1 + q_2 + ... q_J = q.$$

From these conditions we obtain

$$q_j = \frac{\frac{q}{\beta_j}}{\sum_h \frac{1}{\beta_h}},$$

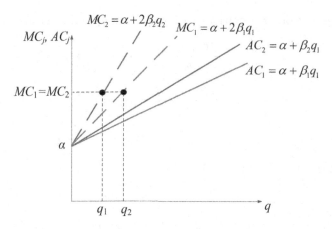

Figure 4.2 $\beta_j > 0$ for every firm.

which coincides with our results for $N = 2$ plants,

$$q_1 = \frac{\frac{q}{\beta_1}}{\frac{1}{\beta_1} + \frac{1}{\beta_2}} = \frac{\beta_2}{\beta_1 + \beta_2} q.$$

Figure 4.2 depicts the average and marginal cost curves for two plants satisfying $\beta_2 > \beta_1$. In particular, the firm manager chooses, for a given aggregate output $q = q_1 + q_2$, the individual output levels q_1 and q_2 that equate the marginal costs across both plants (see vertical axis).

(b) If $\beta_j < 0$ for every plant j, how should output be located among the two plants?

- First, note that $\beta_j < 0$ implies that the average cost $AC_j(q_j) = \alpha + \beta_j q_j$ is decreasing in output. Hence, it is cost-minimizing to concentrate all production on the plant with the smallest $\beta_j < 0$ (the most negative β_j) because average costs (and total costs) are minimized by doing so.

- Figure 4.3 depicts a firm in which both plants exhibit decreasing average costs, but $\beta_2 < \beta_1 < 0$, implying that it is beneficial for the firm to concentrate all output in plant 2. In addition, note that the average cost in plant 1 is positive for all q_1 as long as $\alpha - \beta_1 q_1 > 0$, or $q_1 < \frac{\alpha}{\beta_1}$, where $\frac{\alpha}{\beta_1}$ represents the horizontal intercept of AC_1 in the figure. Similarly for firm 2, where $AC_2 > 0$ for all q_2 as long as $q_2 < \frac{\alpha}{\beta_2}$, where $\frac{\alpha}{\beta_2}$ represents the horizontal intercept of AC_2. Hence, the original condition $q < \frac{\alpha}{\max_j |\beta_j|}$ is equivalent to $q < \min_j \frac{\alpha}{|\beta_j|}$, graphically implying that the aggregate output q lies to the left-hand side to the smallest horizontal intercept.

(c) Suppose that $\beta_j > 0$ for some plants and $\beta_i < 0$ for others.

- Similarly as in part (b), the firm now faces some plants with increasing average costs (those with $\beta_j > 0$) and some plants with decreasing average costs (those with

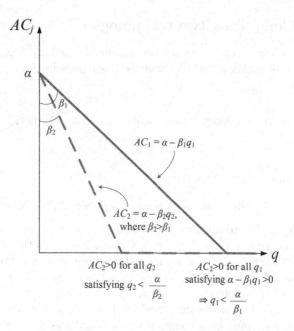

Figure 4.3 $\beta_j < 0$ for every firm.

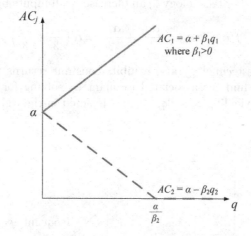

Figure 4.4 $\beta_1 > 0$ and $\beta_2 < 0$.

$\beta_j < 0$). Hence, it is cost-minimizing to concentrate all production on the plant/s with the smallest $\beta_j < 0$, since it benefits from the most rapidly decreasing average costs. Figure 4.4 depicts a firm with plant 1 (2) having increasing (decreasing, respectively) average costs.

Exercise #15 — Comparing two technologies

15. A firm can produce one output q using two inputs, z_1 and z_2 (e.g., labor and capital), by means of two different technologies. Technology 1 is represented by production function

$$q = \min\{z_1, z_2\}$$

for all $z_1, z_2 \geq 0$, while technology 2 is represented by the production function

$$q = \frac{z_1}{3} + \frac{z_2}{3}$$

for all $z_1, z_2 \geq 0$. Input prices are $w_1, w_2 \geq 0$.

(a) Does technology 1 exhibit constant returns to scale? What about technology 2?

- *Technology 1.* For technology 1, $q = \min\{z_1, z_2\}$, we have that either $q = z_1$ (if input 1 is the cheapest, i.e., $z_1 \leq z_2$), or $q = z_2$ (if input 2 is the cheapest, $z_1 > z_2$). In the first case (when $z_1 \leq z_2$), if we increase all inputs by a common factor α, we obtain an output of $\min\{\alpha z_1, \alpha z_2\} = \alpha z_1 = \alpha q$, for any $\alpha \geq 0$ (see the left-hand panel of figure 4.5a). Similarly, when input prices satisfy $z_1 > z_2$, increasing all inputs by the same factor α yields $\min\{\alpha z_1, \alpha z_2\} = \alpha z_2 = \alpha q$. We can thus conclude that increasing all inputs by a common factor α induces an increase in output of exactly α, and therefore technology 1 exhibits constant returns to scale.

- *Technology 2.* For technology 2, an increase in all inputs by a common factor α yields

$$f(\alpha z_1, \alpha z_2) = \frac{\alpha z_1}{3} + \frac{\alpha z_2}{3} = \alpha \left(\frac{z_1}{3} + \frac{z_2}{3} \right) = \alpha f(z_1, z_2),$$

and thus this technology also exhibits constant returns to scale. Note that in this case, we can find the associated isoquant by solving for z_2 in production function $q = \frac{z_1}{3} + \frac{z_2}{3}$, yielding $z_2 = 3q - z_1$, as depicted in the right-hand panel of figure 4.5.

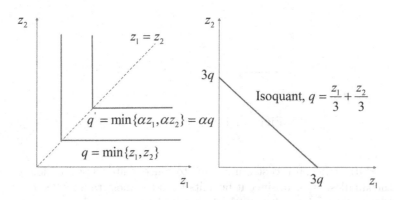

Figure 4.5 (left) Technology 1; (right) technology 2.

(b) Find the cost function $c(w,q)$ for each technology. [*Hint*: You do not need to set up the Lagrangian, using a figure accompanying your explanation is enough.]

- *Technology 1*. This technology represents that the firm uses inputs 1 and 2 in constant proportions (i.e., the firm's isoquants show a kink at $z_1 = z_2$). This implies that, if the firm wants to minimize costs, it will do so by selecting the lowest isocost that "touches" the kink of isoquant associated to production level q, as depicted in figure 4.6.[3]

  Hence, the firm uses the same amount of both inputs, $z_1 = z_2$. In addition, the firm uses one unit of each input in order to produce one unit of output. Therefore, the cost function of reaching output level q is

  $$c(w,q) = w_1 z_1 + w_2 z_1 = (w_1 + w_2)z_1 = (w_1 + w_2)q.$$

- *Technology 2*. This technology represents a linear production function. The firm's isoquants are therefore straight lines. We can, hence, anticipate that the firm operates at either of the corners (using only input 1 or only input 2), or at a continuum of cost-minimizing input combinations. Let us next analyze each case separately.

  (i) If $w_1 > w_2$, then isocost lines are steeper than the isoquant associated with production level q. (Figure 4.7 depicts this case graphically.) Thus, the firm uses input 2 only, i.e., the firm only uses the cheapest input since both inputs are

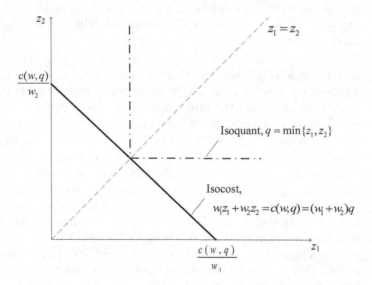

Figure 4.6 Technology 1.

---

[3]Note that we say that the isocost "touches" the isoquant rather than saying that it is "tangent" to the isoquant because in this case the isocost cannot be tangent to the kink, since the slope of the isoquant is not well defined at the kink.

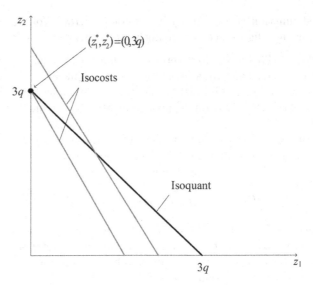

Figure 4.7 Technology 2 when $w_1 > w_2$.

perfectly substitutable in the production process. Hence, when the firm reaches production level q, it must be that $q = \frac{0}{3} + \frac{z_2}{3}$, or $z_2 = 3q$, yielding an input pair $(z_1^*, z_2^*) = (0, 3q)$, as illustrated in figure 4.7. This implies that the firm's cost function is $c(w, q) = 0w_1 + 3qw_2 = 3qw_2$.

(ii) If $w_1 < w_2$, then isocost lines are flatter than the isoquant associated with production level q. Thus, the firm uses input 1 only, i.e., the firm only uses the cheapest input since both inputs are perfectly substitutable in the production process. Hence, when the firm reaches production level q, it must be that $q = \frac{z_1}{3} + \frac{0}{3}$, or $z_1 = 3q$, entailing an input pair $(z_1^*, z_2^*) = (3q, 0)$, as described in figure 4.8. This implies that the firm's cost function is $c(w, q) = 3qw_1 + 0w_2 = 3qw_1$.

(iii) Finally, if $w_1 = w_2$, isocost lines have the same slope as the isoquant associated with production level q. Graphically, the isocost associated with the lowest cost that reaches production level q totally overlaps the isoquant representing that production level, as depicted in figure 4.9. The firm can therefore choose any input combination (z_1, z_2) along the isocost. Intuitively, this implies that the firm is choosing any convex combination between the extreme case in which it only uses input 2 (as in case 1 above) and where it only uses input 1 (as in case 2 above). Hence, the cost function of the firm is a convex combination of the above two cases: $c(w, q) = \lambda 3qw_2 + (1 - \lambda)3qw_1$.

(c) Suppose that the firm wants to produce a special amount of output $\overline{q}$. For which values of w_1 will the firm use technology 1, and for which will the firm use technology 2?

- This exercise asks for a comparison of the cost function under technologies 1 and 2.

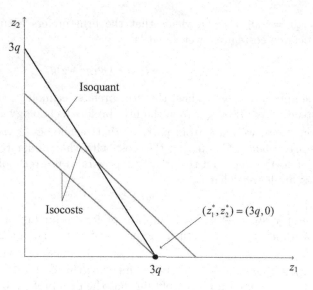

Figure 4.8 Technology 2 when $w_1 < w_2$.

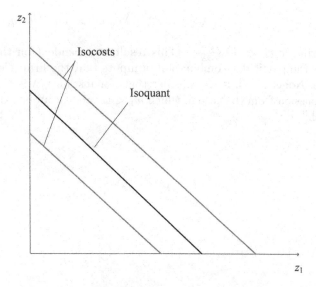

Figure 4.9 Technology 2 when $w_1 = w_2$.

Since the firm's costs under technology 2 depend on input prices, we must divide our analysis into 3 cases:

- If $w_1 < w_2$, we know from part (b) that technology 2 implies a cost function of $c(w, q) = 3qw_1$. Comparing this cost with that under technology 1,

$c(w,q) = (w_1 + w_2)q$, yields that the firm prefers to use technology 1 if its associated costs are lower. That is,

$$3qw_1 > (w_1 + w_2)q,$$

or simply $w_1 > \frac{w_2}{2}$. Thus, the firm prefers technology 1 if $w_2 > w_1 > \frac{w_2}{2}$. If, instead, $w_1 < \frac{w_2}{2} < w_2$, then the firm prefers technology 2.

- If $w_1 > w_2$, we know from part (b) that technology 2 yields a cost function of $c(w,q) = 3qw_2$. Comparing this cost with that under technology 1, $c(w,q) = (w_1 + w_2)q$, we obtain that the firm prefers to use technology 1 if its associated costs are lower. That is,
$$3qw_2 > (w_1 + w_2)q,$$
or simply $w_2 > \frac{w_1}{2}$. Thus, the firm prefers technology 1 if $w_1 > w_2 > \frac{w_1}{2}$. If, instead, $w_2 < \frac{w_1}{2} < w_1$, then the firm prefers technology 2.

- If $w_1 = w_2$, we know from part (b) that Technology 2 yields a cost function of $c(w,q) = \lambda 3qw_2 + (1 - \lambda)3qw_1$. Comparing this cost with that under technology 1, $c(w,q) = (w_1 + w_2)q$, we obtain that the firm prefers to use technology 1 if its associated costs are lower, i.e.,

$$\lambda 3qw_2 + (1 - \lambda)3qw_1 > (w_1 + w_2)q,$$

or simply $w_1 > \frac{w_2(1-\lambda 3)}{2-3\lambda}$. [This result is dependent on the precise value of λ, i.e., the particular combination of inputs that the firm selects along the isocost line. Nonetheless, if we consider that, for instance, λ is close to 1, then all our discussion from the case in which $w_1 < w_2$ above can be extended to this case as well.]

Chapter 5 — Choice under Uncertainty

Summary This chapter examines decision making under uncertainty, beginning by analyzing basic concepts, such as risk premium, the certain equivalent, and the independent axiom. Afterward, it studies the von Neumann–Morgenstern utility function and its application to find the expected utility from different lotteries. We then explore settings in which individual preferences might exhibit two behavioral patterns often observed in experiments: regret and hyperbolic discounting. The chapter then considers optimal savings and investment decisions under uncertainty, and compares them against a context of certainty. Subsequent exercises focus on the theoretical foundations of choice under uncertainty (analyzing, for instance, first- and second-order stochastic dominance, the coefficient of absolute and relative risk aversion, etc.), while the remaining problems are mainly applied. In particular, we explore whether crime is more easily deterred with higher fines or, instead, with better monitoring in two settings: the decision to park in an illegal spot, and the decision on how much income to report to the IRS. We then analyze the problem of an individual choosing how much health insurance to purchase, anticipating that he might become sick in the future. Finally, we study production decisions in agricultural markets, where decision makers are uncertain about future prices.

Exercise #1 — Independence axiom

1. State the independence axiom. Show that if indifference curves in the Machina triangle are *not* parallel straight lines, then the independence axiom is violated. (You can help your discussion by providing a figure.)

   - *Independence axiom.* A preference relation $\succsim$ over the space of simple lotteries $\mathcal{L}$ satisfies the *independence axiom* if for all three lotteries $L, L', L'' \in \mathcal{L}$ and for all $\alpha \in [0,1]$, we have

   $$L \succsim L' \text{ if and only if } \alpha L + (1-\alpha) L' \succsim \alpha L'' + (1-\alpha) L''.$$

   That is, if we mix each of two lotteries with a third one, then the preference ordering of the two resulting lotteries does not depend on (is independent of) the particular third lottery we use.

   - *Nonparallel indifference curves.* In order to show that when indifference curves are not parallel straight lines (as we can see in figure 5.1) the independence axiom is violated, we need to show that

   $$L \succsim L' \text{ does } not \text{ imply } \alpha L + (1-\alpha) L'' \succsim \alpha L' + (1-\alpha) L''.$$

   This is easy to prove for the case in which the individual is indifferent between lotteries L and L', $L \sim L'$. That is, we must show

   $$L \sim L' \text{ does } not \text{ imply } \alpha L + (1-\alpha) L'' \sim \alpha L' + (1-\alpha) L''.$$

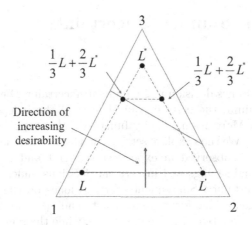

Figure 5.1 Nonparallel indifference curves.

Take the case in which $L \sim L'$, as lotteries L and L' in Figure 5.1, which lie on the same indifference curve. As we can see, the mix of each of these two lotteries with a third lottery L'' leads to compound lotteries $\frac{1}{3}L + \frac{2}{3}L''$ and $\frac{1}{3}L' + \frac{2}{3}L''$, respectively. The possibility of indifference curves which are *not* parallel lines leads to situations like that in the figure, where

$$\frac{1}{3}L + \frac{2}{3}L'' \prec \frac{1}{3}L' + \frac{2}{3}L'',$$

since the decision maker prefers the second compound lottery to the first. Hence, we cannot guarantee that $L \sim L'$ implies

$$\alpha L + (1 - \alpha) L'' \sim \alpha L' + (1 - \alpha) L''.$$

As a consequence, the independence axiom does not hold for indifference curves which are not parallel lines.

Exercise #3 — von Neumann–Morgenstern utility function

3. Let G be the set of compound gambles over a finite set of deterministic payoffs $\{a_1, a_2, ..., a_n\} \subset \mathbb{R}_+$. A decision maker's preference relation $\succsim$ over compound gambles can be represented by utility function $v : G \to \mathbb{R}$. Let $g \in G$, and let probability p_i be associated to the corresponding payoff a_i. Finally, consider that the decision maker's utility function $v(\cdot)$ is given by

$$v(g) = (1 + a_1)^{p_1} (1 + a_1)^{p_2} ...(1 + a_n)^{p_n} = \prod_{i=1}^{n} (1 + a_i)^{p_i}.$$

(a) Show that this is *not* a von Neumann–Morgenstern (vNM) utility function.

- Since $v(g)$ is *not* linear in the probabilities, then $v(g)$ cannot be a vNM expected utility function, with general form

$$v(g) = \sum_{i=1}^{N} p_i u(a_i).$$

(b) Show that the decision maker has the same preference relation as an expected utility maximizer with von Neumann–Morgenstern utility function

$$u(g) = \sum_{i=1}^{n} p_i \ln(1 + a_i).$$

- Since $\ln(\cdot)$ is a monotonic transformation of $v(\cdot)$, both functions represent the same preference relation. Applying the monotonic transformation $u(g) = \ln[v(g)]$ to the original function $v(g)$, we obtain

$$\ln\left(\prod_{i=1}^{n}(1 + a_i)^{p_i}\right) = \sum_{i=1}^{n} p_i \ln(1 + a_i),$$

which represents the initial preference relation over lotteries, and it is linear in the probabilities. Hence, it is a vNM utility function.

(c) Assume now that the decision maker you considered in part (b) has utility function $u(w) = \ln(1 + w)$ over wealth $w \geqslant 0$. Evaluate his risk attitude (concavity in his utility function). Additionally, find the Arrow–Pratt coefficient of absolute risk aversion, $r_A(w, u)$. How does $r_A(w, u)$ change in wealth?

- Given that $u(w) = \ln(1+w)$, where $w \geqslant 0$, then the first- and second-order conditions with respect to w are

$$u'(w) = \frac{1}{1 + w} > 0 \text{ and } u''(w) = -\frac{1}{(1 + w)^2} < 0,$$

which implies that the utility function is concave, as depicted in figure 5.2, and that the decision maker is risk-averse.

- Let us now obtain the Arrow–Pratt coefficient of absolute risk aversion, $r_A(w, u)$, as follows

$$r_A(w, u) = -\frac{u''(w)}{u'(w)} = -\frac{-\frac{1}{(1+w)^2}}{\frac{1}{1+w}} = \frac{1}{1 + w}$$

- Finally, we want to know how this coefficient of absolute risk aversion varies with wealth,

$$\frac{\partial r_A(w, u)}{\partial w} = -\frac{1}{(1 + w)^2},$$

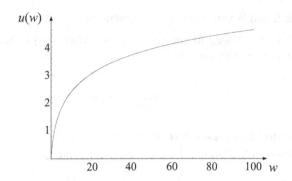

Figure 5.2 Utility function $u(w) = \ln(1 + w)$.

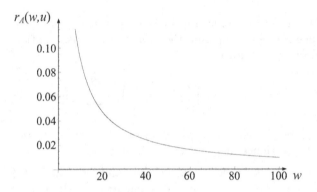

Figure 5.3 Coefficient of absolute risk aversion.

which is negative for all wealth levels $w \geqslant 0$. Hence, the agent becomes less risk-averse as he becomes more wealthy. Figure 5.3 illustrates this coefficient, $r_A(w, u)$, evaluated at different wealth levels.

Exercise #5 — Regret theory

5. Consider the set of deterministic payoffs $\{a_1, a_2, ..., a_n\} \subset \mathbb{R}_+$. Studies in regret-based decision making often consider the following utility function: first, define the highest deterministic payoff that could be reached in gamble g by using function

$$h(g) = \max \{a_k : k \in \{1, 2, ..., n\} \text{ and } p_k > 0\}.$$

Subtracting $h(g)$ from all deterministic outcomes and computing its expected value yields the utility level

$$v(g) = \sum_{i=1}^{n} p_i (a_i - h(g)) = \sum_{i=1}^{n} p_i a_i - h(g).$$

Intuitively, after event i realizes (which provides a payoff a_i to this individual), the "regretful" decision maker compares such monetary payoff with respect to the highest possible payoff he could have obtained from playing this lottery, $h(g)$. Utility functions of this type hence reflect "regret," as individuals experience a disutility from not receiving the highest possible monetary payoff in the lottery.[1]

(a) Compute the expected value of the following two gambles:

$$g^1 = \left(0, 1, 2; \frac{1}{3}, \frac{1}{3}, \frac{1}{3}\right) \text{ and } g^2 = \left(1, 4, 5; \frac{1}{2}, \frac{1}{3}, \frac{1}{6}\right).$$

- First, note that $h(g^1) = \max\{0, 1, 2\}$ since all these events can occur with strictly positive probability in lottery g^1. Then, $h(g^1) = 2$, and therefore the individual's expected utility from playing the first gamble, g^1, is

$$v(g^1) = \frac{1}{3}(0 - 2) + \frac{1}{3}(1 - 2) + \frac{1}{3}(2 - 2) = -1.$$

Similarly, we can find the expected utility from playing the second gamble, g^2. In particular, in this case the highest payoff of the lottery is $h(g^2) = \max\{1, 4, 5\} = 5$, implying that the expected utility from this gamble is

$$v(g^2) = \frac{1}{2}(1 - 5) + \frac{1}{3}(4 - 5) + \frac{1}{6}(5 - 5) = -\frac{7}{3}.$$

Note that the individual experiences a lower expected utility from playing the second than the first lottery. Intuitively, this happens because (1) the distribution of payoffs in the second lottery is more spread than in the first lottery, and this makes the lower payoffs on the second gamble to be compared to a higher possible payoff $h(g^2)$, and (2) because the lowest payoffs on the second gamble are more likely than in the first and, as a consequence, the individual assigns a higher weight in the expected utility calculation to those monetary payoffs in which he is experiencing the biggest regret.

(b) Show that all deterministic outcomes (outcomes with probability 100%) yield the same utility level. That is, $v(a_1) = v(a_2) = ... = v(a_n)$.

- Let us represent by $v(a_i)$ the individual's utility level from a certain deterministic outcome a_i, i.e., $p_{a_i} = 1$. But if outcome a_i occurs with certainty, there is no potential regret. In particular, function $h(g)$ can only find the maximum among all outcomes of the lottery whose probability is strictly greater than zero. Since $p_{a_i} = 1$, then all other outcomes of the lottery receive probability zero, and hence

$$h(g) = \max\{a_k : k \in \{1, 2, ..., n\} \text{ and } p_k > 0\}$$
$$= \max\{a_i\} = a_i.$$

---

[1] Recall that $h(g)$ is unaffected by probability p_i, as it describes the highest payoff receiving a positive probability.

Therefore, the individual's expected utility becomes

$$v(a_i) = \sum_{i=1}^{n} p_i \left(a_i - h(g) \right) = 1 \left(a_i - a_i \right) = 0.$$

Thus, $v(a_1) = v(a_2) = ... = v(a_n) = 0$, regardless of the monetary payoff associated to outcome a_i. If there is just one event to be regretful about, my expected utility is zero!

(c) Show that the preference relation does not satisfy monotonicity if outcomes are deterministic.

- From the definition of monotonicity, we have that

$$(a_1, a_n; \alpha, 1 - \alpha) \succsim (a_1, a_n; \beta, 1 - \beta)$$

for all $\alpha, \beta \in [0, 1]$ if and only if $\alpha > \beta$. So if we make $\alpha = 1$ and $\beta = 0$, then the above condition on monotonicity becomes

$$(a_1, a_n; 1, 0) \succsim (a_1, a_n; 0, 1).$$

Clearly, $a_1 \succsim a_n$ and $a_1 \nprec a_n$, which implies that $a_1 \succ a_n$.

- However, in part (b) we have shown that the individual's utility is the same (and equal to zero) when outcomes are deterministic. In other words, he is indifferent between gambles whose outcomes are deterministic, i.e., $a_1 \sim a_2 \sim ... \sim a_n$. But this contradicts that $a_1 \succ a_n$. Therefore, this "regretful" preference relation cannot satisfy monotonicity.

Exercise #7 — An introductory example on risk aversion

7. Assume that your utility function over income, x, is given by $u(x) = \sqrt{x}$, i.e., a Cobb–Douglas type of function. You have been offered two wage options.

- In the first one you will receive a fixed salary of $54,000.
- In the second one, you will only receive $4,000 as a fixed payment, plus a bonus of $100,000 if the firm is profitable. The probability that the firm goes profitable (and thus you get a total salary of $104,000) is 0.5, while the probability that the firm does not make enough profits is 0.5.

(a) Find the expected value of the lottery induced by accepting the second wage offer.

- The expected value of accepting the second wage offer is

$$EV_{Second} = 0.5(\$4,000) + 0.5(\$104,000) = 2,000 + 52,000 = 54,000.$$

(b) Find the expected utility associated with the second offer.

- The expected utility is

$$EU_{Second} = 0.5\sqrt{4,000} + 0.5\sqrt{104,000} = 192.87.$$

(c) Draw an approximate figure where the following elements are illustrated:

1. Utility function (either concave, linear or convex).
2. Utility level from the first wage offer.
3. Utility level from each of the two possible outcomes of the second wage offer.
4. Expected utility level from the second wage offer.

- Figure 5.4 depicts the decision maker's concave utility function, the utility of the first (certain) wage offer of $54,000 (232.38), the utility of the second (risky) wage offer by separately identifying the utility when the salary is only $4,000 (63.25) and that when the worker receives the bonus, $104,000 (322.5). The figure also depicts the expected utility from accepting the second wage offer, which is graphically illustrated by the mid point of the line connecting the utility in the case in which the decision maker only receives $4,000 and when he receives $104,000.

(d) Using your answers from parts (a) and (b), find the risk premium associated with the second offer.

- We know that the general expression of the risk premium (RP) of a lottery is

$$pu(x_1) + (1 - p)u(x_2) = u(EV - RP).$$

Since the left-hand side is just the expected utility from the lottery, EU, this expression can be move compactly written as

$$EU = u(EV - RP).$$

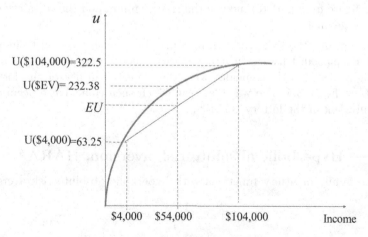

Figure 5.4 Utility function $u(x) = \sqrt{x}$.

Given that we know $EU = 192.87$ from part (b) and that $EV = 54{,}000$ from part (a),

$$192.87 = \sqrt{54{,}000 - RP}.$$

Squaring both sides of this equation and rounding to the nearest integer, yields

$$37{,}199 = 54{,}000 - RP \iff RP = \$16{,}801.$$

In order to intuitively understand the risk premium of a lottery, consider a decision maker who is offered the expected value of the lottery ($54,000), with an associated utility of 232.38 with certainty, or the possibility of playing the lottery (where he obtains an expected utility of 192.87). Needless to say, this risk-averse individual would prefer the expected value of the lottery instead, which, for convenience, coincides with the first wage offer. The risk premium hence measures by how much we need to reduce the certain wage offer of $54,000 in order to make this individual become indifferent between a risk-less offer (of $54,000 − $16,801 = $37,199), or the expected utility of playing the lottery. In other words, a salary below $37,199, despite being certain, would induce the individual decision maker to prefer the risky second wage offer.

(e) What amount of money should the first wage offer propose in order to make you indifferent between accepting the first and the second wage offers?

- The certain amount of money that would make you exactly indifferent between the utility from this certain payment and the utility from accepting the second (uncertain) wage offer is the *certainty equivalent*. As described in our above discussion, the certainty equivalent is obtained from subtracting the risk premium to the certain amount (first wage offer),

$$Certainty\ equivalent = \$54{,}000 - \$16{,}801 = \$37{,}199.$$

(f) In your figure from part (c) include the risk premium and the certainty equivalent of the second wage offer.

- Graphically, the risk premium measures how much we need to move the first wage offer, $54,000, leftward in figure 5.5 to make it map into the utility function at a height that exactly coincides with the expected utility of the lottery, denoted by EU in figure 5.5. The wage level at which such coincidence occurs is the certainty equivalent of the lottery, $37,199.

Exercise #9 — Hyperbolic absolute risk aversion, HARA

9. Consider the family of utility functions with hyperbolic absolute risk aversion (HARA) as follows:

$$u(x) = \frac{1}{\beta - 1}(\alpha + \beta x)^{\frac{\beta - 1}{\beta}},$$

where $\beta \neq 0$ and $\beta \neq 1$. Find the Arrow–Pratt coefficient of absolute risk-aversion, $r_A(x, u)$.

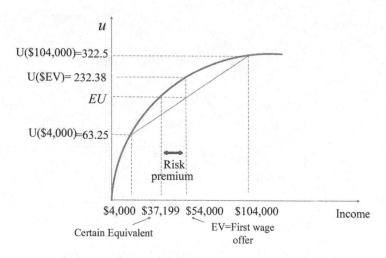

Figure 5.5 Risk premium of the lottery.

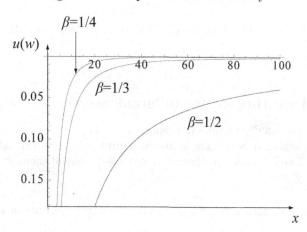

Figure 5.6 HARA utility function.

- First, note that the first derivative of this utility function is $u'(x) = (\alpha + \beta x)^{-\frac{1}{\beta}}$, while the second derivative is $u''(x) = -(\alpha + \beta x)^{-\frac{1+\beta}{\beta}}$. Figure 5.6 depicts this function for different values of β.

- The Arrow–Pratt coefficient of absolute risk-aversion is

$$r_A(x, u) = -\frac{u''(x)}{u'(x)} = -\frac{-(\alpha + \beta x)^{-\frac{1+\beta}{\beta}}}{(\alpha + \beta x)^{-\frac{1}{\beta}}} = \frac{1}{\alpha + \beta x},$$

which is decreasing in wealth, x, as long as $\beta > 0$, but it is increasing if $\beta < 0$. Figure 5.7

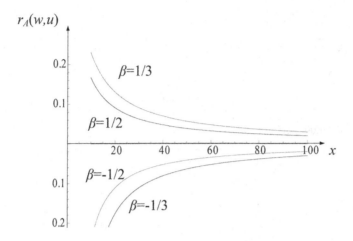

Figure 5.7 $r_A(x, u)$ for the HARA utility function.

depicts the Arrow-Pratt coefficient of absolute risk aversion for different values of parameter β.[2]

Exercise #11 — Investing in two different assets

11. An investor has the von Neumann–Morgenstern utility function $u(c) = -e^{-\alpha c}$, where c is consumption, and where $\alpha > 0$.[3] There are two states of the world, labelled 1 and 2, which are equally likely. There are two (rather extreme) assets, one of them attractive in state 1 and the other in state 2:

- Asset 1 yields one unit of consumption in state 1, but nothing in state 2.

- Asset 2 yields nothing in state 1, but one unit of consumption in state 2.

- The price of the first asset is π_1, while the price of the second asset is π_2, where for simplicity $\pi_1 + \pi_2 = 1$. The investor starts with an endowment of w units of both assets, but seeks to balance her portfolio so as to maximize her expected utility. Denote by x_1 the number of units that he acquires of the first asset, and by x_2 the number of units of the second asset.

---

[2]For more information on the HARA utility function, including behavioral patterns in different investment settings, see its wikipedia entry at the following link: http://en.wikipedia.org/wiki/Hyperbolic_absolute_risk_aversion, and the references included in the link.

[3]Note that this utility function is increasing in consumption, i.e., $\frac{\partial u(c)}{\partial c} = \alpha e^{-\alpha c}$, which is positive for all $c > 0$; and concave since $\frac{\partial^2 u(c)}{\partial c^2} = -\alpha^2 e^{-\alpha c}$ is negative for all $c > 0$.

(a) Formulate the investor's expected utility maximization problem.

- First, note that in state 1, the investor obtains one unit of consumption for every unit of asset x_1 he purchases, and no units of consumption for every unit of asset 2, i.e., $u(c) = -e^{-\alpha c} = -e^{-\alpha x_1}$. In state 2 the opposite happens, leading to a utility of $u(c) = -e^{-\alpha c} = -e^{-\alpha x_2}$. Since both states are equally likely, we can then express the investor's maximization problem as choosing the levels of x_1 and x_2 that solve

$$\max_{x_1, x_2 \geq 0} \frac{1}{2} \cdot \left(-e^{-\alpha x_1}\right) + \frac{1}{2} \cdot \left(-e^{-\alpha x_2}\right)$$

subject to $\pi_1 x_1 + \pi_2 x_2 \leq w$.

(b) Find the utility-maximizing purchases of assets 1 and 2, x_1 and x_2, for this investor.

- Setting up the Lagrangian associated to the above maximization problem,

$$\mathcal{L}(x_1, x_2; \lambda) = \frac{1}{2} \cdot \left(-e^{-\alpha x_1}\right) + \frac{1}{2} \cdot \left(-e^{-\alpha x_2}\right) + \lambda\left[w - \pi_1 x_1 - \pi_2 x_2\right],$$

and solving for the first-order conditions,

$$\frac{\partial \mathcal{L}}{\partial x_1} = \frac{\alpha}{2} e^{-\alpha x_1} - \lambda \pi_1 = 0,$$

$$\frac{\partial \mathcal{L}}{\partial x_1} = \frac{\alpha}{2} e^{-\alpha x_2} - \lambda \pi_2 = 0,$$

$$\frac{\partial \mathcal{L}}{\partial \lambda} = w - \pi_1 x_1 - \pi_2 x_2 = 0.$$

Solving for λ in the first two expressions, and setting them equal to each other, we obtain

$$\frac{e^{-\alpha x_1}}{\pi_1} = \frac{e^{-\alpha x_2}}{\pi_2} \iff e^{-\alpha x_1 + \alpha x_2} = \frac{\pi_1}{\pi_2}.$$

And applying logs,

$$-\alpha x_1 + \alpha x_2 = \ln \pi_1 - \ln \pi_2.$$

Solving for x_1 on the binding budget constraint, we find $x_1 = \frac{w}{\pi_1} - \frac{\pi_2}{\pi_1} x_2$. Plugging this result into the above expression, yields

$$-\alpha \left(\frac{w}{\pi_1} - \frac{\pi_2}{\pi_1} x_2\right) + \alpha x_2 = \ln \pi_1 - \ln \pi_2.$$

Multiplying both sides by $\frac{\pi_1}{\alpha}$,

$$x_2 \left[\pi_1 + \pi_2\right] = w + \frac{\pi_1}{\alpha} \left[\ln \pi_1 - \ln \pi_2\right],$$

and using the property that $\pi_1 + \pi_2 = 1$, then we obtain the optimal amount of asset x_2 that the investor demands,

$$x_2 = w + \frac{\pi_1}{\alpha} \left[\ln \pi_1 - \ln \pi_2 \right].$$

Operating similarly, we can find the optimal amount of asset x_1,

$$x_1 = w + \frac{\pi_2}{\alpha} \left[\ln \pi_2 - \ln \pi_1 \right].$$

(c) How does the holding of assets change with parameter α? Interpret.

     – The demand for assets 1 and 2 found above, x_1 and x_2, is *decreasing* in α. It is easy to show that α is precisely the Arrow–Pratt coefficient of absolute risk-aversion of this investor,

$$r_A(x, u) = -\frac{u''(x)}{u'(x)} = \alpha,$$

which is constant for all wealth levels. Hence, an increase in his risk aversion (measured by α) reduces his demand for any of these two risky assets.

(d) How does the investor's risk aversion and wealth level interact? How sensitive is this result to the specification of the utility function?

     – As the previous section pointed out, the investor's demand for risky assets is independent on his wealth level. This result, however, depends on the particular specification of the investor's utility function. In this case, his utility function has an Arrow–Pratt coefficient of absolute risk-aversion, $r_A(x, u) = \alpha$, which is constant for all wealth levels. Many other utility function can be used which do not satisfy this property, and where the investor would vary his holdings of risky assets when he becomes more risk-averse.

Exercise #13 — Second-order stochastic dominance

13. Consider two cumulative distribution functions over monetary outcomes, $x \in \mathbb{R}_+$, $F(x)$ and $G(x)$. Show that if $G(x)$ is a elementary increase in risk from $F(x)$, then $F(x)$ second order stochastically dominates $G(x)$.

     • Distribution $G(x)$ is considered an *elementary increase in risk* from $F(x)$ if distribution $G(x)$ is generated from $F(x)$ by taking all the probability weight that $F(x)$ assigns to an interval $[x', x'']$ and transferring it to the endpoints of the interval, x' and x'', such that the same mean is preserved. Hence, an elementary increase in risk is a mean preserving spread. Therefore, since $G(x)$ is a mean preserving spread of $F(x)$, then

$$E\left[F(x)\right] = E\left[G(x)\right], \text{ but}$$

$$Var\left[F(x)\right] \leq Var\left[G(x)\right].$$

And as a consequence, $F(x)$ second order stochastically dominates $G(x)$. [Figure 5.8 provides a graphical illustration of a mean preserving spread.]

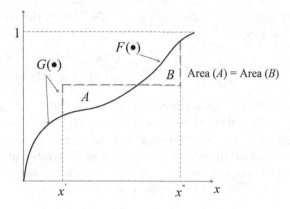

Figure 5.8 Mean-preserving spread.

Exercise #15 — Coefficient of risk aversion

15. Show that the Arrow–Pratt coefficient of absolute risk-aversion is invariant to linear transformations of the utility function $u(\cdot)$.

   • Consider a linear transformation of utility function $u(\cdot)$, i.e., $v = a + bu$, where first- and second-order derivatives are

$$v' = bu' \quad \text{and} \quad v'' = bu''.$$

   Then, the Arrow–Pratt coefficient of absolute risk aversion for the linear transformation v is

$$r_A(x, v) = -\frac{v''(x)}{v'(x)} = -\frac{bu''}{bu'} = -\frac{u''}{u'},$$

   which exactly coincides with the Arrow–Pratt coefficient of absolute risk aversion for the original utility function $u(x)$. Hence, linear transformations still provides the same measure of riskiness as the original utility function.

Exercise #17 — Non constant coefficient of absolute risk aversion

17. Suppose that the utility function is given by

$$u(w) = aw - bw^2,$$

   where $a, b > 0$, and $w > 0$ denotes income.

   (a) Find the coefficient of absolute risk aversion, $r_A(w, u)$. Does it increase or decrease in wealth? Interpret.

- First, note that $u' = a - 2bw$ and $u'' = -2b$. Hence, the Arrow–Pratt coefficient of absolute risk aversion is

$$r_A(w, u) = -\frac{u''(w)}{u'(w)} = \frac{2b}{a - 2bw}.$$

Note that, as w rises, the denominator decreases, and as a consequence $r_A(w, u)$ rises, i.e., the decision maker becomes more risk averse as his wealth increases.

- Importantly, this exercise illustrates that, while the decision maker can have a concave utility function (indeed, $u'' = -2b < 0$, as illustrated in figure 5.9, which depicts utility function $u(w) = aw - bw^2$ evaluated at parameters $a = 80$ and $b = 1$), the Arrow–Pratt coefficient of absolute risk aversion, $r_A(w, u)$, can increase as he becomes richer.

(b) Let us now consider that this decision maker is deciding how much to invest in a risky asset. This risky asset is a random variable R, with mean $\overline{R} > 0$ and variance σ_R^2. Assuming that his initial wealth is w, state the decision maker's expected utility maximization problem, and find first-order conditions.

- First, note that the decision maker's wealth (W in his utility function) is now a random variable $w + xR$, where x is the amount of risky asset that he acquires. Inserting this expression in the decision maker's utility function, and taking expectations, we observe that the decision maker selects his optimal investment in risky asset, x, in order to solve

$$\max_x \ E\left[a\left(w + xR\right) - b\left(w + xR\right)^2\right].$$

And the associated first-order condition with respect to x is

$$E\left[aR - 2bR\left(w + x^*R\right)\right] = 0.$$

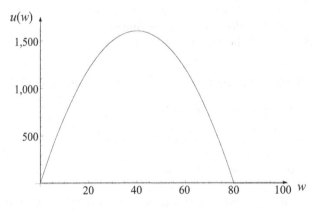

Figure 5.9 Utility function $u(w) = aw - bw^2$.

- We can use the definition of the variance of random variable R, $\sigma_R^2 = E[R^2] - \overline{R}^2$, to obtain $E[R^2] = \overline{R}^2 + \sigma_R^2$. Hence, the above first-order condition can be simplified to

$$E\left[aR - 2bR\left(w + x^* R\right)\right] = a\overline{R} - 2b\overline{R}w - E\left[2bR^2 x^*\right]$$
$$= a\overline{R} - 2b\overline{R}w - 2bx^*\left(\overline{R}^2 + \sigma_R^2\right) = 0.$$

(c) What is the optimal investment in risky assets?

- Solving for x^* in the above expression, we obtain

$$x^* = \frac{(a - 2bw)\,\overline{R}}{2b\left(\overline{R}^2 + \sigma_R^2\right)}.$$

(d) Show that the optimal amount of investment in risky assets is a decreasing function in wealth. Interpret.

- Differentiating x^* with respect to wealth, yields

$$\frac{\partial x^*}{\partial w} = -\frac{\overline{R}}{\left(\overline{R}^2 + \sigma_R^2\right)},$$

which is negative, since $\overline{R}, \sigma_R^2 > 0$. Intuitively, the larger the decision maker's wealth, the lower is the amount of risky assets he wants to hold. This explanation is consistent with his coefficient of absolute risk aversion found at the beginning of the exercise, where we showed that the individual becomes more risk averse as his wealth increases.

Exercise #19 — Coefficient of absolute risk aversion and concave transformations

19. Consider two Bernouilli utility functions $u_1(\cdot)$ and $u_2(\cdot)$, and assume that their Arrow–Pratt coefficients of absolute risk aversion satisfy $r_A(x, u_2) \geq r_A(x, u_1)$ for every monetary amount x. Show that $u_2(\cdot)$ must then be more concave than $u_1(\cdot)$.

- In order to show that utility function $u_2(\cdot)$ is more concave than $u_1(\cdot)$ we need to demonstrate that $u_2(\cdot)$ can be expressed as a concave transformation of $u_1(\cdot)$, that is,

$$u_2(x) = f\left(u_1(x)\right),$$

where $f\left(\cdot\right)$ is an increasing concave function. Differentiating yields

$$u_2'(x) = f'\left(u_1(x)\right) u_1'(x),$$

and differentiating again we obtain

$$u_2''(x) = f'\left(u_1(x)\right) u_1''(x) + f''\left(u_1(x)\right) \left[u_1'(x)\right]^2.$$

Dividing both sides by $u_2'(x)$ yields

$$\frac{u_2''(x)}{u_2'(x)} = f'(u_1(x)) \frac{u_1''(x)}{u_2'(x)} + f''(u_1(x)) \frac{[u_1'(x)]^2}{u_2'(x)},$$

and using expression $u_2'(x) = f'(u_1(x)) u_1'(x)$, we obtain

$$\frac{u_2''(x)}{u_2'(x)} = f'(u_1(x)) \frac{u_1''(x)}{f'(u_1(x)) u_1'(x)} + f''(u_1(x)) \frac{[u_1'(x)]^2}{f'(u_1(x)) u_1'(x)},$$

which simplifies to

$$\frac{u_2''(x)}{u_2'(x)} = \frac{u_1''(x)}{u_1'(x)} + \frac{f''(u_1(x))}{f'(u_1(x))} u_1'(x).$$

Then, using the definition of $r_A(x, u_k)$ for $k = \{1, 2\}$, we find

$$r_A(x, u_2) = r_A(x, u_1) + \frac{f''(u_1(x))}{f'(u_1(x))} u_1'(x).$$

Finally, since $f(\cdot)$ is an increasing concave function, $f'(\cdot) \geq 0$ and $f''(\cdot) \leq 0$, thus implying that $\frac{f''(u_1(x))}{f'(u_1(x))} \leq 0$, and that $r_A(x, u_2) \geq r_A(x, u_1)$ for all x; as required.

- *Parametric example.* Consider $u_1(x) = x^{1/2}$ and the more concave utility function $u_2(x) = x^{1/6}$. We can then find a strictly increasing concave function $f(u) = u^{1/3}$, so that $u_2(x)$ can be expressed as a concave transformation of $u_1(x)$, namely,

$$u_2(x) = [u_1(x)]^{1/3} = \left[x^{1/2} \right]^{1/3} = x^{1/6}.$$

In this context, the Arrow–Pratt coefficients of absolute risk aversion become

$$r_A(x, u_1) = -\frac{-\frac{1}{4x^{3/2}}}{\frac{1}{2x^{1/2}}} = \frac{1}{2x} \quad \text{and} \quad r_A(x, u_2) = -\frac{-\frac{5}{36x^{11/6}}}{\frac{1}{6x^{5/6}}} = \frac{5}{6x},$$

thus yielding $r_A(x, u_2) \geq r_A(x, u_1)$ for all x. (For a graphical representation of a utility function and its concave transformation, see figure 5.29 in the textbook.)

Exercise #21 — Risk aversion

21. Prove that risk aversion is equivalent to the following two points.

(a) $u(\cdot)$ is concave.

- By definition, a decision maker is a risk averter if his expected utility from playing a lottery is weakly lower than his utility from the expected value of the lottery. That is, if preferences admit Bernoulli function representation, risk aversion is captured by Jensen's inequality:

$$\int u(x)dF(x) \leq u\left(\int xdF(x)\right),$$

which implies that $u(x)$ is concave. In fact, several textbooks use Jeusen's inequality in order to define the concavity of any function $f(x)$. In the case in a finite number of states, $x_1, x_2, ..., x_N$, with associated probabilities $\alpha_1, \alpha_2, ..., \alpha_N$ respectively, where $\sum_{i=1}^{N} \alpha_i = 1$, this inequality can be rewritten as

$$u\left(\alpha_1 x_1 + \alpha_2 x_2 + ... + \alpha_N x_N\right) \leq \alpha_1 u\left(x_1\right) + \alpha_2 u\left(x_2\right) + ... + \alpha_N u\left(x_N\right),$$

which also implies the concavity of function $u(\cdot)$.

(b) The certain equivalent of money lottery $F(x)$, $c(F, u)$, satisfies $c(F, u) \leq \int x\, dF(x)$ for every lottery $F(x)$.

- By the definition of the certain equivalent of lottery $F(\cdot)$, $c(F, u)$,

$$u\left(c\left(F, u\right)\right) = \int u(x)dF(x).$$

Recall that the certain equivalent of a lottery defines the amount of money that makes the decision maker indifferent between playing the gamble (left-hand side of the above expression) and accepting such certain amount of money $c(F, u)$ (right-hand side).

- Using Jensen's inequality

$$\int u(x)dF(x) \leq u\left(\int xdF(x)\right),$$

we can substitute the first term by $u\left(c\left(F, u\right)\right)$ from the definition of the certain equivalent, thus yielding

$$u\left(c\left(F, u\right)\right) \leq u\left(\int xdF(x)\right),$$

and since $u(\cdot)$ is nondecreasing,

$$c\left(F, u\right) \leq \int xdF(x) \Leftrightarrow c(F, u) \leqslant EV,$$

which is exactly what we needed to show: the certain equivalent that we must offer a risk-averse individual in order for him to give up the lottery is weakly lower than the expected value of the lottery, $\int dF(x)$.

Exercise #23 — Uncertainty about the future

23. Max Pullman lives for exactly two periods, $t = 0, 1$. Let $c_t \in \mathbb{R}$ denote his consumption in period t. Max's preferences (evaluated at $t = 0$) over two-period consumption streams are represented by function

$$U(c_0, c_1) = u(c_0) + \delta E u(c_1),$$

where δ is a discount factor, $u(\cdot)$ is an increasing and strictly concave utility function, and the E operator denotes his expectation (at $t = 0$) concerning events in period $t = 1$. For simplicity, you can also assume that the marginal utility of consumption is convex, that is, $u''' > 0$.

Suppose that there is initially no uncertainty. Let $w_0 \geq 0$ be Max's income in period 0 and let $w_1 \geq 0$ denote his income in period 1. Max can save or borrow. Let $s \in \mathbb{R}$ denote his saving (notice that s could be negative if he borrows), and let ρ denote the gross return on saving (i.e., $\rho = 1 + r$ where r is the interest rate). Thus, his consumption in period 0 is $w_0 - s$ and his consumption in period 1 is $w_1 + \rho s$. Assume interior solutions throughout the exercise.

(a) Write down necessary and sufficient conditions for Max's choice of saving, s^*, to be positive.

- Max's utility maximization problem is to choose c_0 and c_1 to solve

$$\max_{c_0, c_1} u(c_0) + \delta u(c_1)$$

subject to $c_0 = w_0 - s$ and $c_1 = w_1 + \rho s$.

We can alternatively use the binding constraints to simplify the maximization problem into an unconstrained problem with a single choice variable, as follows:

$$\max_{s} u(w_0 - s) + \delta u(w_1 + \rho s).$$

Taking first-order conditions with respect to s, we obtain

$$-u'(w_0 - s^*) + \delta \rho u'(w_1 + \rho s^*) = 0.$$

Hence, for $s^* > 0$, we require that $-u'(w_0) + \delta \rho u'(w_1) > 0$, as depicted in the vertical intercept of figure 5.10. The figure also shows that expression $-u'(w_0 - s^*) + \delta \rho u'(w_1 + \rho s^*)$ decreases in s, which is guaranteed by the strict concavity of $u(\cdot)$. (Finally, note that expression $-u'(w_0 + s^*) + \delta \rho u'(w_1 + \rho s^*)$ decreases at a decreasing rate, becoming flatter in s as depicted in the figure, if $u''' > 0$.)

- Therefore, since the vertical intercept satisfies $-u'(w_0) + \delta \rho u'(w_1) > 0$ then, solving for ρ we obtain

$$\rho > \frac{u'(w_0)}{\delta u'(w_1)}.$$

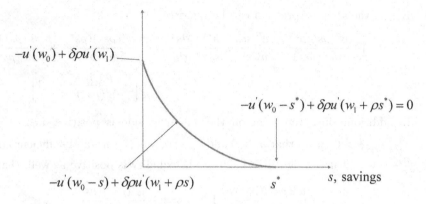

Figure 5.10 Positive savings $s^* > 0$.

- *Intuition:* The gross return on saving ρ (the rate at which Max can transfer consumption from today to tomorrow) must be greater than his marginal rate of substitution evaluated at the endowment (w_0, w_1) (that is, the rate at which he is willing to transfer consumption from today to consumption tomorrow). Otherwise, it would not be profitable for him to save (he would prefer to borrow).

(b) Suppose that $w_1 = 0$ and that the conditions you found in part (a) hold. Find a condition on Max's coefficient of relative risk aversion that is necessary and sufficient for s^* to be (locally) increasing in ρ.

- Evaluating the first-order condition we found in part(a) at $w_1 = 0$, we have

$$\delta \rho u'(\rho s^*) = u'(w_0 - s^*).$$

Differentiating this first-order condition with respect to ρ, we obtain

$$\delta \left[u'(\rho s^*) + u''(\rho s^*) \left(\rho s^* + \rho^2 \frac{\partial s^*}{\partial \rho} \right) \right] = -u''(w_0 - s^*) \frac{\partial s^*}{\partial \rho},$$

and after rearranging,

$$\left[-u''(\rho s^*)\rho^2 \delta - u''(w_0 - s^*) \right] \frac{\partial s^*}{\partial \rho} = \delta \left[u''(\rho s^*)(\rho s^*) + u'(\rho s^*) \right].$$

Dividing both sides of this equality by $u'(w_0 - s^*)$ yields

$$\left[-\frac{u''(\rho s^*)\rho^2 \delta}{u'(w_0 - s^*)} - \frac{u''(w_0 - s^*)}{u'(w_0 - s^*)} \right] \frac{\partial s^*}{\partial \rho} = \delta \left[\frac{u''(\rho s^*)(\rho s^*)}{u'(w_0 - s^*)} + \frac{u'(\rho s^*)}{u'(w_0 - s^*)} \right].$$

Furthermore, from the first-order condition we know that $u'(w_0 - s^*) = \delta \rho u'(\rho s^*) > 0$.

Hence, the above expression can be rewritten as

$$
\left[-\frac{u''(\rho s^*)\rho^2 \delta}{\delta \rho u'(\rho s^*)} - \frac{u''(w_0 - s^*)}{u'(w_0 - s^*)} \right] \frac{\partial s^*}{\partial \rho} = \delta \left[\frac{u''(\rho s^*)(\rho s^*)}{\delta \rho u'(\rho s^*)} + \frac{u'(\rho s^*)}{\delta \rho u'(\rho s^*)} \right]
$$

$$
= \frac{1}{\rho} \left[\frac{u''(\rho s^*)(\rho s^*)}{u'(\rho s^*)} + 1 \right].
$$

In addition, since the term on the left-hand side is positive, i.e., $-\frac{u''(\rho s^*)\rho^2 \delta}{\delta \rho u'(\rho s^*)} - \frac{u''(w_0 - s^*)}{u'(w_0 - s^*)} > 0$, given that $u' > 0$ and $u'' < 0$, a necessary and sufficient condition for $\frac{\partial s^*}{\partial \rho} > 0$ is that the right-hand side of the equality is positive as well, that is

$$
\frac{u''(\rho s^*)(\rho s^*)}{u'(\rho s^*)} + 1 > 0 \iff -\frac{u''(\rho s^*)(\rho s^*)}{u'(\rho s^*)} < 1.
$$

- *Interpretation:* Hence, the Arrow-Pratt's coefficient of relative risk aversion, $r_R(x) = \frac{-u''(x)x}{u'(x)}$, must be lower than one. This property holds for most of the concave utility functions, e.g., for $u(x) = \sqrt{x}$ coefficient $r_R(x)$ becomes r:

$$
{}_R(x) = -\frac{\frac{1}{4x^{3/2}}}{\frac{1}{2x^{1/2}}} = -\frac{1}{2} < 1.
$$

Intuitively, this condition states that for Max to increase his savings as a response of a larger return ρ, his utility function must be sufficiently concave.

(c) Now suppose that Max faces uncertainty over his period 1 income. Specifically, suppose that his period 1 income is given by $w_1 + \tilde{x}$ where $w_1 \geq 0$ and random variable $\tilde{x}$ exhibits an expected value of $E(\tilde{x}) = 0$. Let s^{**} denote Max's new optimal saving in this context. Show that $s^{**} > s^*$. [*Hint:* Suppose that $s^{**} = s^*$ and compare the first-order conditions using Jensen's inequality.]

- Under uncertainty, the first-order condition becomes

$$
-u'(w_0 - s^{**}) + \delta \rho E[u'(w_1 + \tilde{x} + \rho s^{**})] = 0.
$$

By Jensen's inequality, the strict convexity of u' (i.e., $u''' > 0$) implies

$$
-u'(w_0 - s^{**}) + \delta \rho E[u'(w_1 + \tilde{x} + \rho s^{**})] > -u'(w_0 - s^{**}) + \delta \rho u'(w_1 + E(\tilde{x}) + \rho s^*)s^{**}),
$$

and, since $E(\tilde{x}) = 0$, the right-hand side of the inequality can be more compactly expressed as

$$
-u'(w_0 - s^{**}) + \delta \rho u'(w_1 + \rho s^{**})] = 0,
$$

which exactly coincides with the first-order condition of exercise (a) and, hence, it is equal to zero. Hence, the above inequality becomes

$$
-u'(w_0 - s^{**}) + \delta \rho E[u'(w_1 + \tilde{x} + \rho s^{**})] > 0,
$$

indicating that, at a level of savings s^*, the curve $-u'(w_0 - s^*) + \delta \rho E[u'(w_1 + \tilde{x} + \rho s^*)]$ is still positive, i.e., it has not crossed the horizontal axis yet.

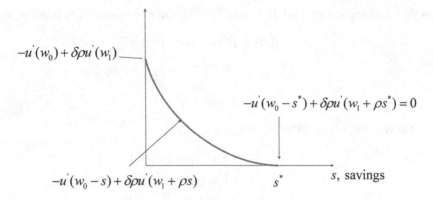

$-u'(w_0) + \delta\rho u'(w_1)$

$-u'(w_0 - s^*) + \delta\rho u'(w_1 + \rho s^*) = 0$

$-u'(w_0 - s) + \delta\rho u'(w_1 + \rho s)$ s^* s, savings

Figure 5.11 Comparing savings s^* and s^{**}.

- Figure 5.11 illustrates this comparison. In particular, the figure depicts the curve $-u'(w_0 - s^*) + \delta\rho u'(w_1 + \rho s^*)]$, which we use in part (a) to identify the level of savings s^*, and curve $-u'(w_0 - s^*) + \delta\rho[u'(w_1 + E(\tilde{x}) + \rho s^*)]$ that we use in part (c) to identify the level of savings s^{**}. Graphically, when evaluating both curves at the same level of savings s^*, we obtain that the latter is above the former, thus implying that $s^{**} > s^*$.

Exercise #25 — Uncertainty in production decisions

25 Consider a firm with initial profits given by $\pi_0 = 15$, and cost function $c(q) = 10 + q^2$. The price at which this firm sells its production is stochastically distributed according to the following probability distribution

$$\tilde{p} = \begin{cases} p_H = \$8 \text{ with probability } \frac{1}{2}, \text{ and} \\ p_L = \$2 \text{ with probability } \frac{1}{2}, \end{cases}$$

where the tilde sign $^\sim$ reflects that the price level is a random variable.

(a) If the firm manager's utility function is given by

$$u(\tilde{\pi}) = E[\tilde{\pi}] - \frac{1}{9}Var(\tilde{\pi}),$$

determine the firm's optimal production level, and the associated equilibrium profits from producing such an output level.

- We first separately find $E[\tilde{\pi}]$ and $Var(\tilde{\pi})$. On one hand, $E(\tilde{\pi})$ is given by

$$E[\tilde{\pi}] = E[\pi_0 + \tilde{p}q - 10 - q^2]$$
$$= 15 + \left(\frac{1}{2}8 + \frac{1}{2}2\right)q - 10 - q^2$$
$$= 5 + 5q - q^2.$$

On the other hand, $Var(\tilde{\pi})$ is given by

$$Var(\tilde{\pi}) = Var[\pi_0 + \tilde{p}q - 10 - q^2]$$
$$= Var[\tilde{p}q] = q^2 Var[\tilde{p}]$$
$$= q^2 \left(\frac{1}{2}(8 - 5)^2 + \frac{1}{2}(2 - 5)^2\right)$$
$$= 9q^2$$

- Therefore, the firm manager's utility function can be expressed as

$$u(\tilde{\pi}) = E[\tilde{\pi}] - \frac{1}{9}Var(\tilde{\pi})$$
$$= \left(5 + 5q - q^2\right) - \frac{1}{9}9q^2$$
$$= 5 + 5q - 2q^2.$$

Hence, the firm manager's maximization problem becomes that of selecting the level of output q that solves

$$\max_{q \geq 0} u(\tilde{\pi}) = 5 + 5q - 2q^2.$$

Taking first order condition with respect to q yields

$$\frac{\partial u(\tilde{\pi})}{\partial q} = 5 - 4q \leq 0,$$

implying that $q = \frac{5}{4}$ at the interior solution. Plugging this result into the objective function $u(\tilde{\pi})$ entails equilibrium profits of

$$u(\tilde{\pi}) = E[\tilde{\pi}] - \frac{1}{9}Var(\tilde{\pi}) = \frac{155}{16} - \frac{1}{9}\frac{225}{16} = \frac{585}{72}.$$

(b) Consider now that the firm manager's utility function is described by $u(\pi) = E[\pi]$. What is now the optimal production level and the associated equilibrium profits?

- In this case, the firm manager is risk neutral. Hence, when selecting the optimal production level, he only considers expected profits. His maximization problem becomes

$$\max_{q \geq 0} u(\tilde{\pi}) = E[\tilde{\pi}] = 5 + 5q - q^2.$$

Taking first-order condition with respect to q yields

$$\frac{\partial u(\widetilde{\pi})}{\partial q} = 5 - 2q \leq 0,$$

implying that $q = \frac{5}{2}$ at the interior solution, i.e., he increases his production decision relative to part (a) where he is risk averse. Plugging this result into the objective function $u(\widetilde{\pi})$ entails equilibrium profits of

$$u(\widetilde{\pi}) = E[\widetilde{\pi}] = 5 + 5\frac{5}{2} - \left(\frac{5}{2}\right)^2 = \frac{45}{4}.$$

Chapter 6 — Partial and General Equilibrium

Summary This chapter explores partial and general equilibrium exercises. We first analyze the equilibrium number of firms that enter a market, and the fact that they are unaffected by a common shock in all prices. Exercises 3 and 4 study the effect that sales taxes impose on equilibrium prices, and how the tax burden is distributed between agents. Then exercise 5 analyzes a perfectly competitive market with firms selling heterogeneous goods, and how equilibrium outcomes are affected by the degree of heterogeneity between firms' products.

We then move to a general equilibrium framework starting with simplicity with economies without production. In particular, exercises 6–9 analyze these types of economies, finding offer curves when individuals have different types of preferences (such as linear, Leontief, and Cobb–Douglas), and characterizing Walrasian equilibrium allocations (WEA) in each case. For completeness, exercise 9 also examines the set of Pareto efficient allocations (PEA) and compares it with WEAs. Exercises 10 and 11 examine, still in a context without production, the effects of having goods being regarded as gross substitutes by consumers on the existence of an equilibrium allocation and its uniqueness. Exercise 12 focuses on the characterization of core allocations in exchange economies (i.e., allocations that cannot be blocked by a coalition of individuals), first for a standard unreplicated economy, and then for a replicated economy. This exercise also connects the "shrinking core" property with the fact that WEAs must be part of the core, regardless of how replicated the economy is. Exercise 13 (15) examines a context with positive (negative) externalities in consumption, which entails that the WEA is not necessarily Pareto efficient—a similar result as that of exercise 14, whereby one consumer exhibits market power. Exercises 15–19 focus on excess demand functions in settings with different preferences, check that they satisfy homogeneity and Walras' law, and evaluate the uniqueness and stability of equilibrium allocations to small perturbations. The rest of the exercises in the chapter extend the above analysis to economies with production, allowing for different production functions, and analyzing both equilibrium and Pareto optimal allocations.

Exercise #1 — Equilibrium number of firms in perfectly competitive markets

1. Consider a perfectly competitive industry with N symmetric firms, each with cost function $c(q) = F + cq$, where $F, c > 0$. Assume that the inverse demand is given by $p(Q) = a - bQ$, where $a > c$, $b > 0$, and where Q denotes aggregate output.

   (a) *Short-run equilibrium.* If exit and entry is not possible in the industry (assuming N firms remain active), find the individual production level of each firm.

   - Each invidual firm i solves the PMP

   $$\max_{q_i \geq 0} (a - bQ)q_i - (F + cq_i) = \left(a - bq_i - b\sum_{j \neq i} q_j \right) q_i - (F + cq_i).$$

Taking first-order conditions with respect to q_i yields

$$a - 2bq_i - b\sum_{j \neq i} q_j - c = 0.$$

and applying symmetry in equilibrium outputs, i.e., $q_1 = q_2 = ... = q_N$, we obtain an individual equilibrium output

$$q_i = \frac{a - c}{b(N + 1)}$$

for every firm $i \in N$. Note that this result is a function of the number of active firms in the industry, N.

- In this setting, the equilibrium market price is

$$p^* = a - b\underbrace{\left(N \cdot \frac{a - c}{b(N + 1)}\right)}_{Q = N \cdot q_i} = \frac{a + Nc}{N + 1}.$$

(b) *Long-run equilibrium.* Consider now that firms have enough time to enter the industry (if economic profits can be made) or to exit (if they make losses by staying in the industry). Find the long-run equilibrium number of firms in this perfectly competitive market.

- In a long-run equilibrium of a perfectly competitive market, we know that firms must be making no economic profits, $\pi = 0$, as otherwise firms would still have incentives to enter or exit the industry. Hence, we first need to find the equilibrium profits that every individual firm i earns by producing the equilibrium output q_i found in part (a). In particular, these profits are

$$\pi_i = (a - b\underbrace{Nq_i}_{Q})q_i - (F + cq_i) = \frac{(a - c)^2}{b(N + 1)^2} - F;$$

setting them equal to zero and solving for N yields the long-run equilibrium number of firms, $\lfloor N^* \rfloor = \frac{a - c}{\sqrt{bF}} - 1$, where $\lfloor N \rfloor$ indicates the highest integer smaller or equal to N. For instance, if $a = b = 1$, $c = \frac{1}{4}$, and $F = \frac{1}{16}$ N^* becomes $N^* = 2$.

- More generally, note that the expression we found for equilibrium profits, π_i, is monotonically decreasing in the number of firms, N, for all parameter values, that is

$$\frac{\partial \pi_i}{\partial N} = -\frac{2(a - c)^2}{b(N - 1)^2} < 0,$$

thus implying that equilibrium profits becomes zero for a sufficiently large number of firms.

Exercise #3 — Per unit taxes versus ad valorem taxes

3. A tax is to be levied on a commodity bought and sold in a competitive market. Two possible forms of tax may be used: In one case, a *per unit* tax is levied, where an amount t is paid per unit bought or sold. In the other case, an *ad valorem* tax is levied, where the government collects a tax equal to τ times the amount the seller receives from the buyer. Assume that a partial equilibrium approach is valid.

   (a) Show that, with a per unit tax, the ultimate cost of the good to consumers and the amounts purchased are independent of whether the consumers or the producers pay the tax. As a guidance, let us use the following steps:

      1. *Consumers.* Let p^c be the competitive equilibrium price when the *consumer* pays the tax. Note that when the consumer pays the tax, he pays $p^c + t$ whereas the producer receives p^c. State the equality of the (generic) demand and supply functions in the equilibrium of this competitive market when the consumer pays the tax.

         - If the per unit tax t is levied on the consumer, then he pays $p+t$ for every unit of the good, and the demand at market price p becomes $x(p+t)$. The equilibrium market price p^c is determinded from equalizing demand and supply:

         $$x(p^c + t) = q(p^c).$$

      2. *Producers.* Let p^p be the competitive equilibrium price when the *producer* pays the tax. Note that when the producer pays the tax, he receives $p^p - t$ whereas the consumer pays p^p. State the equality of the (generic) demand and supply functions in the equilibrium of this competitive market when the producer pays the tax.

         - On the other hand, if the per unit tax t is levied on the producer, then he collects $p-t$ from every unit of the good sold, and the supply at market price p becomes $q(p-t)$. The equilibrium market price p^p is determined from equalizing demand and supply:

         $$x(p^p) = q(p^p - t).$$

   (b) Show that if an equilibrium price p solves your equality in part (a), then $p+t$ solves the equality in (b). Show that, as a consequence, equilibrium amounts are independent of whether consumers or producers pay the tax.

      - It is easy to see that p solves the first equation if and only if $p+t$ solves the second one. Therefore, $p^p = p^c + t$, which is the ultimate cost of the good to consumers in both cases. The amount purchased in both cases is

      $$x(p^p) = x(p^c + t).$$

   (c) Show that the result in part (b) is not generally true with an ad valorem tax. In this case, which collection method leads to a higher cost to consumers? [*Hint:* Use the same steps as above, first for the consumer and then for the producer, but taking into account that now the tax increases the price to $(1+\tau)p$. Then, construct the excess demand function for the case of the consumer and the producer.]

- If the ad valorem tax τ is levied on the consumer, then he pays $(1+\tau)\,p$ for every unit of the good, and the demand at market price p becomes $x\,((1+\tau)\,p)$. The equilibrium market price p^c is determined from equalizing demand and supply:

$$x\,((1+\tau)\,p^c) = q\,(p^c)\,.$$

On the other hand, if the ad valorem tax τ is levied on the producer, he receives $(1+\tau)\,p$ for every unit of the good sold, and the supply at market price p becomes $q\,((1-\tau)\,p)$. The equilibrium market price p^p is determined from equalizing demand and supply:

$$x\,(p^p) = q\,((1-\tau)\,p^p)\,.$$

Consider the excess demand function for this case:

$$z\,(p) = x\,(p) - q\,((1-\tau)\,p)\,. \tag{1}$$

Since the demand curve $x\,(\cdot)$ is nonincreasing and the supply curve $q\,(\cdot)$ is nondecreasing, $z\,(p)$ must be nonincreasing. From (1) we have

$$\begin{aligned}
z\,((1+\tau)\,p^c) &= x\,((1+\tau)\,p^c) - q\,((1-\tau)\,[(1+\tau)\,p^c]) \\
&= x\,((1+\tau)\,p^c) - q\,((1-\tau^2)\,p^c) \geq \\
&\geq x\,((1+\tau)\,p^c) - q\,(p^c) = 0,
\end{aligned}$$

where the inequality takes into account that $q\,(\cdot)$ is nondecreasing.

- Therefore, $z\,((1+\tau)\,p^c) \geq 0$ and $z\,(p^p) = 0$. Since $z\,(\cdot)$ is nonincreasing, this implies that $(1+\tau)\,p^c \leq p^p$. In words, levying the ad valorem tax on consumers leads to a lower cost on consumers than levying the same tax on producers. (In the same way, it can be shown that levying the ad valorem tax on consumers leads to a higher price for producers than levying the same tax on producers).

(d) Are there any special cases in which the collection method is irrelevant with an ad valorem tax? [*Hint:* Think about cases in which the tax introduces the same wedge on consumers and producers (inelasticity). Then prove your statement by using the above argument on excess demand functions.]

- If the supply function $q\,(\cdot)$ is strictly increasing, the argument can be strengthened to obtain the strict inequality: $(1+\tau)\,p^c < p^p$. On the other hand, when the supply is perfectly inelastic, i.e., $q\,(p) = \bar{q}$ =constant, then yield

$$x\,((1+\tau)\,p^c) = \bar{q} = x\,(p^p)\,,$$

and therefore $p^p = (1+\tau)\,p^c$. Here both taxes result in the same cost to consumers. However, producers still bear a higher burden when the tax is levied directly on them:

$$(1-\tau)\,p^p = (1-\tau)\,(1+\tau)\,p^c < p^c.$$

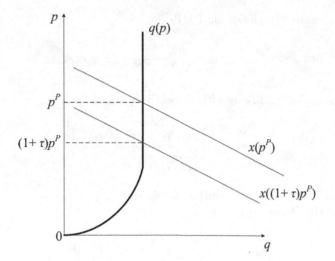

Figure 6.1 Introducing a tax.

These prices are depicted in the next figure, where $x(p)$ reflects the demand function with no taxes and $x((1+\tau)p)$ represents the demand function with the ad valorem tax. While the inelastic supply curve guarantee that sales are unaffected by the tax (remaining at $\overline{q}$ units), the price that the producer receives drops from p^p to $(1+\tau)p^p$. Therefore, the two taxes are still not fully equivalent.

- The intuition behind these results is simple: with a tax, there is always a wedge between the "consumer price" and the "producer price." Levying an ad valorem tax on the producer price, therefore, results in a higher tax burden (and a higher tax revenue) than levying the same percentage tax on consumers.

Exercise #5 — Perfect competition with heterogeneous goods

5. In our discussion of perfectly competitive markets, we considered that all firms produced a homogeneous good. However, our analysis can be easily extended to settings in which goods are heterogeneous. In particular, consider that every firm $i \in N$ faces a inverse demand function

$$p_i(q_i, q_{-i}) = \frac{\theta q_i^{\beta-1}}{\sum_{j=1}^{N} q_j^{\beta}},$$

where q_i denotes firm i's output, q_{-i} the output decisions of all other firms, i.e., $q_{-i} = (q_1, ..., q_{i-1}, q_{i+1}, ..., q_N)$, θ is a positive constant, and parameter $\beta \in (0, 1]$ captures the degree of substitutability. In addition, assume that every firm faces the same cost function $c(q_i) = F + cq_i$, where $F > 0$ denotes fixed costs and $c > 0$ represents marginal costs. Find the individual production level of every firm i, q_i^*, as a function of β. Interpret.

- Every firm i solves the following PMP:

$$\max_{q_i} \frac{\theta q_i^{\beta-1}}{\sum_{j=1}^{N} q_j^{\beta}} q_i - (F + c q_i).$$

Taking first-order conditions with respect to q_i yields

$$\frac{\theta \left[\beta q_i^{\beta-1} \left(\sum_{j=1}^{N} q_j^{\beta} \right) - q_i^{\beta} \left(\beta q_i^{\beta-1} \right) \right]}{\left(\sum_{j=1}^{N} q_j^{\beta} \right)^2} - c = 0.$$

In a symmetric equilibrium, output levels satisfy $q_i^* = q^*$ for every firm $i \in N$, thus simplifying the above expression to

$$\frac{\theta \beta q^{2\beta-1}(N-1)}{N^2 q^{2\beta}} - c = 0.$$

Solving for q^* yields the individual equilibrium output

$$q^* = \frac{\theta \beta (N-1)}{N^2 c}.$$

- *Comparative statics.* Differentiating q^* with respect to the substitutability parameter β, we obtain

$$\frac{\partial q^*}{\partial \beta} = \frac{\theta(N-1)}{N^2 c} > 0.$$

Hence, as goods become more differentiated (higher β), the equilibrium output level q^* rises. However, as more firms operate in this market, the increase in q^* becomes smaller since the derivative $\frac{\partial q^*}{\partial \beta}$ decreases in N, i.e.,

$$\frac{\partial \left(\frac{\partial q^*}{\partial \beta} \right)}{\partial N} = \frac{\theta N^2 c - \theta(N-1)2Nc}{(N^2 c)^2} < 0.$$

Exercise #7 — Finding offer curves for different preferences

7. Consider a two-good economy, where every person has the endowment $\omega = (0, 20)$. For each of the following preferences, solve the individuals UMP in order to find his demand curve. The use the endowment to identify his offer curve.

(a) Cobb–Douglas type: $\alpha \log(x_1) + (1 - \alpha) \log(x_2)$, where $\alpha \in (0, 1)$.

- Setting up the Lagrangian and normalizing the price of good 2, so $p_2 = 1$ and $p_1 = p$, we obtain

$$\mathcal{L} = \alpha \log(x_1) + (1 - \alpha) \log(x_2) + \lambda \left[20 - p x_1 - x_2 \right],$$

which yields first-order conditions

$$\frac{\alpha}{x_1} - \lambda p = 0,$$

$$\frac{1 - \alpha}{x_2} - \lambda = 0,$$

$$20 - px_1 - x_2 = 0.$$

Subtracting the first two equations from the third one, we find $\lambda = \frac{1}{20}$, and so the demands will be

$$x_1 = \frac{20\alpha}{p} \quad \text{and} \quad x_2 = 20(1 - \alpha),$$

and the offer curve will simply be a horizontal straight line at $x_2^h = 20(1 - \alpha)$. Since the offer curve depicts the relationship between the demand of good 2 and good 1, the offer curve in this case is just $x_2 = 20(1 - \alpha)$, i.e., a horizontal straight line with height $20(1 - \alpha)$ in the Edgeworth box.

(b) Perfect substitutes: $ax_1 + x_2$.

- In this case, the consumer demands units of one of the good alone (when the slope of his indifference curve and budget line differs) or any bundle on his budget line (if their slopes coincide). In particular, since the $MRS_{1,2} = \frac{a}{1} = a$, and the price ration is $\frac{p_1}{p_2} = p$, the consumer only demands good 2 if $p > a$, i.e., $x = (0, 20)$; only good 1 if $p < a$, yielding a demand $x = \left(\frac{20}{a}, 0\right)$; and any point on the budget line $px_1 + x_2 = 20$ if $p = a$; as depicted in figure 6.2.

(c) Perfect complements: $\min\{ax_1, x_2\}$.

- Demand will be at the kink of the indifference curve, i.e., $ax_1 = x_2$, which together with the budget constraint $px_1 + x_2 = 20$ yields $px_1 + ax_1 = 20$, or $x_1 = \frac{20}{p+a}$. Hence, the demand for good 2 is $x_2 = ax_1 = a\frac{20}{p+a}$. That is, the offer curve satisfies $x_2 = ax_1$, thus being a straight line from the origin $(0, 0)$ and with a positive slope $a > 0$.

(d) Consider now an economy where all individuals have the Cobb–Douglas preferences of part (a). There are two individuals: consumer A with $\alpha = \frac{1}{2}$ and endowment $\omega = (10, 0)$, and consumer B with $\alpha = \frac{3}{4}$ and $\omega = (0, 20)$. Find the WEA.

- If a person with preferences of $\alpha \log(x_1) + (1 - \alpha) \log(x_2)$ had an income of 10 units of commodity 1 (as opposed to 20 in part (a)) then, by analogy with part (a), demand would be

$$x^1 = \begin{bmatrix} 10\alpha \\ 10p(1 - \alpha) \end{bmatrix},$$

and the offer curve will simply be a vertical straight line at $x_1^h = 10\alpha$. From our demands in part (a) and the equation above, we have $x_1^1 = 10(\frac{1}{2}) = 5$, $x_2^2 = 20(1 - \frac{3}{4}) = 5$. Given

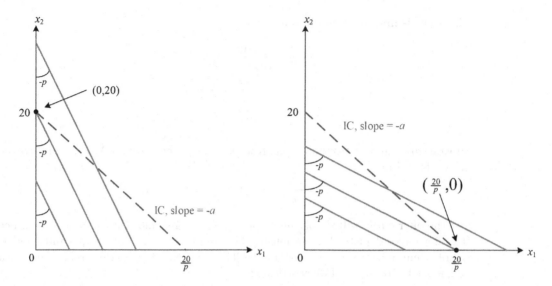

Figure 6.2 Demand when $p > a$ and when $p < a$.

that there are 10 units in total of commodity 1 and 20 units in total of commodity 2, the materials balance condition then means that the equilibrium allocation must be

$$x^1 = \begin{bmatrix} 5 \\ 15 \end{bmatrix} \quad \text{and} \quad x^2 = \begin{bmatrix} 5 \\ 5 \end{bmatrix}.$$

Solving for p from our equilibrium, we find that the equilibrium price ratio must be 3.

Exercise #9 — Pure exchange economy

9. Consider a pure-exchange economy with two individuals, A and B, each with utility function $u^i(x^i, y^i)$ where $i = \{A, B\}$, whose initial endowments are $e^A = (10, 0)$ and $e^B = (0, 10)$, that is, individual A (B) owns all units of good x (y, respectively).

(a) Assuming that utility functions are $u^i(x^i, y^i) = \min\{x^i, y^i\}$ for all individuals $i = \{A, B\}$, find the set of PEAs and the set of WEAs.

- *PEAs.* Since the utility functions are not differentiable we cannot follow the property of $MRS_{x,y}^A = MRS_{x,y}^B$ across consumers. Figure 6.3 helps us identify the set of PEAs. Points away from the $45°$-line, satisfying $y^A = x^A$, such as N, cannot be Pareto efficient since we can still find other points, such as M, where consumer 2 is made better off while consumer 1 reaches the same utility level as under N. Once we are at points on the $45°$-line, such as M, we cannot find other points making at least one

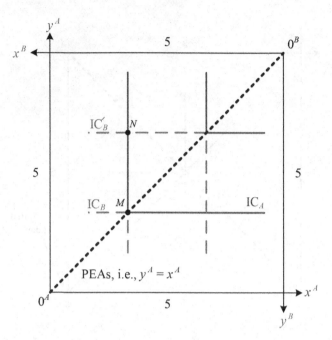

Figure 6.3 Edgeworth box and PEAs.

consumer better off (and keeping the other consumer at least as well off). Hence, the set of PEAs is

$$\{(x^A, y^A), (x^B, y^B) : y^A = x^A \text{ and } y^B = x^B\}.$$

- *WEAs.* Using good 2 as the numeraire, i.e., $p_2 = 1$, the price ratio becomes $\frac{p_1}{p_2} = p_1$. The budget line of both consumers therefore has a slope $-p_1$ and crosses the point representing the initial endowment e in figure 6.4 (where e lies at the lower right-hand corner)

(b) Assuming utility functions of $u^A(x^A, y^A) = x^A y^A$ and $u^B(x^B, y^B) = \min\{x^B, y^B\}$, find the set of PEAs and WEAs.

- *PEAs.* By the same argument as in question (a), the set of PEAs satisfies $y^A = x^A$, as depicted in figure 6.5. Point N cannot be efficient as we can still find other feasible points, such as M, where at least one consumer is made strictly better off (in this case consumer A). At points on the 45°-line, however, we can no longer find alternatives that would constitute a Pareto improvement.

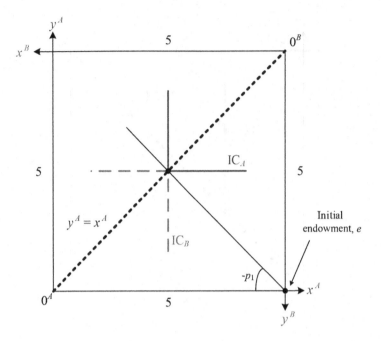

Figure 6.4 Edgeworth box and WEA.

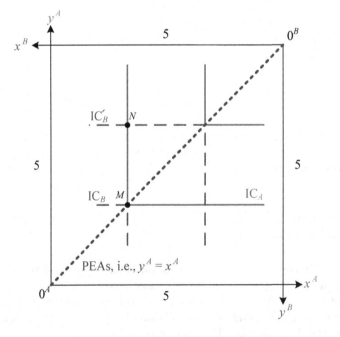

Figure 6.5 Edgeworth box and PEAs.

- *WEAs.* Using good y as the numeraire, $p_y = 1$, so that the price vector becomes $\mathbf{p} = (p_x, 1)$. Hence, *Consumer A's UMP is*

$$\max_{x^A, y^A} \quad x^A y^A$$

subject to $p_x x^A + y^A = 10 p_x$.

After taking first-order conditions,

$$y^A - \lambda^A p_x = 0,$$
$$x^A - \lambda^A = 0,$$
$$p_x x^A + y^A = 10 p_x.$$

Combining the first two FOCs and rearranging, we have

$$p_x x^A = y^A,$$

and substituting this equation into the third FOC yields

$$p_x x^A + p_x x^A = 10 p_x \implies x^A = 5.$$

Then, substituting this back into $p_x x^A = y^A$ gives us

$$y^A = 5 p_x.$$

Consumer B's UMP is not differentiable, but in equilibrium his Walrasian demands satisfy $x^B = y^B$. Substituting this into his budget constraint yields

$$p_x x^B + x^B = 10 \implies x^B = y^B = \frac{10}{p_x + 1}.$$

Furthermore, the feasibility condition for good x entails

$$5 + \frac{10}{p_x + 1} = 10 + 0, \text{ or } p_x = 1.$$

Therefore, the market of good x will clear at an equilibrium price of $p_x = 1$, i.e., $z_x(p_x, 1) = 0$ when $p_x = 1$. Since market y clears when market x does (by Walras' law), $z_y(p_x, 1)$ must also be zero when $p_x = 1$. Summarizing, the equilibrium price $p_x = 1$ yields a WEA

$$\{(5, 5), (5, 5)\}.$$

Exercise #11 — Gross substitutability and uniqueness of equilibrium

11. Consider an economy with I individuals and J goods. Show that if the excess demand functions of all J goods satisfy the gross-substitution property, i.e.,

$$\frac{\partial z_k(\mathbf{p})}{\partial p_j} > 0 \text{ for any two goods } k \neq j,$$

the equilibrium price vector must be unique.

- Without loss of generality, we consider $J = 2$ goods. First, note that excess demand functions satisfy homogeneity of degree zero in prices. That is, if we increase the prices of all goods by a common factor $\lambda > 0$, the excess demands are unaffected. More formally, for any good k, $z_k(p_1, p_2)$ satisfies

$$z_k(\lambda p_1, \lambda p_2) = z_k(p_1, p_2).$$

- On the other hand, the gross-substitution property, $\frac{\partial z_k(\mathbf{p})}{\partial p_j} > 0$ for any two goods $k \neq j$, can also be expressed by saying that, for any two price vectors, $\mathbf{p}, \mathbf{p}' \gg 0$ where the price of good 2 satisfies $p_2' > p_2$ then the excess demand of good 1 increases, i.e., $z_1(\mathbf{p}') > z_1(\mathbf{p})$. Intuitively, a more expensive good 2 increases the Walrasian demand of good 1 and, for a given endowment, its excess demand.

- In order to demonstrate that the equilibrium price vector is unique, we work by contradiction, as follows. Assume that there are two equilibrium price vectors $\mathbf{p} = (p_1, p_2)$ and $\mathbf{p}' = (p_1', p_2')$ satisfying

$$(p_1, p_2) \neq (\lambda p_1', \lambda p_2').$$

In addition, assume that the gross substitutability property (GSP) holds; which is the premise of the proof. Since price vectors (p_1, p_2) and (p_1', p_2') clear both markets (they are equilibrium price vectors) the excess demand functions are both zero:

$$(z_1(\mathbf{p}), z_2(\mathbf{p})) = (z_1(\mathbf{p}'), z_2(\mathbf{p}')) = (0, 0).$$

Since the excess demand functions are homogeneity of degree zero in prices, we can normalize the price vector so that $p_1' = \lambda p_1$, where $\lambda > 1$, and $p_2' = p_2$. Then, to move from price vector p to p', we can increase the price of good 2, the aggregate demand of good 1 must increase by GSP, entailing that its excess demand satisfies $z_1(p') > z_1(p) = 0$. As a consequence, price vector p' cannot be in equilibrium, yielding a contradiction.

- A similar approach applies to economies with more than two commodities, whereby we start increasing the price of one commodity k ($p_k' = \lambda p_k$, where $\lambda > 1$, and $p_l' = p_l$ for all goods $l \neq k$), and then increase the price of each of the $l \neq k$ goods, one at a time, until the aggregate demand for good k increases by the GSP, which induces $z_k(p') > z_k(p) = 0$, as required.

Exercise #13 — Pareto allocations with externalities

13. Consider an economy with two consumers, Ann and Bob, with utility functions

$$u^A(x^A, y^A) = x^A + \left(y^A + \frac{1}{4}\right)^{\frac{1}{2}} \text{ and } u^B(x^B, y^A) = x^B + y^A + \frac{1}{4},$$

where y^A enters Bob's utility (this is not a typo!). Initial endowments satisfy $\mathbf{e}^A = \mathbf{e}^B = (1,1)$. Find the set of PEAs.

- The preferences of Bob reflect that he experiences a positive externality from the units of good y that Ann consumes, i.e., y^A enters positively into Bob's utility function. In such a setting, the use of condition $MRS^A_{x,y} = MRS^B_{x,y}$ will not yield a PEA. To see this, consider the Edgeworth box depicted in figure 6.6, where the indifference curves of Ann are found by solving for y^A in $u^A(x^A, y^A)$, that is,

$$y^A = (u^A - x^A)^2 - \frac{1}{4}$$

while those of Bob are similarly found by solving for y^A in $u^B(x^B, y^A)$,

$$y^A = \left(u^B - \frac{1}{4}\right) - x^B.$$

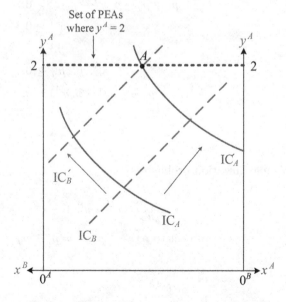

Figure 6.6 PEAs in the presence of externalities.

While Ann's indifference curves are nonlinear in x^A, Bob's is linear in x^B. In addition, since y^B is absent from our analysis, y^A is depicted in both vertical axes, thus implying that the origin for Bob, 0^B is now located in the lower right-hand corner of the figure.

- We can formally prove that $y^B = 0$ in the PEA by finding the contract curve. First, Ann's maximization problem is

$$\max_{x^A, y^A \geq 0} \quad x^A + \left(y^A + \frac{1}{4}\right)^{\frac{1}{2}}$$
$$\text{subject to } p_x x^A + p_y y^A = p_x + p_y$$

with Lagrangian

$$\mathcal{L} = x^A + \left(y^A + \frac{1}{4}\right)^{\frac{1}{2}} + \lambda^A \left(p_x + p_y - p_x x^A - p_y y^A\right) + \mu_x^A x^A + \mu_y^A y^A$$

and first-order conditions

$$1 - p_x \lambda^A + \mu_x^A = 0,$$
$$\frac{1}{2\sqrt{y^A + \frac{1}{4}}} - p_y \lambda^A + \mu_y^A = 0,$$
$$p_x + p_y - p_x x^A - p_y y^A \geq 0,$$
$$x^A \geq 0,$$
$$y^A \geq 0,$$
$$\lambda^A, \mu_x^A, \mu_y^A \geq 0,$$
$$\lambda^A (p_x + p_y - p_x x^A - p_y y^A) = 0,$$
$$\mu_x^A x^A = 0,$$
$$\mu_y^A y^A = 0.$$

Likewise, Bob's maximization problem is

$$\max_{x^B, y^B \geq 0} \quad x^B + y^A + \frac{1}{4}$$
$$\text{subject to } p_x x^B + p_y y^B = p_x + p_y$$

with Lagrangian

$$\mathcal{L} = x^B + y^A + \frac{1}{4} + \lambda^B \left(p_x + p_y - p_x x^B - p_y y^B\right) + \mu_x^B x^B + \mu_y^B y^B$$

and first-order conditions

$$1 - p_x \lambda^B + \mu_x^B = 0,$$
$$-p_y \lambda^B + \mu_y^B = 0,$$
$$p_x + p_y - p_x x^B - p_y y^B \geq 0,$$
$$x^B \geq 0,$$
$$y^B \geq 0,$$
$$\lambda^B, \mu_x^B, \mu_y^B \geq 0,$$
$$\lambda^B (p_x + p_y - p_x x^B - p_y y^B) = 0,$$
$$\mu_x^B x^B = 0,$$
$$\mu_y^B y^B = 0.$$

The proof follows by contradiction. Assume that $y^B > 0$. This requires that $\mu_y^B = 0$ from Bob's ninth FOC. Substituting this into Bob's second FOC yields

$$-p_y \lambda^B = 0,$$

which now requires one of these two parameters to be zero.

(1) If $\lambda^B = 0$ (i.e., Bob's budget constraint does not bind), Bob's first FOC becomes $1 + \mu_x^B = 0$ implying $\mu_x^B = -1$, which contradicts Bob's sixth FOC.

(2) If $p_y = 0$, then Ann's second FOC becomes

$$\frac{1}{2\sqrt{y^A + \frac{1}{4}}} + \mu_y^A = 0 \implies \mu_y^A = -\frac{1}{2\sqrt{y^A + \frac{1}{4}}} < 0,$$

which contradicts Ann's sixth FOC. Hence, any situation in which $y^B > 0$ leads to a contradiction of other FOCs. Thus, $y^B = 0$ which completes our proof.

• As extra practice, you can use Ann's and Bob's first-order conditions from solving their UMPs to find the WEA in this economy. In particular,

$$\{(x^A, y^A, \lambda^A, \mu_x^A, \mu_y^A), (x^B, y^B, \lambda^B, \mu_x^B, \mu_y^B)\} = \left\{ \left(\frac{2}{3}, 2, \frac{1}{3}, 0, 0 \right), \left(\frac{4}{3}, 0, \frac{1}{3}, 0, \frac{1}{3} \right) \right\}$$

with equilibrium prices $(p_x, p_y) = (3, 1)$.

Exercise #15 — When goods are bads

15. An exchange economy consists of two consumers (A and B) with utility function

$$u^i(x_1^i, x_2^i) = x_1^i(4 - x_2^i) \text{ for consumer } i = \{A, B\}.$$

So, the first commodity is a "good" for each consumer, while the second commodity is a "bad" for each consumer. Their initial endowments are $\omega^A = (4, 3)$ and $\omega^B = (1, 0)$.

(a) Find the consumers' Walrasian demand functions.

- *Consumer A.* Starting with consumer A, his maximization problem is

$$\max_{x_1^A, x_2^A \geq 0} \quad x_1^A(4 - x_2^A)$$

$$\text{subject to} \quad p_1 x_1^A + p_2 x_2^A = 4p_1 + 3p_2,$$

and the corresponding Lagrangian is

$$\mathcal{L} = x_1^A(4 - x_2^A) + \lambda^A \left(4p_1 + 3p_2 - p_1 x_1^A - p_2 x_2^A\right).$$

Taking first-order conditions yields

$$4 - x_2^A - \lambda^A p_1 = 0,$$

$$-x_1^A - \lambda^A p_2 = 0,$$

$$4p_1 + 3p_2 - p_1 x_1^A - p_2 x_2^A = 0.$$

Combining the first two first-order conditions, we obtain

$$\frac{p_1}{p_2} = \frac{x_2^A - 4}{x_1^A} \implies p_1 x_1^A = p_2(x_2^A - 4).$$

Substituting this into our third first-order condition gives

$$4p_1 + 3p_2 - p_2(x_2^A - 4) - p_2 x_2^A = 0,$$

and solving for x_2^A gives consumer A's Walrasian demand for good 2,

$$x_2^A = \frac{4p_1 + 7p_2}{2p_2}.$$

Finally, plugging this in to our result from above gives consumer A's Walrasian demand for good 1:

$$p_1 x_1^A = p_2 \left(\frac{4p_1 + 7p_2}{2p_2} - 4\right) \implies x_1^A = \frac{4p_1 - p_2}{2p_1}.$$

- *Consumer B.* Consumer B's UMP is

$$\max_{x_1^B, x_2^B \geq 0} \quad x_1^B(4 - x_2^B)$$

$$\text{subject to} \quad p_1 x_1^B + p_2 x_2^B = p_1,$$

and the corresponding Lagrangian is

$$\mathcal{L} = x_1^B(4 - x_2^B) + \lambda^B \left(p_1 - p_1 x_1^B - p_2 x_2^B\right).$$

Taking first-order conditions yields

$$4 - x_2^B - \lambda^B p_1 = 0,$$
$$-x_1^B - \lambda^B p_2 = 0,$$
$$p_1 - p_1 x_1^B - p_2 x_2^B = 0.$$

Combining the first two first-order conditions, we obtain

$$\frac{p_1}{p_2} = \frac{x_2^B - 4}{x_1^B} \implies p_1 x_1^B = p_2(x_2^B - 4).$$

Substituting this into our third first-order condition gives

$$p_1 - p_2(x_2^B - 4) - p_2 x_2^B = 0,$$

and solving for x_2^A gives consumer B's Walrasian demand for good 2,

$$x_2^B = \frac{p_1 + 4p_2}{2p_2}.$$

Finally, plugging this in to our result from above gives consumer B's demand for good 1:

$$p_1 x_1^B = p_2 \left(\frac{p_1 + 4p_2}{2p_2} - 4 \right) \implies x_1^B = \frac{p_1 - 4p_2}{2p_1}.$$

(b) Show that an allocation is Pareto optimal if and only if $x_1^A + x_2^A = 4$.

- When deriving the demands for both consumers, we found two equations for the price ratios (immediately after combining the first and second first-order conditions, for each consumer):

$$\frac{p_1}{p_2} = \frac{x_2^A - 4}{x_1^A} = \frac{x_2^B - 4}{x_1^B}.$$

Using the feasibility conditions,

$$x_1^A + x_1^B = 5,$$
$$x_2^A + x_2^B = 3,$$

we can substitute for x_1^B and x_2^B in our above expression

$$\frac{x_2^A - 4}{x_1^A} = \frac{(3 - x_2^A) - 4}{5 - x_1^A}.$$

Then, solving this expression for x_2^A gives the contract curve

$$x_2^A = 4 - x_1^A \implies x_1^A + x_2^A = 4,$$

and all allocations on the contract curve are Pareto efficient.

(c) Draw the Edgeworth box.

- Since good 2 is a bad, we find that consumer A's utility is increasing as he moves towards the lower right-hand corner of the Edgeworth box, whereas consumer B's utility increases as he moves to the upper left-hand corner of the Edgeworth box, as shown in figure 6.7.

(d) Find the competitive equilibria in this economy (remembering that good 2 is a bad).

- Before starting our analysis, the knowledge that one of the goods is actually a "bad" should give some initial intuition about the price ratio. Since both consumers would prefer to not have good 2 at all, we can anticipate that they would be willing to pay the other consumer to take that good away, implying that $p_2 < 0$. Other than that, the rest of the analysis should be standard. We can substitute the Walrasian demands found in part (a) into the feasibility constraints. Using good 1's feasibility constraint,

$$x_1^A + x_1^B = \frac{4p_1 - p_2}{2p_1} + \frac{p_1 - 4p_2}{2p_1} = 5.$$

Letting good 1 be the numeraire, i.e., setting $p_1 = 1$, we obtain

$$\frac{4 - p_2}{2} + \frac{1 - 4p_2}{2} = 5.$$

Solving for p_2 yields an equilibrium price of $p_2 = -1$.

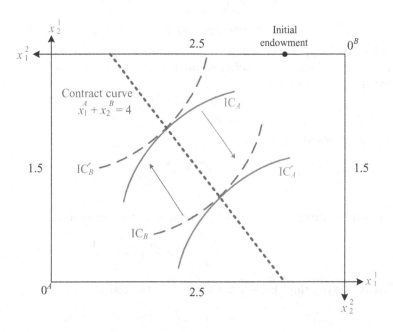

Figure 6.7 Edgeworth box and the contract curve.

- We can substitute all of these prices back into our demands to yield our equilibrium values

$$x_1^A = \frac{4p_1 - p_2}{2p_1} = \frac{5}{2}, \quad x_2^A = \frac{4p_1 + 7p_2}{2p_2} = \frac{3}{2} \quad \text{for consumer } A, \text{ and}$$

$$x_1^B = \frac{p_1 - 4p_2}{2p_1} = \frac{5}{2}, \quad x_2^B = \frac{p_1 + 4p_2}{2p_2} = \frac{3}{2} \quad \text{for consumer } B.$$

(e) What happens to the set of competitive equilibria in the economy if consumer A is given the right to dump her endowment of the second good on consumer B without compensating consumer B?

- If consumer A can dump her endowment of the second good on consumer B without compensating him, the new endowments become $\omega^A = (4, 0)$ and $\omega^B = (1, 3)$. This endowment satisfies the $x_1^A + x_2^A = 4$ Pareto efficiency requirement, and thus neither consumer can do any better through trading without hurting the other consumer. Hence, no trade will take place between consumer A and consumer B. This effect can be seen in figure 6.8.

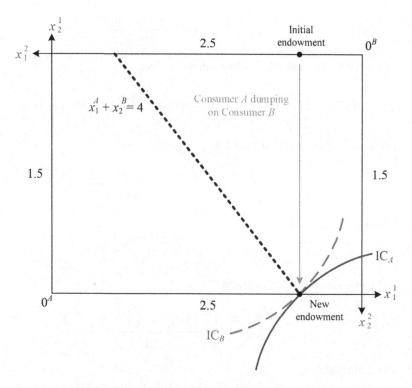

Figure 6.8 WEA when we allow for dumping from consumer A to B.

Exercise #17 — Excess demand in Cobb–Douglas preferences

17. Consider an economy with 2 consumers, A and B, and 2 goods, 1 and 2. The utility function of A is

$$U^A = \gamma \log(x_1^A) + (1 - \gamma) \log(x_2^A),$$

where x_i^A is consumption of good i by A. A has endowments $\omega^A = (\omega_1^A, \omega_2^A) = (2, 1)$. For consumer B,

$$U^B = \gamma \log(x_1^B) + (1 - \gamma) \log(x_2^B)$$

and $\omega^B = (\omega_1^B, \omega_2^B) = (3, 2)$, where $\gamma \in (0, 1)$.

(a) Find the Walrasian demands of consumers A and B.

- The budget constraint of any consumer i, $i = A, B$, is given by

$$p_1 x_1^i + p_2 x_2^i = p_1 \omega_1^i + p_2 \omega_2^i.$$

Solving this for x_2^i yields

$$x_2^i = \frac{p_1 \omega_1^i + p_2 \omega_2^i - p_1 x_1^i}{p_2},$$

and substituting into the utility function gives

$$U^i = \gamma \log(x_1^i) + (1 - \gamma) \log \left(\frac{p_1 \omega_1^i + p_2 \omega_2^i - p_1 x_1^i}{p_2} \right).$$

The first-order condition for x_1^i is

$$\frac{\gamma}{x_1^i} - (1 - \gamma) \frac{p_1}{p_2} \left(\frac{p_2}{p_1 \omega_1^i + p_2 \omega_2^i - p_1 x_1^i} \right) = 0.$$

Solving for x_1^i yields

$$x_1^i = \gamma \left(\frac{p_1 \omega_1^i + p_2 \omega_2^i}{p_1} \right),$$

and using the budget constraint,

$$x_2^i = \frac{p_1 \omega_1^i + p_2 \omega_2^i - p_1 \gamma \left(\frac{p_1 \omega_1^i + p_2 \omega_2^i}{p_1} \right)}{p_2},$$

which simplifies to

$$x_2^i = (1 - \gamma) \left(\frac{p_1 \omega_1^i + p_2 \omega_2^i}{p_2} \right).$$

Lastly, use the values of the endowments to replace ω_1^i and ω_2^i, yielding Walrasian demands

$$x_1^A = \gamma \left(\frac{2p_1 + p_2}{p_1} \right) \qquad x_2^A = (1 - \gamma) \left(\frac{2p_1 + p_2}{p_2} \right)$$

for consumer A, and

$$x_1^B = \gamma \left(\frac{3p_1 + 2p_2}{p_1} \right) \qquad x_2^B = (1 - \gamma) \left(\frac{3p_1 + 2p_2}{p_2} \right)$$

for consumer B.

(b) Choosing good 2 as the numeraire, graph the excess demand for good 1 as a function of p_1.

- If good 2 is the numeraire, then $p_2 = 1$. The excess demand for good 1, $z_1(p_1)$, is defined as

$$z_1(p_1) = x_1^A + x_1^B - \omega_1^A - \omega_1^B.$$

From the Walrasian demands found in part (a), and since $\omega_1^A = 2$ and $\omega_1^B = 3$,

$$z_1(p_1) = \gamma \left(\frac{2p_1 + 1p_2}{p_1} \right) + \gamma \left(\frac{3p_1 + 2p_2}{p_1} \right) - 5,$$

which, considering that $p_2 = 1$ simplifies to

$$z_1(p_1) = \gamma \left(\frac{5p_1 + 3}{p_1} \right) - 5.$$

This is graphed in figure 6.9 for different values of parameter γ. For instance, if $\gamma = 0.5$, the competitive equilibrium price p_1 satisfying $z_1(p_1) = 0$, i.e., that in which $z_1(p_1)$ crosses the horizontal axis, is $p_1 = \$0.6$ whereas when γ increases to $\gamma = 0.75$, the competitive equilibrium price also increases to $p_1 = \$1.8$. Intuitively, parameter γ captures the relative preference for good 1 by both consumers, as the utility function can be alternatively written as a Cobb–Douglas type, $U^i = (x_1^i)^\gamma (x_2^i)^{1-\gamma}$. Hence, a more intense preference for good 1 increases its relative price p_1 in equilibrium.

(c) Calculate the competitive equilibrium allocation. Verify that this is the point where excess demand is zero.

- The demand is equal to supply when excess demand is zero, or

$$z_1(p_1) = \gamma \left(\frac{2p_1 + 1p_2}{p_1} \right) + \gamma \left(\frac{3p_1 + 2p_2}{p_1} \right) - 5 = 0,$$

which, considering that $p_2 = 1$, simplifies to

$$z_1(p_1) = \gamma \left(\frac{5p_1 + 3}{p_1} \right) - 5 = 0.$$

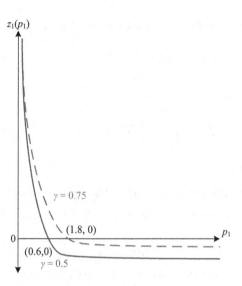

Figure 6.9 Excess demand $z_1(p_1)$.

Solving for p_1 yields an equilibrium price of

$$p_1 = \frac{3}{5}\frac{\gamma}{1-\gamma}.$$

As suggested in part (b), an increase in the parameter reflecting the preference for good 1, γ, increases the relative price ratio (which recall that it is relative to a normalized $p_2 = 1$) in equilibrium, since $\frac{\partial p_1}{\partial \gamma} = \frac{3}{5}\frac{1}{(1-\gamma)^2} > 0$, and is depicted in figure 6.10.

Exercise #19 — Excess demand functions: homogeneity and Walras' law

19. Excess demand functions must satisfy homogeneity of degree zero in prices, that is, increasing all prices by a common factor $\lambda > 0$ does not affect the excess demand function, $z_k(\mathbf{p}) = z_k(\lambda\mathbf{p})$ for all $\lambda > 0$; and Walras' law, $\mathbf{p} \cdot z(\mathbf{p}) = 0$. Check if the following functions satisfy these two properties, and thus are/are not legitimate excess demand functions.

   (a) $z_1(\mathbf{p}) = -p_2 + \frac{10}{p_1}$, $z_2(\mathbf{p}) = p_1$, and $z_3(\mathbf{p}) = -\frac{10}{p_3}$.

   - This is not a legitimate excess demand function since it does not satisfy homogeneity of degree zero in prices. In particular,

$$z_1(\lambda\mathbf{p}) = -\lambda p_2 + \frac{10}{\lambda p_1} \neq z_1(\mathbf{p}).$$

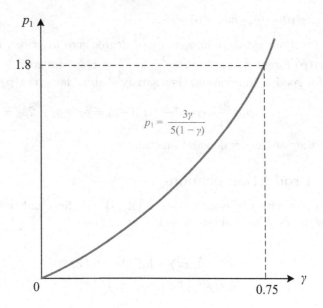

Figure 6.10 Equilibrium price p_1 as a function of γ.

However, it satisfies Walras' law since

$$p_1 \cdot \left(-p_2 + \frac{10}{p_1}\right) + p_2 \cdot p_1 + p_3 \cdot \left(-\frac{10}{p_3}\right) = p_1 p_2 + 10 - p_1 p_2 - 10 = 0.$$

(b) $z_1(\mathbf{p}) = \frac{p_2 + p_3}{p_1}$, $z_2(\mathbf{p}) = \frac{p_1 + p_3}{p_2}$, and $z_3(\mathbf{p}) = \frac{p_1 + p_2}{p_3}$.

- These functions satisfy homogeneity of degree zero in prices. In particular, given their symmetry, $z_k(\mathbf{p}) = \frac{p_i + p_j}{p_k}$, where $i \neq j \neq k$ and $i, j, k = \{1, 2, 3\}$. Then, increasing all prices by the same factor λ yields

$$z_k(\lambda \mathbf{p}) = \frac{\lambda p_i + \lambda p_j}{\lambda p_k} = \frac{\lambda (p_i + p_j)}{\lambda p_k} = \frac{p_i + p_j}{p_k} = z_k(\mathbf{p}).$$

However, they do not satisfy Walras' law and are thus not legitimate excess demand functions. In order to show this, multiply them by their respective prices, which yields

$$\sum_{i=1}^{3} p_i z_i(\mathbf{p}) = p_1 \cdot \frac{p_2 + p_3}{p_1} + p_2 \cdot \frac{p_1 + p_3}{p_2} + p_3 \cdot \frac{p_1 + p_2}{p_3}$$

$$= (p_2 + p_3) + (p_1 + p_3) + (p_1 + p_2) = 2p_1 + 2p_2 + 2p_3 \neq 0.$$

(c) $z_1(\mathbf{p}) = \frac{p_3}{p_1}$, $z_2(\mathbf{p}) = \frac{p_3}{p_2}$, and $z_3(\mathbf{p}) = -2$.

- These functions satisfy homogeneity of degree zero in prices, i.e., $z_1(\lambda\mathbf{p}) = \frac{\lambda p_3}{\lambda p_1} = \frac{p_3}{p_1} = z_1(\mathbf{p})$ for good 1, $z_2(\lambda\mathbf{p}) = \frac{\lambda p_3}{\lambda p_2} = \frac{p_3}{p_2} = z_2(\mathbf{p})$ for good 2, and $z_3(\lambda\mathbf{p}) = -2 = z_3(\mathbf{p})$ for good 3. In addition, they satisfy Walras' law, $\mathbf{p} \cdot z(\mathbf{p}) = 0$, since

$$p_1 \cdot \frac{p_3}{p_1} + p_2 \cdot \frac{p_3}{p_2} + p_3(-2) = p_3 + p_3 - 2p_3 = 0.$$

Hence, they are excess demand functions.

Exercise #21 — Production economy

21. Consider an economy with two consumers $i = \{A, B\}$, one firm and two goods $l = 1, 2$. The individual endowments of individuals A and B are $\omega^A = \omega^B = (\frac{1}{2}, \frac{1}{2})$. The utility functions are

$$u^A(x_1^A, x_2^A) = \ln(x_1^A) + \ln(x_2^A),$$
$$u^B(x_1^B, x_2^B) = (x_1^B)^{\frac{1}{4}}(x_2^B)^{\frac{3}{4}}.$$

The firm produces good 2 using good 1 as input, the production function is $y_2 = \sqrt{y_1}$. The consumer B owns the firm (denote π the firm's profit). Good 2 is the numeraire good (i.e., $p_2 = 1$).

(a) Determine the demand for good 1 of the consumers and the firm.

- *Consumer A.* Starting with consumer A's utility maximization problem

$$\max_{x_1^A, x_2^A} \ln(x_1^A) + \ln(x_2^A) + \lambda^A \left[p_1 \left(\frac{1}{2} \right) + p_2 \left(\frac{1}{2} \right) - p_1 x_1^A - p_2 x_2^A \right],$$

with first-order conditions

$$\frac{1}{x_1^A} - \lambda^A p_1 = 0,$$

$$\frac{1}{x_2^A} - \lambda^A p_2 = 0,$$

$$p_1 \left(\frac{1}{2} \right) + p_2 \left(\frac{1}{2} \right) + \pi - p_1 x_1^A - p_2 x_2^A = 0.$$

Combining and rearranging the first two FOCs yields

$$p_1 x_1^A = p_2 x_2^A.$$

Substituting this into the third FOC yields consumer A's demand for good 1:

$$p_1 \left(\frac{1}{2} \right) + p_2 \left(\frac{1}{2} \right) - 2p_1 x_1^A = 0 \implies x_1^A = \frac{p_1 + p_2}{4p_1},$$

and plugging this value back into $p_1 x_1^A = p_2 x_2^A$ yields consumer A's demand for good 2:

$$p_1 \left(\frac{p_1 + p_2}{4p_1} \right) = p_2 x_2^A \implies x_2^A = \frac{p_1 + p_2}{4p_2}.$$

- *Consumer B.* Next, we perform the same task for consumer B. His utility maximization problem is

$$\max_{x_1^B, x_2^B} \; (x_1^B)^{\frac{1}{4}} (x_2^B)^{\frac{3}{4}} + \lambda^B \left[p_1 \left(\frac{1}{2} \right) + p_2 \left(\frac{1}{2} \right) + \pi - p_1 x_1^B - p_2 x_2^B \right],$$

with first-order conditions

$$\frac{1}{4} (x_1^B)^{-\frac{3}{4}} (x_2^B)^{\frac{3}{4}} - \lambda^A p_1 = 0,$$

$$\frac{3}{4} (x_1^B)^{\frac{1}{4}} (x_2^B)^{-\frac{1}{4}} - \lambda^A p_2 = 0,$$

$$p_1 \left(\frac{1}{2} \right) + p_2 \left(\frac{1}{2} \right) - p_1 x_1^A - p_2 x_2^A = 0.$$

Combining and rearranging the first two FOCs yields

$$3p_1 x_1^B = p_2 x_2^B.$$

Substituting this into the third FOC yields consumer B's demand for good 1:

$$p_1 \left(\frac{1}{2} \right) + p_2 \left(\frac{1}{2} \right) + \pi - 4p_1 x_1^B = 0 \implies x_1^B = \frac{p_1 + p_2 + 2\pi}{8p_1},$$

and plugging this value back into $3p_1 x_1^B = p_2 x_2^B$ yields consumer B's demand for good 2:

$$3p_1 \left(\frac{p_1 + p_2 + 2\pi}{8p_1} \right) = p_2 x_2^B \implies x_2^B = \frac{3 (p_1 + p_2 + 2\pi)}{8p_2}.$$

- *Firm.* Lastly, we find the firm's demand for good 1 by setting up its profit maximization problem:

$$\max_{y_1, y_2} \; p_2 y_2 - p_1 y_1$$
$$\text{subject to } y_2 = \sqrt{y_1}.$$

Substituting the constraint, we obtain an unconstrained maximization problem

$$\max_{y_1} \; p_2 \sqrt{y_1} - p_1 y_1,$$

and taking first-order conditions with respect to y_1 yields the firm's demand for good 1:

$$\frac{p_2}{2\sqrt{y_1}} - p_1 = 0 \implies y_1 = \frac{p_2^2}{4p_1^2}.$$

Plugging this value back into $y_2 = \sqrt{y_1}$ yields the firm's supply of good 2:

$$y_2 = \sqrt{\frac{p_2^2}{4p_1^2}} = \frac{p_2}{2p_1}.$$

This also yields a value for the firm's profits, π:

$$\pi = p_2 y_2 - p_1 y_1 = p_2 \frac{p_2}{2p_1} - p_1 \frac{p_2^2}{4p_1^2} = \frac{p_2^2}{4p_1}.$$

(b) Show that there is a unique equilibrium price p_1.

- The market-clearing condition for good 1 is

$$x_1^A + x_1^B + y_1 = 1;$$

substituting our demands from part (a) gives

$$\frac{p_1 + p_2}{4p_1} + \frac{p_1 + p_2 + 2\pi}{8p_1} + \frac{p_2^2}{4p_1^2} = 1$$

Substituting our profit level, $\pi = \frac{p_2^2}{4p_1}$, our numeraire ($p_2 = 1$), and rearranging gives

$$3p_1 + \frac{5}{2} = 5p_1^2.$$

Solving for p_1 yields two solutions, only one of which is positive,

$$p_1 = \frac{3 + \sqrt{59}}{10} \approx 1.068.$$

Hence, the equilibrium price ratio is $p_1 \simeq 1.068$.

(c) Assume that the production function is now $y_2 = y_1$, and thus satisfies constant returns to scale. Determine the equilibrium price and allocation (i.e., the WEA).

- Recall that the isoprofit line $\pi = p_2 y_2 - p_1 y_1$ can be rewritten as $y_2 = \frac{\pi}{p_2} + \frac{p_1}{p_2} y_1$. Since the production function $y_2 = y_1$ satisfies constant returns to scale, output decisions are $y_2 = y_1 = +\infty$ if $p_2 > p_1$, $y_2 = y_1 = 0$ if $p_2 < p_1$, or any point in the line $y_2 = y_1$ if $p_2 = p_1$; as depicted in figure 6.11. (See the chapter on production theory for more details on this type of technology.)

- Let us solve for the equilibrium.

  - In the case $p_2 > p_1$, $y_1 = +\infty$ so that the market for good 1 cannot clear, i.e., $z_1(p) \neq 0$. There is no equilibrium in this case.

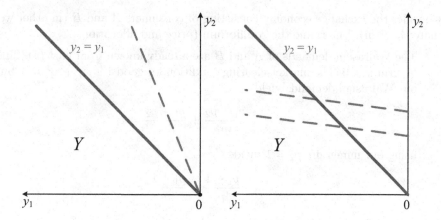

Figure 6.11 Corner solution for infinite production plan.

– In the case $p_2 < p_1$, $y_1 = 0$ (and $\pi = 0$). The market-clearing condition for good 1 becomes $x_1^A + x_1^B = 1$. Substituting the demands from part (a), and the numeraire yields

$$\frac{p_1 + 1}{4p_1} + \frac{p_1 + 1}{8p_1} + 0 = 1,$$

which, solving for p_1 gives $p_1 = \frac{3}{5}$. However, this result entails

$$p_1 = \frac{3}{5} < 1 = p_2,$$

which contradicts our initial assumption of $p_2 < p_1$. Hence, there is no equilibrium in this case either.

– In this case $p_2 = p_1$, and the demands for good 1 of both consumers A and B reduce to $x_1^A = \frac{p_1 + p_1}{4p_1} = \frac{2p_1}{4p_1} = \frac{1}{2}$ and $x_2^B = \frac{p_1 + p_1}{8p_1} = \frac{2p_1}{8p_1} = \frac{1}{4}$ (given that $\pi = 0$, whatever y_1 is). The market-clearing condition for good 1, $x_1^A + x_1^B + y_1 = 1$, thus becomes $\frac{1}{2} + \frac{1}{4} + y_1 = 1$. Solving for y_1, this implies that $y_1 = \frac{1}{4} \geq 0$. Hence, there is only one equilibrium. Using $p_1 = p_2$, i.e., $\frac{p_1}{p_2} = 1$, and $x_1^A = \frac{1}{2}$ and $x_1^B = \frac{1}{4}$, we can find the remaining elements of the WEA,

$$x_2^A = \frac{p_1 + p_1}{4p_1} = \frac{1}{2} \quad \text{and} \quad x_2^B = \frac{3(p_1 + p_1)}{8p_1} = \frac{3}{4},$$

and then $y_2 = y_1 = \frac{1}{4}$.

(d) Consider the exchange economy consisting of consumers A and B (in other words, eliminate the firm). Determine the equilibrium (price and allocation).

- The Walrasian demands of A and B are already known from part (a). Since there is no firm $\pi = 0$. The market-clearing condition for good 1 is $x_1^A + x_1^B = 1$. Substituting our Walrasian demands yields

$$\frac{p_1 + p_2}{4p_1} + \frac{p_1 + p_2}{8p_1} = 1;$$

using our numeraire $p_2 = 1$ yields

$$\frac{p_1 + 1}{4p_1} + \frac{p_1 + 1}{8p_1} = 1.$$

Solving for p_1 yields $p_1 = \frac{3}{5}$. Substituting this back into our demand functions yields our equilibrium quantities $x_1^A = \frac{2}{3}$, $x_2^A = \frac{2}{5}$, $x_1^B = \frac{1}{3}$, and $x_2^B = \frac{3}{5}$

Exercise #23 — Pareto and efficient allocations in the household

23. Consider an economy with two individuals, Ann and Bartholomew, each with utility function

$$u^A(x^A, l^A) = x^A l^A \quad \text{and} \quad u^B(x^B, l^B) = (x^B)^2 l^B,$$

where x denotes a consumption good while l represents hours of leisure. In addition, Ann owns the only firm in this economy and has 20 hours to dedicate to either work (L^A) or leisure (l^A), $20 = L^A + l^A$; whereas Bartholomew does not own any assets in this economy (poor husband!), but has 30 hours to spend, $30 = L^B + l^B$. Ann's firm produces units of good x with labor hours using a Cobb–Douglas production technology $x = \sqrt{L}$, where $L \equiv L^A + L^B$.

(a) Find the set of PEAs.

- Allocations (x^A, l^A) and (x^B, l^B) for consumers and (x, L) for the firm are efficient if they solve

$$\max_{x^A, l^A, x^B, l^B, x, L} x^A l^A,$$

$$\text{subject to } (x^B)^2 l^B \geq \bar{u}^B,$$

$$\left. \begin{array}{c} x^A + x^B \leq x \\ l^A + l^B + L \leq 20 + 30 \end{array} \right\} \text{ feasibility,}$$

$$x \leq \sqrt{L} \quad \text{(technological feasibility).}$$

The Lagrangian of the above maximization problem is

$$\mathcal{L} = x^A l^A + \lambda_1 \left[(x^B)^2 l^B - \bar{u}^B \right] - \lambda_2 \left[x^A + x^B - x \right]$$
$$- \lambda_3 \left[l^A + l^B + L - 50 \right] - \lambda_4 \left[x - \sqrt{L} \right].$$

Before taking FOCs, note that both consumers' utility functions are strictly increasing and preferences are strictly convex, and so is the firm's technology, thus yielding interior solutions. Taking FOCs yields

$$\frac{\partial \mathcal{L}}{\partial x^A} = l^A - \lambda_2 = 0, \qquad \frac{\partial \mathcal{L}}{\partial l^A} = x^A - \lambda_3 = 0, \tag{1}$$

$$\frac{\partial \mathcal{L}}{\partial x^B} = 2\lambda_1 x^B l^B - \lambda_2 = 0, \qquad \frac{\partial \mathcal{L}}{\partial l^B} = \lambda_1 (x^B)^2 - \lambda_3 = 0, \tag{2}$$

$$\frac{\partial \mathcal{L}}{\partial x} = \lambda_2 - \lambda_4 = 0, \qquad \frac{\partial \mathcal{L}}{\partial L} = -\lambda_3 + \frac{1}{2}\lambda_4 \frac{1}{\sqrt{L}} = 0, \tag{3}$$

and the four binding constraints. Dividing the two expressions in (1), we obtain

$$\frac{l^A}{x^A} = \frac{\lambda_2}{\lambda_3}. \tag{4}$$

Operating similarly with the two expressions in (2) yields

$$\frac{2l^B}{x^B} = \frac{\lambda_2}{\lambda_3}. \tag{5}$$

and solving for λ_4 in the two expressions in (3),

$$2\sqrt{L} = \frac{\lambda_2}{\lambda_3}. \tag{6}$$

Combining (4)–(6) yields a double equality

$$\underbrace{\frac{l^A}{x^A}}_{MRS_{l,x}^A} = \underbrace{\frac{2l^B}{x^B}}_{MRS_{l,x}^B} = \underbrace{2\sqrt{L}}_{MRTS_{l,x}}. \tag{7}$$

Hence, a PEA requires that the marginal rate of substitution between the consumption good and leisure coincides across consumers, and, in turn, it must also coincide with the rate at which the firm can transform labor into the consumption good. Condition (7) together with the feasibility conditions in the four binding constraints, characterize the set of PEAs.

(b) Find the set of WEAs.

- A price vector for the single good in the economy, x, and the single input, labor, i.e., (p, w), and an allocation $\{(x^A, l^A), (x^B, l^B), (x, L)\}$ are a WEA if and only if

  1. The price vector (p, w) satisfies

$$x^A(p, w) + x^B(p, w) = x(p, w)$$

and

$$l^A(p, w) + l^B(p, w) + L(p, w) = 50.$$

2. (x^i, l^i) maximizes individual i's UMP, and (x, L) maximizes the firm's PMP. Let us seperately solve UMP_A, UMP_B, and PMP.

- UMP_A. Consumer A solves

$$\max_{x^A, l^A \geq 0} \quad x^A l^A$$

subject to $px^A = \pi + w(20 - l^A)$,

which indicates that Ann can use the profits of the firm she owns, π, and the salary of working $L^A = 20 - l^A$ hours (i.e., the hours she does not dedicate to leisure) to purchase units of good x at a price p. The Lagrangian associated to this UMP_A is

$$\mathcal{L} = x^A l^A - \lambda \left[px^A - \pi - w(20 - l^A) \right].$$

Taking FOCs, we obtain

$$\frac{\partial \mathcal{L}}{\partial x^A} = l^A - p\lambda = 0,$$

$$\frac{\partial \mathcal{L}}{\partial l^A} = x^A - w\lambda = 0,$$

which simplify to

$$\frac{l^A}{x^A} = \frac{p}{w}, \text{ i.e., } MRS_{x,l}^A = \text{ price ratio} \qquad (8)$$

and consumer A's budget line

$$px^A = \pi + w(20 - l^A).$$

Hence, A's demand for good x is

$$px^A = \pi + w \left(20 - \underbrace{\frac{p}{w} x^A}_{l^A} \right),$$

which, solving for x^A, yields

$$x^A = \frac{\pi + 20w}{2p}.$$

Therefore, her labor supply is

$$l^A = \frac{p}{w} x^A = \frac{p}{w} \left(\frac{\pi + 20w}{2p} \right) = \frac{\pi + 20w}{2w}.$$

- UMP_B. Consumer B solves

$$\max_{x^B, l^B \geq 0} \quad (x^B)^2 l^B$$

subject to $px^B = w(30 - l^B)$,

where consumer B has 30 hours at his disposal, but does not enjoy firm profits. The Lagrangian associated to UMP$_B$ is

$$\mathcal{L} = (x^B)^2 l^B - \lambda \left[px^B - w(30 - l^B) \right].$$

Taking FOCs, we obtain

$$\frac{\partial \mathcal{L}}{\partial x^B} = 2x^B l^B - p\lambda = 0,$$

$$\frac{\partial \mathcal{L}}{\partial l^B} = (x^B)^2 - w\lambda = 0,$$

which simplify to

$$\frac{2l^B}{x^B} = \frac{p}{w}, \text{ i.e., } MRS^B_{x,l} = \text{ price ratio,} \tag{9}$$

and his budget line

$$px^B = w(30 - l^B).$$

Hence, consumer B's demand for good x is

$$px^B = w \left(30 - \underbrace{\frac{p}{2w}x^B}_{l^B} \right),$$

which, solving for x^B yields

$$x^B = \frac{20w}{p}.$$

Therefore, his labor supply is

$$l^B = \frac{p}{2w}x^B = \frac{p}{2w}\left(\frac{20w}{p}\right) = 10.$$

- *PMP.* Finally, the firm chooses q and L to solve

$$\max_{q,L \geq 0} \quad pq - wL$$

$$\text{subject to } q \leq \sqrt{L}.$$

However, since the constraint will bind at the optimum, i.e., $q = \sqrt{L}$ we can rewrite the PMP as an unconstrained maximization problem with a single choice variable

$$\max_{L} \quad p\sqrt{L} - wL.$$

Taking FOCs with respect to L yields

$$p\frac{1}{2}\frac{1}{\sqrt{L}} - w = 0, \text{ or } 2\sqrt{L} = \frac{p}{w}, \tag{10}$$

i.e., the marginal rate at which labor can get transformed into units of the consumption good must coincide with the price ratio. Therefore, for a WEA, we need conditions (8)–(10) to hold. In particular, conditions (8) and (9) imply

$$\frac{l^A}{x^A} = \frac{2l^B}{x^B} = \frac{p}{w},$$

i.e., $MRS^A_{x,l} = MRS^B_{x,l} = \frac{p}{w}$; and from condition (10),

$$\frac{l^A}{x^A} = \frac{2l^B}{x^B} = 2\sqrt{L}, \tag{11}$$

i.e., $MRS^A_{x,l} = MRS^B_{x,l} = MRTS_{x,l}$.

- Putting everything together, we can start by combining our feasibility and technological feasibility conditions to obtain

$$x^A + x^B = \sqrt{L}.$$

Multiplying both sides by 2,

$$2(x^A + x^B) = 2\sqrt{L}.$$

allows us to make a substitution from equation (11). Plugging in the second equality from equation (11) yields

$$2(x^A + x^B) = \frac{2l^B}{x^B} = \frac{p}{w}$$

and plugging in the Walrasian demands for x^A and x^B gives

$$2\left(\frac{\pi + 20w}{2p} + \frac{20w}{p}\right) = \frac{p}{w}.$$

Let the price of labor, w, serve as the numeraire, i.e., $w = 1$, and solving the above equation for p yields

$$p = \sqrt{\pi + 60}.$$

Next, using our feasibility constraint for labor,

$$l^A + l^B + L = 50,$$

and since $l^B = 10$,

$$L = 40 - l^A,$$

we can use this equation, and our equation for prices to solve for the profit level, π:

$$\pi = p\sqrt{L} - L = \sqrt{\pi + 60}\sqrt{40 - \underbrace{\frac{\pi + 20}{2}}_{l_A} - \left(40 - \frac{\pi + 20}{2}\right)}.$$

Simplifying,

$$\pi + 60 = 2\sqrt{(\pi + 60)\left(30 - \frac{\pi}{2}\right)}.$$

Squaring both sides,

$$(\pi + 60)^2 = 4(\pi + 60)\left(30 - \frac{\pi}{2}\right),$$

and solving for π yields a profit of $\pi = 20$. Plugging this back into our equation for prices gives

$$p = \sqrt{\pi + 60} = \sqrt{80} \approx 8.94,$$

and substituting this value into the Walrasian demands gives the unique WEA $\{(x^A, l^A), (x^B, l^B), (x, L)\} = \{(2.23, 20), (2.23, 10), (4.47, 20)\}$ with price vector $(p, w) = (8.94, 1)$ and equilibrium profits of $\pi = 20$.

(c) Is the WEA you found in part (b) part of the set of PEAs?

- We only need to check that the WEA from part (b) (1) satisfies condition (7), i.e., $MRS_{x,l}^A = MRS_{x,l}^B = MRTS_{x,l}$, which does as described at the end of the firm's PMP, and (2) satisfies the four feasibility conditions, that is,

$$\frac{l^A}{x^A} = \frac{2l^B}{x^B} = 2\sqrt{L},$$

$$(x^B)^2 l^B \geq \bar{u}^B = 0,$$

$$x^A + x^B = x,$$

$$l^A + l^B + L = 50,$$

$$q = \sqrt{L}.$$

For the first equation, plugging in our values yields $\frac{20}{2.23} = \frac{2 \cdot 10}{2.23} = 2\sqrt{20}$. For the second, consumer B reaches a utility level of $(2.23)^2 * 10 = 50 > 0$. For the third–fifth equations, we find that they hold by definition due to being used to find the WEA in part (b).

Exercise #25 — Effect of distortionary taxes

25. Consider an economy with two individuals $i = \{A, B\}$, each with identical Cobb–Douglas utility function $u(x_1^i, x_2^i) = x_1^i x_2^i$, and initial endowments $e_A = (200, 100)$ and $e_B = (100, 200)$.

(a) Find the Pareto optimal allocation (PEA).

- At the PEA we need that both individuals' MRS coincide, that is, $MRS_{1,2}^A = MRS_{1,2}^B$, or

$$\frac{x_2^A}{x_1^A} = \frac{x_2^B}{x_1^B}.$$

From here, we can use our two feasibility conditions,

$$x_1^A + x_1^B = 300 \implies x_1^B = 300 - x_1^A,$$
$$x_2^A + x_2^B = 300 \implies x_2^B = 300 - x_2^A,$$

and substitute them into our above equation to obtain

$$\frac{x_2^A}{x_1^A} = \frac{300 - x_2^A}{300 - x_1^A}.$$

Simplifying, we are able to obtain the contract curve,

$$x_1^A = x_2^A.$$

Recall that any allocation that lies on the contract curve, and provides a weakly higher utility than the initial allocation for each individual is Pareto efficient. This allows us to define our set of Pareto efficient allocations in figure 6.12.

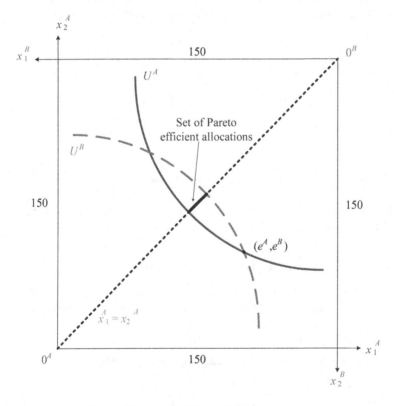

Figure 6.12 Set of PEAs.

In particular, since the utility from the initial bundle for every individual i is $x_1^i x_2^i = 20000$, and $x_1^i = x_2^i$ must hold at the point at which the indifference curve crosses the contract curve, we have that the crossing points satisfy $x_1^i = x_2^i = \sqrt{20000} \simeq 141.42$. Therefore, the PEA is

$$\left\{ (x_1^i, x_2^i) : x_1^i = x_2^i \text{ and } x_j^i \geq \sqrt{20000} \right\}$$

for every good $j = \{1, 2\}$ and every individual $i = \{A, B\}$.

(b) Find the WEA. [For simplicity, you can assume $p_1 = p_2 = 1$.]

- Starting with consumer A's utility maximization problem,

$$\max_{x_1^A, x_2^A} \quad x_1^A x_2^A$$

$$\text{subject to} \quad p_1 x_1^A + p_2 x_2^A = p_1(200) + p_2(100)$$

with first-order conditions

$$x_2^A - \lambda^A p_1 = 0,$$
$$x_1^A - \lambda^A p_2 = 0,$$
$$p_1 x_1^A + p_2 x_2^A = p_1(200) + p_2(100).$$

We can rearrange, then divide the first first-order condition by the second to obtain

$$\frac{p_1}{p_2} = \frac{x_2^A}{x_1^A}, \text{ or } 1 = \frac{x_2^A}{x_1^A},$$

since $p_1 = p_2 = 1$. Using consumer A's third first-order condition (the budget constraint), we have

$$x_1^A + x_2^A = 200 + 100,$$

and substituting,

$$2x_1^A = 300 \implies x_1^{A,*} = 150.$$

From our solution in part (a),

$$x_2^{A,*} = x_1^{A,*} = 150,$$

- Finally, using the feasibility conditions, we obtain the Walrasian demands for consumer B

$$x_1^{B,*} = 300 - x_1^{A,*} = 150,$$
$$x_2^{B,*} = 300 - x_2^{A,*} = 150,$$

which is part of the set of PEAs since $x_1^i = x_2^i$ and $x_j^i \geq \sqrt{20000} \simeq 141.42$ holds for both consumers and both goods.

(c) Assume that the government sets a tax t on purchases of good 1, which is refunded to the consumers as a lump sum payment, $T^i = tx_1^i$. Find the post-tax WEA, and compare it with your results in part (b).

- Starting with consumer A's utility maximization problem,

$$\max_{x_1^A, x_2^A} x_1^A x_2^A$$

subject to $(p_1 + t)x_1^A + p_2 x_2^A = p_1(200) + p_2(100) + T^A$

with first-order conditions

$$x_2^A - \lambda^A(p_1 + t) = 0,$$
$$x_1^A - \lambda^A p_2 = 0,$$
$$(p_1 + t)x_1^A + p_2 x_2^A = p_1(200) + p_2(100) + T^A.$$

We can rearrange, then divide the first first-order condition by the second to obtain

$$\frac{p_1 + t}{p_2} = \frac{x_2^A}{x_1^A}, \text{ or } 1 + t = \frac{x_2^A}{x_1^A}.$$

Using consumer A's third first-order condition (the budget constraint), we have

$$(1 + t)x_1^A + x_2^A = 200 + 100 + T^A,$$

and substituting,

$$2x_1^A = (1 - t)200 + 100 + tx_1^A = 300 - 200t + tx_1^A$$
$$\implies x_1^{A,*} = \frac{300 - 200t}{2 - t}.$$

From our solution in part (a),

$$x_2^{A,*} = x_1^{A,*} = \frac{300 - 200t}{2 - t},$$

and using the feasibility conditions,

$$x_1^{B,*} = 300 - x_1^{A,*} = \frac{300 - 100t}{2 - t},$$
$$x_2^{B,*} = 300 - x_2^{A,*} = \frac{300 - 100t}{2 - t}.$$

(d) Show that the WEA when taxes are absent in part (b) is efficient, whereas the WEA when taxes are present found in part (c) is not necessarily efficient for all values of t.

- The WEA when taxes are absent in part (b) lies on the contract curve and in the Pareto lens as described at the end of part (b). In particular, the WEA without taxes $\left(x_1^A, x_2^A; x_1^B, x_2^B\right) = (150, 150; 150, 150)$ satisfies $x_1^i = x_2^i$ and $x_j^i \geq \sqrt{20000} \simeq 141.42$ for both consumers and for both goods.

- The WEA when taxes are present in part (c) also lies on the contract curve by definition. However, for certain values of t, consumer A would prefer to consume his initial allocation rather than trade at all. For example, when $t = 0$, we obtain the same allocation as in part (b), but if $t = 1$, we obtain the equilibrium allocation $(x_1^A, x_2^A; x_1^B, x_2^B) = (100, 100, 200, 200)$. This would result in individual A receiving a utility of $100 * 100 = 10000$, which is lower than the utility they could receive by consuming their original bundle, 20000. Figure 6.13 shows the range of WEAs, where only those that lie above the U^A curve are Pareto efficient. We can solve for the cutoff value of t that guarantees that the WEA with taxes lies on the lens of

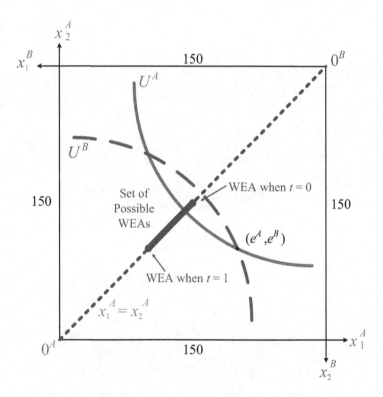

Figure 6.13 WEAs with and without taxes.

Pareto efficient allocations, i.e., it provides a weakly higher utility level than his initial allocation allocation

$$\left(\frac{300 - 200t}{2 - t} \right) \left(\frac{300 - 200t}{2 - t} \right) \geq 20000.$$

Solving this expression for t yields $t \leq 0.293$. Thus, only when the tax is sufficiently low, trade will take place when taxes are present.

Chapter 7 — Monopoly

Summary This chapter first analyzes monopoly pricing under relatively general demand and cost functions, and afterward explores the Lerner index of market power and how to design optimal subsidies that induce the monopolist firm to voluntarily produce the socially optimal level of output. We then consider a monopolist selling two goods that can be complements or substitutes of one another, thus affecting the profit-maximizing production of each of them. We next examine the trade-off that a monopolist faces when producing a durable good: lease the good to customers or directly sell it? Exercises 5 and 6 also explore a similar trade-off where, in particular, the monopolist faces two types of customers (with high and low demand for the good), and needs to decide whether to sell to all customers at a relatively low price or to some of them at a higher price. Exercise 7 extends our analysis to settings in which the monopolist cannot distinguish between each type of customer, and practices second-degree price discrimination, thus offering a menu of price-quantity pairs in order for each type of consumer to self-select the pair intended for him. We then study the production decisions of a monopolist operating at multiple plants, each with different costs, and how the firm optimally distributes its overall production across each plant. Exercise 9 examines a setting where the monopolist can reduce its costs by incurring an investment in a more advanced technology. We then analyze the monopolist's optimal investment and production decisions and compare them with those a social planner would select. In a similar vein, exercise 10 studies learning-by-doing in a monopoly market, where a monopolist production today decreases its future marginal costs, and how the monopolist's production differs from the social planner's. We also examine the production decisions of a monopolist which can benefit from intertermporal network effects in demand. Finally, the chapter considers a natural monopoly, its production decision if left unregulated, and its output level when regulatory authorities allow the monopolist to charge different prices.

Exercise #1 — Monopoly with linear inverse demand

1. Consider a monopolist facing a linear inverse demand curve $p(q) = a - bq$, with cost function $C(q) = F + cq$, where F denotes its fixed costs and c represents the monopolist's (constant) marginal cost and $a > c$.

   (a) Find the monopolist's profit-maximizing output q^m. Given output q^m, what is the market price?

   - The monopolist chooses the output level q that solves

     $$\max_{q} \ (a - bq)q - (F + cq).$$

     Taking first-order conditions with respect to q, we obtain

     $$a - 2bq - c \leq 0,$$

which in the case of interior solutions simplifies to

$$a - 2bq = c.$$

As a remark, note that the left-hand side represents the monopolist's marginal revenue from increasing its production in one unit, while the right-hand side denotes its marginal costs from such increase in production. Solving for q yields a profit-maximizing output of

$$q^m = \frac{a - c}{2b}.$$

- Plugging this output level q^m into the inverse demand function, yields a monopoly price of

$$p^m = a - b\frac{a - c}{2b} = \frac{2a - a + c}{2} = \frac{a + c}{2}.$$

(b) Find the socially optimal output level, q^*. Is it larger or smaller than the profit-maximizing output, q^m, that you found in part (a)?

- At the social optimum, we have that $p(q) = c$, i.e., $a - bq = c$. Solving for q yields a socially optimal output q^* of

$$q^* = \frac{a - c}{b},$$

which is larger than the monopolist's profit-maximizing output q^m. In particular, for this parametric specification with a linear demand and constant marginal costs, $q^* = 2q^m$.

Exercise #3 — Subsidies to monopolists

3. Assume that Alaska Airlines is a monopolist in the route Pullman-Seattle. Washington State Legislature would like to design a policy that induces Alaska Airlines to voluntarily produce an efficient output level. If the firm faces an inverse demand function $p(q)$ with $p'(q) < 0$ and marginal costs $c'(q) > 0$ for all q, show that such a policy must be a subsidy, and determine the exact amount of the subsidy.

- Let t be the tax/subsidy per unit of output. Then the monopolist maximizes

$$\max_{q \geq 0} p(q)q - c(q) - tq,$$

where, at this point, for generality we allow t to be positive (for taxes) or negative (for subsidies). Taking first-order condition with respect to q yields

$$p'(q)q + p(q) - c'(q) - t \leq 0, \text{ with equality if } q > 0.$$

Solving for t (and assuming an interior solution) we obtain

$$t = p'(q)q + p(q) - c'(q). \tag{1}$$

Since we seek to induce an efficient outcome, the monopolist must choose a level of output q that satisfies $p(q) = c'(q)$. This implies that the tax must be $t = p'(q)q$, so that the monopolist's profit-maximizing condition (1) becomes

$$\underbrace{p'(q)q}_{t} = p'(q)q + p(q) - c'(q),$$

which simplifies into the efficient outcome condition

$$p(q) = c'(q).$$

However, we know that $t = p'(q)q < 0$ since $p'(q) < 0$. Therefore, the tax that the government imposes on the monopoly is actually a "negative tax," i.e., a subsidy. Intuitively, the government must subsidize the monopolist in order to induce a larger level of production.

- *Parametric example.* Consider, for instance, that the inverse demand the firm faces is $p(q) = a - bq$ and that the cost function is $c(p) = F + cq$, where F denotes a fixed cost, where $a > c > 0$. The optimal output level q^* in this context satisfies $p(q) = c'(q)$, or $a - bq^* = c$, which yields an output level of $q^* = \frac{a-c}{b}$. In contrast, the monopolist produces $q^m = \frac{a-c}{2b}$. Therefore, the subsidy would need to be

$$t = p'(q^*)q^* = -b\frac{a-c}{b} = c - a,$$

which is a negative tax since $a > c > 0$ holds by definition. Alternatively, a subsidy of $a - c$ provides the monopolist with the incentives to produce the socially optimal output $q^* = \frac{a-c}{b}$. Indeed, if we add this subsidy into the monopolist's profit-maximization problem, we obtain

$$\max_{q \geq 0} p(q)q - c(q) + (a - c)q.$$

Taking first-order conditions with respect to q, yields

$$a - 2bq^m - c + (a - c) = 0,$$

which further simplifies to $a - c = bq^m$. Solving for q, we obtain a monopoly output of $q^m = \frac{a-c}{b}$, which exactly coincides with the socially optimal output $q^* = \frac{a-c}{b}$ the regulator sought to induce.

Exercise #5 — Monopoly with durable goods: leasing versus selling

5. Consider a two-period game where a monopolistic firm wants to sell a durable good, such as land.[1] The durable good will last only two periods, and after that it will become obsolete.

---

[1]This exercise is based on the seminal article by Coase (1972).

There is no depreciation of the good between the two periods. The discount factor δ is identical for all consumers and the firm. The inverse demand function is given by $p = 1 - Q$, where Q denotes aggregate output. Production is assumed to be costless. A resale market exists, since consumers who buy the good in the first period might want to re-sell (or lease) it in the second period.

(a) *Selling the good.* Consider first the case where the firm sells in each period.

1. Starting from the second period, set up the profit-maximization problem for the monopolist, where it selects a production level q_2 given a demand function $p_2 = 1 - q_1 - q_2$. Determine the profit-maximizing output q_2, then identify the resulting market price, p_2, and profits, π_2, during this second period.

   - If the monopolist decides to sell, the quantity sold during period 1 is re-offered in period 2 (remember that a resale market exists). Hence, a monopolist who has produced q_1 units in period 1 will sell in period 2 the quantity q_2 which maximizes its second-period profit

   $$\max_{q_2} \ (1 - q_1 - q_2)q_2.$$

   Taking first-order condition with respect to q_2,

   $$1 - q_1 - 2q_2 = 0,$$

   and solving for q_2 yields $q_2 = \frac{1-q_1}{2}$. Intuitively, second-period production decreases in first-period output, since more consumers have been served in the first period, thus reducing the available demand in the second period. Plugging the second-period output $q_2 = \frac{1-q_1}{2}$ into the inverse demand function, we obtain a second-period price of

   $$p_2 = 1 - q_1 - \frac{1 - q_1}{2} = \frac{1 - q_1}{2},$$

   yielding second-period profits of $\pi_2 = \frac{1-q_1}{2}\frac{1-q_1}{2} = \frac{(1-q_1)^2}{4}$, since production is costless.

2. Given the equilibrium price you found for the monopoly in the second period, p_2, the first-period demand is $p_1 = (1 - q_1) + \delta p_2$, which intuitively represents that the willingness to pay for the good in the first period is given by the current value that the consumer assigns to this good (captured in demand function, $1 - q_1$), plus the discounted value of the good tomorrow (which arises if the current consumer leases the good in the second period at a price p_2). Given this first-period demand, set up the monopolist's profit-maximization problem, where its choice variable is now q_1, and its objective function considers not only first-period but also the discounted value of second-period profits, $\delta\pi_2$. Determine q_1, the ensuing price, p_1, and overall profits across both periods.

- At stage 1, the price consumers will be willing to pay for the good depends on their expectations about p_2. Assume that consumers are rational, and thus, their expectations satisfy $E(p_2) = p_2$. Plugging the second-period price $p_2 = \frac{1-q_1}{2}$ found in the previous part of the exercise into the first-period demand function yields

$$p_1 = (1 - q_1) + \delta p_2 = (1 - q_1) + \delta \frac{1 - q_1}{2} = (1 - q_1)\left(1 + \frac{\delta}{2}\right),$$

where notice that $p_1 > p_2$. Indeed,

$$(1 - q_1)\left(1 + \frac{\delta}{2}\right) > \frac{1 - q_1}{2}$$

simplifies to $\delta > -1$, which holds by definition since $\delta \in [0, 1]$. When the monopolist sells in each period, price falls over time. The monopolist then chooses q_1 as to maximize the present value of the profits from selling the good, π_S, given by

$$\max_{q_1} p_1 q_1 + \delta \pi_2 = \underbrace{(1 - q_1)\left(1 + \frac{\delta}{2}\right) q_1}_{p_1} + \delta \frac{(1 - q_1)^2}{4}.$$

Taking first-order conditions with respect to q_1, we find

$$\frac{(1 - q_1)}{4}[\delta + (4 + \delta)q_1] = 0,$$

and solving for q_1 entails a first-period output of $q_1 = \frac{2}{4+\delta}$. Therefore, the first-period price is

$$p_1 = (1 - q_1)\left(1 + \frac{\delta}{2}\right) = \left(1 - \frac{2}{4 + \delta}\right)\left(1 + \frac{\delta}{2}\right) = \frac{(2 + \delta)^2}{2(4 + \delta)}.$$

yielding overall profits from selling the good of

$$\pi_S = \frac{(2 + \delta)^2}{2(4 + \delta)} \frac{2}{4 + \delta} + \delta \frac{\left(1 - \frac{2}{4+\delta}\right)^2}{4} = \frac{(2 + \delta)^2}{4(4 + \delta)}.$$

3. Show that equilibrium prices decline over time ($p_1 > p_2$).

- As we described in the previous part of the exercise, $p_1 > p_2$, since $(1 - q_1)$ $\left(1 + \frac{\delta}{2}\right) > \frac{1-q_1}{2}$ simplifies to $2 + \delta > 1$, which can be further reduced to $\delta > -1$, which holds by definition since $\delta \in [0, 1]$.

(b) *Leasing the good.* Consider now that the monopolist leases (i.e., rents) the good in each period. Find equilibrium prices and output. In addition, find the monopolist's equilibrium profits from leasing the good, π_L. [*Hint*: When leasing its goods, the monopolist's profits in a given time period t become independent of other-period prices (i.e., p_t and p_k are independent, where $k \neq t$).]

- If, instead, the monopolist decides to lease, then at each time period $t = \{1, 2\}$, it sets a price p_t that solves

$$\max_{p_t} p_t q_t = p_t(1 - p_t).$$

Taking first-order condition with respect to p_t yields $1 - 2p_t = 0$, thus implying prices of $p_1 = p_2 = \frac{1}{2}$, since the profits of a given time period are independent on other period's prices.

- Then, the monopolist produces an output level of

$$q_1 = 1 - p_1 = 1 - \frac{1}{2} = \frac{1}{2}$$

in the first period, and

$$p_2 = 1 - q_1 - q_2 \implies q_2 = (1 - q_1) - p_2 = 1 - \frac{1}{2} - \frac{1}{2} = 0$$

in the second period since we assumed that there is no depreciation.

- The overall profits from leasing, π_L, are then given by

$$\pi_L = \frac{1}{2} \frac{1}{2} + \delta \left(\frac{1}{2} 0 \right) = \frac{1}{4}.$$

(c) *Profit comparison.* Using your results in parts (a) and (b), are profits from leasing, π_L, higher or lower than profits from selling the good, π_S?

- As can be easily checked, $\pi_L > \pi_S$. In particular,

$$\frac{1}{4} > \frac{(2 + \delta)^2}{4(4 + \delta)},$$

which simplifies to $4 + \delta > (2 + \delta)^2$, and which can be further simplified to $\delta(3 + \delta) > 0$, a condition that holds for all discount factors $\delta \in [0, 1]$. Hence, the monopolist prefers to lease rather than sell the durable good.

- *Remark about the Coase paradox:* If we move from the above two-period setting to one with a continuous number of periods (and assume that the monopolist can change its price instantaneously in each of these periods), the monopolist power may vanish. In particular, the monopolist would ideally prefer to sell to customers with the highest willingness to pay, i.e., $p = 1$, in the first period, then move to those with a slightly lower willingness to pay in the subsequent period, e.g., $p = 0.99$, until reaching those whose willingness to pay coincides with the marginal cost. However, customers will anticipate such declining pricing pattern along time, and wait for prices to drop until reaching marginal cost (unless their waiting time is high). As a result, price flexibility along time eliminates the monopolist's monopoly power; a result commonly known as the "Coase paradox" after Coase (1972). For a survey of the literature with several empirical applications, see Waldman (2003).

Exercise #7 — Second-degree price discrimination

7. Consider a setting with two types of consumers $i = \{L, H\}$ (i.e., low- and high-valuation consumers), where a proportion $\gamma \in (0, 1)$ of consumers is of low type while $1 - \gamma$ is of high type. In particular, assume that consumers' utility function is given by

$$u_i(x, p) = \theta_i v(x) - p(x),$$

where $v(x)$ represents the utility from consuming x units, which is symmetric across consumers; θ_i denotes the value that type-i consumer assigns to the good, where $\theta_H > \theta_L$; and $p(x)$ reflects the price the monopolist charges for x units. For simplicity, consider that $v(x) = \frac{1-(1-x)^2}{2}$, which is increasing and concave in x (i.e., $v'(x) = 1 - x$ and $v''(x) = -1 < 0$).

(a) Consider a two-part tariff (F, p) where F denotes a fixed fee while p represents the per-unit price. Solve consumer i's utility-maximization problem, and find his inverse demand function $p_i(x)$.

- Every type-i consumer solves the UMP

$$\max_{x \geq 0} \theta_i v(x) - F - px.$$

   Taking first-order conditions with respect to x, yields $\theta_i(1 - x) = p$. Solving for x, we find the demand for good x, $x_i(p) = 1 - \frac{1}{\theta_i}p$, implying an indirect demand

$$p_i(x) = \theta_i - \theta_i x.$$

- Graphically, this indirect demand originates at θ_H for type-H consumer and at a lower intercept, θ_L, for type-L consumer (indicating his lower willingness to pay), but it reaches the same horizontal intercept for both types of consumers.

(b) Assume that the monopolist could observe the demand of each type of consumer. Find the profit-maximizing pair (F_L, p_L) intended for the low-demand consumer and (F_H, p_H) intended for the high-demand consumer.

- If the monopolist could observe the demand of each type of consumer, he would charge a price equal to marginal cost, $p_i = c \geq 0$ to all $i = \{L, H\}$, and a fee F_i that captures all the consumer surplus of each type of consumer, i.e., $F_i = CS_i(c)$. In this setting, the monopolist profits would be area a from low-type consumers and $a + b$ from high-demand consumers.

(c) *Single two-part tariff.* Let us now assume that the monopolist cannot observe consumer types. If the monopolist is limited to using a single two-part tariff (F, p) for both types of customers, which one would it use?

- From part (a), we know that the indirect demand of type-i consumer is $p_i(x) = \theta_i - \theta_i x$, thus yielding a consumer surplus of

$$CS^i(p) = \frac{\theta_i - p}{2} x_i(p) = \frac{(\theta_i - p)^2}{2\theta_i}.$$

In addition, $CS^H(p) > CS^L(p)$, and thus the monopolist cannot charge a fixed fee F above $CS^L(p)$, since otherwise type-L consumer would not purchase the good. In other words, the highest fee that the monopolist can charge is $F = CS^L(p)$.

- At this point, the only unknown to determine is the per-unit price p. In order to set this price, the monopolist maximizes his expected profits

$$\max_{p \geq 0} \underbrace{\gamma \left[CS^L(p) + (p-c)x_L(p) \right]}_{\text{Profits from low demand}} + \underbrace{(1-\gamma) \left[CS^H(p) + (p-c)x_H(p) \right]}_{\text{Profits from high demand}}$$

$$= \frac{(\theta_L - p)^2}{2\theta_L} + (p-c) \left[\gamma \left(1 - \frac{1}{\theta_L}p \right) + (1-\gamma) \left(1 - \frac{1}{\theta_H}p \right) \right].$$

Taking first-order conditions with respect to p yields

$$\frac{\theta_L(1-\gamma)(c-2p) + \theta_H(c\gamma + p - 2\gamma p)}{\theta_L \theta_H} = 0,$$

and solving for p, we obtain the monopoly price in this two-part tariff,

$$p = \frac{c \left[\gamma \theta_H + (1-\gamma)\theta_L \right]}{2 \left[\gamma \theta_H + (1-\gamma)\theta_L \right] - \theta_H}.$$

- *Numerical example.* For instance, if $\theta_L = 100$, $\theta_H = 150$, $\gamma = 0.7$ and $c = 10$, the (F, p)-pair becomes $(39.38, 11.25)$. Given this two-part tariff:
  - Type-L consumer retains no surplus and purchases $x_L(11.25) = 1 - \frac{1}{100}11.25 = 0.88$ units; whereas
  - Type-H consumer keeps a surplus of

$$CS^H(11.25) - F = 64.17 - 39.38 = 24.79$$

  and purchases $x_L(11.25) = 1 - \frac{1}{150}11.25 = 0.92$ units.

(d) *Two two-part tariffs.* Still under a setting in which the monopolist cannot observe consumers' types, assume that this firm can now offer a menu of two-part tariffs, (F_L, p_L) and (F_H, p_H) intended for the low- and high-demand customer, respectively. That is, each type of customer is now induced to self-select the pair intended for him. Find the profit-maximizing pairs (F_L, p_L) and (F_H, p_H).

- From the explanation of second-degree price discrimination in the main text, we know that the number of units meant to be purchased by the high-demand consumer, q_H, satisfis $\theta_H v'(q_H) = c$, which in this context entails $\theta_H(1 - q_H) = c$, which solving for q_H yields $q_H = \frac{\theta_H - c}{\theta_H}$.
- Similarly, we know that the number of units meant to be purchased by the low-demand consumer, q_L, satisfies the first-order condition

$$v'(q_L) \left[\theta_L - \frac{\gamma}{1-\gamma}(\theta_H - \theta_L) \right] = c,$$

which in this setting implies $(1 - q_L) \left[\theta_L - \frac{\gamma}{1-\gamma} (\theta_H - \theta_L) \right] = c$. Solving for q_L, we obtain

$$q_L = 1 - \frac{c(1 - \gamma)}{\theta_L - \theta_H \gamma}.$$

- As a consequence, the price meant for the high-demand consumer, $p_H = \theta_H(1 - q_H)$, is $p_H = c$; while that for the low-demand consumer, $p_L = \theta_L(1 - q_L)$, is

$$p_L = \frac{\theta_L(1 - \gamma)c}{\theta_L - \gamma\theta_H}.$$

- Finally, the fixed fee intended for the low-demand consumer, F_L, becomes

$$F_L = \theta_L v(q_L) = \theta_L \frac{1 - (1 - q_L)^2}{2} = \frac{\theta_L \left[(\theta_L - \gamma\theta_H)^2 - (1 - \gamma)^2 c^2 \right]}{2(\theta_L - \gamma\theta_H)^2},$$

whereas that intended for the high-demand consumers, F_H, is

$$
\begin{aligned}
F_H &= \theta_H \left[v(q_H) - v(q_L) \right] + F_L \\
&= \theta_H \left[\frac{1 - (1 - q_H)^2}{2} - \frac{1 - (1 - q_L)^2}{2} \right] + F_L \\
&= \frac{(\theta_H - \theta_L) \left[\theta_H(1 - 2\gamma) - \theta_L \right] c^2}{2\theta_H(\theta_L - \gamma\theta_H)^2} + \frac{\theta_L \left[(\theta_L - \gamma\theta_H)^2 - (1 - \gamma)^2 c^2 \right]}{2(\theta_L - \gamma\theta_H)^2},
\end{aligned}
$$

which in the specific case of $\gamma = 1/2$ simplifies to

$$F_H = \frac{\theta_L \left[\theta_H(\theta_H - 2\theta_L)^2 + (3\theta_H - 4\theta_L)c^2 \right]}{2\theta_H(\theta_H - 2\theta_L)^2}.$$

Exercise #9 — Cost reducing investment

9. Consider a monopolist with inverse demand function $p(q) = a - bq$. The monopolist makes two choices: how much to invest in cost reduction, A, and how much to produce, q. If the monopolist invests A units in cost reduction, his (constant) per-unit cost of production is $c(A) = c - \beta\sqrt{A}$, where $c > 0$ is the initial marginal cost, and β denotes the effectiveness of cost-reducing investment. This implies that

$$c'(A) = -\frac{\beta}{2\sqrt{A}} < 0 \quad \text{and} \quad c''(A) = \frac{\beta}{4A^{\frac{3}{2}}} > 0$$

(i.e., investing in cost reduction decreases the monopolist's per-unit cost of production, but at a decreasing rate; as depicted in figure 7.1 for two values of parameter β, where $\beta_2 > \beta_1$). For simplicity, you can assume that $a > c$, and $b > \frac{\beta^2}{2}$.

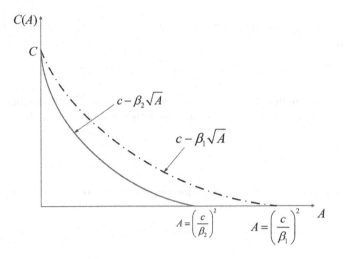

Figure 7.1 Cost function $c(A)$.

(a) *Unregulated monopolist.* Derive the first-order conditions for the monopolist's choices.

- The monopolist will solve

$$\max_{q,A} \ (a - bq) \cdot q - (c - \beta\sqrt{A})q - A$$

Taking first-order condition with respect to q yields

$$a - 2bq^m - (c - \beta\sqrt{A^m}) = 0,$$

and taking first-order condition with respect to A, we obtain

$$\frac{\beta}{2\sqrt{A^m}}q^m - 1 = 0.$$

Simultaneously, solving for q^m and A^m in the above first-order conditions yields

$$q^m = \frac{2(a - c)}{4b - \beta^2} \quad \text{and} \quad A^m = \frac{(a - c)^2\beta^2}{(4b - \beta^2)^2},$$

which is positive for all $b > \frac{\beta^2}{4}$, which holds given the assumption $b > \frac{\beta^2}{2}$ where $\frac{\beta^2}{2} > \frac{\beta^2}{4}$.

- *Ineffective investment, $\beta = 0$.* When $\beta = 0$, the monopolist produces the standard output level $q^m = \frac{a-c}{2b}$ and does not invest on cost-reducing technologies, i.e., $A^m = 0$.
- *Effective investment, $\beta > 0$.* When investing in cost-reducing technologies is effective, the monopolist invests a positive amount in cost-reducing technologies, i.e., $A^m =$

$\frac{(a-c)^2\beta^2}{(4b-\beta^2)^2} > 0$, which reduces its production costs ultimately yielding a larger output level, i.e., q^m increases in the effectiveness of cost-reducing investments, β, since

$$\frac{\partial q^m}{\partial \beta} = \frac{4\beta(a-c)}{(4b-\beta^2)^2}$$

is positive for all parameter values.

(b) *First best.* Compare the monopolist's choices with those of a benevolent social planner who can control both q and A (a "first-best" comparison). Interpret your results.

- The social planner will maximize total surplus,

$$\max_{q,A} \int_0^q (a - bx)dx - (c - \beta\sqrt{A})q - A.$$

Taking first-order condition with respect to q yields

$$a - bq - (c - \beta\sqrt{A}) = 0,$$

and taking first-order condition with respect to A, we obtain

$$\frac{\beta}{2\sqrt{A}}q - 1 = 0.$$

Simultaneously solving for q^{sp} and A^{sp} yields

$$q^{sp} = \frac{2(a-c)}{2b - \beta^2} \quad \text{and} \quad A^{sp} = \frac{(a-c)^2\beta^2}{(2b - \beta^2)^2},$$

which is positive given that $b > \frac{\beta^2}{2}$ by assumption.

- *Ineffective investment, $\beta = 0$.* If cost-reducing technologies are ineffective, $\beta = 0$, then the social planner produces the standard socially optimal output level $q^{sp} = \frac{a-c}{b}$ and invests nothing $A^{sp} = 0$.

- *Effective investment, $\beta > 0$.* In this case, both q^{sp} and A^{sp} increase in β. Moreover, comparing A^{sp} with A^m, we can notice that $A^{sp} > A^m$, suggesting that the monopolist invests less in cost-reducing technologies than the social planner would. In addition, $q^{sp} > q^m$, also indicating that the monopolist production, while increasing in β, is still socially insufficient.

(c) *Second best.* Assume now that the social planner can control for the investment in cost-reducing technologies, A, but *not* for q (i.e., he can implement a "second-best" policy). In particular, suppose that the social planner chooses A and afterwards the monopolist responds choosing q. Compare your results with those in part (b) where the regulator, choosing both A and q, implements a first-best policy.

- Given a level $\widehat{A}$ set by the government, the monopolist will set q to maximize its profits, i.e., it will set q to equate $MR = MC$. Therefore, the governments problem is to maximize social surplus subject to the monopolists's behavior. That is,

$$\max_{q,A} \quad \int_0^q (a - bx)dx - (c - \beta\sqrt{A})q - A$$

$$\text{subject to} \quad a - 2bq = c - \beta\sqrt{A}.$$

The Lagrangian is

$$L = \int_0^q (a - bx)dx - (c - \beta\sqrt{A})q - A - \lambda[a - 2bq - (c - \beta\sqrt{A})],$$

which yields the first-order conditions of

$$a - b\widehat{q} - (c - \beta\sqrt{A}) + 2b\lambda = 0,$$

$$\frac{-2\sqrt{\widehat{A}} + \beta(\widehat{q} - \lambda)}{2\sqrt{\widehat{A}}} = 0, \text{ and}$$

$$a - 2b\widehat{q} - c + \beta\sqrt{\widehat{A}} = 0$$

Simultaneously solving for $\widehat{q}$ and $\widehat{A}$ yields

$$\widehat{q} = \frac{4(a - c)}{8b - 3\beta^2} \quad \text{and} \quad \widehat{A} = \frac{(a - c)^2\beta^2}{(8b - 3\beta^2)^2},$$

which is positive for all $b > \frac{3\beta^2}{8}$, which holds given the assumption $b > \frac{\beta^2}{2}$, where $\frac{\beta^2}{2} > \frac{3\beta^2}{8}$.

- *Comparing first- and second-best policies.* Comparing $\widehat{A}$ and A^{sp}, we see that $\widehat{A} > A^{sp}$. indicating that, in this second-best policy, the social planner needs to select a larger cost-reducing investment in order to induce the monopolist to produce an output level $\widehat{q}$ closer to the social optimal q^{sp} (but still suboptimal). Figure 7.2 illustrates A^{sp} (first best) and $\widehat{A}$ (second best) for parameter values $a = b = 1$ an $c = 0$. (Other parameter values yield similar results.)
  Comparing output levels $\widehat{q}$ and q^{sp}, we find

$$q^{sp} - \widehat{q} = \frac{2(a - c)}{2b - \beta^2} - \frac{4(a - c)}{8b - 3\beta^2} = \frac{2(a - c)(4b - \beta^2)}{16b^2 + 3\beta^4 - 14b\beta^2},$$

which is positive for all $b > \frac{\beta^2}{4}$, which holds given the assumption $b > \frac{\beta^2}{2}$ where $\frac{\beta^2}{2} > \frac{\beta^2}{4}$. Figure 7.3 depicts the first-best output, q^{sp}, and the second-best output, $\widehat{q}$. (For consistency, we use the same parameter values as in figure 7.2.)

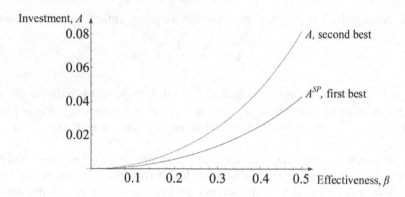

Figure 7.2 First- and second-best investments.

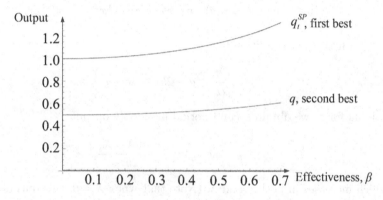

Figure 7.3 First- and second-best output.

Exercise #11 — Monopolist with intertemporal network effects

11. Consider a direct demand function

$$x(p, w) = \alpha - \beta p + \gamma q,$$

where q represents the units of the good purchased in previous periods and $\gamma > 0$ denotes the network effects that exist in this industry. For instance, a larger pool of customers in previous periods makes the good more valuable for current customers, thus producing a rightward shift in the demand function. Network effects arise in industries such as operating systems, game consoles, etc. whereby the larger the population that uses a specific type of device the more useful it becomes for new users who will be able to exchange more files and design more programs. Assume that $\alpha, \beta > 0$. Hence, solving for p, we obtain the indirect utility function

$$p(q) = \frac{\alpha}{\beta} - \frac{1}{\beta}x + \frac{\gamma}{\beta}q.$$

For compactness, let us denote $a \equiv \frac{\alpha}{\beta}, b \equiv \frac{1}{\beta}$, and $\lambda \equiv \frac{\gamma}{\beta}$, which reduces the above inverse demand function to the more familiar expression $p(q) = a - bx + \lambda q$, where now λ measures the network effects. Also assume that marginal costs c are constant and $c < a$.

(a) *Second period.* Determine a monopolist's optimal production level, and the resulting prices, if q units were sold in the market during the previous period. Find the monopoly profits as a function of q in the second period. [*Hint:* For simplicity, assume only two time periods.]

- We start by setting up a profit maximization problem. The monopolist's problem is

$$\max_{x} \pi = p(q) \cdot x - cx = ax - bx^2 + \lambda qx - cx.$$

With a first-order condition,

$$\frac{\partial \pi}{\partial x} = a - 2bx + \lambda q - c = 0.$$

Solving for x, we obtain second-period monopoly output

$$x^*(q) = \frac{(a - c) + \lambda q}{2b},$$

which increases in both q and λ. (Note that when $\lambda = 0$, this output level coincides with that of a standard monopolist without network effects, $\frac{a-c}{2b}$.)

- Plugging $x^*(q)$ into the inverse demand function, we find the second period price

$$p(q) = a - bx + \lambda q = a - b\left(\frac{(a - c) + \lambda q}{2b}\right) + \lambda q = \frac{a + \lambda q + c}{2}.$$

And solving for the monopolist's profits,

$$\pi(q) = p(q) \cdot x(q) - cx(q) = \left(\frac{a + \lambda q + c}{2}\right)\left(\frac{(a - c) + \lambda q}{2b}\right) - c\left(\frac{(a - c) + \lambda q}{2b}\right)$$

$$= \frac{(a + \lambda q - c)^2}{4b}.$$

(b) *First period.* If the monopolist anticipates that no firm will enter into the industry in future periods, how much does the monopolist produce in the first period, assuming a first-period inverse demand curve $p(q) = a - bx$?

- Setting up a profit maximization problem over two separate periods,

$$\max_{q} \pi = p_1(q) \cdot q + p_2(q) \cdot x_2(q) - c(q + x_2(q))$$

$$= (a - bq)q + \left(\frac{a + \lambda q + c}{2}\right)\left(\frac{a + \lambda q - c}{2b}\right) - c\left[q + \left(\frac{a + \lambda q - c}{2b}\right)\right],$$

which simplifies to

$$\left(\frac{\lambda^2}{4b} - b\right)q^2 + \left((a - c)\left(1 + \frac{\lambda}{2b}\right)\right)q + \frac{(a - c)^2}{4b}.$$

Taking first-order conditions with respect to first-period output, q, yields,

$$\frac{\partial \pi}{\partial q} = 2\left(\frac{\lambda^2}{4b} - b\right)q + \left((a - c)\left(1 + \frac{\lambda}{2b}\right)\right) = 0.$$

Solving for q, we obtain the monopolist's first-period output

$$q^* = \frac{a - c}{2b - \lambda}.$$

- Plugging q^* into the second-period output function $x^*(q)$, we obtain

$$x^*(q) = \frac{(a - c) + \lambda\left(\frac{a-c}{2b-\lambda}\right)}{2b} = \frac{a - c}{2b - \lambda},$$

  thus implying that the monopolist seeks to smooth its production decisions in both periods, by producing the same output level, $q^* = x(q^*) = \frac{a-c}{2b-\lambda}$, which is increasing in network effects, λ.

- Similarly as in part (a) of the exercise, note that if network effects are absent, $\lambda = 0$, the output level reduces to $q = \frac{a-c}{2b}$, which also coincides with the standard monopoly output, i.e., the monopolist would produce the same amount of output in both time periods $q^* = x^* = \frac{a-c}{2b}$.

(c) *Social optimum.* Assume that a social planner owned this monopoly. Considering that the social planner maximizes the sum of consumer and producer surplus in both periods, how much would it produce in each period? [*Hint*: Determine $x^{SO}(q)$ first, and then find q^{SO}.]

- *Second period.* Setting up the social planner's second-period maximization problem,

$$\max_{x} \quad \frac{1}{2}\left[(a + \lambda q) - (a + \lambda q - bx)\right]x + \pi(x)$$

$$= \frac{1}{2}bx^2 + (a - bx + \lambda q)x - cx,$$

where the first term represents the consumer surplus (which is independent on network effects) and the last two terms measure the monopolist's second-period profits. Importantly, this implies that a marginal increase in first-period output only raises the monopolist's revenues but does not affect consumer surplus. Simplifying,

$$= -\frac{1}{2}bx^2 + (a - c + \lambda q)x.$$

Taking first-order conditions with respect to x,

$$\frac{\partial S}{\partial x} = -bx + a - c + \lambda q = 0.$$

Solving for x, we obtain the second-period socially optimal output as a function of q,

$$x^{SO}(q) = \frac{a - c + \lambda q}{b},$$

which, similarly to the second-period output function of the unregulated monopolist, it increases in first-period network effects (as measured by λq). Substituting into the inverse demand function,

$$p(q) = a - b\left(\frac{a - c + \lambda q}{b}\right) + \lambda q = c,$$

which indicates that under a social optimum, the price charged for each unit of output would coincide with its marginal cost.

- *First period.* Setting up the social planner's first-period maximization problem,

$$\max_q \quad \frac{1}{2}[a - (a - bq)]q + \pi(q) + \frac{1}{2}\left[(a + \lambda q) - (a + \lambda q - bx^{SO}(q))\right]x^{SO}(q) + \pi(x^{SO}(q))$$

$$= \frac{1}{2}bq^2 + (a - bq)q - cq + \frac{1}{2}b\left(\frac{a - c + \lambda q}{b}\right)^2 + c\left(\frac{a - c + \lambda q}{b}\right) - c\left(\frac{a - c + \lambda q}{b}\right),$$

which also indicates that first-period consumer surplus is independent on λ. Simplifying, we obtain

$$\max_q \quad -\frac{1}{2}bq^2 + (a - c)q + \frac{1}{2}b\left(\frac{a - c + \lambda q}{b}\right)^2.$$

Taking first-order conditions with respect to q,

$$\frac{\partial S}{\partial q} = -bq + a - c + b\left(\frac{a - c + \lambda q}{b}\right)\left(\frac{\lambda}{b}\right) = 0.$$

Solving for q, we obtain the first-period social planner output

$$q^{SO} = \frac{a - c}{b - \lambda}$$

and an associated first-period equilibrium price of

$$p(q) = a - b\left(\frac{a-c}{b-\lambda}\right) = \frac{bc - a\lambda}{b - \lambda}.$$

- Plugging q^{SO} into the second-period social planner's output function $x^{SO}(q)$, yields an output of

$$x^{SO}(q^{SO}) = \frac{a - c + \lambda\left(\frac{a-c}{b-\lambda}\right)}{b} = \frac{a-c}{b-\lambda},$$

which is increasing in network effects, λ. Hence, similarly as the unregulated monopolist in part (b) of the exercise, the regulator produces the same socially optimal output in both periods, i.e., $q^{SO} = x^{SO}(q^{SO})$, and this output is increasing in network effects. In addition, socially optimal output levels are strictly larger than those selected by the unregulated monopolist, i.e., $\frac{a-c}{b-\lambda} > \frac{a-c}{2b-\lambda}$, for all parameter values.

- *Numerical example.* Figure 7.4 depicts the first- and second-period output that the unregulated monopolist selects where, for simplicity, we consider parameter values $a = b = 1$ and $c = 0$ (other parameter values yield similar results). Hence, the monopolist produces $q^* = x(q^*) = \frac{1}{2-\lambda}$. In contrast, the social planner would select $q^{SO} = x^{SO}(q^{SO}) = \frac{1}{1-\lambda}$ in this context, which lies above the monopolist output for all network effects.

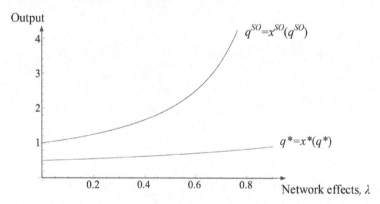

Figure 7.4 Output decisions under network effects.

Chapter 8 — Game Theory and Imperfect Competition

Summary This chapter explores industries where firms sustain some (but not all) market power. Before analyzing equilibrium behavior in those industries, we examine some basic concepts on game theory. Specifically, exercises 1 and 2 study whether strategy profiles surviving the iterative delection of strictly dominated strategies (IDSDS) are also Nash equilibria of the game, and vice versa. Exercise 3 then shows that the order in which we delete strictly dominated strategies in IDSDS does not affect our equilibrium outcome. This is an interesting property, as it implies that one can start deleting strategies for either player without affecting the equilibrium prediction. Exercise 4 focuses on mixed strategies and demonstrates that they do not assign a positive probability weight to strictly dominated strategies. This is also a useful property, as one can first delete all strictly dominated strategies from a game before studying mixed strategies, as the former would never be part of the latter. Exercise 5 considers a bargaining game in which the proposer can only make three possible offers to the responder, and analyzes the mixed strategy Nash equilibrium that arises in this context. In exercise 6 we analyze a larger payoff matrix than previous exercises, as both the column and row player have three different strategies at their disposal, and none of them can be deleted because of being strictly dominated. Hence, the analysis of mixed strategy equilibrium in this setting requires players to randomize over all three strategies. Exercise 7 considers a simultaneous-move game and explores the payoff properties that yield four typical games. Exercise 8 studies a workplace setting in which two workers simultaneously and independently choose whether to work or shirk, and assume that one worker enjoys an information advantage. In this incomplete information context, we find the Bayesian Nash equilibrium of the game, both in pure and mixed strategies. Finally, exercise 9 studies the labor market signaling game and evaluates whether a separating and a pooling strategy profile can be sustained as a perfect Bayesian equilibrium.

In the remainder of the chapter, we examine the application of the above game theory tools to problems in industrial organization. In particular, exercise 10 analyzes necessary and sufficient conditions in a Cournot model with N firms. Then, exercise 11 extends the standard Cournot model to a setting where firms own a share of each other's profits, and analyzes how equilibrium results are affected as firms own larger shares. Afterward, we allow the Cournot model for product differentiation (exercise 12) and introduce fixed costs (which can significantly change some results, as described in exercise 13). A recurrent topic in models of imperfect competition is firms' ability to collude, and how antitrust agencies detect and punish such collusion. We analyze those issues in exercise 14 and explore their extensions in exercises 27 through 30. In particular, exercise 27 examines whether collusion can be more easily sustained if firms use temporary (rather than permanent) punishments on those firms deviating from the collusive agreement. Exercise 28 considers, instead, the possibility that firms use a particularly "nasty" punishment that would reduce firms' profits below those in the unrepeated version of the game, and then evaluates whether cooperation is easier to emerge when firms use such severe punishment. Exercise 29 then allows for impure forms of collusion, whereby firms produce output levels that increase their profits relative to Cournot, but not to the maximal level they could obtain by maximizing their joint profits. Finally, exercise 30 considers firms' incentives to collude when they anticipate that the antitrust authority can observe their collusive practices with a positive probability, i.e., imperfect monitoring. We also explore the effect of mergers on the merging and non-merging firms in exercise 17, and firms' competition in Stackelberg models in exercises 22, 24, and 26.

Exercise #1 — A unique strategy profile that surviving IDSDS must also be NE

1. Consider a n-player game of complete information in which we find that there is only one strategy profile $s^* = (s_1^*, s_2^*, \cdots, s_n^*)$ surviving the iterative deletion of strictly dominated strategies (IDSDS). Show that such strategy profile must also be the unique Nash equilibrium of the game.

   - If strategy s_i^* survives IDSDS for player i, it means that such strategy performs better than some other strategy $s_i \neq s_i^*$ against the surviving strategies of his opponents, s_{-i}, that is,

   $$u_i(s_i^*, s_{-i}) > u_i(s_i, s_{-i}).$$

   In particular, the above inequality holds when the surviving strategy of player i's opponents is s_{-i}^*, that is,

   $$u_i(s_i^*, s_{-i}^*) > u_i(s_i, s_{-i}^*).$$

   Hence, s_i^* is a best response to s_{-i}^*. Since this argument applies to every player i, strategy profile s^* is a Nash equilibrium of the game.

Exercise #3 — Deletion order in IDSDS

3. Show that, in the application of IDSDS, the order in which we delete strictly dominated strategies does not affect the set of strategy profiles surviving IDSDS.

   - Let D_i^N denote the set of strategies of player i that remain after N rounds of IDSDS, i.e, $D_i^N \subset S_i$. Suppose that in round $N+1$ we find that one of the undeleted strategies, $s_i \in D_i^N$, is strictly dominated by s_i^* against $s_{-i} \in D_i^N$, that is,

   $$u_i(s_i^*, s_{-i}) > u_i(s_i, s_{-i}) \quad \text{for all } s_{-i} \in D_i^N. \tag{1}$$

   Intuitively, player i obtains a strictly higher utility level with s_i^* than with s_i regardless of the strategy $s_{-i} \in D_i^N$ that his opponents select. While the above inequality implies that strategy s_i is strictly dominated for player i, and thus should be deleted from D_i^N, let us assume that player i deletes some other strategy different from s_i. We now seek to show that the set of strategy profiles surviving IDSDS is unaffected by the fact that player i did not delete s_i from D_i^N in round $N+1$. That is easy to show, since in round $N+1$

we can find a strategy for player i, s_i^*, that strictly dominates s_i against $s_{-i} \in D_i^{N+1}$, that is,

$$u_i(s_i^*, s_{-i}) > u_i(s_i, s_{-i}) \quad \text{for all } s_{-i} \in D_i^{N+1}, \tag{2}$$

given that D_i^{N+1} is a subset of D_i^N. As a consequence, if (1) holds (2) must also hold, i.e., condition (1) holds under a wider profile of s_{-i} than condition (2) does. In summary, if a strictly dominated strategy s_i is not deleted in the round in which it became strictly dominated, it will be eventually deleted, and thus the set of strategy profiles surviving IDSDS will be unaffected by the order in which one deletes strictly dominated strategies.

Exercise #5 — Equilibrium predictions from IDSDS versus IDWDS

5. While the order of deletion of dominated strategies does not affect the equilibrium outcome when applying IDSDS, it can affect the set of equilibrium outcomes when we delete weakly (rather than strictly) dominated strategies. Use the payoff matrix below to show that the order in which weakly dominated strategies are eliminated can affect equilibrium outcomes.

		Player 2		
		L	M	R
Player 1	U	$2,1$	$1,1$	$0,0$
	C	$1,2$	$3,1$	$2,1$
	D	$2,-2$	$1,-1$	$-1,-1$

- *First route:* Taking the above payoff matrix, first note that, for player 1, strategy U weakly dominates D, since U yields a weakly larger payoff than D for any strategy (column) selected by player 2, that is

$$u_1(U, s_2) \geq u_1(D, s_2) \quad \text{for all } s_2 \in \{L, M, R\}.$$

In particular, U provides player 1 with the same payoff as D when player 2 selects L (a payoff of 2 for both U and D) and M (a payoff of 1 for both U and D), but a strictly higher payoff when player 2 chooses R (in the right-hand column) since $0 > -1$. Once we have deleted D because of being weakly dominated, we obtain the reduced-form matrix depicted below.

		Player 2		
		L	M	R
Player 1	U	$2,1$	$1,1$	$0,0$
	C	$1,2$	$3,1$	$2,1$

We can now turn to player 2, and detect that strategy L strictly dominates R, since it yields a strictly larger payoff than R, regardless of the strategy selected by player 1 (both when he chooses U in the top row, i.e., $1 > 0$ and when he chooses C in the bottom row, i.e., $2 > 1$), or more compactly

$$u_2(s_1, L) \geq u_2(s_2, R) \quad \text{for all } s_1 \in \{U, C\}.$$

Since R is strictly dominated for player 2, it is also weakly dominated. After deleting the column corresponding to the weakly dominated strategy R, we obtain the matrix below.

Player 2

		L	M
	U	2,1	1,1
Player 1	C	1,2	3,1

At this point, notice that we are not done examining player 2, since you can easily detect that M is weakly dominated by strategy L. Indeed, when player 1 selects U (in the top row of the above matrix), player 2 obtains the same payoff from L and M, but when player 1 chooses C (in the bottom row), player 2 is better off selecting L, which yields a payoff of 2, rather than M, which only produces a payoff of 1, i.e., $u_2(s_1, M) \geq u_2(s_1, L)$ for all $s_1 \in \{U, C\}$. Hence, we can delete M because of being weakly dominated for player 1, leaving us with the (further reduced) payoff matrix below.

Player 2

		L
	U	2,1
Player 1	C	1,2

Now we can turn to player 1, and identify that U strictly dominates C (and thus it also weakly dominates C), since the payoffs that player 1 obtains from U, 2, is strictly larger than that from C, 1. Therefore, after deleting C, we are left with a single strategy profile, (U, L), as depicted in the matrix below. Hence, using this particular order in our iterative deletion of weakly dominated strategies (IDWDS) we obtain the unique equilibrium prediction (U, L).

Player 2

		L
Player 1	U	2,1

- *Second route*: Let us now consider the same initial 3×3 matrix, which we reproduce below, and check if the application of IDWDS, but using a different deletion order (i.e., different "route") can lead to a different equilibrium result than that found above (i.e., (U, L)).

Player 2

		L	M	R
	U	2,1	1,1	0,0
Player 1	C	1,2	3,1	2,1
	D	2,−2	1,−1	−1,−1

Unlike in our first route, let us now start identifying weakly dominated strategies for player 2. In particular, note that R is weakly dominated by M, since the former yields a weakly lower payoff than the latter (i.e., it provides a strictly higher payoff when player 1 chooses U in the top row, but the same payoff otherwise). That is,

$$u_2(s_1, M) \geq u_2(s_1, R) \text{ for all } s_1 \in \{U, C, D\}.$$

Once we have deleted R as being weakly dominated for player 2, the remaining matrix becomes that depicted below.

Player 2

		L	M
	U	$2,1$	$1,1$
Player 1	C	$1,2$	$3,1$
	D	$2,-2$	$1,-1$

Turning to player 1, note that we can no longer find weakly dominated strategies: U and D provide the same payoff under a given strategy of player 2, and such payoff is higher than that of C when player 2 selects L but lower when player 2 chooses M.

- Therefore, there are no more weakly dominated strategies for either player, and the equilibrium prediction after using IDWDS is the six remaining strategy profiles: $(U, L), (U, M), (C, L), (C, M), (D, L)$, and (D, M). This equilibrium prediction is, of course, different (and significantly less precise) than what found when we started the application of IDWDS from player 1. Hence, equilibrium outcomes that arise from applying IDWDS are sensitive to the deletion order

Exercise #7 — Four categories of simultaneous-move games

7. Consider the following simultaneous-move game with payoff matrix

Player 2

		A	B
Player 1	A	$u_1(A, A), u_2(A, A)$	$u_1(A, B), u_2(A, B)$
	B	$u_1(B, A), u_2(B, A)$	$u_1(B, B), u_2(B, B)$

In addition, assume that $u_i(A, A) = u_j(A, A)$ and $u_i(B, B) = u_j(B, B)$, and that $u_i(A, B) = u_j(B, A)$ for every player $i = \{1, 2\}$ and $j \neq i$. Find players' strictly dominated strategies and the Nash equilibria of the game (allowing for both pure and mixed strategies) in the following settings. Interpret and relate your results to common games.

(a) $u_i(A, A) > u_i(B, A)$ and $u_i(A, B) > u_i(B, B)$, for every player i.

- Every player i finds B to be strictly dominated by A since $u_i(A, A) > u_i(B, A)$ when his opponent (player $j \neq i$) chooses A, and $u_i(A, B) > u_i(B, B)$ when his opponent chooses B. That is, regardless of the strategy selected by player i's opponent, strategy

A yields player i a strictly higher payoff than strategy B. Hence (A, A) is the only strategy profile surviving IDSDS, and thus becomes the unique NE of the game, which involves the use of strictly dominant strategies by both players. The game has no msNE since every player only assign a positive probability to his undominated strategy, A. Therefore, this game resembles a standard Prisonner's Dilemma game.

(b) $u_i(A, A) > u_i(B, A)$ and $u_i(A, B) < u_i(B, B)$, for every player i.

- In this setting, every player i prefers to respond selecting the same strategy as his opponent, i.e., choose A when his opponent selects A, but B otherwise. Hence, there is no strictly dominated (nor strictly dominant) strategy for either player. In other words, if we rely on IDSDS, the entire matrix would be our most precise equilibrium prediction, i.e., four strategy profiles, $(A, A), (A, B), (B, B)$, and (B, A), survive IDSDS. However, when we apply NE, we can easily show that a more precise equilibrium prediction emerges. In particular, we can underline best response payoffs as follows

Player 2

		A	B
Player 1	A	$\underline{u_1(A, A)}, \underline{u_2(A, A)}$	$u_1(A, B), u_2(A, B)$
	B	$u_1(B, A), u_2(B, A)$	$\underline{u_1(B, B)}, \underline{u_2(B, B)}$

There are two psNE since players are playing mutual best responses: (A, A) and (B, B). Hence, this is a coordination game similar to the Battle of the Sexes game. Note that if $u_i(A, A) > u_i(B, B)$ for every player i, the game would resemble a Pareto coordination game, since the equilibrium outcome (A, A) Pareto dominates (B, B), as (A, A) yields a strictly higher payoff for all players than (B, B) does.

- Let us now find the msNE of this game. Let p denote the probability that player 1 chooses A, and q be the probability that player 2 does. Hence, the value of p that makes player 2 indifferent between A and B is

$$EU_2(A) = EU_2(B),$$
$$pu_2(A, A) + (1 - p)u_2(B, A) = pu_2(A, B) + (1 - p)u_2(B, B).$$

Solving for p, yields

$$p = \frac{u_2(B, B) - u_2(B, A)}{[u_2(A, A) - u_2(A, B)] + [u_2(B, B) - u_2(B, A)]}.$$

The numerator is positive since $u_2(B, B) > u_2(B, A)$ by definition. In addition, the denominator is larger than the numerator given that $u_2(A, A) - u_2(A, B) > 0$ and $u_2(B, B) - u_2(B, A) > 0$, ultimately implying that the probability we found satisfies

$p \in (0, 1)$. Similarly, the value of q that makes player 1 indifferent between choosing A and B is

$$
\begin{aligned}
EU_1(A) &= EU_1(B), \\
qu_1(A, A) + (1 - q)u_1(B, A) &= qu_1(A, B) + (1 - q)u_1(B, B).
\end{aligned}
$$

Solving for q, yields

$$
q = \frac{u_1(B, B) - u_1(B, A)}{[u_1(A, A) - u_1(B, A)] + [u_1(B, B) - u_1(A, B)]}.
$$

The numerator is positive since $u_1(B, B) > u_1(B, A)$. Furthermore, the denominator is larger than the numerator given that $u_1(A, A) - u_1(A, B) > 0$ and $u_1(B, B) - u_1(B, A) > 0$. Hence, probability q satisfies $q \in (0, 1)$. Hence the msNE is

$$
\{(pA, (1 - p)B), (qA, (1 - q)B)\}.
$$

(c) $u_i(A, A) < u_i(B, B)$ and $u_i(A, B) < u_i(B, B)$, for every player i.

- This case is symmetric to the game analyzed in part (a), but has strategy B (A) as strictly dominant (dominated) for both players. Hence, (B, B) is the unique strategy profile surviving IDSDS, and therefore becomes the unique psNE, which has both players using dominant strategies. Hence, the game also resembles a Prisonner's Dilemma game.

(d) $u_i(A, A) < u_i(B, A)$ and $u_i(A, B) > u_i(B, B)$, for every player i.

- This game is symmetric to that in part (b). Similarly as that game, there are no strictly dominant strategies in this case. To see this, note that every player i seeks to respond with the opposite strategy as his opponent's, i.e., player i strictly prefers B when his opponent selects A, but A when his opponent chooses B. Intuitively, there is no strategy that a player would never use regardless of his opponent's strategy choice. Hence, the use of IDSDS does not eliminate any strategies. If we underline best response payoffs for each player in order to identify the NE of the game, we obtain the following matrix:

Player 2

		A	B
Player 1	A	$u_1(A, A), u_2(A, A)$	$\underline{u_1(A, B)}, \underline{u_2(A, B)}$
	B	$\underline{u_1(B, A)}, \underline{u_2(B, A)}$	$u_1(B, B), u_2(B, B)$

yielding that (B, A) and (A, B) are the two psNE of the game. The game then resembles an Anti-coordination game such as the Game of Chicken where, in any psNE, players choose opposite strategies.

- Let us find the msNE of this game. Let p denote the probability that player 1 chooses A, and q be the probability that player 2 does. Hence, the value of p that makes player two indifferent between A and B is

$$EU_2(A) = EU_2(B),$$
$$pu_2(A, A) + (1 - p)u_2(B, A) = pu_2(A, B) + (1 - p)u_2(B, B).$$

Solving for p, yields

$$p = \frac{u_2(B, B) - u_2(B, A)}{[u_2(A, A) - u_2(B, A)] + [u_2(B, B) - u_2(A, B)]}.$$

Since $u_2(B, B) - u_2(B, A) < 0$ and $u_2(A, A) - u_2(A, B) < 0$, in this case both numerator and denominator as negative. However, the absolute value of the denominator is greater than the numerator, implying that the ratio satisfies $p \in (0, 1)$. Similarly, the value of q that makes player 1 indifferent between choosing A and B is

$$EU_1(A) = EU_1(B),$$
$$qu_1(A, A) + (1 - q)u_1(B, A) = qu_1(A, B) + (1 - q)u_1(B, B).$$

Solving for q, yields

$$q = \frac{u_1(B, B) - u_1(B, A)}{[u_1(A, A) - u_1(B, A)] + [u_1(B, B) - u_1(A, B)]}.$$

Since $u_1(B, B) - u_1(B, A) < 0$ and $u_1(A, A) - u_1(A, B) < 0$, we also have that both numerator and denominator as negative, and that the absolute value of the denominator is greater than the numerator, implying that $q \in (0, 1)$. Therefore, the msNE is

$$\{(pA, (1 - p)B), (qA, (1 - q)B)\}.$$

Note that the probabilities we found in this msNE are similar to those of the Coordination game analyzed in part (b). However, since the payoff structure of this game is different, the values of ratios p and q would not coincide with those of part (b). Hence, we should not generally expect players to randomize with the same probabilities in a Coordination and in an Anti-coordination game.

Exercise #9 — Bayesian Nash equilibrium in the workplace

9. Consider the following incomplete-information game: Players 1 and 2 simultaneously and independently choose "Work" or "Shirk", but there is a 0.5 probability that the players are playing the game on the left matrix, and a 0.5 probability that the play on the right matrix. Player 1 knows which game is being played, but player 2 does not. Intuitively, the left-hand (right-hand) matrix represents a setting in which the benefit of having both individuals working is relatively low (high, respectively).

		Player 2	
		Work	Shirk
Player 1	Work	5, 5	−3, 6
	Shirk	6, −3	−1, −1

		Player 2	
		Work	Shirk
Player 1	Work	10, 10	−3, 6
	Shirk	6, −3	−1, −1

(a) Describe the strategy space for each player.

- *Player 1.* The strategy space for the informed player 1 is

$$S_1 = \{w_1w_2, w_1s_2, s_1w_2, s_1s_2\},$$

where each strategy is a pair specifying his action when he plays the left-hand matrix and the right-hand matrix. For instance, w_1s_2 denotes that player 1 only works when playing the left-hand matrix. Since player 1 has two possible actions (work or shirk) in two different matrices (left and right), we obtain a total of four strategies for him.

- *Player 2.* In contrast, the strategy space for the uninformed player 2 is

$$S_2 = \{w, s\}$$

because he cannot condition his strategy on the specific matrix he plays (as he does not know which matrix he plays!).

(b) Depict the Bayesian-normal form representation of the game.

- Since player 1 has four available strategies while player 2 has only two strategies, the Bayesian-normal form representation entails a 4×2 matrix, as follows:

Player 2

	w	s
w_1w_2	$7.5, 7.5$	$-3, 6$
w_1s_2	$5.5, 1$	$-2, 2.5$
s_1w_2	$8, 3.5$	$-2, 2.5$
s_1s_2	$6, -3$	$-1, -1$

Player 1 (labels the rows)

The expected payoffs in each cell follows the procedure described in the text. For instance, for strategy profile (w_1s_2, w) expected payoffs are found as follows:

$$EU_1(w_1s_2, w) = \frac{1}{2}5 + \frac{1}{2}6 = 5.5 \text{ and}$$

$$EU_2(w_1s_2, w) = \frac{1}{2}5 + \frac{1}{2}(-3) = 1$$

because player 1 obtains a payoff of 5 when both players work in the left-hand matrix, and a payoff of 6 when only player 2 works in the right-hand matrix. A similar argument applies to player 2, with payoffs 5 and -3.

(c) Find the Bayesian Nash equilibrium (BNE) of this game, both in pure and mixed strategies.

- First, note that strategy w_1w_2 for player 1 is strictly dominated by s_1w_2, and that w_1s_2 is strictly dominated by s_1s_2. After deleting the strictly dominated strategies w_1w_2 (top row) and w_1s_2 (second row), we obtain the following reduced 2×2 matrix:

Player 2

	w	s
s_1w_2	$8, 3.5$	$-2, 2.5$
s_1s_2	$6, -3$	$-1, -1$

Player 1 (labels the rows)

- *Pure strategy BNE.* We then find the following best responses for each player:
  - $BR_1(w) = s_1w_2$, and $BR_1(s) = s_1s_2$ for player 1; and
  - $BR_2(s_1w_2) = w$, and $BR_2(s_1s_2) = s$ for player 2.
  - The following figure underlines best response payoffs, illustrating that the above best response function entail a mutual best response in two strategy profiles, which are the two BNEs of the game involving pure strategies, (s_1w_2, w) and (s_1s_2, s).

Player 2

		w	s
Player 1	s_1w_2	<u>8,3.5</u>	$-2, 2.5$
	s_1s_2	$6, -3$	<u>−1,−1</u>

- *Mixed strategy BNE.* There is also one mixed strategy BNE that we can find by letting $p\,(1-p)$ denote the probability that player 1 plays s_1w_2 (s_1s_2, respectively). Similarly for player 2, let $q\,(1-q)$ be the probability that he selects w (s, respectively). Recall that we do not need to consider strictly dominated strategies, as they receive zero probability weight in equilibrium. Making player 1 indifferent between s_1w_2 and s_1w_2, we obtain

$$\begin{aligned}
EU_1(s_1w_2) &= EU_1(s_1s_2)\\
8q - 2(1-q) &= 6q - 1(1-q)\\
&\implies q = \frac{1}{3}.
\end{aligned}$$

Similarly, making player 2 indifferent between w and s yields

$$\begin{aligned}
EU_2(w) &= EU_2(s),\\
3.5p - 3(1-p) &= 2.5p - 1(1-p)\\
&\implies p = \frac{2}{3}.
\end{aligned}$$

Hence, the mixed strategy BNE is

$$\left(\underbrace{\frac{2}{3}s_1w_2 \frac{1}{3}s_1s_2}_{\text{Player 1}}, \underbrace{\frac{1}{3}w\frac{2}{3}s}_{\text{Player 2}} \right).$$

Exercise #11 — Cournot with equity swaps

11. Consider a Cournot duopoly with linear inverse demand curve $p(q) = a - q$, where q denotes aggregate output. Both firms have a common constant marginal cost $c > 0$, where $a > c$. Assume that firms do an equity swap of γ, i.e., each firm i receives a share $0 < \gamma \leq \frac{1}{2}$ in firm j's profits, where $j \neq i$.

(a) Find the Cournot equilbrium output, (q_1^C, q_2^C).

- Firm i's profit-maximization problem (PMP) is given by

$$\max_{q_i} \underbrace{(1-\gamma)(a - q_i - q_j - c)q_i}_{\text{Firm } i\text{'s profit}} + \underbrace{\gamma(a - q_i - q_j - c)q_j}_{\text{Firm } j\text{'s profit}}.$$

Taking first-order conditions with respect to q_i yields

$$(1-\gamma)(a - q_i - q_j - c) - (1-\gamma)q_i - \gamma q_j = 0.$$

In a symmetric equilibrium $q_i^C = q_j^C = q^C$, which lets us simplify the above expression as follows:

$$(1-\gamma)(a - 2q^C - c) - (1-\gamma)q^C - \gamma q^C = 0,$$

which, solving for q^C, yields

$$q^C = \frac{(1-\gamma)(a-c)}{3 - 2\gamma}.$$

(b) Evaluate equilibrium output q_i^C at $\gamma = 0$ and $\gamma = \frac{1}{2}$. Interpret.

- When firms do not benefit from each other's profits, $\gamma = 0$, equilibrium output q^C becomes $\frac{a-c}{3}$, thus coinciding with that under the standard Cournot model with linear inverse demand curve $p(q) = a - q$. In contrast, when firms fully share their profits, $\gamma = 1/2$, equilibrium output q^C becomes $\frac{a-c}{4}$, thus coinciding with half of monopoly output (or cartel output).

(c) Determine if q_i^C increases or decreases in γ.

- Differentiating q^C with respect to share γ yields

$$\frac{\partial q^C}{\partial \gamma} = -\frac{a-c}{3-2\gamma} + \frac{2(1-\gamma)(a-c)}{(3-2\gamma)^2},$$

which simplifies to

$$-\frac{a-c}{(3-2\gamma)^2},$$

which is clearly negative since $a > c$ by definition. Intuitively, as firms share more of each other's profits, their individual PMP resembles the joint PMP in a cartel, leading each of them to reduce its production.

- For illustrative purpose, figure 8.1 depicts q^C as a function of the profit share γ. For simplicity, we consider $a = 1$ and $c = 0$ which yields a output $q^C = \frac{1-\gamma}{3-2\gamma}$.

(d) Find equilibrium profits, π^C, and determine whether they increase or decrease in γ.

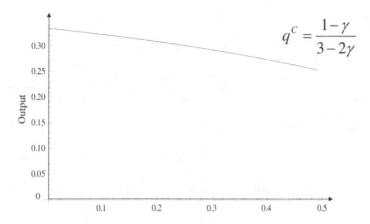

Figure 8.1 Output q^C as a function of γ.

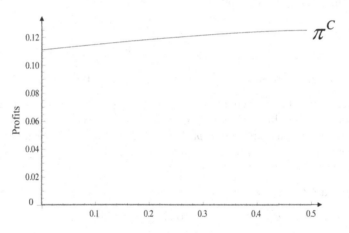

Figure 8.2 Profits π^C as a function of γ.

- Equilibrium profits are $\pi^C = \frac{(1-\gamma)(a-c)^2}{(3-2\gamma)^2}$, which increase in γ since

$$\frac{\partial \pi^C}{\partial \gamma} = \frac{(1 - 2\gamma)(a - c)^2}{(3 - 2\gamma)^3}$$

is positive given that $\gamma \leq \frac{1}{2}$ by definition. Intuitively, as firms take more into account each other's profits, their individual profits approach those they would obtain under a cartel agreement, which are larger than under a standard Cournot model.

- Figure 8.2 plots π^C where, similarly as for the equilibrium output, we consider parameter values $a = 1$ and $c = 0$.

Exercise #13 — Cournot competition with product differentiation (Deneckere 1983)

13. Consider a Cournot duopoly with product differentiation, in which each firm $i = \{1, 2\}$ faces inverse demand curve

$$p_i(q_i, q_j) = 1 - q_i - \theta q_j,$$

where $j \neq i$ and parameter θ satisfies $\theta \in (0, 1]$, that is, if $\theta = 0$ products are fully differentiated; however, if $\theta = 1$ firms sell a completely homogeneous product. For simplicity, assume no production costs.

(a) If firms compete during infinite periods, find the minimal discount factor $\bar{\delta}$ that sustains a cooperative outcome in which firms maximize their joint profits (i.e., collusive agreement).

- We explore a Nash reversion strategy in which firms start producing the cooperative (cartel) output, q^{Coop}, and continue to do so as long as all firms produced q^{Coop} in all previous periods. Otherwise, every firm i reverts to the equilibrium of the unrepeated game, producing the Cournot output q^C, thereafter. Let us first find the exact value of $\frac{q^M}{2}$ and q^C, along with their corresponding profits.

- *Cooperation.* In order to maximize their joint profits, firms must solve

$$\max_{q_1, q_2} (1 - q_1 - \theta q_2)q_1 + (1 - q_2 - \theta q_1)q_2.$$

Taking first-order conditions with respect to q_1 yields $1 - 2q_1 - 2\theta q_2 = 0$. In addition, since the equilibrium must be symmetric, i.e., $q_1 = q_2 = q$, we obtain $1 - 2q - 2\theta q = 0$, or solving for q,

$$q^{Coop} = \frac{1}{2(1 + \theta)}.$$

In this setting, the profits of each firm are given by

$$
\begin{aligned}
\pi^{Coop} &= (1 - q^{Coop} - \theta q^{Coop})q^{Coop} \\
&= \left(1 - \frac{1}{2(1 + \theta)} - \theta \frac{1}{2(1 + \theta)}\right) \frac{1}{2(1 + \theta)} \\
&= \frac{1}{4(1 + \theta)}.
\end{aligned}
$$

- *Deviation.* Consider now that, instead, firm i unilaterally deviates from the cooperative outcome, while its rival still produces $q_j^{Coop} = \frac{1}{2(1+\theta)}$. In this setting, firm i's PMP becomes

$$\max_{q_i} \left(1 - q_i - \theta \frac{1}{2(1 + \theta)}\right) q_i,$$

where note that q_j is evaluated at $q_j^{Coop} = \frac{1}{2(1+\theta)}$. Taking first-order conditions with respect to q_i yields

$$1 - \frac{\theta}{2(1+\theta)} - 2q_i = 0,$$

and solving for q_i we obtain firm i's optimal deviation

$$q_i^{Dev} = \frac{2+\theta}{4(1+\theta)}.$$

In this context, firm i's profits from deviating are

$$
\begin{aligned}
\pi_i^{Dev} &= \left(1 - q_i^{Dev} - \theta\frac{1}{2(1+\theta)}\right) q_i^{Dev} \\
&= \left(1 - \frac{2+\theta}{4(1+\theta)} - \theta\frac{1}{2(1+\theta)}\right) \frac{2+\theta}{4(1+\theta)} \\
&= \left(\frac{2+\theta}{4(1+\theta)}\right)^2.
\end{aligned}
$$

- *Cournot equilibrium.* Upon detecting a deviation, the Nash reversion strategy calls both firms to revert to the Cournot equilibrium thereafter. In that setting, every firm i solves the PMP

$$\max_{q_i} (1 - q_i - \theta q_j)q_i.$$

Taking first-order conditions with respect to q_i yields

$$1 - 2q_i - \theta q_j = 0,$$

and by symmetry in the Cournot equilibrium, i.e., $q_i^C = q_j^C = q^C$, we obtain $q^C = \frac{1}{2+\theta}$, which yields Cournot profits of

$$
\begin{aligned}
\pi^C &= \left(1 - q_i^C - \theta q_j^C\right) q_i^C \\
&= \left(1 - \frac{1}{2+\theta} - \theta\frac{1}{2+\theta}\right) \frac{1}{2+\theta} \\
&= \frac{1}{(2+\theta)^2}.
\end{aligned}
$$

- *Payoff comparison.* In any given period $t \geq 1$ after a history of cooperation during all previous periods, every firm i keeps cooperating if

$$\frac{1}{1-\delta}\pi^{Coop} \geq \pi^{Dev} + \frac{\delta}{1-\delta}\pi^C.$$

Multiplying both sides by $(1 - \delta)$ yields $\pi^{Coop} \geq (1 - \delta)\pi^{Dev} + \delta\pi^C$. Solving for δ, we obtain

$$\delta \geq \frac{\pi^{Dev} - \pi^{Coop}}{\pi^{Dev} - \pi^C} \equiv \bar{\delta}.$$

In particular,

$$\bar{\delta} \equiv \frac{\pi^{Dev} - \pi^{Coop}}{\pi^{Dev} - \pi^C} = \frac{\left(\frac{2+\theta}{4(1+\theta)}\right)^2 - \frac{1}{4(1+\theta)}}{\left(\frac{2+\theta}{4(1+\theta)}\right)^2 - \left(\frac{1}{2+\theta}\right)^2} = \frac{(2+\theta)^2}{8 + \theta(8 + \theta)}.$$

- *Incentives to punish.* Finally, we need to check that, after a history in which a defection occured in previous periods, every firm i has incentives to revert to the equilibrium output of the unrepeated Cournot model, q^C (i.e., to implement the punishment embodied in the NRS). Since firm j selects q^C, firm i's profits from also choosing q^C are π^C, whereas its profits from a different output level $\widehat{q} \neq q^C$ are

$$\widehat{\pi} = (1 - \widehat{q} - \theta q^C)\widehat{q},$$

which is lower than π^C. In particular, the best response of firm i to firm j's output q^C is q^C as well, i.e., q^C maximizes firm i's profits given $q_j = q^C$, while output level $\widehat{q}$ does not. Hence, $\pi^C > \widehat{\pi}$, ultimately implying that, upon observing a defection from either firm, firm i prefers to respond with output level q^C (as prescribed by the Nash reversion strategy) than using any other output level $\widehat{q} \neq q^C$.

(b) Check if the minimal discount factor sustaining cooperation, $\bar{\delta}$, increases or decreses in parameter θ.

- Differentiating $\bar{\delta}$ with respect to the parameter representing product differentiation, θ, yields

$$\frac{\partial \bar{\delta}}{\partial \theta} = \frac{4\theta(2 + \theta)}{[8 + \theta(8 + \theta)]^2} > 0.$$

Intuitively, as goods become more homogeneous (larger θ), the minimal discount factor supporting cooperation increases, thus shrinking the set of discount factors $\delta \in (\bar{\delta}, 1]$ for which cooperation can emerge.[1] Intuitively, as goods become more homogeneous (higher θ), firms' incentives to deviate away from the cooperative outcome are more intense, since the deviating firm can capture a larger market share.

---

[1]In particular, if $\theta = 0$ products are fully differentiated and $\bar{\delta} = \frac{1}{2}$, whereas if $\theta = 1$ firms sell a completely homogeneous product and $\bar{\delta}$ increases (although not by much) to $\bar{\delta} = 0.53$.

Exercise #15 — Antitrust efforts and collusion

15. Consider two perfectly symmetric firms that sell a differentiated good and consider collusion. The fully collusive price in the market is given by p_m, and gives each firm a profit π_m. Firms have the same discount factor δ. They play the Bertrand game an infinite number of periods.

    There also exists an antitrust authority, which investigates the industry in every period. If firms collude, the authority will find them guilty with probability $p \in (0,1)$ and will accordingly impose on them a fine F, which satisfies $F > \delta\pi_n$. If they are found colluding, assume that the authority will prevent them from colluding in the future. In that case, they will forever earn market profit $\pi_n > 0$ each, where the subscript n stands for Nash equilibrium profits. If firms do not collude, they cannot be fined.

    (a) Focus on simple NRS. Under which condition on the common discount factor, δ, can collusion be sustained?

    - *Payoff from collusion.* If the antitrust authority investigates the sector in every period, the present discounted value of collusion, V^C, is given by

    $$V^C = p(\pi_m - F + \frac{\delta}{1-\delta}\pi_n) + (1-p)(\pi_m + \delta V^C),$$

    where the term in the left-hand side illustrates that, if the antitrust authority detects collusion today (which happens with probability p), the payoff that a representative firm obtains is $\pi_m - F$ today and a non-collusive profit π_n thereafter. The term in the right-hand side, in contrast, describes that, if the antitrust authority does not detect collusive practices today (which occurs with probability $1-p$), the representative firm obtains a profit π_m from colluding today, while tomorrow the same expected payoff arises (where the firm can/cannot be detected to practice collusion), as captured by the continuation payoff V^C. [This continuation payoff is analog to that in dynamic optimization models in Macroeconomics when you set up Bellman equations.] Solving for V^C we obtain
    $$V^C = \frac{\pi_m - \pi_n - Fp}{1-(1-p)\delta} + \frac{\pi_n}{1-\delta}.$$

    - *Payoff from deviation.* If the representative firm deviates from the collusive agreement, it obtains a one-shot deviation profit of π_d, but this triggers a non-collusive payoff π_n thereafter (as embodied in the punishment of the NRS). Hence, the discounted stream of payoffs from deviating today is, as usual,

    $$\pi_d + \frac{\delta}{1-\delta}\pi_n.$$

    - *Incentives to collude.* Therefore, the firm chooses to respect the collusive agreement if and only if
    $$V^C = \frac{\pi_m - \pi_n - Fp}{1-(1-p)\delta} + \frac{\pi_n}{1-\delta} > \pi_d + \frac{\delta}{1-\delta}\pi_n.$$

If we solve for the discount factor, δ, we find that the minimal discount factor that supports collusion is

$$\delta > \frac{\pi_d - \pi_m + Fp}{\pi_d - \pi_n + p(\pi_n - \pi_d)} \equiv \bar{\delta}.$$

(b) How is collusion affected by an increase in fines, F, and better monitoring, higher probability of being caught, p?

- The higher p and F the less likely for collusion to be sustained at equilibrium, other things being equal. In particular, increasing fines makes makes the minimal discount factor sustaining cooperation more demanding,

$$\frac{\partial \bar{\delta}}{\partial F} = \frac{p}{\pi_d - \pi_n + p(\pi_n - \pi_d)} > 0,$$

and similarly, improving monitoring (higher probability of detecting collusion, p) also increases the minimal discount factor $\bar{\delta}$,

$$\frac{\partial \bar{\delta}}{\partial p} = \frac{\overbrace{F(\pi_d - \pi_n + p(\pi_n - \pi_d))}^{>0} - \overbrace{(\pi_n - \pi_d)}^{<0} \overbrace{(\pi_d - \pi_m + Fp)}^{>0}}{(\pi_d - \pi_n + p(\pi_n - \pi_d))^2} > 0.$$

Exercise #17 — Profitable and unprofitable mergers

17. Consider an industry with n identical firms competing à la Cournot. Suppose that the inverse demand function is $P(Q) = a - bQ$, where Q is total industry output, and $a, b > 0$. Each firm has a marginal costs, c, where $c < a$, and no fixed costs.

(a) *No merger.* Find the equilibrium output that each firm produces at the symmetric Cournot equilibrium. What is the aggregate output and the equilibrium price? What are the profits that every firm obtains in the Cournot equilibrium? What is the equilibrium social welfare?

- At the symmetric equilibrium with n firms, we have that each firm i maximizes

$$\max_{q_i} \ (a - bQ_{-i} - bq_i) \, q_i - cq_i,$$

where $Q_{-i} \equiv \sum_{j \neq i} q_j$ denotes the aggregate production of all other $j \neq i$ firms. Taking first-order conditions with respect to q_i, we obtain

$$a - bQ_{-i} - 2bq_i^* - c = 0.$$

And at the symmetric equilibrium $Q_{-i} = (n-1)q_i^*$. Hence, the above first-order conditions become $a - b(n-1)q_i^* - 2bq_i^* - c = 0$ or $a - c = b(n+1)q_i^*$. Solving for q_i^*, we find that the individual output level in equilibrium is

$$q_i^* = \frac{a - c}{(n + 1) b}.$$

Hence, aggregate output in equilibrium is $Q^* = nq_i^* = \frac{n}{(n+1)}\frac{a-c}{b}$; the equilibrium price is

$$p^* = a - bQ^* = a - b\frac{n}{(n+1)}\frac{a-c}{b} = \frac{a+cn}{n+1}.$$

And equilibrium profits that every firm i obtains are

$$\pi_i^* = (p^* - c)\, q_i^* = \frac{(a-c)^2}{(n+1)^2 b}.$$

The level of social welfare with n firms, W_n, is defined by $W_n = \int_0^Q [a - bQ]dQ - cQ$. Calculating the integral, i.e., $\int_0^Q [a - bQ]dQ = aQ - \frac{b}{2}Q^2$, and substituting for $Q = \frac{n}{(n+1)}\frac{a-c}{b}$ yields a social welfare

$$W_n = \frac{n(n+2)(a-c)^2}{2n(n+1)^2}.$$

(b) *Merger.* Now let m out of n firms merge. Show that the merger is profitable if and only if it involves a sufficiently large number of firms.

- Assume that m out of n firms merge. While before the merger there are n firms in this industry, after the merger there are $n - m + 1$. In order to examine whether the merger is profitable for the m merged firms, we need to show that the profit after the merger, π_{n-m+1}, satisfies $\pi_{n-m+1} \geq m\pi_n$. That is,

$$\frac{(a-c)^2}{(n-m+2)^2} \geq m\frac{(a-c)^2}{(n+1)^2}.$$

  Solving for n, we obtain that $n < m - \sqrt{m} - 1$, as depicted in the (n, m)-pairs below the line $m - \sqrt{m} - 1$ in figure 8.3.
  And note that this condition is compatible with the fact that the merger must involve a subset of all firms, i.e., $m \leq n$; as depicted in the points below the 45° line. For instance, in an industry with $n = 100$ firms, the condition we found determines that this merger is only profitable if at least 89 firms merge.

- An alternative interpretation of the above condition can be found by, first, solving for m, which yields that $m > n + \frac{3-\sqrt{5+4n}}{2} \equiv \overline{m}$; and second, finding the market share that this minimal number of firms represents, i.e., $\overline{\alpha} = \frac{\overline{m}}{n} = \frac{3+2n-\sqrt{5+4n}}{2n}$. Importantly, this minimal market share is close to 80%, e.g., when $n = 2$ it becomes $\overline{\alpha} = 0.84$, and when $n = 10$ it is $\overline{\alpha} = 0.81$. This result is due to Salant, Switzer and Reynolds (1983), and it is usually referred as the "80% rule," intuitively indicating that the market share of the merged firms must be at least 80% for their merger to be profitable.

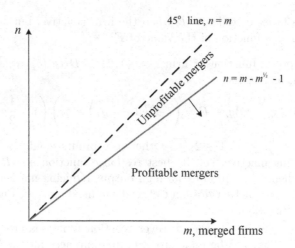

Figure 8.3 Profitable mergers satisfy $n < m - \sqrt{m} - 1$.

(c) Are the profits of the nonmerged firms larger when m of their competitors merge than when they do not?

- The number of firms producing the Cournot output decreases (since the merged firms produce a smaller output), implying that each of the *nonmerged firms* earns larger profits after the merger. This condition holds for mergers of any size, i.e., both when condition $n < m - \sqrt{m} - 1$ and otherwise. This surprising result is often referred to as the "merger paradox" as it is the nonmerged firms the ones seeing their profits increase for all parameter values. For instance, when $n > m - \sqrt{m} - 1$, the nonmerged firms increase their profits while those merging do not.

(d) Show that the merger reduces consumer welfare.

- Since the equilibrium price $p^* = \frac{a+cn}{n+1}$ is decreasing in n, i.e., $\frac{\partial p^*}{\partial n} = \frac{c-a}{(n+1)^2} < 0$ the merger increases the equilibrium price. Similarly, since $W_n = \frac{n(n+2)(a-c)^2}{2b(n+1)^2}$ is increasing in n given that

$$\frac{\partial W_n}{\partial n} = \frac{(a-c)^2}{b(n+1)^3} > 0,$$

equilibrium social welfare is reduced as a consequence of the merger. In other words, W_n and the number of firms n move in the same direction, implying that if n decreases due to the merger welfare is also reduced.

Exercise #19 — Fixed costs and discontinuities

19. Two symmetric firms compete à la Cournot in a market with demand $P(Q) = 1 - Q$, where Q denotes aggregate output. Production costs are given by $C(q) = F$ if $q > 0$ and $C(0) = 0$,

that is, every firm faces a fixed cost F when the firm is active, but zero otherwise. Find the Cournot equilibria as a function of the value of F.

- The best response function of firm $i = \{1, 2\}$ is $BRF_i(q_j) = \frac{1}{2} - \frac{1}{2}q_j$ which yields a positive profit as long as

$$(1 - q_i - q_j)q_i - F = \left(1 - \left(1 - \frac{1}{2}q_j\right) - q_j\right)\left(1 - \frac{1}{2}q_j\right) - F > 0,$$

or, solving for q_j, $q_j < 1 - 2\sqrt{F}$. Otherwise, profits would be negative and firm i is better offstaying inactive, i.e., its best response function is $BRF_i(q_j) = 0$. Intuitively, this occurs when firm j produces a high output reducing market prices, and ultimately yielding a small profit that does not exceed the fixed cost, F. Figure 8.4 depicts firm i's best response function.

We have a Cournot equilibria wherever reaction functions cross. Then we distinguish different cases. They can be understood taking into account the following:

- In the standard Cournot equilibrium ($F = 0$), equilibrium output is $q_i = \frac{1}{3}$ for every firm i, this implying that individual profits are $\frac{1}{9}$. It will still be an equilibrium if $F \leq \frac{1}{9}$.

- The other equilibrium that may arise is that in which one firm produces the monopoly output $\left(\frac{1}{2}\right)$ and the other firm does not want to produce. This will be the case if $\frac{1}{16} \leq F$, because

$$\max_q \left(1 - q - \frac{1}{2}\right)q = \frac{1}{16}.$$

- Finally when the fixed costs are greater than the monopoly profits $\left(\frac{1}{4}\right)$, no firm wants to produce. We are left with four cases each giving a different solution:

  - *Case* 1: If $1 - 2\sqrt{F} > \frac{1}{2}$, or in terms of the fixed cost, F, $0 \leq F < \frac{1}{16}$, fixed costs are low enough that best response functions cross only once at $q_1 = q_2 = \frac{1}{3}$.

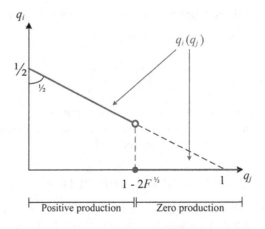

Figure 8.4 Firm i's best response function.

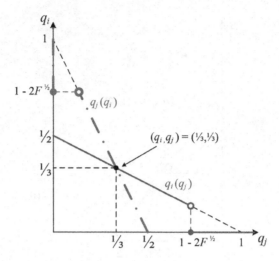

Figure 8.5 Equilibrium when fixed costs are low, $F < \frac{1}{16}$.

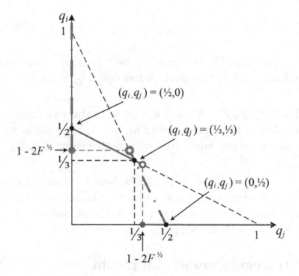

Figure 8.6 Equilibrium when fixed costs are moderately low, $\frac{1}{16} \le F \le \frac{1}{9}$.

Figure 8.5 depicts this case, where cutoff $1 - 2\sqrt{F}$ lies to the right-hand side of $\frac{1}{2}$ since $F < \frac{1}{16}$, thus yielding discontinuities on the best response functions beyond the unique crossing point.

Note that this case embodies the standard Cournot model without fixed costs ($F = 0$) as a special case.

– *Case 2*: If $\frac{1}{3} \le 1 - 2\sqrt{F} \le \frac{1}{2}$, or $\frac{1}{16} \le F \le \frac{1}{9}$. Figure 8.6 depicts this case, where cutoff $1 - 2\sqrt{F}$ lies between $\frac{1}{3}$ and $\frac{1}{2}$, thus giving rise to three different crossing

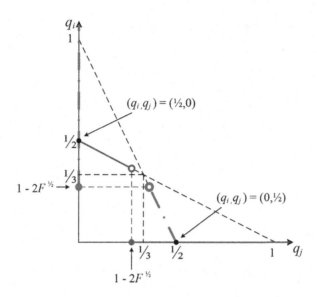

Figure 8.7 Equilibrium when fixed costs are moderately high, $\frac{1}{9} \leq F \leq \frac{1}{4}$.

points between firm i's and firm j's best response functions, each identifying one Nash equilibrium of the Cournot game, $(q_1 = q_2 = \frac{1}{3})$, $(q_1 = \frac{1}{2}, q_2 = 0)$ and $(q_1 = 0, q_2 = \frac{1}{2})$.

- *Case 3*: If $0 \leq 1 - 2\sqrt{F} < \frac{1}{3}$, or $\frac{1}{9} < F \leq \frac{1}{4}$. In this case, cutoff $1 - 2\sqrt{F}$ is smaller than $\frac{1}{3}$, thus hindering the emergence of an interior equilibria as depicted in Figure 8.7. In particular, only two equilibria arise in this context, $(q_1 = \frac{1}{2}, q_2 = 0)$ and $(q_1 = 0, q_2 = \frac{1}{2})$.

- *Case 4*: If $1 - 2\sqrt{F} < 0$ or $F > \frac{1}{4}$. The best response functions collapse to the axis (i.e., every firm i produces a zero output regardless of its competitor's output q_j), as depicted in Figure 8.8. As a consequence, the unique crossing point (and equilibrium output pair) has both firms producing a zero output at the origin, $(q_1 = 0, q_2 = 0)$.

Exercise #21 — Strategic managerial incentives

21. Consider a Cournot duopoly with linear demand $p = a - Q$ and constant marginal costs c, where $a, c \geq 0$. Suppose that each owner gives its manager an incentive contract which is a convex combination of profits (π_i) and sales (S_i):

$$\lambda_i \pi_i + (1 - \lambda_i) S_i.$$

Study the two-stage game in which first owners choose λ_i, and then managers, upon observing the offered contracts, compete à la Cournot (recall that sales are defined as simply total revenue, not profits).[2]

---

[2]This exercise is inspired by Fershtman and Judd (1987).

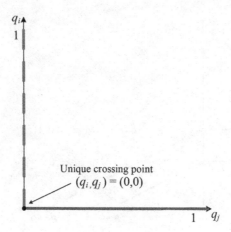

Figure 8.8 Equilibrium when fixed costs are high, $F > \frac{1}{4}$.

- *Second period (Cournot competition).* In the second period, every manager i's problem is

$$\max_{q_i} \; \lambda_i \pi_i + (1 - \lambda_i) S_i = \lambda_i \left[(a - q_i - q_j)q_i - cq_i \right] + (1 - \lambda_i) \left[(a - q_i - q_j)q_i \right]$$
$$= (a - q_i - q_j)q_i - cq_i \lambda_i.$$

Taking first-order conditions with respect to q_i yields

$$a - 2q_i - q_j - c\lambda_i = 0.$$

Solving this expression for q_i gives manager i's best response function

$$q_i(q_j) = \frac{a - c\lambda_i}{2} - \frac{q_j}{2}.$$

Intuitively, not that, relative to a standard Cournot exercise where managers maximize profits alone ($\lambda_i = 1$), this best response function originates at a higher vertical intercept, but still maintains the same slope. That is, a decrease in λ_i (giving more importance to sales in the manager's compensation) produces a parallel outward shift in firm i's best response function, as depicted in figure 8.9. Ultimately, manager i has more incentives to raise q_i for any q_j of its opponent.

Solving simultaneously for both managers 1 and 2 yield equilibrium values of

$$q_i^* = \frac{a - 2c\lambda_i + c\lambda_j}{3}$$

with prices

$$p^* = a - \frac{a - 2c\lambda_1 + c\lambda_2}{3} - \frac{a - 2c\lambda_2 + c\lambda_1}{3} = \frac{a + c\lambda_1 + c\lambda_2}{3}.$$

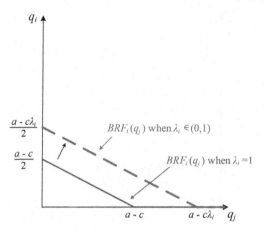

Figure 8.9 Parallel shift of the best response function.

- *First stage (incentive contract).* In the first period, the owner's problem is to choose the profit share λ_i he offers to the manager in order to maximize the firm's profits,

$$\max_{\lambda_i} \quad pq_i - cq_i = \left(\frac{a + c\lambda_i + c\lambda_j}{3}\right)\left(\frac{a - 2c\lambda_i + c\lambda_j}{3}\right) - c\left(\frac{a - 2c\lambda_i + c\lambda_j}{3}\right).$$

Taking first-order conditions with respect to λ_i yields

$$\frac{c}{3}\left(\frac{a - 2c\lambda_i + c\lambda_j}{3}\right) - \frac{2c}{3}\left(\frac{a + c(\lambda_i - 3) + c\lambda_j}{3}\right) = 0$$

which simplifies to

$$2(a + c(\lambda_i - 3) + c\lambda_j) = a - 2c\lambda_i + c\lambda_j.$$

- Invoking symmetry, $\lambda_i^* = \lambda_j^* = \lambda^*$ the first-order condition simplifies further to

$$2(a + c(2\lambda - 3)) = a - c\lambda,$$

and solving this expression for λ gives our equilibrium value of

$$\lambda^* = \frac{6c - a}{5c}.$$

which is increasing in marginal costs, c, and decreasing in a. Figure 8.10 plots λ^* as a function of c, where for simplicity we assume $a = 1$.[3] Note that when $c < \frac{1}{6}$ (and generally $c < \frac{a}{6}$) the optimal share is zero, i.e., $\lambda^* = 0$; whereas λ^* approaches 1 when $c \to a$.

---

[3]In particular, the figure depicts $\max\left\{0, \frac{6c-1}{c}\right\}$ as the profit share λ^* must satisfy $\lambda^* \in [0, 1]$ by definition.

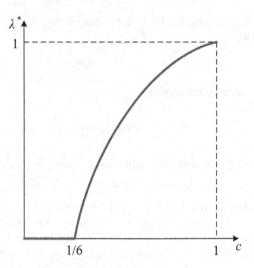

Figure 8.10 λ^* as a function of c.

Exercise #23 — Fixed costs with collusion (Bernheim and Whinston 1990)

23. Consider a market with two firms with inverse demand given by $p(Q) = 1 - Q$, where $Q = q_1 + q_2$, and the cost function is given by: $C(q) = cq + F$ if $q > 0$ and 0 otherwise. This market game is repeated infinite times. Obtain the discount factor that sustains the collusive outcome when competing à la Bertrand: both firms set the monopoly price and share equally demand. Assume that firms use "trigger strategies." (In the static equilibrium, assume that although both firms set the same price, all demand goes to one firm).

- First, since we are competing in prices, we can rewrite our inverse demand function as a demand function $D(p) = 1 - p$. To determine the monopoly price and quantity, we must solve

$$\max_p \ p(1 - p) - [c(1 - p) + F]$$

with first-order condition

$$1 - 2p + c = 0.$$

Solving this expression for p gives our equilibrium monopoly price

$$p = \frac{1 + c}{2},$$

and plugging this expression back into our demand function gives our equilibrium monopoly quantity

$$Q = 1 - p = \frac{1-c}{2}$$

with equilibrium monopoly profits

$$\pi^m = pQ - [cQ + F] = \frac{(1-c)^2}{4} - F.$$

Note that if both firms were to split the monopoly profits, they would each receive $\pi^{Coop} = \frac{(1-c)^2}{8} - F$ since they both must pay the fixed cost.

- The optimal deviation in this case would be to set $p^{Dev} = p - \varepsilon$, and capture all of the monopoly profits. This would trigger a Nash Reversion Strategy (NRS) of marginal cost pricing (i.e., $p = c$ for all future periods). This would lead to profits of $-F$ for each firm for the foreseeable future, and hence they would set their output quantities to 0 and get 0 profits in all future periods. Therefore, to sustain cooperation, we must have

$$\frac{1}{1-\delta}\pi^{Coop} > \pi^m + \frac{\delta}{1-\delta} \cdot 0,$$

$$\frac{1}{1-\delta}\left(\frac{(1-c)^2}{8} - F\right) > \frac{(1-c)^2}{4} - F + \frac{\delta}{1-\delta} \cdot 0,$$

and solving this expression for δ gives

$$\delta > \frac{(1-c)^2}{2(1-c)^2 - 8F} \equiv \bar{\delta}.$$

If $F = 0$, we obtain the well-known result ($\delta > \bar{\delta} = \frac{1}{2}$). However, as fixed costs increase the minimal discount factor $\bar{\delta}$ increases, implying that collusion becomes harder to sustain. Figure 8.11 depicts the minimal discount factor $\bar{\delta}$ required to sustain collusion as a function of F when $c = 3$, i.e., $\bar{\delta} = \frac{4}{8-8F}$.

Exercise #25 — Cournot game revisited

25. In a duopoly market, let the inverse demand curve be

$$p(Q) = \frac{a}{1 + bQ},$$

where $Q = q_1 + q_2$ denotes aggregate output, and $a, b > 0$. Let average and marginal cost be c, with $0 \le c < a$.

(a) Find best response functions. Interpret.

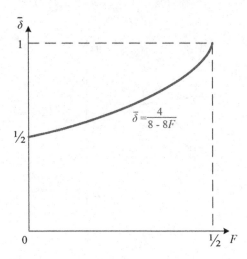

Figure 8.11 Minimal discount factor $\bar{\delta}$ as a function of F.

- Firm i's maximization problem is

$$\max_{q_i} \ \pi_i(q_i, q_j) = p(Q) \cdot q_i - cq_i = \frac{a}{1 + b(q_i + q_j)} q_i - cq_i.$$

Taking first-order conditions with respect to q_i yields

$$a\frac{(1 + bq_j)}{(1 + bq_i + bq_j)^2} - c = 0.$$

Solving this expression for q_i gives firm i's best response function

$$q_i(q_j) = \frac{-(1 + bq_j) + \sqrt{\frac{a}{c}(1 + bq_j)}}{b}.$$

- Differentiating the best response function with respect to q_j, we find its slope

$$\frac{\partial q_i(q_j)}{\partial q_j} = \frac{1}{2}\left[\sqrt{\frac{a}{c(1 + bq_j)}} - 2\right].$$

It can be seen that if $q_j = 0$, this derivative reduces to

$$\frac{\partial q_i(q_j)}{\partial q_j} = \frac{1}{2}\left[\sqrt{\frac{a}{c}} - 2\right].$$

Therefore, the slope of the best response function at its origin is positive if $\sqrt{\frac{a}{c}} > 2$, or $\frac{a}{c} > 4$, zero if $\frac{a}{c} = 4$, and negative if $\frac{a}{c} < 4$. Figure 8.12a and 8.12b show two seperate cases of best response functions for different parameter values.

a.   b.

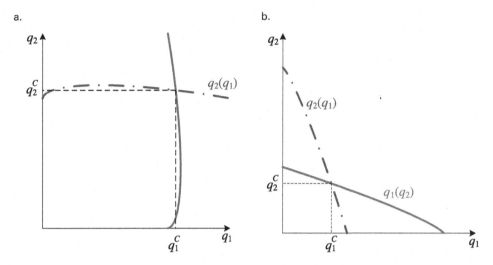

Figure 8.12 a. BRF when $a = 225$, $b = \frac{1}{2}$ and $c = 25$. b. BRF when $a = 225$, $b = \frac{1}{2}$ and $c = 100$.

(b) For what value of q_2 is the slope of firm 1's best response function equal to zero?

- Setting the derivative of firm 1's best response function equal to zero,

$$\frac{1}{2}\left[\sqrt{\frac{a}{c(1+bq_2)}} - 2\right] = 0.$$

and solving this expression for q_2 yields

$$q_2 = \frac{a - 4c}{4bc}$$

(c) Find equilibrium outputs

- We can impose symmetry on the best response function ($q_1^* = q_2^* = q$), which reduces to

$$q = \frac{-(1+bq) + \sqrt{\frac{a}{c}(1+bq)}}{b}.$$

Solving this expression for q gives our equilibrium value of

$$q^* = \frac{\frac{a-4c}{c} + \sqrt{\left(\frac{a-4c}{c}\right)^2 b^2 + 16b^2\left(\frac{a-c}{c}\right)}}{8b}.$$

Exercise #27 — Collusion with temporary reversion

27. Consider the setting in example 8.15. Under which conditions of the discount factor, δ, can cooperation be sustained if NRS prescribes a temporary, rather than permanent reversion to the Nash equilibrium during three consecutive periods?

- Recall from example 8.10, that firm i's payoff from collusion is $\frac{(a-c)^2}{8b}$ per period, whereas, from deviating, he would receive $\frac{9(a-c)^2}{64b}$ for the first period, the Cournot payoff, $\frac{(a-c)^2}{9b}$, for the three periods following, and would revert to the collusive payoff afterward. In order for cooperation to be sustained, in each period the payoff from cooperating must exceed the payoff from deviating, then being punished. Consider a period where all firms have been cooperating up to that point. The condition for cooperation to continue is

$$\frac{(a-c)^2}{8b} + \delta\frac{(a-c)^2}{8b} + \delta^2\frac{(a-c)^2}{8b} + \delta^3\frac{(a-c)^2}{8b} + \delta^4\frac{(a-c)^2}{8b} + \dots$$
$$> \frac{9(a-c)^2}{64b} + \delta\frac{(a-c)^2}{9b} + \delta^2\frac{(a-c)^2}{9b} + \delta^3\frac{(a-c)^2}{9b} + \delta^4\frac{(a-c)^2}{8b} + \dots.$$

This can be simplified to

$$\frac{(a-c)^2}{8b} + \delta\frac{(a-c)^2}{8b} + \delta^2\frac{(a-c)^2}{8b} + \delta^3\frac{(a-c)^2}{8b}$$
$$> \frac{9(a-c)^2}{64b} + \delta\frac{(a-c)^2}{9b} + \delta^2\frac{(a-c)^2}{9b} + \delta^3\frac{(a-c)^2}{9b}$$

and further rearranged to

$$\delta\left(\frac{1}{8} - \frac{1}{9}\right) + \delta^2\left(\frac{1}{8} - \frac{1}{9}\right) + \delta^3\left(\frac{1}{8} - \frac{1}{9}\right) > \frac{9}{64} - \frac{1}{8}$$
$$(\delta + \delta^2 + \delta^3)\left(\frac{1}{72}\right) > \frac{1}{64} \implies \delta + \delta^2 + \delta^3 > \frac{9}{8}.$$

Note that solving for δ we obtain three roots: two irrational numbers and $\delta \gtrsim 0.5842$. Alternatively, plotting the equation $\delta + \delta^2 + \delta^3 = \frac{9}{8}$ in the admissible range of $\delta \in [0, 1]$, we find that $\delta + \delta^2 + \delta^3 = \frac{9}{8}$ only crosses the horizontal axis once (to be precise, from below), at exactly $\delta = 0.5842$.

- Now consider a period where a deviation has been previously detected. Since the strategy prescribes that the Nash equilibrium of the stage game be played, there is no optimal deviation, and thus, cooperation during a punishment phase is optimal for all values of δ.

Exercise #29 — Impure forms of cooperation

29. Consider the setting where two firms, competing in prices, face the linear demand curve $Q = a - bp$ and marginal costs $c > 0$. Rather than colluding at the monopoly price, p^m, these firms attempt to collude at some price $p \in (c, p^m)$ in order to sustain easier collusion. Assume that if there is a deviation, both firms return to marginal cost pricing. Find the minimal discount factor sustaining cooperation as a function of p.

- The aggregate equilibrium profit in this economy from colluding is

$$\pi^{Coop} = p(a - bp) - c(a - bp) = (p - c)(a - bp)$$

for which each firm gets half

$$\pi = \frac{\pi^{Coop}}{2} = \frac{(p - c)(a - bp)}{2}.$$

- The optimal deviation from colluding would be to set $p^d = p - \varepsilon$, allowing the deviator to capture all of the profits, π^{Coop}. Hence, to sustain collusion, we must have

$$\frac{1}{1 - \delta} \frac{\pi^{Coop}}{2} > \pi^{Coop} + \frac{\delta}{1 - \delta} \times \underbrace{\pi^{Bertrand}}_{0}.$$

Rearranging,

$$\frac{1}{1 - \delta} \frac{(p - c)(a - bp)}{2} > (p - c)(a - bp),$$

solving for δ, yields

$$\frac{1}{1 - \delta} > 2 \implies \delta > \frac{1}{2},$$

which is the same result as when the monopoly price is chosen. Hence, there is a continuum of collusive prices $p \in (c, p^m]$ sustainable in the infinitely repeated version of the Bertrand game, all under the condition $\delta \in (\frac{1}{2}, 1]$.

Chapter 9 — Externalities and Public Goods

Summary This chapter examines settings in which the actions of one agent affect the welfare of other individual or firm in the economy, where this effect is not transmitted via prices. In the first exercise, we consider speeding decisions of individual drivers, and how they do not internalize the negative externality that their speeding imposes on other drivers (through an increase in the probability of suffering a car accident). The second exercise studies how pollution is affected by income—the so-called Kuznetz's curve—using a relatively general approach and afterward applying a parametric example. In exercises 4 and 5, we examine the regulator's task to induce socially optimal emission levels by imposing an emission fee—first to a monopolist, and afterward to a duopoly—measuring under which conditions the market failure arising from the externality dominates that emerging from lack of competition in that industry. Exercise 6 then studies two firms, whose production simultaneously generates a positive and a negative externality, their individual output levels, and how their production decision, consumer surplus, profits and welfare are affected if the firms choose to merge. We then examine regulation of pollutant emissions when the government has accurate information about the disutility consumers experience from pollution, but is imperfectly informed about how firms' profits increase in emissions. In particular, the regulator's use of quotas and emission fees gives rise to inefficiencies in this setting, thus implying that the regulator must choose the policy instrument that entails the smallest welfare loss (i.e., the second best policy). Exercise 7 takes a small detour to examine the problem of the commons, showing that an excessive level of exploitation will arise in the unregulated equilibrium, relative to the socially optimal outcome. We then consider two different contexts in which the presence of externalities yields equilibrium results that differ from the social optimum: (1) a setting in which a firm's production generates a smelly gas and how, under relatively general properties on the cost function, the government can use quotas or emission fees to reduce the level of the externality; and (2) a situation where an individual's consumption of one good generates a negative externality on other individuals' wellbeing. The chapter then analyzes the private contributions to provide a public good, their best response function, and how their individual contributions differ from those a social planner would select. It also considers the effect of reference points in equilibrium contributions. We finish with four applications to environmental economics: (1) the so-called Porter hypothesis, whereby firms may have incentives to invest in clean technologies; (2) the analysis of settings in which the social planner might prefer Cournot rather than Bertrand competition between the firms that operate in a polluting industry; (3) the study of mergers in industries subject to environmental regulation, and the analysis of whether firms have more incentives to merge when facing such regulation than when they do not; and (4) the regulation of a polluting industry in which firms sell differentiated products.

Exercise #1 — Externalities and car accidents

1. Consider an economy with two individuals $i = \{1, 2\}$ with the following quasi-linear utility function

$$u_i(s^i, q^i) = v^i(s^i) + \alpha w^i,$$

where s^i denotes the speed at which individual i drives his car, w^i is his wealth, and $\alpha > 0$. The utility that individual i obtains from driving fast is $v^i(s^i)$, which is increasing but concave in speed, whereby $\frac{\partial v^i(s^i)}{\partial s^i} > 0$ and $\frac{\partial^2 v^i(s^i)}{(\partial s^i)^2} < 0$. Driving fast, however, increases the probability of suffering a car accident, represented by $\gamma(s^i, s^j)$. This probability is increasing both in the speed at which individual i drives, s^i, and the speed at which other individuals drive, s^j, where $j \neq i$. Hence, the speed of other individuals imposes a negative externality on driver i, since it increases his risk of suffering a car accident. If individual i suffers an accident, he bears a cost of $c^i > 0$, which intuitively embodies the cost of fixing his car, health-care expenses, etc.

(a) *Unregulated equilibrium.* Set up individual i's expected utility maximization problem. Take first-order conditions with respect to s^i, and denote the (implicit) solution to this first-order condition as $\widehat{s}^i$.

- With probability $\gamma(s^i, s^j)$, the individual suffers a car accident, and thus his utility is $v^i(s^i) + \alpha w^i - c^i$, and with probability $1 - \gamma(s^i, s^j)$ he does not suffer the accident, leaving his utility level at $v^i(s^i) + \alpha w^i$.

- Hence, his expected utility is

$$\gamma(s^i, s^j)[v^i(s^i) + \alpha w^i - c^i] + (1 - \gamma(s^i, s^j))[v^i(s^i) - \alpha w^i],$$

which reduces to $v^i(s^i) + \alpha w^i - \gamma(s^i, s^j)c^i$. Hence, every individual i maximizes his expected utility by choosing an speed level s^i that solves

$$\max_{s^i} \ v^i(s^i) + \alpha w^i - \gamma(s^i, s^j) \times c^i.$$

Taking first-order conditions with respect to s^i we obtain

$$\frac{\partial v^i(s^i)}{\partial s^i} - \frac{\partial \gamma}{\partial s^i}c^i = 0. \tag{1}$$

Hence, driver i independently selects the speed, $\widehat{s}^i$, that solves $\frac{\partial v^i(s^i)}{\partial s^i} = \frac{\partial \gamma}{\partial s^i}c^i$.

- Intuitively, driver i increases his speed s^i until the point where the additional utility from marginally increasing s^i, $\frac{\partial v^i(s^i)}{\partial s^i}$, coincides with its associated expected individual cost from speed, i.e., a higher probability of suffering a car accident times its associated cost, as measured by $\frac{\partial \gamma}{\partial s^i}c^i$.

- *Parametric example.* Consider, for instance, a utility from driving fast of $v(s^i) = \sqrt{s^i}$ (which is increasing and concave in s^i, as required), and that the probability of suffering a car accident is $\gamma(s^i, s^j) = \beta_i s^i + \beta_j s^j$, where $\beta_i > \beta_j$ (indicating that my own speed increases the probability that I suffer a car accident more than other drivers' speeds). First-order condition (1) in this context becomes

$$\frac{1}{2\sqrt{s^i}} = \beta_i c^i,$$

and solving for s^i, we obtain an equilibrium speed of $\widehat{s}^i = \frac{1}{4(\beta_i c^i)^2}$ for every individual driver $i = \{1, 2\}$.

(b) *Social optimum.* Set up the social planner's expected welfare maximization problem. Take first-order conditions with respect to s^1 and s^2. Denote the (implicit) solution to this first-order condition as $\bar{s}^i$.

- The social planner solves the expected welfare maximization problem

$$\max_{s^1, s^2} \ v^1(s^1) + \alpha w^1 + v^2(s^2) + \alpha w^2 - \gamma(s^1, s^2) \times (c^1 + c^2)$$

Taking first-order conditions with respect to s^1, we obtain that $\bar{s}^1$ solves

$$\frac{\partial v^1(s^1)}{\partial s^1} = \frac{\partial \gamma}{\partial s^1}(c^1 + c^2), \qquad (2)$$

and similarly with respect to s^2, we obtain that $\bar{s}^2$ solves

$$\frac{\partial v^2(s^2)}{\partial s^2} = \frac{\partial \gamma}{\partial s^2}(c^1 + c^2). \qquad (3)$$

Intuitively, at the social optimum every driver i increases his speed s^i until the point where the additional utility from marginally increasing s^i coincides with its associated expected social cost from speed, measured by not only the higher probability of him suffering a car accident but also by the higher probability that the other individual $j \neq i$ suffers a car accident because of the speed s^i of individual i.

(c) *Comparison.* Show that drivers have individual incentives to drive too fast, relative to the socially optimal speed, i.e., show that $\widehat{s}^i > \bar{s}^i$.

- Comparing expressions (1) and (2), yields

$$\frac{\partial v^1(\widehat{s}^1)}{\partial s^1} < \frac{\partial v^1(\bar{s}^1)}{\partial s^1}.$$

Since $\frac{\partial^2 v^i(s^i)}{(\partial s^i)^2} < 0$ by definition, $\frac{\partial v^i(s^i)}{\partial s^i}$ is a decreasing function. Therefore, the speed that individual 1 independently selects, $\widehat{s}^1$, is excessive from a social point of view, i.e., $\widehat{s}^1 > \bar{s}^1$. Similarly, comparing (1) and (3), we have that $\widehat{s}^2 > \bar{s}^2$. Intuitively, every driver does not internalize the negative externality that his speed imposes on other drivers (in the form of a higher probability of suffering a car accident) when he independently selects his driving speed.

- Figure 9.1 represents the marginal utility, $\frac{\partial v^i(s^i)}{\partial s^i}$, and marginal expected costs, individual marginal costs, $\frac{\partial \gamma}{\partial s^i} c^i$, and social marginal costs, $\frac{\partial \gamma}{\partial s^i}(c^i + c^j)$, to support the above explanation. Since the social marginal cost curve is higher for any speed level s^i than the individual marginal cost curve, the former crosses the marginal utility curve at a lower speed level, i.e., $\overline{s}^i < \widehat{s}^i$. Intuitively, the social planner internalizes the externality that additional speed imposes on other drivers (who could suffer a car accident due to the speed of driver i), and thus reduces the speed of both drivers.

  – Note that for simplicity, we consider that the marginal utility decreases in s^i at a constant rate, i.e., $\frac{\partial^2 v^i(s^i)}{\partial s^{i2}}$ is constant in s^i or, alternatively, $\frac{\partial^3 v^i(s^i)}{(\partial s^i)^3} = 0$; implying that the marginal utility curve is a straight line. In addition, we also assume that further increases in speed s^i imply a constant increase in the probability of an accident, i.e., $\frac{\partial^2 \gamma}{(\partial s^i)^2} > 0$ but constant or, alternatively, that $\frac{\partial^3 \gamma}{(\partial s^i)^3} = 0$. This property entails the marginal cost curve is also a straight line.

  – *Parametric example.* Continuing with the previous example in which $v^i(s^i) = \sqrt{s^i}$ and $\gamma(s^i, s^j) = \beta_i s^i + \beta_j s^j$, the socially optimal speed that the social planner would select, $\overline{s}^i$, is that satisfying

$$\frac{1}{2\sqrt{\overline{s}^i}} = \beta_i(c^i + c^j),$$

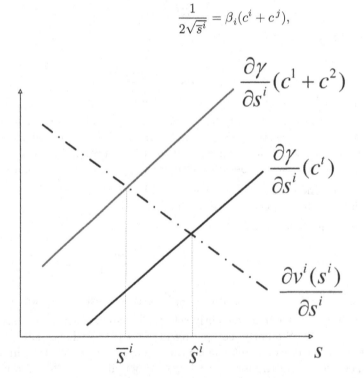

Figure 9.1 Efficient and socially optimal speed.

and solving for $\overline{s}^i$ yields $\overline{s}^i = \frac{1}{4[\beta_i(c^i+c^j)]^2}$, which clearly falls below the speed level independently selected by every driver $\widehat{s}^i = \frac{1}{4(\beta_i c^i)^2}$.

(d) *Restoring the social optimum.* Let us now evaluate the effect of speeding tickets (fines) to individuals driving too fast, i.e., to those drivers with a speed $\widehat{s}^i$ satisfying, $\widehat{s}^i > \overline{s}^i$. What is the dollar amount of the fine m^i that induces every individual i to fully internalize the externality he imposes onto others?

- Comparing (1) and (2) for driver 1, we must impose a fine of $m^1 = c^2$ in order to guarantee that (1) coincides with (2). Intuitively, this fine induces driver 1 to internalize the negative externality (higher chances of suffering a car accident and, in this case, an associated monetary cost of repairs) that he imposes on driver 2. Similarly comparing (1) and (3) for driver 2, we must impose a fine of $m^2 = c^1$ in order to guarantee that (1) coincides with (3).

(e) Let us now consider that individuals obtain a utility from driving fast, $v^i(s^i)$, only in the case that no accident occurs. Repeat steps (*a*) through (*c*), finding the optimal fine m^i that induces individuals to fully internalize the externality.

- *Equilibrium speed.* In this section of the exercise, driver i only obtains utility from driving fast, $v^i(s^i)$, when no accident occurs. Given that the probability that an accident does *not* occur is $1 - \gamma(s^1, s^2)$, the utility of driver i is

$$\underbrace{[1 - \gamma(s^1, s^2)]\left(v^i(s^i) + \alpha w^i\right)}_{\text{No accident}} + \underbrace{\gamma(s^i, s^j)(\alpha w^i - c^i)}_{\text{Accident}},$$

which can be rearranged as

$$v^i(s^i) + \alpha w^i - \gamma(s^i, s^j)\left[c^i + v^i(s^i)\right].$$

Taking first-order conditions with respect to s^i, we obtain that the individual driver i independently selects the speed $\overline{s}^i$ that solves

$$\frac{\partial v^i(s^i)}{\partial s^i}\left[1 - \gamma(s^i, s^j)\right] = \frac{\partial \gamma}{\partial s^i}(c^i + v^i(s^i)), \qquad (4)$$

where conveniently separates the marginal utility of driving faster in the left-hand side, which only arises if driver i does not suffer a car accident, an event with probability $1 - \gamma(s^i, s^j)$; and its associated marginal cost in the right-hand side, which captures the higher probability of suffering a car accident, $\frac{\partial \gamma}{\partial s^i}$, and its two costs: one explicit, c^i, and one implicit, namely, the utility from driving that driver i would have to give up (since he can only benefit from driving when he does not suffer a car accident).

- *Parametric example.* Following with the on-going parametric example, the above first-order condition (4) becomes

$$\frac{1}{2\sqrt{\overline{s}^i}}\left[1 - (\beta_i \overline{s}^i + \beta_j \overline{s}^j)\right] = \beta_i(c^i + \sqrt{\overline{s}^i}),$$

and similarly for driver j. Before solving for $\overline{s}^i$ in order to driver i's best response function, let us assume (in order to keep our parametric example compact) that $\beta_i = \beta_j = \frac{1}{2}$ and $c^i = c^j = \frac{2}{3}$. In this context, solving for $\overline{s}^i$ we obtain

$$\overline{s}^i(\overline{s}^j) = 2 - 3\overline{s}^j - \frac{4}{3}\sqrt{\overline{s}^j}.$$

Since both drivers are symmetric, $\overline{s}^i = \overline{s}^j$, we can solve for $\overline{s}^i$ yielding a symmetric equilibrium speed level of $\overline{s}^i = 0.313$.

- *Socially optimal speed.* The social planner's maximization problem in this case becomes

$$\max_{s^1, s^2} \ v^1(s^1) + \alpha w^1 - \gamma(s^1, s^2)\left[c^1 + v^1(s^1)\right] + v^2(s^2) + \alpha w^2 - \gamma(s^1, s^2)\left[c^2 + v^2(s^2)\right].$$

Taking first-order conditions with respect to s^i, we obtain that the socially optimal speed, $\widehat{s}^i$, solves

$$\frac{\partial v^i(s^i)}{\partial s^i}\left[1 - \gamma(s^i, s^j)\right] = \frac{\partial \gamma}{\partial s^i}\left[c^i + v^i(s^i)\right] + \frac{\partial \gamma}{\partial s^i}\left[c^j + v^j(s^j)\right]. \qquad (5)$$

- *Comparison.* Comparing expressions (4) and (5), we obtain that the fine m^i that induces every individual i to internalize the externality that his driving imposes on others is

$$m^i = c^j + v^j(s^j).$$

Intuitively, now an increase in the speed of driver i not only increases the probability that driver j suffers a car accident, and thus needs to incur a cost of c^j, it also reduces the utility from driving that driver j can only experience if he is not involved in a car accident.

  - *Parametric example.* Following with the on-going parametric example, the above first-order condition (4) becomes

$$\frac{1}{2\sqrt{\widehat{s}^{ii}}}\left[1 - (\beta_i \widehat{s}^i + \beta_j \widehat{s}^j)\right] = \beta_i\left[(c^i + \sqrt{\widehat{s}^i}) + (c^j + \sqrt{\widehat{s}^j})\right],$$

Before solving for $\widehat{s}^i$ in order to driver i's best response function, let us assume (in order to keep our parametric example compact) that $\beta_i = \beta_j = \frac{1}{2}$ and $c^i = c^j = \frac{2}{3}$. In this context, we can simultaneously solve for $\widehat{s}^i$ and $\widehat{s}^j$ obtaining $\widehat{s}^i = \widehat{s}^j = 0.157$, which is indeed a lower speed than when drivers independently choose their own driving speed, $\overline{s}^i = 0.313$.

Exercise #3 — Positive and negative externalities

3. Consider an economy with two firms which produce a homogeneous good. Firm 1 produces q_1 units of the good, and its cost function is $c_1(q_1, q_2) = 2q_1^2 + 5q_1 + q_2$, while firm 2 produces

q_2 units of the same good and its cost function is $c_2(q_2, q_1) = q_2^2 + 3q_2 - 4q_1$. Note that every firm i's costs depends on its rival's output, q_j, where $j \neq i$. Finally, inverse market demand is given by $p(Q) = 34 - Q$, where $Q = q_1 + q_2$ denotes aggregate output.

(a) *Unregulated equilibrium.* Considering that every firm independently and simultaneously selects its production level, determine equilibrium output q_1 and q_2. What are the associated profits for each firm? Measure consumer surplus, profits and social welfare.

- Since $\frac{\partial c_1(q_1, q_2)}{\partial q_2} = 1 > 0$ and $\frac{\partial c_2(q_2, q_1)}{\partial q_1} = -4 < 0$, firm 2 generates a negative externality on firm 1 (i.e., q_2 increases firm 1's costs), while firm 1 produces a positive externality on firm 2. In order to determine the equilibrium level of q_1 and q_2, we need to separately consider each firm's profit-maximization problem. First, firm 1 chooses the level of q_1 that solves

$$\max_{q_1 \geq 0} \ (34 - q_1 - q_2)\, q_1 - \left(2q_1^2 + 5q_1 + q_2\right).$$

Taking first-order condition with respect to q_1, we obtain $29 - 6q_1 - q_2 = 0$. Solving for q_1 we find firm 1's best response function, $q_1(q_2) = \frac{29 - q_2}{6}$. Similarly, firm 2 solves

$$\max_{q_2 \geq 0} \ (34 - q_1 - q_2)\, q_2 - \left(q_2^2 + 3q_2 - 4q_1\right),$$

and taking first-order condition with respect to q_2, we have $31 - q_1 - 4q_2 = 0$. Thus, solving for q_2 we obtain firm 2's best response function, $q_2(q_1) = \frac{31 - q_1}{4}$. Plugging $q_2(q_1)$ into $q_1(q_2)$, we find the equilibrium output levels $q_1^* = \frac{85}{23} \simeq 3.69$ and $q_2^* = \frac{157}{23} \simeq 6.82$. Therefore, the aggregate supply is $Q^S(p) = q_1^* + q_2^* = \frac{242}{23} \simeq 10.52$, with an equilibrium price of $p = 34 - \frac{242}{23} = \frac{540}{23} \simeq \$23.47$.

- Equilibrium profits are therefore $\pi_1 = 34.14$ and $\pi_2 = 107.97$ for firm 1 and 2, respectively, and aggregate profits are $\pi = 142.11$.

- Consumer surplus is, hence, given by the area of the triangle below the inverse demand curve and above the equilibrium price of $23.47.

$$CS = \frac{1}{2}(34 - 23.47) \cdot 10.52 = 55.39.$$

Thus, social welfare is $W = CS + \pi = 197.5$.

- Finally, notice that this output allocation is inefficient: firm 1 (the agent who generates the positive externality) produces too little, whereas firm 2 (the agent who causes the negative externality) produces too much. We formally show this result in the next question, where firms are allowed to merge and thus internalize the positive and negative externalities of their production decisions.

(b) *Merger.* Assume that the government is aware of these mutual externalities between firm 1 and 2, but does not want to directly regulate their production by the imposition of quotas or fees. Instead, the regulator allows both firms to merge. Determine the equilibrium level of q_1 and q_2 that the newly merged firm will choose, and check if firm 1 and 2 have incentives to merge.

- This merge is equivalent to a horizontal integration, whereby firms choose the level of q_1 and q_2 in order to maximize their joint profits, as follows:

$$\max_{q_1 \geq 0, q_2 \geq 0} \ (34 - q_1 - q_2)(q_1 + q_2) - (2q_1^2 + 5q_1 + q_2) - (q_2^2 + 3q_2 - 4q_1).$$

Taking first-order conditions with respect to q_1 and q_2, we obtain

$$33 - 6q_1 - 2q_2 = 0, \quad \text{and}$$
$$30 - 2q_1 - 4q_2 = 0,$$

where we can simultaneously solve for q_1 and q_2 to find $q_1 = \frac{18}{5} = 3.6$ and $q_2 = \frac{57}{10} = 5.7$.

- Thus, the production of firm 2 (which generates a negative externality on firm 1) is significantly reduced, from 6.28 to 5.7 units. Aggregate supply is hence $Q^S(p) = \frac{93}{10} = 9.3$ units, with an equilibrium price of $p = 34 - 9.3 = \$24.7$. Aggregate output thus decreases and the equilibrium price increases as a consequence, from \$23.47 to \$24.7.

- Equilibrium profits are therefore $\pi_1 = 39.3$ and $\pi_2 = 105.6$ for firm 1 and 2, respectively, and aggregate profits are $\pi = 144.9$. Aggregate profits increase as a result of the merger, and hence firms have incentives to merge. (While aggregate profits increase, the individual profits of firm 2 decrease, suggesting that firm 2 will only be attracted to merge if firm 1 compensates it.)

(c) *Comparisons.* Compare consumer surplus, profits and welfare after the merger (as you found in part b) and before the merger (as found in part a). Does the merger ameliorate the negative externality that the production of firm 2 generates? Does social welfare increase as a result of the merger?

- After the merge, consumer surplus is

$$CS = \frac{1}{2}(34 - 24.7) \cdot 9.3 = 43.24.$$

Thus, social welfare is $W = CS + \pi = 188.14$.

- Comparing our results in parts (a) and (b), we can summarize that, as a result of the merger firms are better off, they not only maximize joint profits, as in a standard cartel exercise, but, in addition, they solve the mutual externality problem they face in part (a). However, the merger leads firms to reduce aggregate production, which increases market prices, ultimately reducing consumer surplus (and aggregate welfare). Hence, while the mutual externalities are internalized by the merger, their monopolistic effects yield a net welfare loss.

Exercise #5 — Regulating externalities under incomplete information

5. Consider a polluting firm with profit function $\pi(q) = 10q - q^2$, where q denotes units of the externality-generating activity (for instance, q can represent units of output if each unit

generates one unit of pollution). Pollution damage to consumers is given by the convex damage function $d(q) = 3q^2$. Let us analyze a context in which the regulator does not observe the firm's profit function, but observes the damage which additional pollution causes on consumers. In particular, the regulator estimates that marginal profits are

$$\frac{\partial \pi(q, a)}{\partial q} = 10 - 2aq,$$

where the random parameter a takes two equally likely values, $a = 1$ or $a = \frac{1}{2}$. (Note that in our above description we assume that the firm privately observes that the realization of parameter a is $a = 1$, thus yielding a marginal profit function of $10 - 2q$.) We will first determine which is the best quota and emission fee that the regulator can design given that he operates under incomplete information. Afterwards, we will evaluate the welfare that arises under each of these policy instruments, to determine which is better from a social point of view.

(a) *Unregulated equilibrium.* Find the equilibrium amount of pollution, q^E, if the firm is unregulated and no bargaining occurs between the affected consumers and the firm.

- In this setting, the firm maximizes its profits by solving

$$\max_q \pi(q).$$

Taking first-order conditions with respect to q, yields $\frac{\partial \pi(q^E)}{\partial q} \leq 0$. Since $\frac{\partial \pi(q)}{\partial q} = 10 - 2q$ by definition, then

$$\frac{\partial \pi(q^E, \alpha)}{\partial q} = 10 - 2q^E \leq 0, \text{ with equality for } q^E > 0.$$

Solving for q^E, we obtain an equilibrium amount of pollution (in interior solutions) of $q^E = 5$ units.

(b) *Setting a quota.* In this incomplete information setting, determine which is the best quota x_q that a social planner can select in order to maximize the expected value of aggregate surplus.

- The firm must produce an output level exactly equal to the quota. The social planner determines the optimal quantity $\widehat{q}$ by choosing the value of q that maximizes the expected value of aggregate surplus (since the social planner does not know the precise realization of parameter a),

$$\max_q E_a[\pi(q, a)] - d(q).$$

And taking first-order condition with respect to q, we obtain

$$E_a\left[\frac{\partial \pi(\widehat{q}, a)}{\partial q}\right] - \frac{\partial d(\widehat{q})}{\partial q} \leq 0.$$

We can now substitute the functional forms for the marginal damage for consumers, $\frac{\partial d(q)}{\partial q}$, and the expected marginal profits for the firm, $\frac{\partial \pi(q,a)}{\partial q}$, yielding

$$\frac{1}{2}(10 - 2 \cdot \widehat{q}) + \frac{1}{2}\left(10 - 2 \cdot \frac{1}{2} \cdot \widehat{q}\right) - 6\widehat{q} \leq 0,$$

which reduces to

$$5 - \widehat{q} + 5 - \frac{1}{2} \cdot \widehat{q} - 6\widehat{q} \leq 0, \text{ or } \widehat{q} \geq \frac{4}{3}.$$

(c) *Setting an emission fee.* Find the best tax t^* that this social planner can set under the context of incomplete information described above.

- Given a tax t^*, the government predicts firm's expected best response function by maximizing its expected profits.

$$\max_t \ E_a[\pi(q,a)] - tq.$$

Taking first-order condition with respect to t, yields

$$E_a\left[\frac{\partial \pi(q,a)}{\partial q}\right] - t = 0,$$

and plugging our functional forms, we obtain

$$5 - q + 5 - \frac{1}{2} \cdot q = t,$$

which yields an output function $q(t) = \frac{20 - 2t}{3}$. Provided this expected output function, we can now find the optimal tax that the social planner imposes, anticipating the firm's expected best response function, as follows:

$$\max_t \ E_a[\pi(q(t),a)] - d(q(t)).$$

Taking first-order conditions with respect to t, and applying the chain rule, yields

$$E\left[\frac{\partial \pi(q(t),a)}{\partial q} \cdot \frac{\partial q(t)}{\partial t}\right] = \frac{\partial d(q(t))}{\partial q} \cdot \frac{\partial q(t)}{\partial t},$$

where we use the chain rule. Intuitively, the regulator equals the marginal disutility of additional pollution to consumers (which he can perfectly assess), as represented in the right-hand side of the equality; and the expected marginal profits from additional pollution for the firm (which he cannot observe), represented in the left-hand side of the above expression.

- Since $q\left(t\right) = \frac{20-2t}{3}$ then the derivative $\frac{\partial q(t)}{\partial t} = -\frac{2}{3}$ is a constant, that can be taken out of the expectation operator. That is,

$$\frac{\partial q(t)}{\partial t} E\left[\frac{\partial \pi(q(t), a)}{\partial q}\right] = \frac{\partial d\left(q\left(t\right)\right)}{\partial q} \cdot \frac{\partial q(t)}{\partial t}.$$

Therefore, we can cancel out the $\frac{\partial q(t)}{\partial t}$ term on both sides of the equality, which yields

$$E\left[\frac{\partial \pi(q(t), a)}{\partial q}\right] = \frac{\partial d\left(q\left(t\right)\right)}{\partial q}.$$

Substituting the functional form of our marginal benefit and marginal profit functions, the above first-order condition becomes

$$\frac{1}{2}\left(10 - 2 \cdot q\left(t\right)\right) + \frac{1}{2}\left(10 - 2 \cdot \frac{1}{2} \cdot q\left(t\right)\right) = 6q\left(t\right),$$

$$q\left(t\right) = \frac{4}{3}.$$

Substituting $q\left(t\right) = \frac{20-2t}{3}$, we can finally find the optimal tax t^* that solves

$$\frac{20 - 2t^*}{3} = \frac{4}{3}, \text{ or } t^* = 8.$$

(d) *Policy comparison.* Compare the emission fee and the quota in terms of their associated deadweight loss. Under which conditions an uninformed regulator prefers to choose the emission fee?

- We need to compare the expected difference in losses in order to determine when a tax or a quota instrument is better. Figure 9.2 illustrates the welfare loss associated to tax t^*, which induces an externality level of $q\left(t^*\right)$.
  The figure considers that the regulator sets a tax based on the certain marginal disutility from the externality and the expected marginal profit. However, the realization of parameter a implies that the real and expected marginal profits do not coincide, thus giving rise to a welfare loss associated to a suboptimal tax due to the regulator's imprecise information.

- If the regulator, instead, imposes a quota, $\hat{q}$, figure 9.3 illustrates the associated welfare loss.

- *Welfare loss from the fee.* In order to compute the welfare loss from the tax, WL_t, we first need to find the socially optimal level of externality, q^{SO}, given the true $a = 1$. In particular, q^{SO} solves

$$\frac{\partial d(q^{SO})}{\partial q} = \frac{\partial \pi(q^{SO})}{\partial q},$$

$$6q^{SO} = 10 - 2q^{SO},$$

$$q^{SO} = \frac{5}{4}.$$

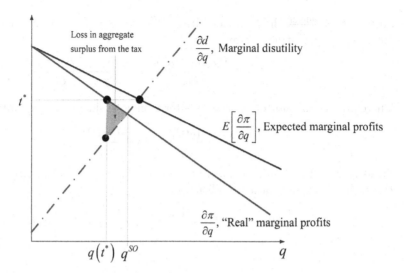

Figure 9.2 Welfare loss from a tax.

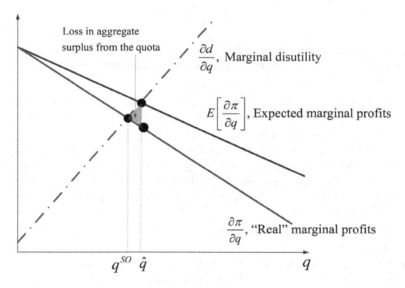

Figure 9.3 Welfare loss from a quota.

Moreover, given an emission fee, the firm maximizes profits. That is, it chooses the level of q that maximizes its profits (net of tax payments), as follows:

$$\max_{q} \pi\left(q\right) - q \cdot t.$$

The firm, hence, takes first-order condition with repect to q, yielding

$$\frac{\partial \pi(q)}{\partial q} - t = 0.$$

Since the firm knows its true marginal profit $\frac{\partial \pi(q)}{\partial q} = 10 - 2q$, the above expression becomes $10 - 2q - t = 0$, which yields an output function $q(t) = 5 - \frac{1}{2}t$. Given that $t^* = 8$, such fee induces an externality level of

$$q(t^*) = 5 - \frac{t^*}{2} = 1.$$

Finally, we need to evaluate the marginal disutility function $\frac{\partial d(q)}{\partial q} = 6q$ at $q(t^*) = 1$, which yields

$$\frac{\partial d(q)}{\partial q} = 6q(t^*) = 6.$$

Hence, the WL_t is given by the area of the shaded triangle in figure 9.2,

$$\begin{aligned}
WL_t &= \frac{1}{2}\left[q^{SO} - q(t^*)\right] \cdot \left[t^* - 6q(t^*)\right] \\
&= \frac{1}{2}\left[\frac{5}{4} - 1\right] \cdot [8 - 6] \\
&= \frac{1}{4}.
\end{aligned}$$

- *Welfare loss from the quota.* If, in contrast, the regulator uses a quota of $\hat{q} = \frac{4}{3}$, then we first need to evaluate the real marginal profits of the quota, that is,

$$10 - 2q = 10 - 2 \times \frac{4}{3} = \frac{30}{3} - \frac{8}{3} = \frac{22}{3}.$$

Second, we need to evaluate the expected marginal profit, $\frac{1}{2}(10 - 2 \cdot q) + \frac{1}{2}\left(10 - 2 \cdot \frac{1}{2} \cdot q\right)$, at the quota $\hat{q} = \frac{4}{3}$, i.e.,

$$\frac{1}{2}\left(10 - 2 \cdot \frac{4}{3}\right) + \frac{1}{2}\left(10 - 2 \cdot \frac{1}{2} \cdot \frac{4}{3}\right) = 8.$$

Therefore, the welfare loss from the quota is the area of the shaded triangle in figure 9.3. That is,

$$\begin{aligned}
WL_q &= \frac{1}{2}(\hat{q} - q^{SO})\left[8 - \frac{22}{3}\right] \\
&= \frac{1}{2}(\frac{4}{3} - \frac{5}{4})\left[\frac{24}{3} - \frac{22}{3}\right] \\
&= \frac{1}{36}.
\end{aligned}$$

- *Comparing welfare losses.* Comparing WL_t and WL_q, we obtain that

$$WL_t = \frac{1}{4} > \frac{1}{36} = WL_q.$$

Hence, setting a quota is better than imposing an emission fee in this case.[1]

Exercise #7 — Entry in the commons

7. Consider a common pool resource initially operated by a single firm during two periods, appropriating x_i units in the first period and q_i units in the second period. In particular, assume that its first-period cost function is $\frac{x_i^2}{\theta}$ where $\theta > 0$, while second-period cost function is $\frac{q_i^2}{\theta-(1-\beta)x_i}$. Intuitively, parameter θ reflects the initial abundance of stock, i.e., a large θ decreases the firms' first- and second-period costs; while β denotes the regeneration rate of the resource. Hence, if regeneration is complete, $\beta = 1$, first- and second-period costs coincide, but if regeneration is null, $\beta = 0$, second period costs become $\frac{q_i^2}{\theta-x_i}$ and thus every unit of first-period appropriation x_i increases the firm's second-period costs. For simplicity, assume that every unit of output is sold at a price of \$1 at the international market.[2] Last, assume that second-period profits are discounted at a rate $\delta \in [0, 1]$.

   (a) Assuming no entry during both periods (i.e., the incumbent operates alone in both periods), find the profit-maximizing second-period appropriation, q_i^{NE}, and its first-period appropriation, x_i^{NE}, where superscript NE denotes no entry. [*Hint*: Use backward induction.]

   - *Second period.* Operating by backward induction, let us first analyze the second period. For a given first-period appropriation x_i, with price equal to 1, the incumbent's profit maximization problem is

$$\max_{q_i \geq 0} \quad q_i - \frac{q_i^2}{\theta - (1-\beta)x_i}.$$

   Taking first-order conditions with respect to q_i yields

$$1 - \frac{2q_i}{\theta - (1-\beta)x_i} = 0.$$

   Solving for q_i we obtain

$$q_i(x_i) = \frac{\theta - (1-\beta)x_i}{2},$$

   which is increasing in the initial abundance of the stock, θ, and in its regeneration rate, β, but decreasing in first-period appropriation, x_i.

---

[1] For more details about the welfare properties of emission fees and quotas under contexts in which the regulator is imperfectly informed, see Weitzman (1974).

[2] This exercise is based on Espinola-Arredondo and Munoz-Garcia (2013). The exercise, however, focuses on a complete information setting, whereas the article examines how the presence of incomplete information affect equilibrium appropriation, and ultimately welfare levels.

- *First period.* Given the optimal second-period appropriation function $q_i(x_i)$ we found above, the incumbent selects the level of x_i to solve the discounted sum of first and second periods profits.

$$\max_{x_i \geq 0} \underbrace{\left[x_i - \frac{x_i^2}{\theta} \right]}_{\text{First period}} + \underbrace{\delta \left[q_i(x) - \frac{q_i^2(x)}{\theta - (1-\beta)x_i} \right]}_{\text{Second period}}.$$

Taking first-order conditions with respect to x_i yields

$$\frac{1}{4}\left(4 - \delta(1-\beta) - \frac{8x_i}{\theta} \right) = 0,$$

and solving for x_i, we obtain

$$x_i^{NE} = \frac{\theta \left(4 - (1-\beta)\delta \right)}{8}.$$

Therefore, evaluating $q_i^{NE}(x_i)$ at x_i^{NE} yields a second-period appropriation of

$$\begin{aligned}
q_i^{NE}\left(x_i^{NE}\right) &= \frac{\theta - (1-\beta)x_i}{2} \\
&= \frac{\theta - (1-\beta) \cdot \frac{\theta(4-(1-\beta)\delta)}{8}}{2} \\
&= \frac{\theta\left[4 + 4\beta + (1-\beta)^2\delta \right]}{16}.
\end{aligned}$$

(b) Assume that entry occurs in the second period, and that the second-period cost function for both incumbent and entrant becomes $\frac{(q_i+q_j)q_i}{\theta-(1-\beta)x_i}$. Find the profit-maximizing second-period appropriation, q_i^E and q_j^E, and first-period appropriation, x_i^E, where superscript E denotes entry.

- *Second period.* When entry occurs in the second period, the incumbent's second-period profit-maximization problem becomes

$$\max_{q_i \geq 0} \quad q_i - \frac{(q_i + q_j)q_i}{\theta - (1-\beta)x_i}$$

Taking first-order conditions and solving for q_i, we obtain the incumbent's best response function

$$q_i(q_j, x_i) = \frac{\theta - (1-\beta)x_i}{2} - \frac{1}{2}q_j.$$

Note that when $q_j = 0$, this function reduces to $q_i(0, x_i) = \frac{\theta-(1-\beta)x_i}{2}$, thus coinciding with the second-period appropriation level when entry does not ensue that we found in part (a). However, if $q_j > 0$, the incumbent's second-period appropriation decreases.

- By symmetry, the entrant's best response function is

$$q_j \left(q_i, x_i \right) = \frac{\theta - (1 - \beta) \, x_i}{2} - \frac{1}{2} q_i.$$

Simultaneously solving for q_i and q_j, yields

$$q_i^E \left(x_i \right) = q_j^E \left(x_i \right) = \frac{\theta - (1 - \beta) \, x_i}{3}.$$

- *First period.* Given these profit-maximizing second-period appropriation functions, the incumbent selects x_i in order to maximize the discounted sum of profits

$$\max_{x_i \geq 0} \underbrace{\left[x_i - \frac{x_i^2}{\theta} \right]}_{\text{First period}} + \delta \underbrace{\left[q_i^E \left(x \right) - \frac{\left[q_i^E \left(x \right) + q_j^E \left(x \right) \right] q_i^E \left(x \right)}{\theta - (1 - \beta) \, x_i} \right]}_{\text{Second period}}.$$

Taking first-order conditions with respect to x_i, yields

$$1 - \delta \frac{1}{9} (1 - \beta) - \frac{2x_i}{\theta} = 0.$$

Solving for x_i we obtain the first-period appropriation in equilibrium

$$x_i^E = \frac{\theta \left[9 - (1 - \beta) \, \delta \right]}{18}.$$

We can finally substitute x_i^E into $q_i^E \left(x_i \right)$ and $q_j^E \left(x_i \right)$, which yields a second-period appropriation level of

$$q_i^E \left(x_i^E \right) = q_j^E \left(x_i^E \right) = \frac{\theta - (1 - \beta) \left(\frac{\theta[9 - (1-\beta)\delta]}{18} \right)}{3}$$

$$= \frac{\theta \left[9 + \delta + \beta \left(9 - (2 - \beta) \, \delta \right) \right]}{54}.$$

Exercise #9 — Voluntary contributions to a public good with Cobb–Douglas preferences

9. Consider a setting with N individuals, each of them simultaneously and independently deciding how many dollars to contribute to a public good. Assume that each individual has a Cobb–Douglas utility function $u(x_i, G) = x_i^{1-\alpha} G^\alpha$ where $G = \sum_{j=1}^n g_j$ denotes aggregate contributions and $\alpha \in (0, 1)$ for all $i = 1, ..., N$. For simplicity, normalize the price of the public good.

   (a) Set up the utility maximization problem of agent i. Find the demand functions denoted $(x_i(\cdot), G(\cdot))$, for the private and public good.

- Agent i's maximization problem is

$$\max_{x_i, g_i} \ x_i^{1-\alpha} G^\alpha = x_i^{1-\alpha} \underbrace{\left(g_i + \sum_{i \neq j} g_j \right)^\alpha}_{G}$$

$$\text{subject to} \quad px_i + g_i = \omega_i,$$

since $\frac{p_2}{p_2} = 1$ and $\frac{p_1}{p_2} \equiv p$. Inserting the constraint into the objective function, we obtain the following (unconstrained) problem

$$\max_{x_i} \ x_i^{1-\alpha} \left(\omega_i - px_i + \sum_{i \neq j} g_j \right)^\alpha$$

Differentiating with respect to x_i, we find

$$(1-\alpha)x_i^{-\alpha} \left(\omega_i - px_i + \sum_{i \neq j} g_j \right)^\alpha - \alpha p x_i^{1-\alpha} \left(\omega_i - px_i + \sum_{i \neq j} g_j \right)^{\alpha-1} = 0$$

which, after regarranging, yields

$$(1-\alpha) \left(\omega_i + \sum_{i \neq j} g_j \right) = px_i$$

or

$$\underbrace{\omega_i - px_i}_{g_i} = \alpha \left(\omega_i + \sum_{i \neq j} g_j \right) - \sum_{i \neq j} g_j$$

Using $px_i + g_i = \omega_i$ on the left-hand side of the above equation, or $g_i = \omega_i - px_i$, we find consumer i's demand for the public good:

$$g_i = \alpha \omega_i - (1-\alpha) \sum_{i \neq j} g_j$$

- Intuitively, this expression is consumer i's best response function, as it identifies the utility-maximizing contribution he makes to the public good as a function of the donation of all other donors, $\sum_{i \neq j} g_j$. As usual, an increase in other donors' contributions decreases individual i's donation by $(1-\alpha)$. If no other contributor donates the public good, i.e., $\sum_{i \neq j} g_j = 0$, his donation becomes a fraction of his wealth, i.e., $g_i^* = \alpha \omega_i$.

(b) Suppose that individuals are ranked according to wealth, whereby $\omega_1 \geq \omega_2 \geq \ldots \geq \omega_n$. Find conditions on ω_i and α for an equilibrium in which $g_2^* = \ldots = g_n^* = 0$ and agent 1 is the only contributor (only the richest individual contributes).

- To solve this, we only need to find conditions for which agent 2 will contribute 0 to the public good. If he does not contribute, then all other agents $j > 2$, having less wealth than agent 2, will not contribute to the public good either.

- For agent 2, she will contribute zero to the public good if

$$g_2^* = \alpha\omega_2 - (1 - \alpha)g_1^* \leq 0,$$

and solving this expression for g_1^* yields $g_1^* \geq \frac{\alpha}{1-\alpha}\omega_2$. Likewise, we have agent 1's contribution to the public good $g_1^* = \alpha\omega_1$. Hence, in order for agent 2 to not contribute to the public good, we must have

$$g_1^* = \alpha\omega_1 \geq \frac{\alpha}{1 - \alpha}\omega_2,$$

or, solving for ω_1,

$$\omega_1 \geq \frac{1}{1 - \alpha}\omega_2.$$

For instance, if $\alpha = \frac{1}{2}$, then $\omega_1 \geq 2\omega_2$, i.e., individual 1 must be twice as rich as individual 2 (the second richest individual in the population) for him to be the only donor.

(c) Let G_k denote aggregate donations in equilibrium when the total wealth W is divided equally among k individuals.

1. Suppose first that we divide the wealth W among 2 individuals. Find aggregate donations in this case, G_2, and show that they are lower than aggregate donations when a single individual holds all the wealth, whereby $G_2 < G_1$.

   - When a single individual holds all the wealth, $\omega_1 = W$, his contribution becomes $g_1^* = \alpha W$, which coincides with aggregate donations, i.e., $G_1 = g_1^* = \alpha W$.

   - For two individuals, their equilibrium bundles can be shown from part (a) as

$$x_i^* = \frac{(1 - \alpha)\left(\frac{W}{2} + g_j\right)}{p} \quad \text{for the private good, and}$$

$$g_i^* = \alpha\frac{W}{2} - (1 - \alpha)g_j \quad \text{for the public good, where } i, j = 1, 2 \text{ and } i \neq j$$

We can aggregate the individual contributions to the public good to find

$$G_2 = \sum_{k=1}^{2} g_k^* = \alpha W - (1 - \alpha)\overbrace{(g_1 + g_2)}^{G_2}$$

and solving for G_2 yields

$$G_2 = \frac{\alpha W}{2 - \alpha} < \alpha W = G_1$$

as required.

2. More generally, suppose that the wealth is divided into k equal shares $\frac{W}{k}$ among k consumers. Compute the equilibrium value of G_k and show that $G_k \to 0$ when $k \to +\infty$. (The smallest amount of public production is supplied when everyone is a contributor).

- From part (a),

$$x_i^* = \frac{(1 - \alpha)\left(\frac{W}{k} + \sum_{i \neq j} g_j\right)}{p} \quad \text{for the private good, and}$$

$$g_i^* = \alpha \frac{W}{k} - (1 - \alpha) \sum_{i \neq j} g_j \quad \text{for the public good, where } i, j = 1, 2 \text{ and } i \neq j.$$

And aggregating the individual donations to the public good, we find

$$G_k = \sum_{k=1}^{k} g_k^* = \alpha W - (1 - \alpha)(k - 1)G_k,$$

where the $(k-1)G_k$ term comes from the fact that for all k agents, $k-1$ provisions of the public good are added together, with each individual provision omitted exactly once. This creates $k - 1$ complete sets of the provision. Solving for G_k yields an aggregate contribution of

$$G_k = \frac{\alpha W}{1 + (1 - \alpha)(k - 1)}.$$

- Evaluating the limit of G_k as $k \to +\infty$, we obtain

$$\lim_{k \to +\infty} \frac{\alpha W}{1 + (1 - \alpha)(k - 1)} = 0$$

as required.

Exercise #11 — Externalities in consumption

11. Consider two consumers with utility functions over two goods, x_1 and x_2, given by

$$u_A = \log(x_1^A) + x_2^A - \frac{1}{2}\log(x_1^B) \quad \text{for consumer } A, \text{ and}$$

$$u_B = \log(x_1^B) + x_2^B - \frac{1}{2}\log(x_1^A) \quad \text{for consumer } B,$$

where the consumption of good 1 by individual $i = \{A, B\}$ creates a negative externality on individual $j \neq i$ (see the third term, which enters negatively on each individual's utility function). For simplicity, consider that both individuals have the same wealth, m, and that the price for both goods is 1.

(a) *Unregulated equilibrium.* Set up consumer A's utility maximization problem, and determine his demand for goods 1 and 2, as x_1^A and x_2^A. Then operate similarly to find consumer B's demand for good 1 and 2, as x_1^B and x_2^B.

- Consumer A chooses x_1^A and x_2^A to solve

$$\max_{(x_1^A, x_2^A)} \ \log(x_1^A) + x_2^A - \frac{1}{2}\log(x_1^B)$$

subject to $x_1^A + x_2^A = M.$

The Lagrangian for this optimization problem is

$$\mathcal{L} = \log(x_1^A) + x_2^A - \frac{1}{2}\log(x_1^B) + \lambda^A(M - x_1^A - x_2^A),$$

which yields first-order conditions

$$\frac{\partial \mathcal{L}}{\partial x_1^A} = \frac{1}{x_1^A} - \lambda^A = 0,$$

$$\frac{\partial \mathcal{L}}{\partial x_2^A} = 1 - \lambda^A = 0,$$

$$\frac{\partial \mathcal{L}}{\partial \lambda} = M - x_1^A - x_2^A = 0.$$

Solving for x_1^A, we obtain $\frac{1}{x_1^A} = 1$, i.e., $x_1^A = 1$, which implies $M - 1 - x_2^A = 0$, or $x_2^A = M - 1$. Hence, consumer A's optimal consumption is

$$x_1^A = 1 \ \text{ and } \ x_2^A = M - 1.$$

A similar argument applies to consumer B,

$$x_1^B = 1 \ \text{ and } \ x_2^B = M - 1.$$

(b) *Social optimum.* Calculate the socially optimal amounts of x_1^A, x_2^A, x_1^B and x_2^B, considering that the social planner maximizes a utilitarian social welfare function, namely, $W = U_A + U_B$.

- The socially optimal consumption in this case solves

$$\max_{(x_1^A, x_2^A)} \ U^A + U^B \ \text{ subject to } x_1^A + x_2^A = M \text{ and } x_1^B + x_2^B = M.$$

The Lagrangian for this social planner's problem is

$$\mathcal{L} = \frac{1}{2}\log(x_1^A) + \frac{1}{2}\log(x_1^B) + x_2^A + x_2^B + \lambda^A(M - x_1^A - x_2^A) + \lambda^B(M - x_1^B - x_2^B).$$

Taking first-order conditions, we find the socially optimal consumption profile:

$$x_1^A = \frac{1}{2} \text{ and } x_2^A = M - \frac{1}{2},$$

$$x_1^B = \frac{1}{2} \text{ and } x_2^B = M - \frac{1}{2}.$$

Intuitively, the social planner recommends a lower consumption of good 1 (the good that generates the negative externality), and an increase in the consumption of good 2, for both individuals.

(c) *Restoring efficiency.* Show that the social optimum you found in part (b) can be induced by a tax on good 1 (so the after-tax price becomes $1 + t$) with the revenue returned equally to both consumers in a lump-sum transfer.[3]

- With tax t^A placed on good 1 and with lump-sum transfer T^A, consumer A solves

$$\max_{(x_1^A, x_2^A)} \log(x_1^A) + x_2^A - \frac{1}{2}\log(x_1^B)$$

subject to $(1 + t^A)x_1^A + x_2^A = M + T^A$,

where note that the price of good 1 increased from 1 to $(1+t^A)$, but this consumer also sees his wealth increase by the lump sum T^A. The Lagrangian for this optimization problem is

$$\mathcal{L} = \log(x_1^A) + x_2^A - \frac{1}{2}\log(x_1^B) + \lambda^A(M + T^A - (1 + t^A)x_1^A - x_2^A).$$

Taking first-order conditions, we obtain

$$\frac{\partial \mathcal{L}}{\partial x_1^A} = \frac{1}{x_1^A} - \lambda^A(1 + t^A) = 0,$$

$$\frac{\partial \mathcal{L}}{\partial x_2^A} = 1 - \lambda^A = 0,$$

$$\frac{\partial \mathcal{L}}{\partial \lambda} = M + T^A - (1 + t^A)x_1^A - x_2^A = 0.$$

---

[3]Similarly as in the exercises about a polluting monopoly or oligopoly subject to emission fees, we assume that tax revenue is entirely returned to the agents being taxed as a lump-sum transfer. This assumption guarantees that the tax is revenue neutral, yet it helps modify agents' incentives ultimately correcting the externality, i.e., inducing the social optimum.

Simultaneously solving for x_1^A and x_2^A, we find that consumer A's consumption bundles after introducing the tax become

$$x_1^A = \frac{1}{1+t^A} \quad \text{and} \quad x_2^A = M + T^A - 1.$$

Similarly we find the optimal consumption of consumer B who pays tax t^B on good 1 and receives T^B as a lump-sum transfer:

$$x_1^B = \frac{1}{1+t^B} \quad \text{and} \quad x_2^B = M + T^B - 1.$$

- *Comparison.* Comparing the optimal consumption levels found in part (b) with the equilibrium outcomes found in part (c), the tax imposed on any individual $i = A, B$ must hence satisfy

$$\frac{1}{2} = \frac{1}{1+t^i},$$

which would guarantee that equilibrium and socially optimal amounts coincide. Solving for the tax t^i yields $t^i = \$1$. Hence, by setting a tax of $t^i = \$1$ on the consumption of good 1, and returning the tax revenue to this individual in a lump-sum transfer, efficiency is restored, yielding a consumption

$$x_1^i = \frac{1}{1+1} = \frac{1}{2} \quad \text{of good 1,}$$

and

$$x_2^i = M + T^i - 1$$
$$= M + \frac{1}{2} - 1 = M - \frac{1}{2} \quad \text{of good 2,}$$

as described in the socially optimal amounts found in part (b).

Exercise #13 — Reference points in public good games

13. Consider a sequential public good game where a first mover (player 1) is asked to submit a donation, $g_1 \in [0,1]$, for the provision of a public good, and observing her donation, a follower (player 2) responds selecting his own contribution, $g_2 \in [0,1]$. In particular, leader and follower's utility functions are

$$u_1(g_1, g_2) = w - g_1 + [m(g_1 + g_2)]^{0.5}.$$
$$u_2(g_1, g_2) = w - g_2 + [m(g_1 + g_2)(1 + \alpha(g_1 - g_1^R))]^{0.5}.$$

Both of these functions are linear in money, w. The nonlinear part of their utility function takes into account the utility derived from the total public good provision $G = g_i + g_j$ (relevant for both players), but for the follower also considers the distance $\alpha\left(g_1 - g_1^R\right)$ which compares the first mover's actual donation against a reference point, g_1^R. For simplicity, assume that the follower uses the same reference contribution g_1^R to evaluate all donations of the leader. Finally, $m \geq 0$ denotes the return every player obtains from total contributions to the public good. In particular, note that when $\alpha = 0$, the follower only cares about private and public good consumption. However, when $\alpha > 0$, he experiences a higher utility from contributing to the public good when the leader's donation is higher than the reference point, $g_1 > g_1^R$, but a lower utility otherwise, $g_1 < g_1^R$.

(a) Find the follower's best response function, $g_2(g_1, g_1^R)$, and explain how it is affected by changes in his reference point g_1^R.

- The follower's utility maximization problem is

$$\max_{g_2 \geq 0} w - g_2 + \left[m(g_1 + g_2)\left[1 + \alpha\left(g_1 - g_1^R\right)\right]\right]^{0.5}.$$

  Differentiating with respect to g_2, and manipulating, we find the follower's best response function

$$g_2(g_1, g_1^R) = \begin{cases} \frac{m\left(1 - \alpha g_1^R\right)}{4} + \left(\frac{\alpha m - 4}{4}\right) g_1 & \text{if } g_1 \in \left[0, \frac{m\left(\alpha g_1^R - 1\right)}{\alpha m - 4}\right), \\ 0 & \text{if } g_1 \geq \frac{m\left(\alpha g_1^R - 1\right)}{\alpha m - 4}. \end{cases}$$

- Figure 9.4 compares the second mover's best response function when he is concerned about reference points, $g_2(g_1, g_1^R)$, and when he is not, $g_2(g_1)$.
  Specifically, the introduction of reference points into the follower's utility function induces a counterclockwise rotation in his best response function, with center at $g_1 = g_1^R$, making $g_2(g_1, g_1^R)$ steeper than $g_2(g_1)$, i.e., contributions become more strategically complementary. Hence, the second mover reduces his donation when the first mover's contribution is below her reference donation $g_1 < g_1^R$, but increases his contribution otherwise $g_1 > g_1^R$, which could be understood as if he "reciprocates" the first mover's contributions.

(b) Find the leader's equilibrium donation in this sequential public good game. Under which conditions such donation is strictly positive? Interpret.

- Regarding the first mover (player 1), he inserts the follower's best response function, $g_2(g_1, g_1^R)$, into his utility function, to obtain $u_1(g_1, g_2) = w - g_1 + \left[m\left(g_1 + g_2(g_1, g_1^R)\right)\right]^{0.5}$. Taking first-order conditions with respect to his donation, g_1, and solving for g_1 yields an equilibrium contribution of $g_1^* = \frac{16\left(\alpha g_1^R - 1\right) + \alpha^2 m^2}{16\alpha}$. This expression is only positive if $\frac{16\left(\alpha g_1^R - 1\right) + \alpha^2 m^2}{16\alpha} > 0$ or, solving for α, $\alpha > \frac{4\left(\sqrt{4\left(g_1^R\right)^2 + m^2} - 2g_1^R\right)}{m^2} \equiv \bar{\alpha}$.

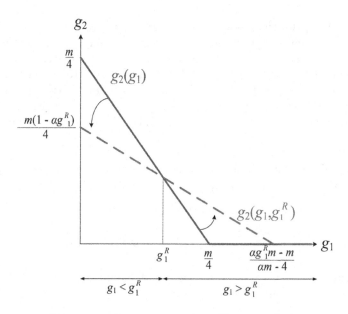

Figure 9.4 Comparing $g_2(g_1, g_1^R)$ and $g_2(g_1)$.

- If, in contrast, α satisfies $\alpha \leq \bar{\alpha}$, the first mover submits a zero contribution in equilibrium. Note that $\alpha \leq \bar{\alpha}$ embodies $\alpha = 0$ as a special case, thus indicating that the first donor submits a zero contribution when the follower is unconcerned about reference points. This is common result in sequential public good games, whereby the leader leaves the follower with all the burden of contributions to the public good. In particular, the follower donates $g_2 = \frac{m}{4}$ when the leader does not contribute, $g_1 = 0$ and he is unconcerned about reference points, $\alpha = 0$.

- However, when the follower's concerns are sufficiently high, $\alpha > \bar{\alpha}$, the leader is induced to submit positive contributions that can trigger larger donations from the follower (given his reciprocating behavior described in the previous section of the exercise).

Exercise #15 — Adding regulation to the Salant et al. (1984) model

15. Consider an industry with N firms competing a la Cournot, facing linear demand $p(Q) = a - bQ$, and with symmetric and constant marginal cost of production c, where $a > c > 0$. Firms' incentives to merge in this type of industry were analyzed by Salant et al. (1984). In this exercise, we briefly study how the results on that article are affected if firms are subject to environmental regulation.

   (a) *Benchmark (no regulation).* Assume that firms are subject to no regulation. Assume that $M \subset N$ firms merge. Find the critical number of firms that makes post-merger profits larger than pre-merger profits, and label it M^{NR} where the superscript NR indicates no regulation. Then identify the critical market share that induces firms to profitably merge, $\alpha^{NR} = \frac{M^{NR}}{N}$.

- At the symmetric equilibrium with N firms, we have that each firm i maximizes

$$\max_{q_i} \quad (a - bQ_{-i} - bq_i)\, q_i - cq_i,$$

where Q_{-i} denotes the aggregate production of all other $j \neq i$ firms. Taking first-order conditions with respect to q_i, we obtain

$$a - bQ_{-i} - 2bq_i - c = 0.$$

And at the symmetric equilibrium, $q_i = q_j$. Hence, the above first-order conditions become

$$a - b\,(n - 1)\, q_i - 2bq_i - c = 0.$$

Solving for q_i, we find that the individual output level in equilibrium without regulation is

$$q_i^{NR} = \frac{a - c}{b\,(1 + N)}.$$

The aggregate output in equilibrium without regulation is then $Q^{NR} = Nq_i^{NR} = \frac{N}{N+1}\frac{a-c}{b}$, while the equilibrium price is

$$p^{NR} = a - bQ^{NR} = \frac{a + cN}{N + 1}.$$

In this setting, equilibrium profits without regulation become

$$\pi_i^{NR,NM} = \frac{(a - c)^2}{b\,(1 + N)^2},$$

which is the standard profit in Cournot games of individual output squared, i.e., $\pi_i^{NR,NM} = b\left(q_i^{NR}\right)^2$.

- Let us now assume that $M \subset N$ firms merge. While before the merger there are N firms in this industry, after the merger there are $N - M + 1$. Hence, profits when M out of N firms merge are

$$\pi_i^{NR,M} = \frac{(a - c)^2}{b\,(2 - M + N)^2}.$$

As a consequence, every firm i prefers to merge rather than not merge if and only if $\pi_i^{NR,M} \geq M\pi_i^{NR,NM}$, that is,

$$\frac{(a - c)^2}{b\,(2 - M + N)^2} \geq M\frac{(a - c)^2}{b\,(1 + N)^2}.$$

Solving for N, we find that $N < -1 - \sqrt{M} + M$. Or equivalently, $M \geq M^{NR} \equiv \frac{3+2N-\sqrt{5+4N}}{2}$. Therefore, the critical market share that induces firms to profitably merge, $\alpha^{NR} = \frac{M^{NR}}{N}$, is

$$\alpha^{NR} = \frac{M^{NR}}{N} = \frac{3 + 2N - \sqrt{5 + 4N}}{2N}.$$

(b) *Environmental regulation.* Consider now that firms are subject to an emission fee τ per unit of output, with the social planer's welfare function being $SW = CS + PS + T - Env$, where CS (PS) denotes consumer (producer) surplus, T captures tax revenue, and $Env = dQ^2$ represents the environmental damage, which is assumed to be convex in aggregate output, and $d > 0$. Repeat your analysis of part (a) in this setting where firms are subject to environmental regulation. That is, first find the critical number of firms that makes post-merger profits larger than pre-merger profits (label it M^R where the superscript R indicates regulation), and then identify the critical market share that induces firms to profitably merge, $\alpha^R = \frac{M^R}{N}$.

- In this case, at the symmetric equilibrium with N firms, we have that each firm i maximizes

$$\max_{q_i} \quad (a - bQ_{-i} - bq_i) q_i - (c + \tau) q_i.$$

We can easily find that individual equilibrium output under regulation becomes

$$q_i^R = \frac{a - c - \tau}{b(1 + N)}.$$

Now, let's first find the aggregate socially optimal output. The social welfare function is

$$\frac{1}{2} [a - (a - bQ)] Q + [(a - bQ) Q - (c + \tau) Q] + \tau Q - dQ^2.$$

Differentiating with respect to Q yields

$$a - c - (b + 2d) Q.$$

And solving for Q, we obtain the socially optimal output $Q^{SO} = \frac{a-c}{b+2d}$. By symmetry, every firm produces a equal share of the socially optimal output, i.e., $q_i^{SO} = \frac{Q^{SO}}{N} = \frac{a-c}{(b+2d)N}$. Hence, the socially optimal fee that induces firms to produce an aggregate output Q^{SO} solves

$$\frac{a - c - \tau}{b(1 + N)} = \frac{a - c}{(b + 2d) N},$$

which gives us $\tau^{SO} = \frac{(a-c)(2dN-b)}{(b+2d)N}$. Clearly, τ^{SO} is increasing in the number of firms N, i.e., as the number of firms increases the regulator needs to curb a larger amount of pollution by setting a more stringent fee. Therefore, equilibrium profits under regulation are

$$\pi_i^{R,NM} = \frac{b\,(a-c)^2}{(b+2d)^2\,N^2}.$$

Hence, profits when M out of N firms merge are the following (recall that, since when M firms merge, there are only $N - M + 1$ firms active):

$$\pi_i^{R,M} = \frac{b\,(a-c)^2}{(b+2d)^2\,(1-M+N)^2}.$$

Therefore, under regulation, every firm i prefers to merge rather than not merge if and only if $\pi_i^{R,M} \geq M\pi_i^{R,NM}$, or

$$\frac{b\,(a-c)^2}{(b+2d)^2\,(1-M+N)^2} \geq M\frac{b\,(a-c)^2}{(b+2d)^2\,N^2}.$$

Solving for N, yields $N < -\sqrt{M} + M$; or equivalently, $M \geq M^R \equiv \frac{1+2N-\sqrt{1+4N}}{2}$. Therefore, the critical market share that induces firms to profitably merge is

$$\alpha^R = \frac{M^R}{N} = \frac{1+2N-\sqrt{1+4N}}{2N}.$$

(c) *Comparison.* Compare the critical shares that make mergers profitable without regulation, α^{NR}, and with regulation, α^R. Which one is higher? Interpret.

- We can compute the difference $\alpha^{NR} - \alpha^R$, which yields

$$\frac{3+2N-\sqrt{5+4N}}{2N} - \frac{1+2N-\sqrt{1+4N}}{2N} = \frac{2+\sqrt{1+4N}-\sqrt{5+4N}}{2N},$$

and after solving for N, is positive for all $N > -0.25$. Since the number of firms satisfies $N \geq 2$ by definition, we can conclude that $\alpha^{NR} > \alpha^R$ for all admissible values of N. Given that, in addition, shares α^{NR} and α^R lie in the interval $[0,1]$, we can conclude that

$$1 > \alpha^{NR} > \alpha^R > 0.$$

This ranking gives rise to three regions in the (α, N)–quadrant, as depicted in Figure 9.5:

1. Region A: When the market share is relatively low, i.e., α lies in $\alpha^R \geq \alpha > 0$, firms do not have incentives to merge regardless of the regulatory setting, i.e., both when environmental policy is present and when it is absent;

2. Region B: When the market share is intermediate, i.e., α lies in $\alpha^{NR} \geq \alpha > \alpha^R$, firms find it profitable to merge under regulation, but do not have incentives to merge when regulation is absent; and

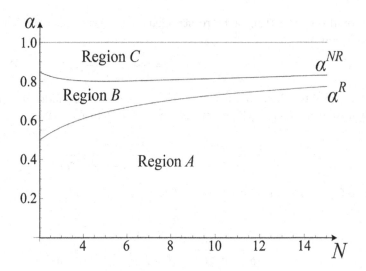

Figure 9.5 Incentives to merge with/without regulation.

3. Region C: When the market share is relatively high, i.e., α lies in $1 \geq \alpha > \alpha^{NR}$, firms find it profitable to merge regardless of the regulatory settings.

- *Intuition:* First, note that, under no regulation, a merger reduces aggregate output, and thus increases market price, but has no effects on the emission fee (since firms are not subject to fees both before and after the merger). Under regulation, mergers do not entail the above positive effect on profits since aggregate output remains at the socially optimal level Q^{SO}. However, the merger reduces the number of firms in the industry, ultimately decreasing the emission fee τ^{SO} imposed by the regulator. In summary, mergers produce a positive effect on profits, but such effect originates from different sources when regulation is present and absent. Our above results (i.e, $\alpha^{NR} > \alpha^{R}$), therefore, suggest that the positive effect of a merger when regulation is present (lower emission fees) dominates its positive effect when regulation is absent (lower aggregate output and increasing market price), ultimately providing firms with more incentives to merge when they face environmental regulation than otherwise.

Chapter 10 — Contract Theory

Summary This chapter considers settings of contracting under asymmetric information and presents exercises in three main areas: moral hazard, the lemons problem, and adverse selection. We start with exercises on moral hazard, first with discrete conditional probabilities (exercise 1) and then with continuous conditional probabilities (exercises 2 and 3). Exercises 4 through 6 then apply moral hazard to three settings: a credit market (to show the existence of credit rationing due to asymmetric information between the lender and the clients), the provision of unemployment benefits (to show that it is optimal for government agencies to decrease the generosity of these benefits over time), and finally to insurance markets. Exercise 7 explores a common wage scheme in applied settings—linear contracts—whereby the principal provides a fixed payment plus a bonus conditional on the agent's observed output. Exercise 8 considers a similar linear contract but allows the principal to condition the agent's compensation not only on the agent's observed output (e.g., sales) but also on the output of other agents, as the latter can serve as a signal of the agent's effort. Exercise 9 analyzes moral hazard in teams of agents and the the free-riding problem that emerges, and presents a wage scheme that can alleviate such a problem. We then switch focus to lemons problems. Exercise 10 illustrates the market failure that arises when agents are asymmetrically informed, and exercise 11 shows that such inefficiency can be solved if the seller offers quality certificates with its product. Exercise 12 extends the lemons problem by allowing for the product to break down after the buyer acquires it, demonstrating that the warranties as a signal of quality can reduce information inefficiencies. For the rest of the chapter, we explore variations of the principal–agent model and adverse selection problems. In particular, exercise 13 analyzes a standard principal–agent problem between a risk-neutral firm manager and a risk-averse worker, first evaluating optimal effort and wages under symmetric information, and then contrasting our results with those arising under asymmetric information. Exercise 17 applies the adverse selection model to a monopoly's goal of screening consumers with different willingness to pay for its product. For completeness, we find monopoly profits under uniform pricing (i.e., setting the same price for all customers), under a single two-part tariff, and under a menu of two-part tariffs; and finally compare profits in each pricing regime. Exercise 18 explores a similar setting, but showing that the monopolist can use product quality to screen customers. Exercises 20 and 21 apply the adverse selection model to labor markets and study the principal's use of efficiency wages to induce the agent to exert a high effort. Finally, exercise 22 considers a principal hiring two subsequent agents (the first agent conducts R&D in a new drug, while the second brings the drug to the market), and identifies the optimal contract in this setting.

Exercise #1 — Moral hazard

1. Consider a principal hiring an agent. The principal can observe the profits that emerge from the agent's effort, but cannot directly observe the amount of effort that the agent exerts. For

simplicity, assume that the agent can only exert two levels of effort, high or low (H or L), yielding only two levels of profits, 300 or 0, with the following conditional probabilities:

Profits

		$x = 300$	$x = 0$
Effort	e_L	$1/2$	$1/2$
	e_H	$3/4$	$1/4$

The principal's profit function is $\pi(x, w) = x - w$, where x indicates the outcome (300 or 0) and w is the salary that he pays to the agent. The agent's utility function is $u(w, e) = \sqrt{w} - c(e)$, where the cost of effort $c(e)$ becomes $c(e_H) = 1$ when he exerts a high effort level but zero otherwise, i.e., $c(e_L) = 0$. Assume that the agent's reservation utility is $\overline{u} = 5$.

(a) Consider that the principal is the only firm in the industry competing for the agent. Set up the principal's problem and find the equilibrium wage and effort.

- Let us separately find the expected profits of the principal: first of inducing a low effort and second of inducing a high effort.

- *Low effort.* If the principal induces a low effort, his problem becomes

$$\max_{w_H, w_L} \ \frac{1}{2}(300 - w_H) + \frac{1}{2}(0 - w_L)$$

$$\text{subject to} \ \frac{1}{2}\sqrt{w_H} + \frac{1}{2}\sqrt{w_L} \geq \frac{3}{4}\sqrt{w_H} + \frac{1}{4}\sqrt{w_L} - 1, \tag{IC_L}$$

$$\frac{1}{2}\sqrt{w_H} + \frac{1}{2}\sqrt{w_L} \geq \overline{u} = 5. \tag{PC_L}$$

Setting up the Lagrangian,

$$L = \frac{1}{2}(300 - w_H) + \frac{1}{2}(0 - w_L)$$

$$+ \lambda_1^L \left(\frac{1}{2}\sqrt{w_H} + \frac{1}{2}\sqrt{w_L} - 5 \right)$$

$$+ \lambda_2^L \left(\frac{1}{4}\sqrt{w_L} - \frac{1}{4}\sqrt{w_H} + 1 \right).$$

Taking FOCs with respect to w_H and w_L yields

$$\frac{\partial L}{\partial w_H} = -\frac{1}{2} + \frac{\lambda_1^L}{4\sqrt{w_H}} - \frac{\lambda_2^L}{8\sqrt{w_H}} = 0, \tag{1}$$

$$\frac{\partial L}{\partial w_L} = -\frac{1}{2} + \frac{\lambda_1^L}{4\sqrt{w_L}} + \frac{\lambda_2^L}{8\sqrt{w_L}} = 0. \tag{2}$$

and the Kuhn–Tucker slackness conditions are

$$\lambda_1^L \left(\frac{1}{2}\sqrt{w_H} + \frac{1}{2}\sqrt{w_L} - 5 \right) = 0, \quad \text{and} \qquad (3)$$

$$\lambda_2^L \left(\frac{1}{4}\sqrt{w_H} - \frac{1}{4}\sqrt{w_L} - 1 \right) = 0. \qquad (4)$$

- We consider four different cases associated with the Lagrangian multipliers as follows:

(i) When $\lambda_1 = \lambda_2 = 0$, the above FOC (1) and (2) become

$$\frac{\partial L}{\partial w_H} = \frac{\partial L}{\partial w_L} = -\frac{1}{2} \neq 0$$

such that the optimality conditions are not satisfied.

(ii) When $\lambda_1 = 0$ but $\lambda_2 > 0$, the above FOC (1) becomes

$$\sqrt{w_H} = -\frac{\lambda_2}{4},$$

which would entail a complex number for w_H.

(iii) When $\lambda_1 > 0$ but $\lambda_2 = 0$, FOC (1) and (2) simplify to

$$\sqrt{w_H} = \sqrt{w_L} = \frac{\lambda_1}{2}$$

such that $w_H = w_L \equiv w$. Substituting this result into (3), yields $\sqrt{w} = 5$, which entails salaries of $w_H = w_L = 25$.

(iv) When $\lambda_1 > 0$ and $\lambda_2 > 0$, Kuhn–Tucker conditions (3) and (4) become

$$\frac{1}{2}\sqrt{w_H} + \frac{1}{2}\sqrt{w_L} = 5, \quad \text{and}$$

$$\frac{1}{4}\sqrt{w_H} - \frac{1}{4}\sqrt{w_L} = 1,$$

respectively. We rewrite the binding constraints in matrix form,

$$\begin{bmatrix} 1 & 1 \\ 1 & -1 \end{bmatrix} \begin{bmatrix} \sqrt{w_H} \\ \sqrt{w_L} \end{bmatrix} = \begin{bmatrix} 10 \\ 4 \end{bmatrix}.$$

Since the determinant of $\begin{bmatrix} 1 & 1 \\ 1 & -1 \end{bmatrix}$ is -2, the matrix has full rank and we can obtain a unique solution for w_H and w_L. In particular,

$$\begin{bmatrix} \sqrt{w_H} \\ \sqrt{w_L} \end{bmatrix} = -\frac{1}{2} \begin{bmatrix} -1 & -1 \\ -1 & 1 \end{bmatrix} \begin{bmatrix} 10 \\ 4 \end{bmatrix} = \begin{bmatrix} 7 \\ 3 \end{bmatrix}.$$

such that $w_H = 49$ and $w_L = 9$.

- The principal chooses the wage schedule that maximizes his expected profit if he is to induce low effort from the agent. Specifically, the principal's expected profit under the fixed wage schedule in case (iii) is

$$\frac{1}{2}(300 - 25) + \frac{1}{2}(0 - 25) = 125,$$

whereas his expected profit under the outcome-dependent wage schedule in case (iv) is

$$\frac{1}{2}(300 - 49) + \frac{1}{2}(0 - 9) = 121.$$

Hence, the principal opts for the fixed wage schedule and sets the equilibrium wage to be $w_H^* = w_L^* = 25$, which induces the agent to exert a low effort since his PC_L condition binds

$$\frac{1}{2}\sqrt{25} + \frac{1}{2}\sqrt{25} = 5,$$

and his IC_L slacks

$$\frac{1}{2}\sqrt{25} + \frac{1}{2}\sqrt{25} = 5 \geq 4 = \frac{3}{4}\sqrt{25} + \frac{1}{4}\sqrt{25} - 1.$$

- *High effort.* If the principal induces instead a high effort, his problem is

$$\max_{w_H, w_L} \quad \frac{3}{4}(300 - w_H) + \frac{1}{4}(0 - w_L)$$

$$\text{subject to} \quad \frac{3}{4}\sqrt{w_H} + \frac{1}{4}\sqrt{w_L} - 1 \geq \frac{1}{2}\sqrt{w_H} + \frac{1}{2}\sqrt{w_L}, \qquad (IC_H)$$

$$\frac{3}{4}\sqrt{w_H} + \frac{1}{4}\sqrt{w_L} - 1 \geq \overline{u} = 5. \qquad (PC_H)$$

Setting up the Lagrangian,

$$L = \frac{3}{4}(300 - w_H) + \frac{1}{4}(0 - w_L)$$

$$+ \lambda_1 \left(\frac{3}{4}\sqrt{w_H} + \frac{1}{4}\sqrt{w_L} - 6 \right)$$

$$+ \lambda_2 \left(\frac{1}{4}\sqrt{w_H} - \frac{1}{4}\sqrt{w_L} - 1 \right).$$

Taking FOCs:

$$\frac{\partial L}{\partial w_H} = -\frac{3}{4} + \frac{3\lambda_1}{8\sqrt{w_H}} + \frac{\lambda_2}{8\sqrt{w_H}} = 0, \qquad (5)$$

$$\frac{\partial L}{\partial w_L} = -\frac{1}{4} + \frac{\lambda_1}{8\sqrt{w_L}} - \frac{\lambda_2}{8\sqrt{w_L}} = 0. \qquad (6)$$

and the Kuhn–Tucker slackness conditions

$$\lambda_1 \left(\frac{3}{4}\sqrt{w_H} + \frac{1}{4}\sqrt{w_L} - 6 \right) = 0, \quad \text{and} \tag{7}$$

$$\lambda_2 \left(\frac{1}{4}\sqrt{w_H} - \frac{1}{4}\sqrt{w_L} - 1 \right) = 0. \tag{8}$$

- We consider four different cases associated with the Lagrangian multipliers as follows:
  (i) When $\lambda_1 = \lambda_2 = 0$, the above FOC (5) and (6) become

$$\frac{\partial L}{\partial w_H} = -\frac{3}{4} \neq 0,$$

$$\frac{\partial L}{\partial w_L} = -\frac{1}{4} \neq 0,$$

such that the optimality conditions are not satisfied.

  (ii) When $\lambda_1 = 0$ but $\lambda_2 > 0$, the above FOC (6) becomes

$$-\frac{1}{4} - \frac{\lambda_2}{8\sqrt{w_L}} = 0, \quad \text{or} \quad \sqrt{w_L} = -\frac{\lambda_2}{2},$$

which would entail a complex number for w_L.

  (iii) When $\lambda_1 > 0$ but $\lambda_2 = 0$, FOC (5) and (6) simplify to

$$\sqrt{w_H} = \sqrt{w_L} = \frac{\lambda_1}{2}$$

such that $w_H = w_L \equiv w$. Substituting this result into (7), yields $\sqrt{w} = 6$, which entails salaries of $w_H = w_L = 36$, and induces the agent to exert a low effort (rather than the high effort required in this context).

  (iv) When $\lambda_1 > 0$ and $\lambda_2 > 0$, Kuhn–Tucker conditions (7) and (8) become

$$\frac{3}{4}\sqrt{w_H} + \frac{1}{4}\sqrt{w_L} = 6,$$

$$\frac{1}{4}\sqrt{w_H} - \frac{1}{4}\sqrt{w_L} = 1.$$

We rewrite the binding constraints in matrix form,

$$\begin{bmatrix} 3 & 1 \\ 1 & -1 \end{bmatrix} \begin{bmatrix} \sqrt{w_H} \\ \sqrt{w_L} \end{bmatrix} = \begin{bmatrix} 24 \\ 4 \end{bmatrix}.$$

Since the determinant of $\begin{bmatrix} 3 & 1 \\ 1 & -1 \end{bmatrix}$ is -4, the matrix has full rank and we can obtain a unique solution for w_H and w_L:

$$\begin{bmatrix} \sqrt{w_H} \\ \sqrt{w_L} \end{bmatrix} = -\frac{1}{4} \begin{bmatrix} -1 & -1 \\ -1 & 3 \end{bmatrix} \begin{bmatrix} 24 \\ 4 \end{bmatrix} = \begin{bmatrix} 7 \\ 3 \end{bmatrix},$$

which yields salaries of $w_H = 49$ and $w_L = 9$.

- The principal chooses the wage schedule that maximizes his expected profit, and that induces the agent to exert a high effort. Only the wage schedule found in case (iv) induces such effort level, which expected profit of

$$E\left[\pi^H\right] = \frac{3}{4}(300 - w_H) + \frac{1}{4}(0 - w_L) = \$186.$$

In this setting, the agent's expected utility is

$$\frac{3}{4}\sqrt{w_H} + \frac{1}{4}\sqrt{w_L} - 1 = \frac{3}{4}\sqrt{49} + \frac{1}{4}\sqrt{9} - 1 = 5,$$

which confirms the bindness of the PC_H, whereby the agent receives his reservation utility in expectation.

- Finally, notice that the principal prefers to induce a high than a low effort since expected profits satisfy $E\left[\pi^H\right] = \$186 > \$125 = E\left[\pi^L\right]$.

(b) In the setting of part (a), assume that the government forces the principal to pay a fixed salary, that is, a salary that is not affected by the firm's profit realization. Find the salary w that the principal offers in this context, and the effort that such a fixed salary induces. Then compare the agent's utility and the firm's profits in both scenarios.

- When the principal pays a fixed salary, $w_H = w_L = w$, the agent is induced to exert a low effort, since effort is costly, and increasing his effort does not alter his salary. Anticipating a low effort from the agent, the principal pays the fixed salary found optimal in part (a), $w_H = w_L = w = \$25$, which yields a utility of $5 for the agent (which coincides with his utility when he was induced to exert a high effort), and expected profits of $125 for the firm (lower than when a high effort was induced). In summary, the information of fixed salaries does not benefit the worker (he obtains his reservation utility with fixed and flexible salaries) but harms the firm as its profits are lower.

Exercise #3 — Moral hazard—continuous probabilities

3. Consider a moral hazard problem between a principal (firm manager) and an agent (worker) where the principal cannot observe the effort that the agent exerts. Suppose that the principal is risk neutral, the agent is risk-averse, and the utility of the agent's "outside option" is zero. Let there be two (monetary) outcomes arising from the agent's effort, x_B and x_G, where $x_G > x_B \geq 0$; and two effort levels that the agent can exert, e and e', where $e' > e \geq 0$. Let $p(e)$ and $p(e')$ denote the probabilities of the good outcome, x_G, when the agent exerts the low effort, e, or the high effort, e', respectively. (The probability of the bad outcome is then $1 - p(e)$ after exerting low effort e, and $1 - p(e')$ after exerting a high effort e'.) Assume that the agent's disutility from exerting the high effort level e' is -1, while his disutility from the low effort level e is zero. Let w_B and w_G denote the salary that the principal pays to the agent if the outcomes are x_B and x_G, respectively. Show that if the principal seeks to induce the agent to exert a low effort, e, then the optimal contract requires a fixed wage $w = w_B = w_G$.

- The principal's problem is

$$\max_{w_B, w_G} \quad (1 - p(e))(x_B - w_B) + p(e)(x_G - w_G)$$

$$\text{subject to} \quad (1 - p(e))u(w_B) + p(e)u(w_G) \geq 0. \tag{PC}$$

Setting up the Lagrangian,

$$L = (1 - p(e))(x_B - w_B) + p(e)(x_G - w_G) + \lambda[(1 - p(e))u(w_B) + p(e)u(w_G)].$$

Taking FOC with respect to salaries w_B and w_G yields

$$\frac{\partial L}{\partial w_B} = 1 - p(e) - \lambda(1 - p(e))u'(w_B) = 0,$$

$$\frac{\partial L}{\partial w_G} = p(e) - \lambda p(e)u'(w_G) = 0.$$

Solving for λ in both FOCs we obtain

$$\lambda = \frac{1}{u'(w_B)} \quad \text{and} \quad \lambda = \frac{1}{u'(w_G)},$$

setting them equal to each other, yields

$$u'(w_B) = u'(w_G) \implies w_B = w_G = w,$$

entailing that, when the principal seeks to induce a low effort, it is optimal for him to offer a fixed salary to the agent, i.e., a wage that is not affected by the outcome realization.

- *Alternative proof.* We can rewrite the above profit maximization problem as follows

$$\max_{w_B, w_G} \quad (1 - p(e))(x_B - w_B) + p(e)(x_G - w_G)$$

$$= [(1 - p(e))x_B + p(e)x_G] - [(1 - p(e))w_B + p(e)w_G],$$

thus presenting expected profits in terms of outcomes (first bracket), and then in terms of wages (second bracket). Since the principal's choice variables are salaries w_B and w_G, the above profit maximization problem is equivalent to the following cost minimization problem:

$$\min_{w_B, w_G} \quad (1 - p(e))w_B + p(e)w_G.$$

In addition, by the concavity of the utility function, i.e., $u' > 0$ and $u'' \leq 0$, we have that

$$u\left[(1 - p(e))w_B + p(e)w_G\right] \geq (1 - p(e))u(w_B) + p(e)u(w_G) \geq 0.$$

That is, the utility of the expected wage is weakly higher than the expected utility from wages w_B and w_G. The above condition holds with equality. Otherwise, the principal could further reduce the payment to the agent while still inducing his participation until his payoff exactly coincides with his reservation utility, which is zero in this case. In particular, the above condition holds with equality only when salaries in the bad and good outcomes coincide, $w_B = w_G = w$, since

$$u\left[(1 - p(e))w + p(e)w\right] = u(w) \quad \text{and}$$
$$(1 - p(e))u(w) + p(e)u(w) = u(w),$$

entailing that $u(w) \geq 0$. In this context, the principal reduces the fixed salary w to satisfy $u(w) = 0$ strictly, i.e., $w = u^{-1}(0)$. [As a remark, note that this alternative proof demonstrates both the necessity and sufficiency of the fixed salary $w_B = w_G = w$, while the above proof based on FOCs only demonted necessity.]

- *Example*: Assume that the agent's utility function is $v(w, e) = u(w) - c(e)$, where $u(w) = \sqrt{w}$, and the cost of effort is increasing and convex, i.e., $c'(e) > 0$ and $c''(e) \leq 0$. Using the above result, the principal sets a fixed salary $w_B = w_G = w$ that solves $w = u^{-1}(0)$, which in this context entails $w = u^{-1}(0) = 0^2 = 0$, i.e., the wage that yields a zero utility is $w = \$0$. Note that this result holds regardless of the probability of the good and bad outcome after effort level $e \geq 0$, and regardless of the principal's profit function.

Exercise #5 — Moral hazard with two periods (Hopenhayn and Nicolini 1997)

5. Many countries offer unemployment benefits (UB), but some analysts argue that these programs reduce the incentives of beneficiaries to find a job, and propose to decrease the generosity and/or duration of the UB. Let us analyze these incentives as part of a moral hazard problem between a risk-neutral principal (employer) and the risk-averse agent (worker) who interact during two periods. The UB is received during two periods while the worker is unemployed, UB_t where $t = \{1, 2\}$. If, in contrast, the worker is employed in period t he pays T_t in payroll taxes (e.g., social security) and receives no UB. Further assume that, if the worker finds a job in period $t = 1$, he keeps it in period $t = 2$ (so he pays T_t in the second period). In particular, following Hopenhayn and Nicolini (1997), in each period t, the worker exerts a search effort to find a job (which entails a search cost $c > 0$) or not (with no cost). If he searches, the probability of finding a job is p_t; if he does not search, his probability of finding a job decreases to q_t, where $q_t < p_t$ for all $t = \{1, 2\}$.

If he finds a job, the worker's payoff becomes $u(w - T_t) - c$ if he searched and $u(w - T_t)$ if he did not. If he does not find a job, he receives UB_t, yielding a utility of $u(UB_t) - c$ if he searched, and $u(UB_t)$ if he did not search for a job. The worker is risk averse, i.e., $u' > 0$ and $u'' < 0$, his reservation utility is assumed to be zero, and there is no discounting.

(a) Write down the government's problem (setting the generosity of UB_1 and UB_2, and payroll taxes T_1 and T_2) in order to induce the worker to search during both periods. Interpret. [*Hint*: You need one PC condition, two IC conditions: one for worker to prefer search today and tomorrow rather than only tomorrow, and another for the worker to prefer to search tomorrow regardless of his today's decision.]

- Since T_1 and T_2 enter positively into the regulator's objective function while UB_1 and UB_2 enter negatively, the regulator's problem becomes

$$\max_{T_1,T_2,UB_1,UB_2} \quad p_1(T_1+T_2) + (1-p_1)p_2(-UB_1+T_2)$$

$$+(1-p_1)(1-p_2)(-UB_1-UB_2)$$

subject to

$$p_1[u(w-T_1)+u(w-T_2)-c]+(1-p_1)p_2[u(UB_1)+u(w-T_2)-2c]$$
$$+(1-p_1)(1-p_2)[u(UB_1)+u(UB_2)-2c] \geq 0, \qquad \text{(PC)}$$
$$p_1[u(w-T_1)+u(w-T_2)-c]+(1-p_1)p_2[u(UB_1)+u(w-T_2)-2c]$$
$$+(1-p_1)(1-p_2)[u(UB_1)+u(UB_2)-2c] \geq$$
$$q_1[u(w-T_1)+u(w-T_2)] \qquad \text{(IC}_1\text{)}$$
$$+(1-q_1)p_2[u(UB_1)+u(w-T_2)-c]$$
$$+(1-q_1)(1-p_2)[u(UB_1)+u(UB_2)-c],$$

and

$$(1-p_2)u(UB_2)+p_2u(w-T_2)-c \geq \qquad \text{(IC}_2\text{)}$$
$$(1-q_2)u(UB_2)+q_2u(w-T_2).$$

The government receives payroll taxes of T_1+T_1 when the worker finds a job in period $t=1$, which happens with probability p_1; only receives $-UB_1+T_2$ if he finds a job in period $t=2$ (since the government provides UB_1 to the worker during the first period); and pays $-UB_2-UB_1$ if the worker never finds a job. Regarding worker's PC condition, note that if he searches for a job in period 1, he finds it with probability p_1 entailing a payoff of $u(w-T_1)+u(w-T_1)-c$.

If he doesn't find a job in period 1, but finds it in period 2, his utility is $u(UB_1)+u(w-T_2)-2c$. Finally, if he never finds a job despite searching for it in both periods, his utility is $u(UB_1)+u(UB_2)-2c$. The left-hand side of the PC condition can then be interpreted as the expected utility of searching for a job during both periods, and thus becomes the left-hand side of IC$_1$ condition, indicating that the worker prefers to search during both periods than only during the last period. On the right-hand side of IC$_1$ the worker can find a job in $t=1$, despite no searching, but if he doesn't find a job in $t=1$, he searches for a job in $t=2$, which helps him find a job with probability p_2.

In order to understand IC$_2$, note that, regardless of the previous history, we must also check that an unemployed worker at $t=2$ has incentives to search at that period, yielding $u(w-T_2)$ if he finds a job and $u(UB_2)$ if he does not, rather than not searching for a job.

(b) Take first-order conditions on the government's problem, and show that the genorosity of the UB decreases over time.

- Note first that the IC_2 condition can be simplified to $(p_2-q_2)[-u(UB_2)+u(w-T_2)] \geq c$ or, given that worker is risk averse, i.e., $u' > 0$ and $u'' < 0$, $w-T_2 > UB_2$. Let

λ be the Lagrange multiplier for PC, λ_1 the multiplier for IC_1, and λ_2 for IC_2. We can take FOC with respect to UB_1 and UB_2 to obtain

$$\frac{\partial L}{\partial UB_1} = -(1-p_1)p_2 - (1-p_1)(1-p_2)$$

$$+\lambda(1-p_1)u'(UB_1) - \lambda_1(p_1 - q_1)u'(UB_1) = 0$$

and

$$\frac{\partial L}{\partial UB_2} = -(1-p_1)(1-p_2) + \lambda(1-p_1)(1-p_2)u'(UB_2)$$

$$-\lambda_1(p_1 - q_1)(1-p_2)u'(UB_2) - \lambda_2(p_2 - q_2)u'(UB_2) = 0.$$

Rearranging the first FOC yields

$$\frac{1}{u'(UB_1)} = \lambda - \lambda_1\frac{p_1 - q_1}{1 - p_1}. \tag{A}$$

Similarly, rearranging the second FOC, we get

$$\frac{1}{u'(UB_2)} = \lambda - \lambda_1\frac{p_1 - q_1}{1 - p_1} - \lambda_2\frac{p_2 - q_2}{(1-p_1)(1-p_2)}. \tag{B}$$

The right-hand side of (A) is greater than that of (B) since $p_t > q_t$ for every $t = \{1,2\}$. Therefore the left-hand side of (A) must also be greater than the left-hand side of (B), that is,

$$\frac{1}{u'(UB_1)} > \frac{1}{u'(UB_2)} \iff u'(UB_2) > u'(UB_1),$$

which entails that $UB_2 < UB_1$ given that $u' > 0$ and $u'' \leq 0$. In words, the generosity of the UB decreases over time.

- Let us now take FOC with respect to payroll taxes T_1, and T_2,

$$\frac{\partial L}{\partial T_1} = p_1 - \lambda p_1 u'(w - T_1) - \lambda_1(p_1 - q_1)u'(w - T_1) = 0,$$

$$\frac{\partial L}{\partial T_2} = p_1 + p_2(1 - p_1) - \lambda\left[p_1 + (1-p_1)p_2\right]u'(w - T_2)$$

$$-\lambda_1(1-p_2)(p_1 - q_1)u'(w - T_2) - \lambda_2(p_2 - q_2)u'(w - T_2) = 0.$$

Rearranging these FOCs in a similar fashion as in the previous steps, we obtain

$$\frac{1}{u'(w - T_1)} = \lambda + \lambda_1\frac{p_1 - q_1}{p_1}, \tag{C}$$

$$\frac{1}{u'(w - T_2)} = \lambda + \lambda_1\frac{(1-p_2)(p_1 - q_1)}{p_1 + p_2(1 - p_1)} + \lambda_2\frac{p_2 - q_2}{p_1 + p_2(1 - p_1)}. \tag{D}$$

The right-hand side of expression (C) is larger than that of (D) as long as λ_2 satisfies $\lambda_2 < \frac{p_2(p_1-q_1)\lambda_1}{p_1(p_2-q_2)}$, i.e., if providing incentives to search for a job in the second period is not too costly for the government. In this case, we have that

$$\frac{1}{u'(w-T_1)} > \frac{1}{u'(w-T_2)} \iff u'(w-T_2) > u'(w-T_1),$$

entailing $w - T_2 < w - T_1$ or $T_2 > T_1$. That is, payroll taxes are higher in the second period.

Exercise #7 — Moral hazard under linear contracts

7. Consider the following type of contracts frequently used in applied settings, where the principal offers a fixed payoff F, plus a bonus per unit of observed outcome, such as sales or units of output. We here focus on the case in which the principal observes units of output, q. For a given effort $e \geq 0$, output is $q = e + \varepsilon$, where shock ε is normally distributed around zero, $\varepsilon \sim N(0, \sigma^2)$. The cost of effort is $c(e)$ which we assume to be increasing and convex. Hence, after a level of output q is observed, the agent receives a salary $w(q) = F + bq$, and his utility is $u(w(q) - c(e))$, where $u(x)$ is a CARA utility function $u(x) = -e^{-x}$ and $x \in \mathbb{R}_+$. The principal is risk neutral, and thus his utility is $q - w(q)$. Suppose for simplicity that the agent's reservation utility (i.e., his outside option) is -1. [Note that the CARA utility function $u(x) = -e^{-x}$ originates at -1 when $x = 0$, and increases in x approaching zero when $x \to \infty$.]

(a) The principal's problem is

$$\max_{w(q),e} \quad E[q - w(q)]$$

$$\text{subject to} \quad E[u(w(q) - c(e))|e] \geq u(0), \tag{PC}$$

$$e \in \arg\max_{e' \geq 0} \ E[u(w(q) - c(e'))|e']. \tag{IC}$$

In words, the principal seeks to maximize his expected profit subject to the voluntary participation of the agent (PC) and the agent's utility-maximizing choice of effort (IC). The $E[\cdot]$ operator indicates that, for a given effort e, the realized output is stochastic since $q = e + \varepsilon$, where $\varepsilon \sim N(0, \sigma^2)$.

Using the first-order approach, characterize the optimal contract, given by a triplet (F, b, e). [*Hint*: Express the agent's expected utility in PC and IC in terms of his certainty equivalent, which in this context is $-\frac{\sigma^2}{2}$. That is, $E[u(w(q)-c(e))|e] = F+be-\frac{b^2}{2}\sigma^2-c(e)$ since $w(q) = F + bq$.]

- The principal's problem can be written as follows

$$\max_{F,b,e} \ E[e - w(q)] = e - (F + be)$$

$$\text{subject to } F + be - \frac{b^2}{2}\sigma^2 - c(e) \geq -1, \tag{PC}$$

$$e \in \arg\max_{e' \geq 0} \; F + be' - \frac{b^2}{2}\sigma^2 - c(e'), \tag{IC}$$

where the principal chooses the optimal value of the fixed payment, F, and the bonus, b, that induce the agent to select the effort level e that maximizes the principal's expected profits, subject to the PC and IC constraints.

- First, the PC constraint must be binding. Otherwise, the principal could lower the fixed payment F to the agent and still induce participation. Solving for F in the binding PC yields,

$$F = c(e) + \frac{b^2}{2}\sigma^2 - be - 1,$$

which helps us express the principal's objective function as

$$e - \left(c(e) + \frac{b^2}{2}\sigma^2 - be - 1 \right) - be = e - c(e) - \frac{b^2}{2}\sigma^2 + 1.$$

Second, using the first-order approach, i.e., taking the derivative of the IC constraint with respect to e, we find that

$$b - c'(e) = 0.$$

Hence, the IC constraint can be written as $b = c'(e)$. Therefore, the principal's problem reduces to

$$\max_{b,e} \quad e - c(e) - \frac{b^2}{2}\sigma^2 + 1$$

$$\text{subject to } b = c'(e).$$

Substituting $b = c'(e)$ into the objective function (last term) yields the following unconstrained problem:

$$\max_{e} \quad e - c(e) - \frac{(c'(e))^2}{2}\sigma^2.$$

Taking FOC with respect to e, we obtain

$$1 - c'(e^*) - c'(e^*)c''(e^*)\sigma^2 = 0. \tag{FOC_e}$$

Solving for $c'(e^*)$, and using the IC constraint again, i.e., $b = c'(e)$, we find that the principal offers a bonus

$$b^* = \frac{1}{1 + c''(e^*)\sigma^2},$$

which is decreasing in the variability of realized output, σ^2. Intuitively, the higher the variability of output, the more likely it is that the agent's output depends on good luck (e.g., a low effort e received a large positive shock ε yielding a high observed output).

(b) Find the optimal effort e^*, the fixed payment F^*, and the bonus b^*, in the context where the cost of effort is $c(e) = \theta e^2$, where $\theta > 0$, and $\varepsilon \sim N(0,1)$.

- In this setting, $c'(e) = 2\theta e$ and $c''(e) = 2\theta$. Hence, the above FOC_e becomes

$$1 - 2\theta e^* - 4\theta^2 e^* = 0,$$

which, solving for e^*, yields an optimal effort of

$$e^* = \frac{1}{2\theta(1 + 2\theta)}.$$

In this context, we can evaluate the above expression of bonus b^* to obtain

$$b^* = \frac{1}{1 + 2\theta},$$

since $c''(e) = 2\theta$ and $\sigma^2 = 1$. Finally, the fixed payment F^* can be found from the (binding) PC condition, $F = c(e) + \frac{b^2}{2}\sigma^2 - be - 1$, evaluated at e^*

$$F^* = \theta\left(e^*\right)^2 + \frac{1}{2(1 + 2\theta)^2} - \frac{e^*}{1 + 2\theta} - 1$$

$$= -\frac{16\theta^2(1 + \theta) + 2\theta + 1}{4\theta(1 + 2\theta)^2}.$$

which means that there is an entry fee (the agent needs to pay the principal in order to participate in the contract, and thus have access to a bonus). Note that effort e^* and the bonus b^* are both decreasing in θ, while the fixed payment F^* is increasing in θ as long as

$$\frac{\partial F^*}{\partial \theta} = \frac{1 + 6\theta - 8\theta^2}{4\theta^2(1 + 2\theta)^3} > 0,$$

which holds for all $\theta < 0.89$. Otherwise, the fixed payment F^* decreases in θ. [For instance, if we restrict parameter θ to satisfy $\theta > 1$, then F^* is unambiguously decreasing in θ.]

(c) How would your above results change if the agent knows ε (i.e., the exact shock on his effort) after signing the contract but before choosing his effort? How would the agent's effort change if the variance σ^2 increases?

- The solution would not change if the agent knows ε. This can be seen from the fact that the IC constraint is independent of ε. Intuitively, this is because the contract is linear: incentives are unchanged if output increases by a fixed amount ε. For more details on this result, see Holmstrom and Milgrom (1987).[1]

- As the variance σ^2 increases, the bonus that the agent receives, $b^* = \frac{1}{1+c''(e^*)\sigma^2}$, decreases. Hence, by the IC $b = c'(e)$, we obtain that $c'(e)$ must also decrease. Since the cost function is increasing and convex in effort, this entails that the agent's optimal effort e^* must decrease in σ^2. Intuitively, as luck plays a more important role in the transformation of effort into outcomes, not only the bonus offered decreases, but so does the agent's optimal effort.

Exercise #9 — Moral hazard in teams (Holmstrom 1982)

9. In this exercise we analyze a standard free-rider problem of team production. First, we show that when each worker's effort is unobservable but the benefits from the project are equally distributed among all agents, equilibrium effort is suboptimal relative to the social optimal (first best), as workers free ride on each others' effort. Secondly, we analyze if the presence of a principal can help the team reach a first best outcome.

Consider n agents working in a partnership to produce aggregate output

$$Q = Q(e_1, e_2, \cdots, e_n),$$

where $e_i \in [0, \infty)$ is the agent i's effort. Assume that function $Q(\cdot)$ satisfies

$$\frac{\partial Q}{\partial e_i} > 0, \ \frac{\partial^2 Q}{\partial e_i^2} < 0, \ \text{and} \ \frac{\partial^2 Q}{\partial e_i \partial e_j} \geq 0.$$

That is, every agent i's effort is productive, but at a decreasing rate. In addition, the marginal contribution of each agent's effort to the project increases in other agent's efforts, i.e., efforts are strategic complements of each other.

Suppose that each agent is risk-neutral: with wage w_i and effort e_i, the agent i's utility is

$$w_i - c_i(e_i)$$

with $c_i(\cdot)$ strictly increasing and convex in effort. Since each agent's effort or individual output is not observable, a contract in the partnership can only depend on the aggregate output:

$$w(Q) = (w_1(Q), w_2(Q), \cdots, w_n(Q)).$$

We require each wage function $w_i(\cdot)$ to be differentiable (almost everywhere). All agents in the partnership share the aggregate output in the following sense:

$$\sum_{j=1}^{n} w_j(Q) = Q \text{ for each } Q.$$

---

[1]Holmstrom, B., and P. Milgrom (1987), "Aggregation and Linearity in the Provision of Intertemporal Incentives," *Econometrica*, 55(2): 303–28.

Note that there exists a positive externality among agents: if all agents are rewarded when Q increases, then one agent working hard will increase the reward to all other $n-1$ agents as well. This provides a possible source for free-riding incentives, and an inefficient outcome.

(a) Find the social optimum outcome, and compare it against the Nash equilibrium outcome.

- *Social optimum:* The first-best profile of efforts $\hat{e} = (\hat{e}_1, \cdots, \hat{e}_n)$ has a social planner considering aggregate welfare, and solving the following problem

$$\max_{e_1, \cdots, e_n} \sum_{j=1}^{n} \left[w_j(Q) - c_j(e_j) \right].$$

Taking FOC with respect to each effort e_i yields

$$\sum_{j=1}^{n} \frac{\partial w_j(Q(\hat{e}))}{\partial Q} \cdot \frac{\partial Q(\hat{e})}{\partial e_i} - c_i'(\hat{e}_i) =$$

$$\sum_{j=1}^{n} w_j'(Q(\hat{e})) \cdot \frac{\partial Q(\hat{e})}{\partial e_i} - c_i'(\hat{e}_i) = 0 \quad \text{for every agent } i,$$

or, rearranging,

$$\sum_{j=1}^{n} w_j'(Q(\hat{e})) \cdot \frac{\partial Q(\hat{e})}{\partial e_i} = c_i'(\hat{e}_i).$$

That is, at the social optimum, every agent i increases his effort e_i until his marginal disutility, $c_i'(\hat{e}_i)$, coincides with the marginal benefit that his effort entails for the entire group, or social marginal benefit $SMB \equiv \sum_{j=1}^{n} w_j'(Q(\hat{e})) \cdot \frac{\partial Q(\hat{e})}{\partial a_i}$.

- *Nash equilibrium:* We next show that when actions are not contractible, the first-best is no longer achievable. In particular, every agent takes other agents' effort levels $e_{-i} = (e_1, \cdots, e_{i-1}, e_{i+1}, \cdots, e_n)$ as given, and solves his individual utility maximization problem

$$\max_{e_i} \ w_i(Q) - c_i(e_i).$$

Taking FOC with respect to agent i's effort, and applying the chain rule, we obtain

$$\frac{dw_i(Q(e_i, e_{-i}))}{\partial Q} \cdot \frac{\partial Q(e_i, e_{-i})}{\partial e_i} = c_i'(e_i) \quad \text{for each } i.$$

In words, in equilibrium agent i increases his effort level e_i until the point in which his marginal disutility, $c_i'(e_i)$, coincides with his private marginal benefit, $MB_i \equiv \frac{dw_i(Q(e_i, e_{-i}))}{\partial Q} \cdot \frac{\partial Q(e_i, e_{-i})}{\partial e_i}$. As a consequence, he selects an inefficient effort relative to the social optimum, as depicted in figure 10.1. In particular, since $0 < \frac{dw_i(Q(e_i, e_{-i}))}{\partial Q} < 1$ the social marginal benefit lies above the private marginal benefit, $SMB_i \geq MB_i$. Together with the convexity of $c_i(e_i)$, entails that private effort is socially insufficient, $e_i < \hat{e}_i$.

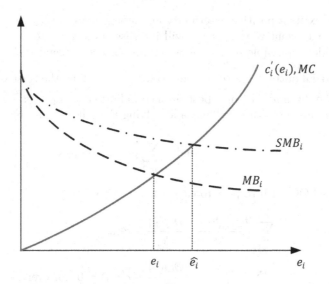

Figure 10.1 Equilibrium and optimal effort levels.

(b) How can a principal induce the socially optimal outcome in this setting? Let us next consider a relaxation of the budget-balance condition

$$\sum_{j=1}^{n} w_j(Q) = Q$$

so that a payment $B > 0$ goes to a principal that the team hired, implying

$$\sum_{j=1}^{n} w_j(Q) < Q.$$

In particular, consider an incentive scheme that pays every agent i a reward $w_i(Q) = \bar{w}_i$ if total output coincides or exceeds the first-best level, $Q \geq Q_{FB}$, but zero otherwise, where $\sum_{i=1}^{n} \bar{w}_i = Q_{FB}$, and $\bar{w}_i > c_i(e_i^{FB})$ for every agent i. Importantly, the principal does not observe the agents' efforts levels, but only the aggregate output Q, and whether it exceeds the first-best level, Q_{FB}. Show that such incentive scheme induces a Nash Equilibrium in which agents choose an aggregate effort level that coincides with the first-best.

- Such incentive scheme is a Nash equililibrium. To see why, consider agent i. Taking the actions of all other agents as given, $e_{-i} = e_{-i}^{FB}$, we can now check if agent i also prefers to choose $e_i = e_i^{FB}$ or instead deviate. If agent i deviates upwards, $e_i > e_i^{FB}$, his cost of effort increases but his reward doesn't (his reward is still $\bar{w}_i$), so he does not have incentives to deviate. If he deviates downwards, $e_i < e_i^{FB}$, he saves the cost of effort but his reward drops to zero. In particular, his utility from $e_i = e_i^{FB}$ is

$\bar{w}_i - c_i(e_i^{FB})$, while by deviating to $e_i < e_i^{FB}$ his utility becomes $0 - c_i(e_i)$. Hence, agent i does not want to deviate if

$$\bar{w}_i - c_i(e_i^{FB}) > 0 - c_i(e_i)$$

or,

$$\bar{w}_i > c_i(e_i^{FB}) - c_i(e_i).$$

His optimal deviation would thus be $e_i = 0$. That is, if slacking entails a zero reward, then his optimal deviation is to slack completely, which entails a zero cost of effort, $c(0) = 0$. In such a case, the above inequality becomes

$$\bar{w}_i > c_i(e_i^{FB}),$$

which holds by definition. Hence, agent i does not have incentive to deviate from the first-best effort level $e_i = e_i^{FB}$.

Exercise #11 — Solving the lemons problem by offering quality certificates

11. Consider a lemons problem with cars of two qualities, high or low, with corresponding probability r and $1 - r$. Let θ_B and θ_S be the valuation that buyer and seller, respectively, assign to a car of quality $\theta = \{H, L\}$. As usual in this model, if both seller and buyer could observe the car's quality, an exchange could occur because the buyer assigns a larger value to that type of car than the seller does, i.e., $H_B > H_S > L_B > L_S > 0$. The seller sets a price in the first period, and the buyer responds by accepting or rejecting the price. Assume a large number of buyers.

   (a) *Symmetric information.* If the buyer and seller could observe the car's quality θ, what equilibrium prices would emerge?
       • The buyer accepts any price p that yields a positive utility $\theta_B - p \geq 0$, or $\theta_B \geq p$ for every car type $\theta = \{H, L\}$. Anticipating such a decision rule from the buyer, the seller sets a price p that solves

$$\max_{p \geq 0} \quad p - \theta_S$$

$$\text{subject to} \quad \theta_B \geq p. \tag{PC}$$

   The buyer's PC binds, since otherwise the seller could profitably raise the price and still achieve voluntary participation. Hence, $\theta_B = p$. (Alternatively, since seller's objective function is monotonically increasing in p, he raises p until $p = \theta_B$.) Therefore, the seller sets price of $p = \theta_B$, which entails: (1) $p_H = H_B$ for the high-quality car; and (2) $p_L = L_B$ for the low-quality car, and the prices are accepted by the buyer.

   (b) *Asymmetric information.* If the buyer could not observe the car's quality (but the seller observes it), which equilibrium price emerges?

- In this setting, the buyer's expected value from a car is

$$EV_B \equiv rH_B + (1-r)L_B .$$

If $EV_B \geq H_S$, the seller of high-quality cars can set a price $p = EV_B$ which is accepted by the buyer, and which leads to positive profits since $p > H_S$. The seller of a low-quality car can operate similarly, setting a price $p = EV_B$, which also leads to positive profits since $p > L_S$. Both types of cars are then traded in this context, confirming that the buyer's expected car quality is EV_B.

If $EV_B < H_S$, the seller of low-quality cars can set prices as above, but that of high-quality cars does not find that practice profitable since that would entail a price

$$p = EV_B < H_B,$$

leading to losses. Hence, only low-quality cars are exchanged. That happens, in particular, when

$$rH_B + (1-r)L_B < H_S,$$

rearranging,

$$r(H_B - L_B) < H_S - L_B,$$

and solving for r,

$$r < \frac{H_S - L_B}{H_B - L_B} \equiv \hat{r}.$$

Therefore, when the proportion of high-quality cars r satisfies $r < \hat{r}$, only low-quality cars are traded at a price $p = L_B$; while if $r \geq \hat{r}$ both types of cars are traded at a price $p = EV_B$.

(c) *Costly certificates.* Consider that in the model of part (b), the proportion of high-quality cars, r, is sufficiently low to yield an equilibrium in which only low-quality cars are traded. Assume now that car sellers can acquire certificates reporting that the quality of the car they sell is $q \in \mathbb{R}_+$, at a cost $c_L(q) = q$ when the true car quality is low, and $c_H(q) = \frac{1}{4}q$ when its true quality is high. Intuitively, the cost of acquiring a certificate stating a quality level q is higher for the low-quality car than for the high-quality car as it requires a more detailed inspection of the car by a mechanic in order to confirm that its quality is q. (Nevertheless, these certificates do not affect the original true quality of the car.)

Find if a separating equilibrium can be sustained whereby the seller with high-quality cars acquires certificates of quality q_H while that of low-quality cars acquires certificates of quality q_L, where $0 \leq q_L < q_H$. For simplicity, let us assume $H_B = 4, H_S = 3, L_B = 2$ and $L_S = 1$. [*Hint:* Since the separating equilibrium would convey the car quality to potential buyers, the price of cars with certificate q_H (q_L) must be H_B (L_B, respectively) as under asymmetric information].

- The values of certificates q_H and q_L that support the existence of a separating equilibrium in which H-cars are certified with q_H and L-cars are certified with q_L are given by the following PC and IC conditions:

$$H_B - (H_S + \frac{1}{4}q_H) \geq 0, \tag{PC$_H$}$$

$$L_B - (L_S + q_L) \geq 0, \tag{PC$_L$}$$

$$H_B - (H_S + \frac{1}{4}q_H) \geq L_B - (H_S + \frac{1}{4}q_L), \tag{IC$_H$}$$

$$L_B - (L_S + q_L) \geq H_B - (L_S + q_H). \tag{IC$_L$}$$

Since $H_B = 4, H_S = 3, L_B = 2$, and $L_S = 1$, the above conditions become

$$4 - (3 + \frac{1}{4}q_H) \geq 0 \quad \text{or} \quad q_H \leq 4,$$

$$2 - (1 + q_L) \geq 0 \quad \text{or} \quad q_L \leq 1,$$

$$4 - (3 + \frac{1}{4}q_H) \geq 2 - (3 + \frac{1}{4}q_L) \quad \text{or} \quad q_H \leq 8 + q_L,$$

$$2 - (1 + q_L) \geq 4 - (1 + q_H) \quad \text{or} \quad q_H \geq 2 + q_L.$$

And since $q_H \leq 4$ is more restrictive than $q_H \leq 8 + q_L$, the set of (q_H, q_L)-pairs that support a separating equilibrium must at least satisfy:

$$2 + q_L \leq q_H \leq 4 \quad \text{and} \quad q_L \leq 1.$$

Figure 10.2 plots the above four conditions in the (q_H, q_L).

- *Off-the-equilibrium deviations.* Note that in order to find the separating PBE, we need to consider not only the equilibrium certificate q_L and q_H but also deviations towards any quality certificate q located off-the equilibrium path, i.e., $q \neq q_L \neq q_H$. For instance, the low-quality seller prefers to acquire certificate q_L than any other certificate $q < q_H$. Formally,

$$L_B - (L_S + q_L) > L_B - (L_S + q).$$

Note that in the right-hand side of the inequality, we consider that, when a seller offers a certificate q such that $q < q_H$, the buyer interprets that the car must be of low quality. Let us next show this result.

Proof. Let us work by contradiction. Suppose that when the buyer observes a car certified with $q < q_H$ he believes that the car is of *high* quality. In this case, the seller of a high-quality car would not have incentives to offer a q_H certificate. Instead, he would prefer the cheaper certificate $q < q_H$ which still signals its high quality. But then, we cannot be at a separating PBE where the high-quality seller offers a certificate q_H; a contradiction. Hence, when the buyer observes a car with a quality certificate $q < q_H$, he interprets that the car is low-quality, offering as a consequence L_B. Q.E.D.

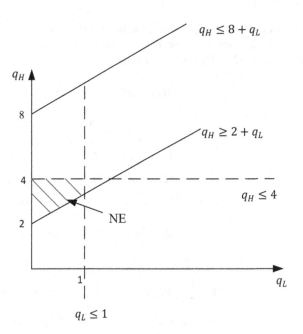

Figure 10.2 Region of (q_H, q_L)–pairs satisfying the PC and IC conditions

- Continuing with the I.C. condition for the low-quality seller that we wrote above:

$$L_B - (L_S + q_L) > L_B - (L_S + q),$$

$$2 - (1 + q_L) \geq 2 - (1 + q),$$

which reduces to $q_L \leq q$. In words, the low-quality seller prefers q_L rather than any other certificate $q \neq q_L \neq q_H$ if and only if q_L is lower than any other certificate! In summary, $q_L \leq q$ can only hold when $q_L = 0$.

- Now we need to identify the I.C. condition for the low-quality seller in the case of a deviation towards an off-the-equilibrium certificate q such that $q > q_H$ (upward deviation):

$$L_B - (L_S + q_L) \geq H_B - (L_S + q).$$

Note that since $q > q_H$ buyers identify the car is a H-type and offer H_B. Then,

$$2 - (1 + q_L) \geq 4 - (1 + q),$$

which reduces to $q \geq 2 + q_L$. But this inequality does not bring more information than that contained at original IC's.

- Consider now a downward deviation to an off-the-equilibrium certificate $q < q_H$, the high-quality seller prefers certificate q_H to q if:

$$H_B - \left(H_S + \frac{1}{4}q_H\right) \geq L_B - \left(H_S + \frac{1}{4}q\right).$$

In the right-hand side of the inequality, we considered, similarly as for the low-quality seller, that a car certified with $q < q_H$ are interpreted as low-quality cars and the buyer only offers L_B for it. This yields $q_H \leq 8 + q$, which is redundant as it provides a similar information as IC_H when we evaluated the high-quality seller incentives to deviate from q_H to q_L. If, instead, the high-quality seller were to deviate upwards toward an off-the-equilibrium certificate $q > q_H$, buyers would still infer a high-quality from its car, but the seller would incur a larger cost since $q > q_H$. Therefore, the high-quality seller does not have incentives to deviate to $q > q_H$.

- Summarizing, the relevant I.C conditions for the values of q_H and q_L that support a PBE (separating equilibrium) are defined by

$$q_L = 0 \quad \text{and} \quad 8 \geq q_H \geq 2.$$

Furthermore, from the PC conditions we know that

$$q_L \leq 1 \quad \text{and} \quad q_H \leq 4.$$

Hence, the values of q_H and q_L that support PBE (seperating) equilibra are

$$q_L = 0 \quad \text{and} \quad q_H \in [2, 4].$$

Figure 10.3 uses the NE outcomes depicted in figure 10.2 and shades all $(q_L, q_H)-$ pairs (along the vertical axis) that can be sustained as separating PBEs.

- *Equilibrium refinement.* Let us next apply, Cho and Krep's (1987) Intuitive Criterion in order to discard those separating PBEs based on insensible off-the-equilibrium beliefs by the buyer.

  - *First step.* First, consider the separating equilibrium $(q_L, q_H) = (0, 4)$, i.e., that in which the high-quality seller acquires the highest certificate, and consider a deviation towards any lower certificate in the interval $q \in [2, 4)$. We then need to restrict buyer's (receiver) beliefs after observing certificate $q \in [2, 4)$, deleting all those types of sellers for which this certificate can never be equilibrium dominated:

$$\Theta^{**}(q) := \left\{ \theta \in \Theta \mid u^*(\theta) \leq \max_{s \in S^*(\Theta, q)} u(s, q | \theta) \right\}.$$

In this case, we see that a certificate $q \in [2, 4)$ is equilibrium dominated for the seller of low-quality cars:

$$u^*(Low) > \max_{s \in S^*(\Theta, q)} u(s, q | Low) \quad \text{for all } q \in [2, 4].$$

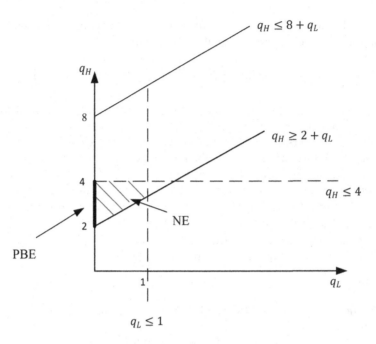

Figure 10.3 Separating PBEs.

But it is never equilibrium dominated for the seller of high-quality cars:

$$u^*(High) > \max_{s \in S^*(\Theta, q)} u(s, 4|High) \quad \text{for all } q \in [2, 4].$$

Therefore, after observing $q \in [2, 4)$, the buyer restricts his beliefs to $\Theta^{**}(q) = \{High\}$.

— *Second step.* Once buyers' beliefs have been restricted to $\Theta^{**}(q) = \{High\}$, we need to find whether there exists a message q sent by a seller of high-quality cars such that

$$u^*(High) > \min_{s \in S^*(\Theta^{**}(q), q)} u(s, q|High).$$

Indeed, if a seller of high-quality cars is sending $q_H = 4$ in equilibrium, once $\Theta^{**}(q) = \{High\}$, we can always find a message, such as $q = 2$, that improves his profits.

$$u^*(High) < \min_{s \in S^*(\Theta^{**}(2), 2)} u(s, 2|High).$$

Intuitively, any certificate $q \in [2, 4)$ can only be profitably sent by the high-quality seller, and thus buyers respond paying a price H_B. Therefore, the high-quality seller has incentives to deviate from $q_H = 4$ to any lower (and cheaper) certificate $q \in [2, 4]$. Hence, the seperating PBE $(q_L, q_H) = (0, 4)$ violates the Intuitive Criterion. Intuitively, since the cost of inspection at $q_H = 2$ is weakly larger than the price differential $H_B - L_B = 2$, low-quality sellers do not have incentives to masquerade as high-quality sellers.

- This argument can be similarly extended to all separating PBEs (q_L, q_H) where $q_H > 2$. The only separating PBE remaining, and that survives the Intuitive Criterion, is $(q_L, q_H) = (0, 2)$. In this separating PBE the low-quality seller behaves as under symmetric information (No certificate, and selling its car at $p = L_B$), while the high-quality seller exerts the least-costly separating effort (i.e., he acquires the smallest amount of quality certificate $q_H = 2$), which signals the quality of his cars, thus allowing him to charge a price $p = H_B$.

Exercise #13 — Principal–agent problem

13. Consider a situation where a principal has profit function

$$u^p(e, w) = \beta e - w,$$

where e denotes the effort that agent (e.g., employee) exerts, which is transformed into profits at a rate $\beta > 1$, and w represents the salary that principal pays the agent. While the principal cannot observe the agent's type θ_i, where $i = \{L, H\}$ and $\theta_L = 1$ and $\theta_H = 2$, he knows the frequency of worker with high-type, p, and low-type, $1 - p$. Utility function of each agent is

$$u^i(e, w) = w - \theta_i e^2,$$

where $i = \{L, H\}$. Intuitively, the agent's utility increases in the salary that he receives, but decreases in the effort he exerts. Hence, the second term $\theta_i e^2$ can be interpreted as the agent's cost of effort, which is increasing and convex in effort, and where the (absolute and marginal) cost of effort is larger for the high type than for the low-type since $\theta_H > \theta_L$. The reservation utility of the agents is zero.

(a) *Symmetric information.* Find the contract(s) that will be offered by the principal when he can observe the agent's type.

- Since the principal can observe each agent's type, he solves, for every worker type θ_i,

$$\max_{w_i, e_i} \quad \beta e_i - w_i$$

$$\text{subject to } w_i - \theta_i e_i^2 \geq 0. \tag{PC}$$

As usual, the PC constraint must be binding, i.e, $w_i = \theta_i e_i^2$ for all $i = \{L, H\}$. Otherwise, the firm manager could still lower salaries and extract a larger surplus. We can thus substitute the binding PC constraint into the principal's objective function, to obtain the following unconstrained problem:

$$\max_{e_i} \quad \beta e_i - \theta_i e_i^2.$$

Taking the FOC with respect to e_i yields

$$\beta - 2\theta_i e_i = 0,$$

which, solving for e_i, helps us obtain the optimal effort level under symmetric information

$$e_i = \frac{\beta}{2\theta_i} \quad \text{for all } i = \{L, H\}.$$

That is, since $\theta_L = 1$ and $\theta_H = 2$, effort levels are $e_L = \frac{\beta}{2}$ and $e_H = \frac{\beta}{4}$, thus prescribing a higher effort level for the worker with a low disutility from effort, i.e., $e_L > e_H$. Salaries in this context become $w_i = \theta_i e_i^2$, which entail

$$w_H = 2\left(\frac{\beta}{4}\right)^2 = \frac{\beta^2}{8} \quad \text{and} \quad w_L = \left(\frac{\beta}{2}\right)^2 = \frac{\beta^2}{4}.$$

(b) *Asymmetric information.* Find the contract(s) that the principal offers when he cannot observe the types of each agent.

- In this case, the principal will maximize his expected utility

$$\max_{w_L, w_H, e_L, e_H} \quad p(\beta e_H - w_H) + (1-p)(\beta e_L - w_L)$$

subject to the participation constraints for each agent

$$w_L - e_L^2 \geq 0, \tag{PC$_L$}$$

$$w_H - 2e_H^2 \geq 0, \tag{PC$_H$}$$

and the incentive compatibility constraints for each agent

$$w_L - e_L^2 \geq w_H - e_H^2, \tag{IC$_L$}$$

$$w_H - 2e_H^2 \geq w_L - 2e_L^2, \tag{IC$_H$}$$

From the above equations,

$$w_L - e_L^2 \geq w_H - e_H^2 > w_H - 2e_H^2.$$

This indicates that the PC_H is binding. So we can now set up our Lagrangean as follows:

$$\begin{aligned}
\mathcal{L} = {} & p(\beta e_H - w_H) + (1-p)(\beta e_L - w_L) \\
& + \lambda_1(w_H - 2e_H^2) \\
& + \lambda_2(w_L - e_L^2 - w_H + e_H^2) + \lambda_3(w_H - 2e_H^2 - w_L + 2e_L^2).
\end{aligned}$$

Taking the FOCs,

$$\frac{\partial \mathcal{L}}{\partial w_H} = -p + \lambda_1 - \lambda_2 + \lambda_3 = 0 \Longrightarrow \lambda_3 - \lambda_2 = p - \lambda_1,$$

$$\frac{\partial \mathcal{L}}{\partial w_L} = -(1-p) + \lambda_2 - \lambda_3 = 0 \Longrightarrow \lambda_2 - \lambda_3 = 1 - p,$$

$$\frac{\partial \mathcal{L}}{\partial e_H} = p\beta - 4\lambda_1 e_H + 2\lambda_2 e_H - 4\lambda_3 e_H = 0 \Longrightarrow e_H = \frac{p\beta}{2\,(2\lambda_1 - \lambda_2 + 2\lambda_3)},$$

$$\frac{\partial \mathcal{L}}{\partial e_L} = (1-p)\beta + 4\lambda_3 e_L - 2\lambda_2 e_L = 0 \Longrightarrow e_L = \frac{(1-p)\beta}{2\,(\lambda_2 - 2\lambda_3)}.$$

In addition, from the first and second FOC, we obtain that $p - \lambda_1 = p - 1$, or $\lambda_1 = 1$, thus confirming that its associated constraint, PC_H, binds, i.e., $w_H - 2e_H^2 = 0$. We can then use this result into the expression of IC_H to obtain that

$$\underbrace{w_H - 2e_H^2}_{0} \geq w_L - 2e_L^2,$$

which means that the high-type agent would receive a negative utility should he select the contract meant for the low-type. Hence, the IC_H must slack (i.e., hold strictly) entailing that its associated Lagrange multiplier is nil, $\lambda_3 = 0$. Using the second FOC, $\lambda_2 - \lambda_3 = 1 - p$, we then find that $\lambda_2 = 1 - p > 0$.

- We can now evaluate the effort levels found in the last two FOCs at $\lambda_1 = 1$, $\lambda_3 = 0$, and $\lambda_2 = 1 - p$, which yields

$$e_H = \frac{p\beta}{2\,(2 - (1-p))} = \frac{p\beta}{2(1+p)} \quad \text{and}$$

$$e_L = \frac{(1-p)\beta}{2(1-p)} = \frac{\beta}{2}.$$

Let us now compare these effort levels against those under complete information found in part (a), where we obtained that $e_H = \frac{\beta}{4}$ for the high type and $e_L = \frac{\beta}{2}$ for the low type. Therefore, the effort level of the high-type agent is lower under incomplete than complete information since $\frac{p\beta}{2(1+p)} < \frac{\beta}{4}$ simplifies to $p \leq 1$, which holds by definition; but the effort level of the low-type agent coincides across information settings. In other words, there is "no distortion" for the low-type worker (the most efficient worker), while there is distortion in the effort required from the high disutility of effort worker. (In addition, note that while $e_H = \frac{p\beta}{2(1+p)}$ increases in p, it lies below $e_L = \frac{\beta}{2}$ for all values of p, including at $p = 1$.) Regarding salaries, we find that

$$w_L = e_H^2 + e_L^2 = \left[\frac{p\beta}{2(1+p)}\right]^2 + \frac{\beta^2}{4}, \text{ and}$$

$$w_H = 2e_H^2 = \frac{p^2\beta^2}{2(1+p)^2}.$$

In addition, note that when $p = 1$, our results converge to the finding under symmetric information of part (a), i.e., effort levels become $e_H = \frac{\beta}{4}$ and $e_L = \frac{\beta}{2}$, and salaries are $w_L = \frac{\beta^2}{16} + \frac{\beta^2}{4} = \frac{5\beta^2}{16}$ and $w_H = \frac{\beta^2}{8}$.

- *Information rents.* We can finally evaluate the information rents of each type of agent, by comparing his utility under asymmetric information (where it can be positive) and symmetric information (where it was zero). In particular, since PC_H binds, the high-type does not retain information rents. However, the low-type agent obtains a utility level of

$$u_L = w_L - e_L^2 = \underbrace{\left(e_H^2 + e_L^2\right)}_{w_L} - e_L^2 = e_H^2 = \left[\frac{p\beta}{2(1+p)}\right]^2,$$

which is positive under all parameter values, and thus larger than his zero utility level under symmetric information. His information rent is thus $\left[\frac{p\beta}{2(1+p)}\right]^2$, which is increasing in the probability of the agent being of high type, p. Intuitively, as the proportion of low-cost agents decreases, they require a higher salary for the principal to distinguish them from the high-cost agents.

- *Numerical example.* Consider that $p = \frac{1}{3}$, and $\beta = 32$. Then the optimal efforts under symmetric information are

$$e_L = 16 \text{ and } e_H = 8,$$

while under asymmetric information they are

$$e_L = 16 \text{ and } e_H = 4.$$

Similarly, salaries under symmetric information are

$$w_L = 256 \text{ and } w_H = 128,$$

whereas under asymmetric information

$$w_L = 272 \text{ and } w_H = 32.$$

Exercise #15 — A special type of principal–agent problem

15. Consider a principal–agent model with a finite number of actions (e.g., a finite number of effort levels). Assume that the probability of each outcome is independent of the agent's action. In this context, how much should the principal pay? What happens to the likelihood ratio?

- Since the number of actions is finite, consider, without loss of generality, two effort levels e_L and e_H. Let p_i^L be the probability of outcome i occuring when the agent exerts effort e_L and p_i^H the probability of outcome i when he chooses e_H. If the probability of each outcome is independent of the agent's effort level, then $p_i^L = p_i^H$ for every outcome i. This means that the likelihood ratio becomes $\frac{p_i^L}{p_i^H} = 1$ for every outcome i.

Recall that the FOC from the principal–agent problem yields

$$\frac{1}{u'(w_i)} = \lambda + \mu\left(1 - \frac{p_i^L}{p_i^H}\right).$$

If the likelihood ratios are all 1, then the above FOC collapses to $\frac{1}{u'(w_i)} = \lambda$, entailing $u'(w_i) = \frac{1}{\lambda}$. Using the inverse $u^{-1}(.)$ on both sides yields a salary

$$w_i = u^{-1}\left(\frac{1}{\lambda}\right) \quad \text{for all outcomes } i.$$

Therefore, the principal pays the same salary for every realized outcome i. Since the wage is then fixed (unaffected by the outcome), the agent will respond by taking the least costly action, e_L. This is optimal because choosing a costlier action would have no effect on his salary.

Exercise #17 — Screening—monopoly pricing

17. Consider a setting of a monopolist seeking to sell a product to a consumer, who can be of two types, each type being equally likely. Cutomer type $i = \{H, L\}$ has a quasi-linear utility function

$$u_i(x, y) = \alpha_i \sqrt{x} + y,$$

where α_i denotes his preference for quality (where $\alpha_H > \alpha_L$), x represents the quality of a particular good the monopolist sells, and y is money (representing consumption of all other goods). A monopolist offers the item at a price p as a take-it-or-leave-it offer to consumers. The cost of producing one unit of quality is \$1 for the monopolist. Assume that the reservation utility of both types of consumers is zero. Since the monopolist cannot observe each type of consumer (i.e., the realization of parameter α_i), it needs to screen customers by offering a menu that induces each type of consumer to self select the offer meant for him. That is, we seek to identify conditions under which separating equilibria can arise. In the following sections of the exercise we first show that other pricing strategies such as linear pricing or single two-part tariff (rather than a menu of tariffs) yield a lower profit for monopolist.

(a) *Uniform pricing.* Suppose that the monopolist can only offer every type of customer the same uniform price. What would be the profit-maximizing price and profit?

- We can use backward induction in this setting, by first finding consumer i's demand at a price p (second stage), and then identifying the price that the seller sets in the first stage. After observing a price and quality pair (p, x), consumer type i solves:

$$\max_x \quad \alpha_i \sqrt{x} - px.$$

Taking FOCs with respect to x yields

$$\frac{\alpha_i}{2\sqrt{x}} - p = 0.$$

Solving for x, we find that consumer i's demand for quality is $x_i(p) = \frac{\alpha_i^2}{4p^2}$. Such demand increases in consumer i's preference for quality, α_i, but decreases in the price set by the monopolist. Hence, aggregate demand becomes $x_H(p) + x_L(p) = \frac{\alpha_H^2}{4p^2} + \frac{\alpha_L^2}{4p^2}$.

- Anticipating such an aggregate demand, the monopolist sets a uniform price (a unique price to all types of customers) that maximizes its profits,

$$\max_{p \geq 0} \ (p-1)\left[\frac{\alpha_H^2}{4p^2} + \frac{\alpha_L^2}{4p^2}\right].$$

Taking FOC with respect to p yields

$$-\frac{\alpha_H^2}{4p^2} - \frac{\alpha_L^2}{4p^2} + \frac{2\alpha_H^2}{4p^3} + \frac{2\alpha_L^2}{4p^3} = 0.$$

Solving for p, we obtain a uniform price of $p^U = 2$, which entails an equlibrium profit of

$$\pi^U = (p^U - 1)\left[\frac{\alpha_H^2}{4p^2} + \frac{\alpha_L^2}{4p^2}\right] = \frac{\alpha_H^2 + \alpha_L^2}{16} > 0.$$

(b) *Single two-part tariff.* Suppose the monopolist can offer a single two-part tariff pricing consisting of an initial fee T and a unit price p (which does not depend on quantity sold). What is the profit maximizing (T, p)-pair for the monopolist?

- *Serving both types of customers.* When the monopolist wants to include all types of consumers, we need that the low-type consumer prefers to participate, i.e., $T \leq S_L(p)$, where $S_L(p)$ represents the surplus for the low-valuation customers, as we next define for any type i,

$$S_i(p) \equiv u_i(x_i(p), y) - px_i(p)$$

$$= \alpha_i\sqrt{\frac{\alpha_i^2}{4p^2}} - p\frac{\alpha_i^2}{4p^2} = \frac{\alpha_i^2}{4p}.$$

We also require a similar condition to hold for the high-type consumer, $T \leq S_H(p) = \frac{\alpha_H^2}{4p}$. However, $S_L(p) \leq S_H(p)$ for every $p \geq 0$ given that $\alpha_L < \alpha_H$ by definition, implying that we only need to impose the condition on the low-type. Therefore, the monopolist's profit maximization problem becomes

$$\max_{p \geq 0} \ T + (p-1)\left[\frac{1}{2}x_L(p) + \frac{1}{2}x_H(p)\right]$$

$$\text{subject to } T \leq S_L(p). \tag{PC$_L$}$$

In addition, note that PC_L must bind. Otherwise, the monopolist would have incentives to increase the fee T and still achieve participation of the low type. Hence, $T = S_L(p) = \frac{\alpha_L^2}{4p}$, implying that the above problem can be expressed as the following unconstrained maximization problem:

$$\max_{p \geq 0} \quad \frac{\alpha_L^2}{4p} + (p-1)\left[\frac{\alpha_H^2}{8p^2} + \frac{\alpha_L^2}{8p^2}\right].$$

Taking FOC with respect to p yields

$$-\frac{\alpha_H^2}{8p^2} - \frac{\alpha_L^2}{4p^2} - \frac{\alpha_L^2}{8p^2} + \frac{\alpha_H^2}{4p^3} + \frac{\alpha_L^2}{4p^3} = 0.$$

Solving for p, we obtain

$$p^{ST} = \frac{2(\alpha_H^2 + \alpha_L^2)}{3\alpha_L^2 + \alpha_H^2},$$

and plugging p^{ST} into the fee $T^{ST} = \frac{\alpha_L^2}{4p^{ST}}$ yields

$$T^{ST} = \frac{\alpha_L^2}{4p^{ST}} = \frac{\alpha_L^2(3\alpha_L^2 + \alpha_H^2)}{8(\alpha_H^2 + \alpha_L^2)},$$

entailing profits of

$$\pi^{ST} = \frac{\alpha_L^2(3\alpha_L^2 + \alpha_H^2)}{8(\alpha_H^2 + \alpha_L^2)} + \left(\frac{2(\alpha_H^2 + \alpha_L^2)}{3\alpha_L^2 + \alpha_H^2} - 1\right)\left(\frac{\alpha_H^2 + \alpha_L^2}{8}\right)\left(\frac{3\alpha_L^2 + \alpha_H^2}{2(\alpha_H^2 + \alpha_L^2)}\right)^2$$

$$= \frac{(3\alpha_L^2 + \alpha_H^2)^2}{32(\alpha_L^2 + \alpha_H^2)}.$$

- *Serving only the high-type customer.* We need to check if the monopolist profits from serving both types of customers are larger than its profits from selling to the high-type customer alone. Let's next find the tariff and price if the monopolist only seeks to sell to the high-type customer. In this context, its maximization problem becomes

$$\max_{p \geq 0} \quad T + (p-1)x_H(p)$$

$$\text{subject to} \quad T \leq S_H(p). \qquad (\text{PC}_H)$$

Note that now the only PC constraint we consider is that of the high type, where $S_H(p) = \frac{\alpha_H^2}{4p}$. Since PC_H must bind (otherwise the monopolist could increase the fee T and still achieve participation), we have that $T = S_H(p) = \frac{\alpha_H^2}{4p}$. Therefore, the monopolist's problem becomes the following unconstrained program:

$$\max_{p \geq 0} \quad \frac{\alpha_H^2}{4p} + (p-1)\frac{\alpha_H^2}{4p^2}.$$

Taking FOC with respect to p, we obtain

$$-\frac{\alpha_H^2}{2p^2} + \frac{\alpha_H^2}{2p^3} = 0;$$

solving for p yields $p^H = 1$. Then, the fee in this context is $T^H = \frac{\alpha_H^2}{4p} = \frac{\alpha_H^2}{4}$, entailing profits of

$$\pi^H = \frac{\alpha_H^2}{4}.$$

- *Comparison.* Finally, comparing the profits using a single two-part tariff that serves both customers, π^{ST}, against those from selling to the high-type customer alone, π^H, we find that $\pi^{ST} < \pi^H$ if

$$\frac{\left(3\alpha_L^2 + \alpha_H^2\right)^2}{32\left(\alpha_L^2 + \alpha_H^2\right)} < \frac{\alpha_H^2}{4}.$$

This inequality simplifies to

$$7\left(x\right)^2 + 2x - 9 > 0,$$

where, for compactness, we denote $x \equiv \left(\frac{\alpha_H}{\alpha_L}\right)^2$. Solving for x, we obtain two roots, $x > -9/7$ and $x > 1$. Since $\alpha_H > \alpha_L$ by definition, $x > 1$ holds, entailing that the above inequality is satisfied, ultimately implying that $\pi^{ST} < \pi^H$. In order to illustrate the above result, we next provide a numerical example.

- *Numerical example.* Consider $\alpha_L = 2$ and $\alpha_H = 3$. Evaluating equilibrium results, we obtain that when the monopolist serves both types

$$p^{ST} = \frac{26}{21} \simeq 1.24,\ T^{ST} = \frac{1}{p^{ST}} \simeq 0.808\ \text{and}\ \pi^{ST} = \frac{441}{416} \simeq 1.06.$$

If the monopolist decides to serve only to high-type consumers, then

$$p^H = 1,\ T^H = 2.25\ \text{and}\ \pi^H = 2.25.$$

Hence, the monopolist only serves the high-type consumers.

(c) *Menu of two-part tariffs.* Let us now find the menu of offers (contracts), (x_L, T_L) and (x_H, T_H), meant for low-type and high-type customer, respectively.

- Unlike in previous sections, under a menu of two-part tariffs there is no need for unit prices, p, since, upon separation of consumers, the tariff itself captures all consumer surplus.
- The problem for the monopolist is now the following:

$$\max_{x_H, T_H, x_L, T_L} T_H - x_H + T_L - x_L$$

$$\text{subject to} \ \ \alpha_L \sqrt{x_L} - T_L \geq 0, \tag{PC_L}$$

$$\alpha_H \sqrt{x_H} - T_H \geq 0, \tag{PC_H}$$

$$\alpha_L \sqrt{x_L} - T_L \geq \alpha_L \sqrt{x_H} - T_H, \tag{IC_L}$$

$$\alpha_H \sqrt{x_H} - T_H \geq \alpha_H \sqrt{x_L} - T_L \tag{IC_H}$$

as usual in screening problems, we include the participation constraint for each types of customers, along with the incentive compatibility conditions for each customer.

- Since $\alpha_H \sqrt{x_H} - T_H \geq \alpha_H \sqrt{x_L} - T_L > \alpha_L \sqrt{x_L} - T_L$, the PC_L constraint binds, i.e., $\alpha_L \sqrt{x_L} = T_L$ or $\alpha_L \sqrt{x_L} - T_L = 0$. As a consequence, the IC_L slacks because

$$\underbrace{\alpha_L \sqrt{x_L} - T_L}_{0 \text{ since } PC_L \text{ binds}} \geq \alpha_L \sqrt{x_H} - T_H$$

Therefore, the low-type buyer will not mimic the high type buyer. Last, note that since PC_H slacks, IC_H should bind. Otherwise, the seller could lower the units sold to the high-type buyer to decrease his payoff, and still achieve participation. Thus, we can write the binding IC_H as follows

$$\alpha_H \sqrt{x_H} - T_H = \alpha_H \sqrt{x_L} - T_L$$

and, after solving for tariff T_H, we obtain

$$T_H = T_L + \alpha_H \left(\sqrt{x_H} - \sqrt{x_L} \right)$$
$$= \alpha_L \sqrt{x_L} + \alpha_H \left(\sqrt{x_H} - \sqrt{x_L} \right)$$

since $T_L = \alpha_L \sqrt{x_L}$ by the binding PC_L. We are now ready to use to insert the binding IC_H and PC_L into the above monopolist's problem, which becomes the following (unconstrained) problem

$$\max_{x_H, x_L} \ \underbrace{\alpha_L \sqrt{x_L} + \alpha_H \left(\sqrt{x_H} - \sqrt{x_L} \right)}_{T_H} - x_H + \underbrace{\alpha_L \sqrt{x_L}}_{T_L} - x_L$$

where the number of choice variables decreased from four to two. We can now take FOCs with respect to x_H and x_L, yielding

$$\frac{\partial L}{\partial x_H} = \frac{\alpha_H}{2\sqrt{x_H}} - 1 = 0 \iff x_H = \frac{\alpha_H^2}{4},$$

$$\frac{\partial L}{\partial x_L} = \frac{2\alpha_L - \alpha_H}{2\sqrt{x_L}} - 1 = 0 \iff x_L = \frac{(2\alpha_L - \alpha_H)^2}{4},$$

which implies that the optimal tariffs are

$$T_L = \alpha_L \sqrt{x_L} = \frac{\alpha_L (2\alpha_L - \alpha_H)}{2} \quad \text{and}$$

$$T_H = \frac{\alpha_H^2}{2} - \frac{\alpha_H(2\alpha_L - \alpha_H)}{2} + \frac{\alpha_L(2\alpha_L - \alpha_H)}{2}$$
$$= \frac{2\alpha_H^2 - 3\alpha_L\alpha_H + 2\alpha_L^2}{2}.$$

Therefore, the monopolist's profits from the menu of two-part tariffs is

$$\pi^{MT} = (T_H - x_H) + (T_L - x_L)$$
$$= \left(\frac{2\alpha_H^2 - 3\alpha_L\alpha_H + 2\alpha_L^2}{2} - \frac{\alpha_H^2}{4} \right) + \left(\frac{\alpha_L(2\alpha_L - \alpha_H)}{2} - \frac{(2\alpha_L - \alpha_H)^2}{4} \right)$$
$$= \frac{2\alpha_L^2 + \alpha_H^2 - 2\alpha_L\alpha_H}{2}.$$

- *Numerical example.* Continuing with the above parameter values, $\alpha_L = 2$ and $\alpha_H = 3$, let us find the menu of offers (contracts), (x_L, T_L) and (x_H, T_H).

$$x_H = 2.25 \text{ and } T_H = 4,$$

$$x_L = 0.25 \text{ and } T_L = 1.$$

And profits are $\pi^{MT} = 2.5$.

(d) One can rank the profits of the monopolist in the above three cases without actually calculating them. Explain.

- We have relaxed the constraints in steps. As we move from part (a) to part (c), the monopolist derives more and more rent (surplus) as he develops more sophisticated pricing strategies, i.e., $\pi^U < \pi^H < \pi^{MT}$ (where note that, rather than writing π^{ST} under a single two-part tariff in part (b), we wrote π^H since in that part of the exercise we showed that serving the high-type customers alone was more profitable). This profit ranking holds if

$$\frac{\alpha_L^2 + \alpha_H^2}{16} < \frac{\alpha_H^2}{4} < \frac{2\alpha_L^2 + \alpha_H^2 - 2\alpha_L\alpha_H}{2}.$$

For the first inequality to hold, we need $\alpha_L^2 + \alpha_H^2 < 4\alpha_H^2$, or $\left(\frac{\alpha_L}{\alpha_H} \right)^2 < 3$, which is satisfied since $\frac{\alpha_L}{\alpha_H} < 1$ given that $\alpha_L < \alpha_H$ by definition. For the second inequality to hold, we need $\alpha_H^2 < 4\alpha_L^2 + 2\alpha_H^2 - 4\alpha_L^2\alpha_H^2$, or rearranging $(2\alpha_L - \alpha_H)^2 > 0$, which is always positive. Therefore, the profit ranking $\pi^U < \pi^H < \pi^{MT}$ holds for all parameter values.

- *Numerical example.* Using the same parameter values as the numerical examples of part (b) and (c), we find profits of

$$\pi^U = 0.8125 < \pi^H = 2.25 < \pi^{MT} = 2.5.$$

Exercise #19 — Screening two types of customers

19. A monopolist considers selling its product to buyers with utility function $u(q, \theta) = \theta v(q) - t$, where $v'(q) > 0$ and $v''(q) \leq 0$. In addition, parameter θ indicates the utility that a buyer obtains from consuming q units of the good, and $\theta \in \{\theta_L, \theta_H\}$ where $\theta_L < \theta_H$. The probability that a buyer is of type θ_L is $p \in (0, 1)$, while that of type θ_H is $1 - p$. As usual, $t > 0$ denotes the transfer from the buyer to the seller for all q units that the buyer purchases (not the price per unit, but for the *bulk* of all q units). The cost of producing each unit is constant in q, $c > 0$, and satisfies $c < \theta_L < \theta_H$. You can assume that the utility that a buyer obtains from not buying is simply zero.

(a) *Symmetric information.* Assuming that the monopolist can perfectly observe a buyer's type, identify the pair (q_L, t_L) that it offers to the buyer with type θ_L, and the pair (q_H, t_H) that it offers to the buyer with type θ_H.

- When the monopolist observes a buyer with type θ_i, it solves

$$\max_{q, t \geq 0} t - cq$$

$$\text{subject to } \theta_i v(q) - t \geq 0. \tag{PC}$$

Since the monopolist can increase the transfer until the point in which the buyer is indifferent between buying and not buying the good, the PC constraint binds, thus implying $t = \theta v(q)$. Substituting that information in the objective function yields the following reduced problem (which is unconstrained, and with a single choice variable, q, as the transfer t no longer shows up in the monopolist's problem)

$$\max_{q \geq 0} \theta_i v(q) - cq$$

Taking FOC with respect to q, we obtain

$$\theta_i v'(q) = c \text{ for all } i = \{L, H\}.$$

Intuitively indicating an efficient outcome: the monopolist increases q until the point where the marginal utility that the buyer obtains coincides with the monopolist's marginal cost of production; as depicted in figure 10.4. Hence, q_L solves $\theta_L v'(q) = c$ while q_H solves $\theta_H v'(q) = c$. Using these two output levels, the optimal transfers are

$$t_L = \theta_L v(q_L) \text{ and } t_H = \theta_H v(q_H).$$

- *Example.* For instance, if $v(q) = \sqrt{q}$, optimal output levels solve the FOC

$$\theta_i \frac{1}{2\sqrt{q}} = c, \text{ or } q_i = \frac{\theta_i^2}{4c^2}.$$

Plugging the output levels q_i into $v(q)$ we obtain the optimal transfer $t_i = \theta_i v(q) = \frac{\theta_i^2}{2c}$.

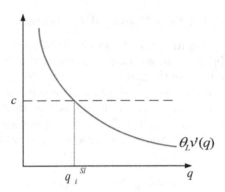

Figure 10.4 Units sold under symmetric information.

(b) *Asymmetric information.* Assuming that the monopolist cannot observe a buyer's type, identify the menu of pairs (q_L, t_L) and (q_H, t_H) that maximize the monopolist's expected profits (and achieve self-selection and participation).

- In this case the monopolist cannot observe the buyer's type, so he maximizes his expected profits, subject to incentive compatibility (IC) and participation constraints (PC), as follows:

$$\max_{q_L, t_L, q_H, t_H \geq 0} \ p \left(t_L - c q_L \right) + (1-p) \left(t_H - c q_H \right)$$

$$\text{subject to} \ \ \theta_H v(q_H) - t_H \geq 0, \qquad\qquad (PC_H)$$

$$\theta_L v(q_L) - t_L \geq 0, \qquad\qquad (PC_L)$$

$$\theta_H v(q_H) - t_H \geq \theta_H v(q_L) - t_L, \qquad\qquad (IC_H)$$

$$\theta_L v(q_L) - t_L \geq \theta_L v(q_H) - t_H. \qquad\qquad (IC_L)$$

First, note that PC_H is redundant, i.e., it does not bind. In order to show this, let us work by contradiction supposing that PC_H binds, i.e., $\theta_H v(q_H) = t_H$. Plugging this result into the IC_H condition yields

$$\underbrace{\theta_H v(q_H) - t_H}_{0} \geq \theta_H v(q_L) - t_L,$$

which can be rearranged as

$$0 \geq \theta_H v(q_L) - t_L > \theta_L v(q_L) - t_L,$$

since $\theta_H > \theta_L$ by definition. However, the above inequality entails that $0 > \theta_L v(q_L) - t_L$ strictly, thus violating the PC_L condition. Hence, PC_H cannot bind, and becomes redundant in the above program.

- We can now simplify our program by using the Lagragian method to see which of the three remaining constraints bind. In particular,

$$
\begin{aligned}
L = {} & p\left(t_L - cq_L\right) + (1-p)\left(t_H - cq_H\right) \\
& + \lambda_1\left[\theta_L v(q_L) - t_L\right] \\
& + \lambda_2\left[\theta_H v(q_H) - t_H - \theta_H v(q_L) + t_L\right] \\
& + \lambda_3\left[\theta_L v(q_L) - t_L - \theta_L v(q_H) + t_H\right].
\end{aligned}
$$

Taking FOCs with respect to t_L and t_H yields

$$
\frac{\partial L}{\partial t_L} = p - \lambda_1 + \lambda_2 - \lambda_3 = 0,
$$

$$
\frac{\partial L}{\partial t_H} = (1-p) - \lambda_2 + \lambda_3 = 0.
$$

From the second FOC we obtain $\lambda_3 = \lambda_2 - (1-p)$. Plugging it into the first FOC, we find

$$
p - \lambda_1 + \lambda_2 - \underbrace{[\lambda_2 - (1-p)]}_{\lambda_3} = 0 \iff \lambda_1 = 1.
$$

Hence, $\lambda_1 > 0$, implying that PC_L holds with equality, i.e., $\theta_L v(q_L) = t_L$. In addition, from the second FOC, $\lambda_2 = \lambda_3 + (1-p)$, entailing that $\lambda_2 > 0$, i.e., even if λ_3 was zero, $(1-p) > 0$ yields $\lambda_2 > 0$. As a consequence, its associated constraint (the IC_H) must bind.

- Therefore, the PC_L and IC_H bind (hold with equality), entailing $\theta_L v(q_L) - t_L = 0$, i.e., $t_L = \theta_L v(q_L)$, and $\theta_H v(q_H) - t_H = \theta_H v(q_L) - t_L$, i.e., $\theta_H\left[v(q_H) - v(q_L)\right] + t_L = t_H$. Plugging $t_L = \theta_L v(q_L)$ into the binding IC_H, yields

$$
\theta_H\left[v(q_H) - v(q_L)\right] + \underbrace{\theta_L v(q_L)}_{t_L} = \theta_H v(q_H) - (\theta_H - \theta_L)v(q_L) = t_H.
$$

In contrast, PC_H and IC_L slack, i.e., they do not hold strictly. Ignoring these two constraints, we can rewrite the above program as

$$
\max_{q_L, q_H \geq 0} \; p\left(\underbrace{\theta_L v(q_L)}_{t_L} - cq_L\right) + (1-p)\left(\underbrace{\theta_H v(q_H) - (\theta_H - \theta_L)v(q_L)}_{t_H} - cq_H\right),
$$

where now we only have two choice variables. Taking FOCs yields

$$
\frac{\partial L}{\partial q_L} = p\left[\theta_L v'(q_L) - c\right] - (1-p)(\theta_H - \theta_L)v'(q_L) = 0,
$$

$$
\frac{\partial L}{\partial q_H} = (1-p)\left[\theta_H v'(q_H) - c\right] = 0.
$$

From the second FOC, we obtain that q_H solves

$$\theta_H v'(q_H) = c,$$

thus coinciding with the FOC under symmetric information. That is, the high-type consumer gets the same output as under symmetric information. This is the common result of "no distortion at the top" we have found in other principal–agent problems. Rearranging the first FOC, we obtain

$$\frac{\theta_L - (1-p)\theta_H}{p} v'(q_L) = c,$$

which entails a downward distortion in the output sold to the low-value buyer, relative to symmetric information, since $\frac{\theta_L - (1-p)\theta_H}{p} < \theta_L$. Figure 10.5 depicts the above FOC, and compares the output under symmetric and asymmetric information.

- *Example.* Using the same utility function $v(q) = \sqrt{q}$ as in part (a) and considering $p = \frac{2}{3}$, the output levels under asymmetric information become

$$q_H = \left(\frac{\theta_H}{2c}\right)^2 \quad \text{and} \quad q_L = \left(\frac{3\theta_L - \theta_H}{4c}\right)^2.$$

While q_H coincides with that of under symmetric information (see parametric example at the end of part a), q_L is lower than under symmetric information since $\left(\frac{3\theta_L - \theta_H}{4c}\right)^2 < \left(\frac{\theta_L}{2c}\right)^2$.

(c) Compare your results in parts (a) and (b).

- *High-value buyer.* He suffers no distortion in output relative to symmetric information ("no distortion at the top"). In order to find his transfer, we can use the fact that IC_H binds, $\theta_H v(q_H) - t_H = \theta_H v(q_L) - t_L$, so that $t_H = \theta_H v(q_H) - (\theta_H - \theta_L)v(q_L)$.

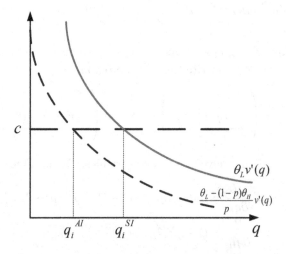

Figure 10.5 Units sold under asymmetric information.

- *Low-value buyer.* In contrast, this type of buyer suffers a downward distortion. In order to find his transfer, we can use the fact that PC_L binds, so that $t_L = \theta_L v(q_L)$.

- *Information rents.* Finally, note that the information rent of the high-value buyer is positive since PC_H does not bind (as shown above). That is,

$$u_H = \theta_H v(q_H) - t_H > \overline{u} = 0$$

as his utility under symmetric information is zero, $\overline{u} = 0$. (In addition, note that the rent $\theta_H v(q_H) - t_H$ can be expressed as $(\theta_H - \theta_L) v(q_L)$, which is increasing in the difference between consumers' valuations.) Hence, since in both information contexts he purchases the same number of units, q_H, the information rent originates from a lower price t_H under asymmetric than symmetric information. Intuitively, in order to induce the high type to select (q_H, t_H) rather than (q_L, t_L), the monopolist must offer the buyer a cheaper price than under symmetric information. More formally, since $\theta_H v(q_H^{SI}) - t_H^{SI} = \overline{u} = 0$ under symmetric information, and $q_H^{SI} = q_H^{AI}$, then $\theta_H v(q_H^{SI}) = \theta_H v(q_H^{AI})$, implying that $t_H^{AI} < t_H^{SI}$, which yields

$$0 = \theta_H v(q_H^{SI}) - t_H^{SI} \leq \theta_H v(q_H^{AI}) - t_H^{AI}.$$

In contrast, the low-value buyer receives a lower output under asymmetric than symmetric information (recall the downward output distortion mentioned above), but receives no information rents since PC_L binds. Then, he must be subject to a more expensive price. That is, if

$$\theta_L v(q_L^{AI}) - t_L^{AI} = \theta_L v(q_L^{SI}) - t_L^{SI} = \overline{u} = 0$$

and $q_L^{SI} > q_L^{AI}$ (downward distortion), then $v(q_L^{SI}) > v(q_L^{AI})$ since $v' > 0$ by definition, which implies $\theta_L v(q_L^{SI}) > \theta_L v(q_L^{AI})$. Hence, the above equality in utility levels across information contexts can only hold if transfers satisfy $t_L^{AI} < t_L^{SI}$.

Exercise #21 — Efficiency wages and the principal–agent problem (Shapiro and Stiglitz 1984)

21. Consider the following explanation of why wages can be above the competitive equilibrium prediction, as suggested by Shapiro and Stiglitz (1984). Assume a risk neutral worker with utility $u(w, e) = w - e$, where effort e is binary $e = \{0, 1\}$. The firm obtains a product αm, where $\alpha > 0$ and where m represents the number of workers choosing an effort $e = 1$. The firm can monitor only one worker, each with equal probability, paying each worker salary w if he exerts a positive effort $e = 1$, but zero otherwise. There are $n > 2$ workers in the firm.

   (a) For a given salary w, under which conditions does each worker choose effort $e = 1$?

   - Each worker compares the utility of exerting a positive effort, $w - 1$, against the utility of slacking, given by the probability that the firm does not monitor him (so the firm is monitoring either of the other $n - 1$ coworkers). The probability of a specific worker i being monitored is $\frac{1}{n}$, thus leaving the probability of any other coworker being monitored as $1 - \frac{1}{n} = \frac{n-1}{n}$. Hence, a worker i exerts effort $e = 1$ if

$$w - 1 \geq \frac{n-1}{n}w \iff nw - n \geq nw - w,$$

which simplifies to $w \geq n$.

(b) Set up the firm's profit maximization problem, find the profit-maximizing salary w and the number of workers n hired.

- From part (a) we know that workers exert a positive effort if and only if $w \geq n$. Given that response, the firm chooses the lowest possible salary, i.e., $w = n$. Hence, the firm's profit maximization problem is

$$\max_{n \geq 0} \ \alpha m - nw = \alpha n - n^2,$$

where the equality is due to the fact that if all workers exert effort $e = 1$, $m = n$; and workers are paid the lowest salary that induces a positive effort $w = n$. Taking FOC with respect to n yields

$$\alpha - 2n \leq 0 \Rightarrow n^* = \frac{\alpha}{2}.$$

Therefore, the firm hires $n^* = \frac{\alpha}{2}$ and pays the salary $w^* = \frac{\alpha}{2}$.

(c) If monitoring was perfect, how do your results in parts (a) and (b) change?

- When monitoring is perfect, if the worker exerts effort $e = 1$, his payoff is still $w - 1$. However, his payoff from slacking is a certain salary of zero because he is caught slacking with certainty. Therefore, every worker exerts a positive effort as long as:

$$w - 1 \geq 0 \ \text{ or } \ w \geq 1.$$

Anticipating the above decision rule by the worker, the firm sets the lowest possible salary that induces positive effort, i.e., $w = 1$. Hence, the firm's profit-maximization problem under perfect monitoring becomes

$$\max_{n \geq 0} \ \alpha m - nw = \alpha n - n,$$

since $m = n$ and $w = 1$. Taking FOC with respect to n yields $\alpha - 1$, which entails a corner solution of $n = 0$ (no workers hired) if $\alpha < 1$, or $n = \infty$ (all workers hired) if $\alpha > 1$.

- In summary, imperfect monitoring yields a salary higher that under perfect monitoring, i.e., salary is $w = n > 2$ when monitoring is imperfect but is lower (at $w = 1$) when monitoring is perfect. Regarding employment levels, if $\alpha > 1$, the firm hires all available workers under perfect monitoring, but plays a more conservative role under imperfect monitoring whereby it only hires $n^* = \frac{\alpha}{2}$ workers.

References

[1] Baye, M., K. Crocker, and J. Ju (1996), Divisionalization, franchising and divestiture incentives in oligopoly, *American Economic Review*, 86, pp. 223–36.

[2] Bernheim, D., and M. Whinston (1990), Multimarket contact and collusive behavior, *Rand Journal of Economics*, 21, pp. 1–26.

[3] Coase, R. (1972), Durability and monopoly, *Journal of Law and Economics*, pp. 143–50.

[4] d'Aspremont, C., and M. Motta (1994), Tougher price-competition or lower concentration: A trade-off for antitrust authorities?, Université Catholique de Louvain, Center for Operations Research and Econometrics, Discussion Paper 1994015.

[5] Deneckere, R. (1983), Duopoly supergames with product differentiation, *Economics Letters*, 11(1–2), pp. 37–42.

[6] Espinola-Arredondo, A., and F. Muñoz-Garcia (2013), Asymmetric information may protect the commons: The welfare benefits of uninformed regulators, *Economics Letters*, 121, pp. 463–66.

[7] Espinola-Arredondo, A., F. Muñoz-Garcia, and J. Bayham (2014), The entry-deterring effects of inflexible regulation, *Canadian Journal of Economics*, 47(1), pp. 298–324.

[8] Fershtman, C., and K. Judd (1987), Equilibrium incentives in oligopoly, *American Economic Review*, 77, pp. 927–40.

[9] Holmstrom, B. (1982), Moral Hazard in Teams, *Bell Journal of Economics*, 13(2): 324–40.

[10] Hopenhayn, Hugo A., and Juan Pablo Nicolini (1997), Optimal Unemployment Insurance, *Journal of Political Economy*, 105(2): 412–38.

[11] Huck, S., K. A. Konrad, and W. Muller (2001), Big fish eat small fish: On merger in Stackelberg markets, *Economic Letters*, 73, pp. 213–17.

[12] Porter, M. E., and C. van der Linde (1995), Toward a new conception of the environment-competitiveness relationship, *Journal of Economic Perspectives*, 9, pp. 97–118.

[13] Salant, S., S. Switzer, and R. Reynolds (1983), Losses due to merger: The effects of an exogenous change in industry structure on Cournot–Nash equilibrium, *Quarterly Journal of Economics*, 87, pp. 185–99.

[14] Shapiro, C., and J. Stiglitz (1984), Equilibrium Unemployment as a Worker Discipline Device, *American Economic Review*, 74(3): 433–44.

[15] Simon, C. P., and L. E. Blume (1994), *Mathematics for Economists*, W.W. Norton Publishing.

[16] Singh, N., and X. Vives (1984), Price and quantity competition in a differentiated duopoly, *Rand Journal of Economics*, 15(4), pp. 546–54.

[17] Stone, R. (1954), Linear expenditure systems and demand analysis: Application to the pattern of British demand, *Economic Journal*, 64, pp. 511–27.

[18] Waldman, M. (2003), Durable goods theory for real world markets, *Journal of Economic Perspectives*, 17(1), pp. 131–54.

[19] Weitzman, M. L. (1974), Prices vs. quantities, *Review of Economic Studies*, 41(4), pp. 477–91.

Printed in the United States
by Baker & Taylor Publisher Services